Law, Social Science, and the Criminal Courts

Law, Social Science, and the Criminal Courts

Alisa Smith, JD, Ph.D.

Carolina Academic Press
Durham, North Carolina

Library of Congress Cataloging-in-Publication Data

Smith, Alisa, 1963–

Law, social science, and the criminal courts / by Alisa Smith.

p. cm.

Includes bibliographical references and index.

ISBN 0-89089-518-X

1. Criminal law—Social aspects—United States. 2. Criminal Procedure—Social aspects—United States. 3. Criminal courts—United States. 4. Law and the social sciences—United States. I. Title.

KF9219.S62 2003

345.73'05—dc22   2003061088

Carolina Academic Press
700 Kent Street
Durham, North Carolina 27701
Telephone (919) 489-7486
Fax (919) 493-5668
E-mail: cap@cap-press.com
www.cap-press.com

In memory of my grandparents,

Emil and Jennie Danella

Dedicated to my children, Skyler Marie and Alec Emile

*and their cousins, Cari, Margaret, Elena, Ashley,
Megan, Kaitlin, Kacey, Cody, and Kyra*

CONTENTS

Law, Social Science, and the Criminal Courts

CHAPTER 1

THE HISTORY OF SOCIAL SCIENCE IN THE LAW

Constitutional questions, it is true, are not settled by even a consensus of present public opinion, for it is the peculiar value of a written constitution that it places in unchanging form limitations upon legislative action, and thus gives a permanence and stability to popular government which otherwise would be lacking. At the same time, when a question of fact is debated and debatable, and the extent to which a special constitutional limitation goes is affected by the truth in respect to that fact, a widespread and long continued belief concerning it is worthy of consideration. We take judicial cognizance of all matters of general knowledge.

–*Muller v. Oregon*, 208 U.S. 412, 420–1 (1907).

Do mandatory arrest policies reduce domestic violence? Is the death penalty racially discriminatory? Do eye-witnesses provide accurate accounts to the jury? Does decision-making differ in six- and twelve-person jury panels? These are prominent questions for the criminal courts; they are also questions that can be answered using social science research. Social science and the law are interrelated in many areas, and the use of social science research to develop policy and resolve legal disputes has become more common.

Although courts have relied more readily on social science to resolve civil rather than criminal matters, some members of the United States Supreme Court have begun to express an interest in social science research as a means to resolve issues related to criminal law and procedure. For example, during the oral argument in *Maryland v. Wilson*, Justice Scalia asked counsel whether data existed to assist in determining the danger or safety associated with ordering passengers from their vehicles during police-citizen traffic encounters. No data existed and the Court permitted law enforcement to order passengers

> **Extralegal materials** are those that are not directly related to the law. These include sociological, psychological, economic, historical and scientific information.

from their cars under the presumption of police dangerousness. In the decision, Chief Justice Rhenquist made the following comment: "It is, indeed, regrettable that the empirical data on a subject as this are sparse, but we need not ignore the data which do exist simply because further refinement would be even more helpful."

This book focuses on criminal law and procedural cases that raise social science questions and the social science research that examines these issues. In some instances the courts have relied on social science and empirical studies to resolve issues, but they have failed to do so in other cases. In some of the latter instances, courts may simply have been unaware of existing empirical research or at the time the case was decided, the research was not yet available.

What are the historical roots of social science use by the courts?

Prior to the late 1800s, legal decision-making was presumed to rest on logic. In 1881, Oliver Wendell Holmes challenged this entrenched presumption by arguing that "the life of the law has not been logic: it has been experience." Holmes maintained that judicial decisions rely on "life experience" but these experiences are simply not mentioned in judicial decisions. Holmes' critique was intended to confront judges with this realization and encourage them to be more forthright in their reliance on life experience. In a later writing, Holmes (1897) envisioned that social science would play a more prominent role in the development and understanding of the law.

A few years later, Louis D. Brandeis was the first lawyer to rely on social science data to support his argument on behalf of the state of Oregon in *Muller v. Oregon*. Brandeis relied on a variety of sources to support Oregon legislation limiting the work day of females employed in factories and laundries to ten hours per day. Brandeis submitted the statements and opinions of a variety of authorities that demonstrated long work days were detrimental to the health and well-being of women and that women were in need of the state's protection against over-work.

As reflected by the quote from the *Muller* decision that introduces this chapter, the United States Supreme Court, for the first time, explicitly relied on "experience" in rendering its decision. The Court recognized that social facts may be resolved by the Court based on **"extralegal" materials**. The social science data advanced by Brandeis influenced the Court to uphold the statute and find it was rationally related to a legitimate state interest. Although the information—opinions and statements of legislative bodies, organizations and individuals—would not be considered "scientific" by today's standards, Brandeis' work was ground-breaking. It was the first time the Court relied on this type of material in rendering a decision.

Roscoe Pound, a renowned jurist, wrote a great deal on using "social interests" in the law. In 1912, Pound wrote an essay for the Harvard Law Review and argued that the development, interpretation, and application of the law should rely more heavily on "social facts." Pound proposed a more advanced and comprehensive intersection of law and social science. He viewed law as a social phenomenon and argued that the development, application and enforcement of the law should be examined.

It is Pound's broader conceptualization of the intersection of social science and the law that is evidenced in the United States Supreme Court's decision in *Brown v. Board of Education*. Fifty years after *Muller v. Oregon*, the Court was presented with social science data demonstrating the harmful psychological effects of segregation on children in public schools. The Court, in holding segregation to be unconstitutional, relied explicitly on seven authoritative, social science articles providing research that segregation was detrimental to the personality and psychological development of children. With this decision, the Court put its stamp of acceptance on the utilization of social science research to resolve legal and policy questions.

What are the conflicts between the law and social science?

Although the Court's 1954 decision in *Brown v. Board of Education* paved the way for social science in the courts, conflicts remain between the two disciplines that hinder broader and wider use of social science to resolve legal issues. In a study of the use of social science data by the United States Supreme Court, Erickson and Simon (1998) identify essential, culture conflicts between the two disciplines. Social scientists and lawyers or legal scholars are different in terms of their customs, values, discourse and approach to problem-solving. According to Erickson and Simon (1998: p. 6), the following dichotomous differences exist between law and social science:

> Science is rational, but the law is irrational. Law is specific while science is abstract. Law produces **idiographic** knowledge while science produces **nomothetic** knowledge. Legal findings are based on certainties and the absence of **reasonable doubt** but social science find-

> **Idiographic:** "An approach to explanation in which we seek to exhaust the idiosyncratic causes of a particular condition or event" (Babbie 2002: 443)
> **Nomothetic:** "An approach to explanation in which we seek to identify a few causal factors that generally impact a class of conditions or events" (Babbie 2002: 445)
> **Reasonable Doubt:** "Reasonable doubt which will justify acquittal is doubt based on reason and arising from evidence or lack of evidence, and it is doubt which reasonable man or woman might entertain, and it is not fanciful doubt, is not imagined doubt, and is not doubt that juror might conjure up to avoid performing unpleasant task or duty" (Black's Law Dictionary).

ings are based on probabilities and generalizations. The law is normative and prescriptive, describing how people should behave, and what ought to be. Social science attempts to be value-free, positive, and descriptive, describing how people do behave.

In terms of pursuing the truth, these two disciplines lie at opposite ends of the spectrum. The law seeks the truth through an adversarial process regarding a single or specific instance and the "truth" is a determinative outcome rendered by a jury or judge. The fact-finder is provided with only legally "relevant" information, thus it is a "closed system" and based on a deductive process. On the other hand, social science is a continuous process of theory testing, empirical generalizations, and observations. There is not a definitive outcome, nor ultimate proof that a theory is true. The social science process is inductive wherein "the body of knowledge upon which conclusions are based is continually growing and conclusions are always subject to revision". (Simon and Erickson 1998). Whereas the legal process is adversarial, the social science process is more cooperative. The social science system is open and is influenced by many different perspectives examining the same phenomena. For example, many have attempted to explain or understand criminal behavior from a variety of perspectives, including biology, psychology, and sociology.

The use of social science information to assist in the resolution of legal disputes has been limited for a number of reasons related to the above differences. First, lawyers are not schooled in social science or the **scientific method**. In other words lawyers and social scientists don't speak the same language. Second, many judges have been reluctant to rest their decisions on social science grounds when a researcher acknowledges that there are **margins of error**

> **Scientific method:** attempts to understand the world in a non-arbitrary and objective way through the testing of hypotheses.
>
> **Margins of Error:** "is a common summary of sampling error…which quantifies uncertainty about a survey result" (ASA, What is a Margin of Error Pamphlet at page 3—http://www.amstat.org/sections/srms/brochures/margin.pdf)
>
> **Precedent:** An adjudged case or decision of a court, considered as furnishing an example or authority for an identical or similar case afterwards arising or a similar question of law. Courts attempt to decide cases on the basis of principles established in prior cases. Prior cases which are close in facts or legal principles to the case under consideration are called precedents. A rule of law established for the first time by a court for a particular type of case and thereafter referred to in deciding similar cases. This is also called **stare decisis** which means to abide by, or adhere to, decided cases. (Black's Law Dictionary).

in making scientific determinations. Social science is in essence abstract and deals in probabilities. Lawyers and judges are used to dealing with certainties and legal **precedent.**

Despite these differences in culture and perhaps the natural antagonism of the two disciplines, the law has slowly come to use social science research to resolve some very important criminal law and procedural issues that impact society. However, in reading this book, it will become evident that the relationship between the law and social science remains a love-hate relationship. Social science remains an underutilized tool by the courts particularly in deciding issues of criminal law and behavior.

In criminal law, the use of social science by the Court in resolving social fact questions has varied. James Acker (1992) examined the use of social science authorities by the Supreme Court in resolving criminal cases in a sample of 240 cases and found that during the thirty years between 1958 and 1987 almost one in seven (13.8%) of randomly selected criminal cases relied on one or more citations to social science research. However, there were a handful of particular types of cases where the Court was more likely to discuss social science, extralegal materials. Acker (1992: 3–4) defined "[s]ocial science evidence"…as information derived from the traditional *methods* of science—through systematic observation and objective measurement, allowing for replication and empirical verification—and within the *subject* purview of the social sciences, including psychology, sociology, psychiatry, economics, political science and

> **Amicus curiae:** "Means, literally, friend of the court. A person with strong interest in or views on the subject matter of an action may petition the court for permission to file a brief, ostensibly on behalf of a party but actually to suggest a rationale consistent with its own views. Such amicus curiae briefs are commonly filed in appeals of a broad public interest; e.g., civil rights cases. Such may be filed by private persons or the government....such brief[s] may be filed only if accompanied by written consent of all parties, or by leave of court granted on motion or at the request of the court..." (Black's Law Dictionary)

criminal justice, but not history." The cases more commonly relying on social science evidence involved Fourth Amendment exclusionary rule (32%), jury size (71.4%), and death penalty (40.5%) issues. He found that not only did the justices cite to this research, but they also discussed and quoted much of the research in their decisions. The use of social science to inform Supreme Court decisions in resolving socio-legal matters may increase as the number of publications devoted to the study of legal and social science questions, the number of law schools offering studies in social science, and the number of briefs, particularly **amicus curiae** briefs that include references to social science information become more prevalent. (Acker 1992; Simon and Erickson 1998).

The debate: Is social science helpful or harmful in resolving legal, social and public policy matters?

Although the United States Supreme Court has relied on extralegal information to decide social policy issues dating back to *Muller* in 1908, there remains debate among scholars about the appropriate use of this type of information. In 2000, the Journal of Criminal Law and Criminology devoted an entire journal to discussions about the use of social science research in resolving constitutional criminal procedure questions (Meares and Harcourt 2000). In the Foreword to that edition, the authors argue that empirical and social scientific evidence is necessary to properly inform criminal procedural questions, though they temper their enthusiasm for extralegal materials by qualifying that this type of evidence should not be relied on exclusively by the Court in making these determinations. In making their case, the authors discuss a number of criminal case issues that could be informed by using empirical social scientific evidence.

Other scholars however have argued that social science evidence is being abused as a way of resolving important policy matters. For example, Leroy

Pelton, a social work scholar, argues that social science evidence which is based on findings drawn from "aggregate-data and group-difference...overlook fairness to each and every individual" and that findings from this type of data "lend themselves to, and are used for, the promotion of a narrow form of utilitarianism...." (Pelton 2000: 62). In making his argument, Pelton discusses the consequences of using empirical social scientific evidence as a way of perpetuating myths and stereotypes about groups. He argues that these policy-decisions have harmed a number of individuals. Specifically he argues:

> Research supporting group stereotypes that, in turn, are used to misinform, initiate, maintain, and extend social policies run the gamut from the mere collection of descriptive statistics to studies employing sophisticated methodology and analysis. Some states now have laws that require vision and other tests for driver's license renewal, only for people over a certain age, based on statistics indicating that elderly people, as a group, are involved proportionately in more fatal accidents than most other age groups. Our eyes are diverted from the injustice of age discrimination to the seeming reasonableness of policies that may, indeed, reduce fatal accidents.

Pelton applies this critical assessment of using aggregate data to other situations, e.g., relying on statistics that demonstrate that young black males commit a disproportionate number of crimes therefore shopkeepers and others would be statistically justified in discriminating against this group. This author qualifies his criticism of using social science evidence as a basis for policy-making by suggesting that there are some uses of social science that are legitimate, however "policies must first be evaluated in terms of agreed-upon principles of justice and fairness; that no amount of social-scientific data can inform such evaluation; and that social scientists should not pretend or represent otherwise."

This is an interesting debate about the use of social science particularly by the Court to confront issues of constitutional law. The United States Constitution is intended to guarantee fundamental rights and provide the minimal protections for individuals against government abuse. How and should aggregate-empirical and social scientific evidence properly inform decisions intended to protect individual liberties? This may be a difficult question to resolve, but one that should be considered in examining the influence of empirical and social scientific evidence in resolving matters that impact society.

Included in this chapter are excerpts from *Muller v. Oregon*, *Brown v. Board of Education* and Meares and Harcourt's *Foreward: Transparent adjudication and social science research in constitutional criminal procedure* in the Journal of Criminal Law and Criminology.[1]

Muller v. Oregon
208 U.S. 412 (1908)(Excerpt)

MR. JUSTICE BREWER delivered the opinion of the court.

On February 19, 1903, the legislature of the State of Oregon passed an act...[which states]:

> "SEC. 1. That no female (shall) be employed in any mechanical es-
> tablishment, or factory, or laundry in this State more than ten hours
> during any one day. The hours of work may be so arranged as to per-
> mit the employment of females at any time so that they shall not work
> more than ten hours during the twenty-four hours of any one day."
> Section 3 made a violation of the provisions of the prior sections a
> misdemeanor, subject to a fine of not less than $10 nor more than $25.

On September 18, 1905, an information was filed...charging that the defendant "on the 4th day of September, A.D. 1905, in the county of Multnomah
and State of Oregon, then and there being the owner of a laundry, known as
the Grand Laundry, in the city of Portland, and the employer of females
therein, did then and there unlawfully permit and suffer one Joe Haselbock,
he, the said Joe Haselbock, then and there being an overseer, superintendent
and agent of said Curt Muller, in the said Grand Laundry, to require a female,
to wit, one Mrs. E. Gotcher, to work more than ten hours in said laundry on
said 4th day of September, A.D. 1905, contrary to the statutes in such cases
made and provided, and against the peace and dignity of the State of Oregon."

A trial resulted in a verdict against the defendant, who was sentenced to
pay a fine of $10. The Supreme Court of the State affirmed the conviction,
State v. Muller, 48 Oregon, 252, whereupon the case was brought here on writ
of error.

The single question is the constitutionality of the statute under which the
defendant was convicted so far as it affects the work of a female in a laundry.
That it does not conflict with any provisions of the state constitution is settled by the decision of the Supreme Court of the State. The contentions of the
defendant, now plaintiff in error, are thus stated in his brief:

---

1. Throughout the text, most footnotes in cases and articles have been omitted.

"(1) Because the statute attempts to prevent persons, sui juris, from making their own contracts, and thus violates the provisions of the Fourteenth Amendment, as follows: " 'No State shall make or enforce any law which shall abridge the privileges or immunities of citizens of the United States; nor shall any State deprive any person of life, liberty, or property, without due process of law; nor deny to any person within its jurisdiction the equal protection of the laws.' "(2) Because the statute does not apply equally to all persons similarly situated, and is class legislation. "(3) The statute is not a valid exercise of the police power. The kinds of work proscribed are not unlawful, nor are they declared to be immoral or dangerous to the public health; nor can such a law be sustained on the ground that it is designed to protect women on account of their sex. There is no necessary or reasonable connection between the limitation prescribed by the act and the public health, safety or welfare."

It is the law of Oregon that women, whether married or single, have equal contractual and personal rights with men.... It thus appears that, putting to one side the elective franchise, in the matter of personal and contractual rights they stand on the same plane as the other sex. Their rights in these respects can no more be infringed than the equal rights of their brothers. We held in *Lochner v. New York*, 198 U.S. 45, that a law providing that no laborer shall be required or permitted to work in a bakery more than sixty hours in a week or ten hours in a day was not as to men a legitimate exercise of the police power of the State, but an unreasonable, unnecessary and arbitrary interference with the right and liberty of the individual to contract in relation to his labor, and as such was in conflict with, and void under, the Federal Constitution. That decision is invoked by plaintiff in error as decisive of the question before us. But this assumes that the difference between the sexes does not justify a different rule respecting a restriction of the hours of labor.... In the brief filed by Mr. Louis D. Brandeis, for the defendant in error, is a very copious collection of all these matters, an epitome of which is found in the margin.[1]

---

1. The following legislation of the States impose restrictions in some form or another upon the hours of labor that may be required of women: Massachusetts: chap. 221, 1874, Rev. Laws 1902, chap. 106, §24; Rhode Island: 1885, Acts and Resolves 1902, chap. 994, p. 73; Louisiana: §4, Act 43, p. 55, Laws of 1886, Rev. Laws 1904, vol. 1, p. 989; Connecticut: 1887, Gen. Stat. revision 1902, §4691; Maine: chap. 139, 1887, Rev. Stat. 1903, chap. 40, §48, p. 401; New Hampshire: 1887, Laws 1907, chap. 94, p. 95; Maryland: chap. 455, 1888, Pub. Gen. Laws 1903, art. 100, §1; Virginia: p. 150,1889–1890, Code 1904, tit. 51A, chap. 178A, §3657b; Pennsylvania: No. 26, p. 30, 1897, Laws 1905, No. 226, p. 352; New York: Laws 1899, §1, chap. 560, p. 752, Laws 1907, chap. 507, §77, subdiv. 3, p. 1078;

The legislation and opinions referred to in the margin may not be, technically speaking, authorities, and in them is little or no discussion of the constitutional question presented to us for determination, yet they are significant of a widespread belief that woman's physical structure, and the functions she performs in consequence thereof, justify special legislation restricting or qualifying the conditions under which she should be permitted to toil. Constitutional questions, it is true, are not settled by even a consensus of present public opinion, for it is the peculiar value of a written constitution that it places in unchanging form limitations upon legislative action, and thus gives a permanence and stability to popular government which otherwise would be lacking. At the same time, when a question of fact is debated and debatable, and the extent to which a special constitutional limitation goes is affected by the truth in respect to that fact, a widespread and long continued belief concerning it is worthy of consideration. We take judicial cognizance of all matters of general knowledge…

That woman's physical structure and the performance of maternal functions place her at a disadvantage in the struggle for subsistence is obvious. This

---

Nebraska: 1899, Comp. Stat. 1905, § 7955, p. 1986; Washington: Stat. 1901, chap. 68, § 1, p. 118: Colorado: Acts 1903, chap. 138, § 3, p. 310; New Jersey: 1892, Gen. Stat. 1895, p. 2350, §§ 66, 67; Oklahoma: 1890, Rev. Stat. 1903, chap. 25, art. 58, § 729; North Dakota: 1877, Rev. Code 1905, § 9440; South Dakota: 1877, Rev. Code (Penal Code, § 764), p. 1185; Wisconsin: § 1, chap. 83, Laws of 1867, Code 1898, § 1728; South Carolina: Acts 1907, No. 233, p. 487. In foreign legislation Mr. Brandeis calls attention to these statutes: Great Britain: Factories Act of 1844, chap. 15, pp. 161, 171; Factory and Workshop Act of 1901, chap. 22, pp. 60, 71; and see 1 Edw. VII, chap. 22. France, 1848; Act Nov. 2, 1892, and March 30, 1900. Switzerland, Canton of Glarus, 1848; Federal Law 1877, art. 2, § 1. Austria, 1855; Acts 1897, art. 96a, §§ 1–3. Holland, 1889; art. 5, § 1. Italy, June 19, 1902, art. 7. Germany, Laws 1891.

Then follow extracts from over ninety reports of committees, bureaus of statistics, commissioners of hygiene, inspectors of factories, both in this country and in Europe, to the effect that long hours of labor are dangerous for women, primarily because of their special physical organization. The matter is discussed in these reports in different aspects, but all agree as to the danger. It would of course take too much space to give these reports in detail. Following them are extracts from similar reports discussing the general benefits of short hours from an economic aspect of the question. In many of these reports individual instances are given tending to support the general conclusion. Perhaps the general scope and character of all these reports may be summed up in what an inspector for Hanover says: "The reasons for the reduction of the working day to ten hours—(a) the physical organization of women, (b) her maternal functions, (c) the rearing and education of the children, (d) the maintenance of the home—are all so important and so far reaching that the need for such reduction need hardly be discussed."…

is especially true when the burdens of motherhood are upon her. Even when they are not, by abundant testimony of the medical fraternity continuance for a long time on her feet at work, repeating this from day to day, tends to injurious effects upon the body, and as healthy mothers are essential to vigorous offspring, the physical well-being of woman becomes an object of public interest and care in order to preserve the strength and vigor of the race.

Still again, history discloses the fact that woman has always been dependent upon man. He established his control at the outset by superior physical strength, and this control in various forms, with diminishing intensity, has continued to the present. As minors, though not to the same extent, she has been looked upon in the courts as needing especial care that her rights may be preserved. Education was long denied her, and while now the doors of the school room are opened and her opportunities for acquiring knowledge are great, yet even with that and the consequent increase of capacity for business affairs it is still true that in the struggle for subsistence she is not an equal competitor with her brother. Though limitations upon personal and contractual rights may be removed by legislation, there is that in her disposition and habits of life which will operate against a full assertion of those rights. She will still be where some legislation to protect her seems necessary to secure a real equality of right. Doubtless there are individual exceptions, and there are many respects in which she has an advantage over him; but looking at it from the viewpoint of the effort to maintain an independent position in life, she is not upon an equality. Differentiated by these matters from the other sex, she is properly placed in a class by herself, and legislation designed for her protection may be sustained, even when like legislation is not necessary for men and could not be sustained. It is impossible to close one's eyes to the fact that she still looks to her brother and depends upon him. Even though all restrictions on political, personal and contractual rights were taken away, and she stood, so far as statutes are concerned, upon an absolutely equal plane with him, it would still be true that she is so constituted that she will rest upon and look to him for protection; that her physical structure and a proper discharge of her maternal functions—having in view not merely her own health, but the well-being of the race—justify legislation to protect her from the greed as well as the passion of man. The limitations which this statute places upon her contractual powers, upon her right to agree with her employer as to the time she shall labor, are not imposed solely for her benefit, but also largely for the benefit of all. Many words cannot make this plainer. The two sexes differ in structure of body, in the functions to be performed by each, in the amount of physical strength, in the capacity for long-continued labor, particularly when done standing, the influence of vigorous health upon the future well-being of the race, the self-reliance which enables one to assert full rights, and in the capacity to maintain the struggle for subsistence. This difference justifies a difference in legislation and upholds that which is designed to compensate for some of the burdens which rest upon her.

For these reasons, and without questioning in any respect the decision in *Lochner v. New York*, we are of the opinion that it cannot be adjudged that the act in question is in conflict with the Federal Constitution, so far as it respects the work of a female in a laundry, and the judgment of the Supreme Court of Oregon is affirmed.

Brown v. Board of Education
347 U.S. 483 (1954)(Excerpt)

OPINION BY: MR. CHIEF JUSTICE WARREN

These cases come to us from the States of Kansas, South Carolina, Virginia, and Delaware. They are premised on different facts and different local conditions, but a common legal question justifies their consideration together in this consolidated opinion. In each of the cases, minors of the Negro race, through their legal representatives, seek the aid of the courts in obtaining admission to the public schools of their community on a nonsegregated basis. In each instance, they had been denied admission to schools attended by white children under laws requiring or permitting segregation according to race. This segregation was alleged to deprive the plaintiffs of the equal protection of the laws under the Fourteenth Amendment. In each of the cases other than the Delaware case, a three-judge federal district court denied relief to the plaintiffs on the so-called "separate but equal" doctrine announced by this Court in *Plessy* v. *Ferguson*, 163 U.S. 537. Under that doctrine, equality of treatment is accorded when the races are provided substantially equal facilities, even though these facilities be separate. In the Delaware case, the Supreme Court of Delaware adhered to that doctrine, but ordered that the plaintiffs be admitted to the white schools because of their superiority to the Negro schools.

The plaintiffs contend that segregated public schools are not "equal" and cannot be made "equal," and that hence they are deprived of the equal protection of the laws. Because of the obvious importance of the question presented, the Court took jurisdiction.... [After substantial argument and discussion, the history of the Fourteenth Amendment was found not to be a conclusive determinant on an issue of public education].....In the first cases in this Court construing the Fourteenth Amendment, decided shortly after its adoption, the Court interpreted it as proscribing all state-imposed discriminations against the Negro race. The doctrine of "separate but equal" did not make its appearance in this Court until 1896 in the case of *Plessy* v. *Ferguson, supra,* involving not education but transportation. American courts have since labored with the doctrine for over half a century. In this Court, there have been six cases involving the "separate but equal" doctrine in the field of public education. In *Cumming* v. *County Board of Education,* 175 U.S. 528, and *Gong Lum* v. *Rice,* 275 U.S. 78, the validity of the doctrine itself was not challenged. In more recent cases, all on the graduate school level, inequality was found in that specific benefits enjoyed by white students were denied to Negro students of the same educational qualifications. *Missouri ex rel. Gaines* v. *Canada,* 305 U.S. 337; *Sipuel* v. *Oklahoma,* 332 U.S. 631; *Sweatt* v. *Painter,* 339 U.S. 629; *McLaurin* v. *Oklahoma State Regents,* 339 U.S. 637. In none of these cases was it necessary to re-examine the doctrine to grant relief to the Negro plaintiff. And in *Sweatt* v. *Painter, supra,* the Court expressly reserved decision on the question whether *Plessy* v. *Ferguson* should be held inapplicable to public education.

In the instant cases, that question is directly presented. Here, unlike *Sweatt* v. *Painter,* there are findings below that the Negro and white schools involved have been equalized, or are being equalized, with respect to buildings, curricula, qualifications and salaries of teachers, and other "tangible" factors. Our decision, therefore, cannot turn on merely a comparison of these tangible factors in the Negro and white schools involved in each of the cases. We must look instead to the effect of segregation itself on public education.

In approaching this problem, we cannot turn the clock back to 1868 when the Amendment was adopted, or even to 1896 when *Plessy* v. *Ferguson* was written. We must consider public education in the light of its full development and its present place in American life throughout the Nation. Only in this way can it be determined if segregation in public schools deprives these plaintiffs of the equal protection of the laws.

Today, education is perhaps the most important function of state and local governments. Compulsory school attendance laws and the great expenditures for education both demonstrate our recognition of the importance of education to our democratic society. It is required in the performance of our most basic public responsibilities, even service in the armed forces. It is the very foundation of good citizenship. Today it is a principal instrument in awakening the child to cultural values, in preparing him for later professional training, and in helping him to adjust normally to his environment. In these days, it is doubtful that any child may reasonably be expected to succeed in life if he is denied the opportunity of an education. Such an opportunity, where the state has undertaken to provide it, is a right which must be made available to all on equal terms.

We come then to the question presented: Does segregation of children in public schools solely on the basis of race, even though the physical facilities and other "tangible" factors may be equal, deprive the children of the minority group of equal educational opportunities? We believe that it does.

In *Sweatt* v. *Painter, supra,* in finding that a segregated law school for Negroes could not provide them equal educational opportunities, this Court relied in large part on "those qualities which are incapable of objective measurement but which make for greatness in a law school." In *McLaurin* v. *Oklahoma State Regents, supra,* the Court, in requiring that a Negro admitted to a white graduate school be treated like all other students, again resorted to intangible considerations: "…his ability to study, to engage in discussions and exchange views with other students, and, in general, to learn his profession." Such considerations apply with added force to children in grade and high schools. To separate them from others of similar age and qualifications solely because of their race generates a feeling of inferiority as to their status in the community that may affect their hearts and minds in a way unlikely ever to be undone. The effect of this separation on their educational opportunities was well stated by a finding in the Kansas case by a court which nevertheless felt compelled to rule against the Negro plaintiffs:

> "Segregation of white and colored children in public schools has a detrimental effect upon the colored children. The impact is greater when it has the sanction of the law; for the policy of separating the races is usually interpreted as denoting the inferiority of the negro group. A sense of inferiority affects the motivation of a child to learn. Segregation with the sanction of law, therefore, has a tendency to [retard] the educational and mental development of negro children and to deprive them of some of the benefits they would receive in a racial[ly] integrated school system."

Whatever may have been the extent of psychological knowledge at the time of *Plessy* v. *Ferguson*, this finding is amply supported by modern authority.[11] Any language in *Plessy* v. *Ferguson* contrary to this finding is rejected.

---

11. K. B. Clark, *Effect of Prejudice and Discrimination on Personality Development* (Midcentury White House Conference on Children and Youth, 1950); Witmer and Kotinsky, *Personality in the Making* (1952), c. VI; Deutscher and Chein, The Psychological Ef-

We conclude that in the field of public education the doctrine of "separate but equal" has no place. Separate educational facilities are inherently unequal. Therefore, we hold that the plaintiffs and others similarly situated for whom the actions have been brought are, by reason of the segregation complained of, deprived of the equal protection of the laws guaranteed by the Fourteenth Amendment. This disposition makes unnecessary any discussion whether such segregation also violates the Due Process Clause of the Fourteenth Amendment....*It is so ordered.*

T. Meares and B. Harcourt, *Foreword: Transparent adjudication and social science research in constitutional criminal procedure*
Journal of Criminal Law and Criminology
volume 90, page 733 (2000) (Excerpt). *

In this Foreword, we call for increased attention to social science research in constitutional criminal procedure adjudication. In most criminal procedure cases...the Court's decision-making process and opinions would be greatly improved if the justices discussed and referenced the relevant empirical research. By addressing social science data, the Court would articulate more explicitly the values of interest—for example, how effective Miranda warnings are in apprising accused persons of their right to silence, or how reliable fleeing from the police is in predicting criminal behavior. This, in turn, would make more transparent the interpretive choices that underlie the balancing of liberty and order interests

.... [T]he turn to social science does not tilt the playing field in any particular ideological direction [and] it [does not] guarantee a right answer. In the first place, social science evidence is often in dispute and calls for interpretive judgment itself. But more importantly, the outcome under a balancing-of-interests approach is determined by a normative assessment of the order/liberty relationship, and not simply by quantifying the values of interest. In this sense, we are not arguing that empirical evidence will resolve constitutional litigation, nor that social science will constrain the Court's decision-making—al-

---

fects of Enforced Segregation: A Survey of Social Science Opinion, 26 *J. Psychol.* 259 (1948); Chein, What are the Psychological Effects of Segregation Under Conditions of Equal Facilities?, 3 *Int. J. Opinion and Attitude* Res. 229 (1949); Brameld, Educational Costs, in *Discrimination and National Welfare* (MacIver, ed., 1949), 44–48; Frazier, *The Negro in the United States* (1949), 674–681. And see generally Myrdal, *An American Dilemma* (1944).

* Reprinted with permission of T. Meares, author.

though, if treated respectfully, it will of course preclude the Court from making decisions based on improper empirical findings. What we are arguing, instead, is that it will improve the quality of the Court's decision-making in constitutional criminal procedure and render more transparent and open to criticism the Court's opinions.

We anticipate at least three major criticisms and will address these in conclusion. The first has to do with institutional competence. Many may respond that courts are simply not capable of dealing with complicated and conflicting social science data. Judges and lawyers, for the most part, are not trained to assess social science evidence and may not have advanced degrees in the social sciences. To make matters worse, a lot of the empirical research that is likely to reach the courts may be funded or conducted by ideologically motivated groups. How are the courts to deal with such studies?

In the article that originated the concept of social authority, John Monahan and Laurens Walker offer a set of guidelines for courts to use to assess social science research. Monahan and Walker point to critical review as a mechanism by which courts could evaluate social science research, and they discuss methods by which courts could assess the validity and generalizability of social science findings—including the question of research sponsorship. Monahan and Walker point out, moreover, that courts are unlikely to undertake these evaluations by themselves and on their own initiative. The authors suggest instead that the adversarial process itself will address some concerns about the ability of courts to adequately appraise social science research.

Once courts, and the Supreme Court in particular, more forthrightly indicate an interest in social science relevant to criminal procedure questions, litigating parties will be quick to make arguments regarding the strengths and weaknesses of empirical research. It also follows from our argument here that social scientists and the professional organizations to which they belong should be more involved in amicus brief writing presenting issues within their competence, which would further add to the strength and validity of social science research presented to the Court.

A second likely criticism is that most of the values of interest—especially personal liberty and efficient law enforcement—are incommensurable and therefore cannot properly be compared. Some scholars may respond to our proposal that any balancing of liberty and order will inevitably favor the government because one individual's interest in precluding an intrusion on her space and time will always lose out against the enormity of society's collective interest. Lawrence Tribe, for instance, has argued that "in that kind of calculus, the costs will always seem weightier than the benefits. The benefits will be elusive, intangible, diffuse." As Dorf suggests, "Liberals distrust law and economics because it undervalues "soft" variables...." These values, some may argue, are incommensurate among themselves and as against the interests of law enforcement. In a similar vein, Weisselberg argues, in the *Miranda* context, that [a] cost/benefit analysis is utterly unsuited to the task, for there is no single metric that can encompass *Miranda*'s costs and its benefits.... [O]ne cannot establish empirically the ordering of Fifth Amendment values...and the needs of law enforcement. These values, interests, and needs are incommensurate; they cannot be measured along the same scale.

With respect to the specific argument that an individual's particular interest is never weighty enough to overcome society's collective interest in safety and order, we need only point out that aggregated societal interests appear on both sides of the balance, not just on the side of safety. As a result, it is not entirely correct that social order will always be weightier than individual liberties. But the concern about the incommensurability of the costs and benefits of different levels of government respect for individual interests in privacy, autonomy and property is more difficult to address.

One answer is that acknowledging this kind of incommensurability does not necessarily preclude the comparability of society's interests in both liberty and order. Those who criticize the use of empirical evidence to inform the Court's balancing analysis are not primarily concerned with this more pragmatic approach. After all, this very approach produced the *Miranda* opinion in the first place. Recall that *Miranda*'s chief supporters characterize the opinion in this way. Rather, critics are concerned that the particular values they most cherish will be muted if decision makers use empirical evidence to create a cardinal scale against which law enforcement needs and various constitutional values can be arrayed—a scale that critics do not believe exists.

We believe this concern about empirical evidence is somewhat misplaced. These values, we contend, inevitably are and must be compared in complex criminal procedure cases. Without some evidence, the Court's pronouncements about the impact of its decisions amount to little more than bald assertions of "common sense" or "intuition." Rather than fearing the utilization of empirical and social science evidence in balancing order and liberty interests, the Court and the advocates appearing before it should strive to measure these values to the very best of their ability.

Finally, a third criticism is that our approach makes it too easy for judges to insert their own ideological predispositions into the resolution of the empirical questions. Some may argue that the real decision-making process will actually be hidden in technical and purportedly "neutral" discussions of the social science data. Worse yet, it will have the aura of "science" and "objectivity" and will therefore be more insulated from criticism. Rather than being more transparent, some may argue, the reliance on science will mask or minimize the normativity and insulate it from attack.

There is, undoubtedly, such a risk. A court deciding [a case] could, of course, fudge or nudge the science....But that would not insulate the opinion from criticism. It would in fact expose the decision-making process to further criticism from advocates and the public. In some cases, it is precisely the exposure of the underlying social science that will afford more accountability and transparency, and may allow for more criticism and revision. In some cases, social science may counteract bias, or at least highlight it....Our firm conviction is that the inevitable obstacles of institutional competence, incommensurability, and scientific myth do not derail our proposal. To conclude, we suspect, and we hope, that more infusion of social science will likely highlight potential biases, will inspire judges to make more narrow, limited and provisional decisions, and, at a minimum, will hold judges more accountable.

A list of other cases and articles relevant to this topic

Acker, J. (1990). Social science in Supreme Court criminal cases and briefs: The actual and potential contribution of social scientists as amici curiae. *Law and Human Behavior* 14: 25.

Acker, J. (1992). Affirmed: Using social science research evidence in appellate court decision making. *Criminal Justice Bulletin* 7(3): 1–6.

Davis, K. C. (1942). An approach to problems of evidence in the administrative process. *Harvard Law Review* 55: 364.

Monahan, J. and L. Walker (1986). Social authority: Obtaining, evaluating, and establishing social science in law. *University of Pennsylvania Law Review* 134: 477–517.

Monahan, J. and L. Walker (1987). Social frameworks: A new use of social science in law. *Virginia Law Review* 73: 559.

Discussion and Review Questions

1. Why have the courts been reluctant to use social science evidence? Do you agree that a greater reliance on empirical social scientific evidence would improve the social and policy decision-making by the Court? Why or why not?

2. Using Lexis-Nexis, Westlaw or Findlaw.com, locate recent criminal law cases where the trial court relied on social science to resolve an issue.

What type of case was it, and how was social science used to assist in deciding the issue or case?

References

Articles

Acker, J. (1990). Thirty years of social science in Supreme Court criminal cases. *Law and Policy* 12: 1–23.

Acker, J. (1992). Affirmed: Using social science research evidence in appellate court decision making. *Criminal Justice Bulletin* 7 (3): 1–6.

Babbie, E. (2002). *The Basics of Social Research.* Belmont, CA: Wadsworth Publishing Company.

Erickson, R. J. and R. J. Simon (1998). *The Use of Social Science Data in Supreme Court Decisions.* Chicago, IL: University of Illinois Press.

Holmes, O. W. (1881). *The Common Law.*

Holmes, O. W. (1897). The Path of the Law, *Harvard Law Review* 10: 457–469.

MacHovec, Frank (1987). *The Expert Witness Survival Manual.* Springfield, IL: Thomas.

Meares, T. and B. Harcourt (2000). Foreword. Transparent adjudication and social science research in constitutional criminal procedure. *Journal of Criminal Law and Criminology* 90: 733.

Monahan, J. and L. Walker. (1986). Social authority: Obtaining, evaluating, and establishing social science in law. *University of Pennsylvania Law Review* 134 (3): 477–517.

Pelton, L. H. (2000). Misinforming public policy: The illiberal uses of social science. *Society* 37: 61.

Pound, R. (1912). The Scope and Purpose of Sociological Jurisprudence. *Harvard Law Review* 25: 489.

Tanford, A. J. (1990). The limits of a scientific jurisprudence: The Supreme Court and psychology. *Indiana Law Journal* 66: 136–73.

Case Citations

Brown v. Board of Education, 347 U.S. 483 (1954)
Maryland v. Wilson, 519 U.S. 408 (1997)
Muller v. Oregon, 208 U.S. 41 (1907)

CHAPTER 2

SOCIAL SCIENCE AS EVIDENCE IN COURT

The reality of everyday life is taken for granted as reality. It does not require additional verification over and beyond its simple presence....But even the unproblematic sector of everyday reality is so only until further notice, that is, until its continuity is interrupted by the appearance of a problem.

–Berger, Peter L. and Thomas Luckmann (1966). *The Social Construction of Reality.* Doubleday Publishers.

The life of the law has not been logic: it has been experience.

–Oliver Wendell Holmes, Jr. (1881). *The Common Law.* Boston: Little, Brown and Co.

What is reality? What is knowledge? Berger and Luckmann, in the quote above, describe how reality is taken for granted until accepted beliefs are questioned. Oliver Wendell Holmes likewise recognized that much of the law is based on life experience as opposed to a pure logic. As experience, beliefs and knowledge are challenged, what is taken as reality will also change. In chapter one, the decision of *Brown v. Board of Education* reflects one such change that affected law and society. In *Brown*, the fundamental assumption that "separate but equal" school facilities were not harmful (as held in the prior decision of *Plessy v. Ferguson*) to children was questioned and the Court relying on psychological studies, demonstrating such harm, reversed its previous decision and mandated the integration of schools.

Much of what we know or think we know is based on life experience, intuition, authoritative sources as well as science. As suggested in the quote from Berger and Luckman, much of what we take for granted or as reality may not

> **Scientific method:** "is an approach to acquiring knowledge that uses observations to develop a hypothesis and then empirically tests the hypothesis by making additional, systematic observations. Typically, the new observations lead to a new hypothesis, and the cycle continues" (Gravetter and Forzano 2003: 18).

necessarily be true. Judges and attorneys in the legal system routinely rely on "logic" or assumptions about human behavior in resolving legal disputes and social science, in some instances, has informed judicial decision-making and perhaps improved legal conclusions. When social scientists undertake the study of what is real, they do so by utilizing a particular method of study—called the **scientific method.**

Attaining knowledge through science is very different from knowledge through experience, tradition, logic or intuition (Babbie 2002). Unlike these forms of understanding the world, the **scientific method** "is an approach to acquiring knowledge that uses observations to develop a hypothesis and then empirically tests the hypothesis by making additional, systematic observations. Typically, the new observations lead to a new hypothesis, and the cycle continues" (Gravetter and Forzano 2003: 18).

In this chapter, we discuss the use of social science as a method of understanding reality and how the introduction of this evidence impacts legal decisions that in turn effect society.

What type of social scientific evidence is used to resolve legal disputes?

There are three types of evidence used by courts and policy-makers in resolving disputes and creating law. They have been called adjudicative facts, legislative facts and social framework evidence.(Davis 1942; Monahan and Walker 1998). The first two types of evidence were identified and defined by Professor Kenneth Culp Davis in 1942. The third type of evidence, which is actually a combination of adjudicative and legislative facts, was identified and defined more recently by Monahan and Walker in 1987.

Adjudicative fact evidence concerns issues arising during a trial and information necessary to assist the jury in determining questions about "who-what-where-when-why." These facts are case-specific and do not address greater questions of changing a law. Those are called "legislative facts" and will be discussed momentarily. Use of social scientific evidence to determine case-specific facts is least controversial. (Monahan and Walker 1998) Professor Davis defined adjudicative facts in 1942 as follows:

> When [a court] finds facts concerning immediate parties—what the parties did, what the circumstances were, what the background conditions were--the [court] is performing an adjudicative function, and the facts may conveniently be called adjudicative facts. (Davis 1942).

A Florida court has referred to this type of fact as "a plain, garden-variety fact." (Monahan and Walker 1998 citing *Bowling v. Dept. of Ins.*, 394 So. 2d 165 (Fla. 1st DCA 1981).

In criminal cases, examples of the use of adjudicative facts can be found involving issues of pre-trial publicity and the prosecution of pornography or obscenity cases. In cases where there has been a great deal of publicity about a crime, social scientists have been asked by lawyers to assess whether defendants can get a fair trial in the place the crime was committed and will be prosecuted. In accusations about pornography, community standards and assessments are essential. Social science experts engage in a variety of methods, including the use of surveys and telephone interviews, to determine whether an unbiased jury could be chosen from a community subjected to a great deal of media attention for a particular case and to determine the community standards concerning obscenity. The legal issues concerning the admissibility of social science evidence in cases of obscenity will be discussed briefly.

The prosecution of obscenity and pornography cases has been riddled with conflict. The question concerning what is obscene and therefore not protected by the First and Fourteenth Amendments to the Constitution has been a question not easily determined by the courts. The Court has held "hard-core pornography" is not protected by the First Amendment. However, what is "hard-core pornography?" In an oft-quoted statement on this issue, Supreme Court Justice Stewart stated in *Jacobellis v. Ohio*, "I shall not today attempt to further define the kinds of material I understand to be embraced within the shorthand description; and perhaps I could never succeed in intelligibly doing so. *But I know it when I see it*, and the motion picture involved in this case is not [hard-core pornography.]"

Social science has been utilized to assist courts and juries in deciding the difference between protected speech or art and that which is unprotected obscenity. In *Miller v. California*, the United States Supreme Court developed a test for the trier-of-fact to determine what constitutes obscene materials:

(a) whether the average person, applying contemporary community standards, would find that the work, taken as a whole, appeals to the prurient interests, (b) whether the work depicts or describes, in a patently offensive way, sexual conduct specifically defined by the applicable state law; and (c) whether the work, taken as a whole, lacks serious literary, artistic, political or scientific value.

The first two prongs of the *Miller* test—prurient interest and patent offensiveness—involve issues of fact for the jury to decide applying contemporary community standards. *Pope v. Illinois.* In *Hamling v. United States,* the Court explained that jurors were not to apply their personal views or values in making decisions about obscenity, but that they were expected to apply what they believed was the community standard. Thus, it seems imperative that jurors be provided with outside information to assist them in making these decisions (Clark 1993) and in 1973, the Court held that the use of expert witnesses by the defense was approved. (*Kaplan v. California*). In *Miller,* the Court explicitly stated that expert testimony could be used to assist the jury in determining "community standards." (Clark 1993). A social science survey in obscenity litigation has been used in court to assist the judge or jury[1] in determining "community standards" in a few states and Canada. (Clark 1993).

"The three most common types of evidence offered to prove community standards are expert opinion testimony, public opinion surveys, and comparable materials available in the community". (Peterson 1998: 639). However, expert opinion testimony is subject to exclusion by the court on the ground that it is not scientific and not necessary to assist a jury. (*Paris Adult Theatre I*; *United States v. Pryba*). Similarly, comparable materials evidence has also been regularly excluded by the courts. (Peterson 1998). Courts have held that availability of other materials does not necessarily prove their acceptance by the community. (Peterson 1998; *United States v. Pryba*). On the other hand, courts have acknowledged the potential importance of community surveys and this is the most common form of expert testimony used to assess community standards.(Clark 1993; Peterson 1998). However, there are stringent standards for the admission of this testimony and evidence. (*United States v. Various Articles of Merchandise*).

---

1. Defendants and prosecutors may agree to waive trial by jury. In those cases, it is the judge—not a jury—that is the trier of fact.

> **First Amendment** (1719): Congress shall make no law respecting an establishment of religion, or prohibiting the free exercise thereof; or abridging the freedom of speech, or of the press; or the right of the people peaceably to assemble, and to petition the Government for a redress of grievances.
>
> **Sixth Amendment** (1791): In all criminal prosecutions, the accused shall enjoy the right to a speedy and public trial, by an impartial jury of the State and district wherein the crime shall have been committed, which district shall have been previously ascertained by law, and to be informed of the nature and cause of the accusation; to be confronted with the witnesses against him; to have compulsory process for obtaining witnesses in his favor, and to have the Assistance of Counsel for his defence.

Legislative fact evidence is defined by Davis as follows:
When a [court] wrestles with a question of law or policy, it is acting legislatively, just as judges have created the common law through judicial legislation, and the facts which inform its legislative judgment may conveniently be denominated legislative facts. (Davis 1942: 402).

The determination by the courts of legislative facts influences more than just the parties in litigation and it is much more controversial than the assessment of adjudicative facts. Rules of evidence have been designed to address adjudicative facts, not legislative facts that influence "the content of legal doctrine". (Monahan and Walker 1998: 174).

Although utilized in other types of cases, the most common use of legislative facts involves decisions of constitutional law. Specifically decisions on the "**First**, **Sixth**, **Eighth**, and **Fourteenth** Amendments have often invoked social science to support a finding of 'legislative fact'". (Monahan and Walker 1998: 179).

> **Eighth Amendment** (1791): Excessive bail shall not be required, nor excessive fines imposed, nor cruel and unusual punishments inflicted.
>
> **Fourteenth Amendment** (1868) (in part): Section 1....No State shall make or enforce any law which shall abridge the privileges or immunities of citizens of the United States; nor shall any State deprive any person of life, liberty, or property, without due process of law; nor deny to any person within its jurisdiction the equal protection of the laws....

Some examples where the Court has relied on social science to support a finding of "legislative fact" include the previously discussed decisions of *Muller v. Oregon* as well as *Brown v. Board of Education*. There are a wide variety of other criminal constitutional issues invoking the use of "legislative facts." Whether state's can regulate obscene material under the First Amendment is a question of legislative fact. In the last section concerning adjudicative facts, we saw how issues relating to "community standards" relate to adjudicative facts; but the question about whether states may create laws infringing on one's freedom of speech is a question of "legislative fact" as well. (Monahan and Walker 1998: 224). Issues relating to the constitutional minimum number of persons necessary for a jury to render a verdict in a criminal case and the video-taping of witness testimony involve defendants' rights and raise questions of legislative fact. Finally, there are several issues concerning the constitutionality of the death penalty that involve legislative fact questions—proportionality issues, racial discrimination issues, and deterrent effect issues. Most of these issues and the use of social science evidence to resolve the attendant legal disputes are discussed throughout this book.

Although several Supreme Court cases have addressed the issue of the number of persons necessary to constitute a jury under the Sixth Amendment to the United States Constitution (and these will be discussed in greater detail later), consider their first decision on this issue in *Williams v. Florida* as an example. In this case, Williams was convicted of robbery by a six-person jury. Since Florida provided only a six- as opposed to a twelve-person jury, the question before the Court concerned the constitutionality, under the Sixth Amendment guarantee of a trial by "jury," of the necessity of a trial by twelve persons. The Court held that the twelve-person panel was not a necessary ingredient of "trial by jury" and the six-member jury used in Florida was not in violation of the Constitution. In arriving at this conclusion—this legislative fact—the Court relied on social science evidence that demonstrated there was no real difference between decisions made by groups of six versus twelve. Specifically the Court stated:

> What few experiments have occurred—usually in the civil area—indicate that there is no discernable difference between the results reached by the two different-sized juries. In short, neither currently available evidence nor theory, suggests that the 12-man jury is necessarily more advantageous to the defendant than a jury composed of fewer members. (*Williams v. Florida* footnotes omitted).

In footnotes 48 and 49 to these statements, the Court cited several experimental studies conducted to evaluate the influence of six-person juries on decision-making. In essence, the Court arrived at this conclusion based on these studies. Interestingly and as scholars who engaged in studies following the *Williams* decision stated, the Court relied on negligible evidence of "no discernable difference" at best. (Saks 1974; Zeisel and Diamon 1974). Researchers asserted there were a host of problems with the social scientific evidence ranging from the Court's inaccurate discussion of the findings, inadequate sampling in the research studies, and questionable methodology. (Saks 1974).

Despite its empirical weakness, the importance of its decision for our purposes is that the United States Supreme Court relied on social science evidence to render a decision that had an impact beyond the parties in the case. The Court's decision that six-member juries were consistent with the guarantee of the Sixth Amendment gave its stamp of approval for state courts to utilize less than twelve-person juries in criminal cases.

> *Social framework evidence* is defined by Monahan and Walker as follows: General research results [that] are used to construct a frame of reference or background context for deciding a factual issue crucial to the resolution of a specific case. (Monahan and Walker 1987: 559).

Monahan and Walker call this type of evidence a "hybrid." It is a "use of social science...research that appears to have the general, broadly-based characteristics usually associated with lawmaking [but] is used to determine case-specific issues, a function usually conceived as fact-finding". (Monahan and Walker 1998: 354). Thus, this type of evidence is a mix of legislative and adjudicative fact evidence. One example of social framework evidence includes testimony about "battering and its effects." With this type of evidence, experts educate juries concerning general testimony and may not make specific reference to a particular or specific person. In other words, they would provide general testimony about battered victims' reactions without specific reference to the victim. In this chapter an excerpt from Monahan and Walker's (1987) *Social framework: A new use of social science in law* is included.

L. Walker and J. Monahan,
Social frameworks: A new use of social science in law. *
Virginia Law Review volume 73, page 559 (Excerpt)(1987)

OVER the past half-century it has become commonplace for courts and commentators to distinguish two uses of social science in law. Social science is said either to prove "legislative facts" that concern general questions of law and policy, or to prove "adjudicative facts" that pertain only to the case at hand. The choice of procedures to introduce research findings has depended heavily on the assignment of the research to one of these two categories. In this article, we identify a new generic use of social science in law that is emerging from recent cases. In this third use, research findings presented in court are neither legislative nor adjudicative facts themselves. Rather, empirical information is being offered that incorporates aspects of both of the traditional uses: general research results are used to construct a frame of reference or background context for deciding factual issues crucial to the resolution of a specific case. We call this new use of social science in law the creation of *social frameworks.....*

I. An emerging use of empirical research

A. The legislative-adjudicative distinction

In 1942, Kenneth Culp Davis published what proved to be a remarkably influential article in which he proposed a distinction between "adjudicative facts" and "legislative facts." According to Davis, facts concerning the immediate parties to a law suit were "adjudicative facts," and facts relating to the determination of law and policy were "legislative facts." For Davis, the distinction suggested a need to modify traditional common law rules of evidence when the objective of introducing evidence is the development of information for choosing among legal rules. Though the legislative-adjudicative distinction was developed in the context of administrative law, a broader application ensued and today the usefulness of the distinction is widely recognized.

Two recent examples will illustrate the use of social science research for these purposes. In *United States v. Leon,* the United States Supreme Court considered the question of whether the exclusionary rule should be modified to admit evidence seized by the police in good faith reliance upon a search warrant that is subsequently held to be defective. A majority held that the ex-

---

    * reprinted with the permission of the copyright holder and Copyright Clearance Center.

clusionary rule was "a judicially created remedy," designed to deter violations of the fourth amendment. Whether this remedy should be modified by creating an exception where the police have acted in good faith, the court stated, "must be resolved by weighing the costs and benefits" of creating the exception. This weighing process was accomplished, in part, by reviewing the findings of social science research concerning the effects of the exclusionary rule on the disposition of felony arrests. None of these studies involved the immediate parties to the *Leon* case. Rather, the research was used exclusively and explicitly for the purpose of considering whether to alter an existing rule of law. In *Leon*, therefore, social science research was plainly used to determine a "legislative fact."

Contrast this use of social science with the way research was used in *Processed Plastic v. Warner Communications*. Warner Communications had a registered copyright in "The Dukes of Hazzard" television series and had licensed several toy companies to manufacture replicas of a car that figured prominently in the series. The Processed Plastic Company, which was not licensed by Warner Communications, began to market a toy car that had many of the same physical characteristics as the car used in the television series. Warner Communications moved for a preliminary injunction to stop the sale of the cars made by Processed Plastic. At a hearing, Warner introduced a social science survey of random groups of children in which eighty-two percent of the children, when presented with a Processed Plastic car, identified it as the " 'Dukes of Hazzard' car." The trial court ruled, and the United States Court of Appeals for the Seventh Circuit affirmed, that these data demonstrated that Processed Plastic had violated the Lanham Act by creating consumer confusion. The study introduced in this case did not concern any rule of law. Indeed, neither of the parties challenged the meaning or application of the copyright or trademark statutes involved. Instead, the research pertained to the immediate parties to the case, and to no one else. The use of social science research in *Processed Plastic* is a clear example of its use to determine an "adjudicative fact."

B. Anomalous uses of social science

Most of the uses of social science in court fall into either the "legislative fact" or "adjudicative fact" categories. Within the past several years, however, courts have increasingly begun to use research in ways that do not correspond to either of the traditional classifications. There are strong indications that a new, third use of social science in law is emerging. Notable examples can be found in cases concerning eyewitness identification, assessments of dangerousness, battered women, and sexual victimization.

The only evidence that connected the defendant in *State v. Chapple* to the crime of murder was the testimony of two eyewitnesses. At trial, the defense offered the testimony of a research psychologist to rebut the testimony of the state's witnesses. In the offer of proof, the expert testified to published studies on factors such as the speed with which memory decays over time, the effects of stress on eyewitness accuracy, and the relationship between the confidence of a witness in his or her identification and the accuracy of that identification. The trial judge granted a motion to suppress the social science testimony, but the Arizona Supreme Court reversed and remanded the case for a new trial, stating that "there were a number of substantive issues of ultimate fact on which the expert's testimony would have been of significant assistance."

The defendant in *State v. Davis* was also charged with murder, and pleaded guilty. At a penalty trial to determine whether the defendant would be executed or serve a mandatory thirty-year minimum sentence, defense counsel offered the testimony of a sociologist as evidence in support of mitigation of the sentence. The expert, according to the offer of proof, would have testified to published studies and government statistics demonstrating that murderers have the lowest rate of recidivism of all criminals, and that, considering the crime rate among persons of the age the defendant would be when released from prison a minimum of thirty years hence, it was extremely unlikely that the defendant would again be a threat to society. As in *Chapple,* the trial court granted a motion to suppress the testimony, stating that "the statistical approach doesn't tell us anything at all about a given defendant." The New Jersey Supreme Court reversed, however, holding that social science research "may, in effect, encapsulate ordinary human experience and provide an appropriate frame of reference for a jury's consideration."

In addition to eyewitness identification and predictions of dangerousness, apparently anomalous uses of social science research have occurred with respect to the "battered woman syndrome." In *State v. Kelly,* the defendant was convicted of the reckless manslaughter of her husband. She claimed at trial that she was acting in self-defense, fearing that her husband would kill her. The defense presented evidence that the husband had beaten the defendant on many prior occasions. The defense also sought to call a psychologist to testify to the findings of several researchers who had published reports on the state of mind "of other women who had been in similarly abusive relationships." Here, too, the trial judge suppressed the testimony and the state supreme court reversed and remanded the case for a new trial, stating that "the proffered expert testimony [may be] not only relevant, but critical" to the defendant's case.

Finally, in *State v. Myers* the defendant was found guilty of criminal sexual conduct involving a child. Over the objection of defense counsel, the prosecution had been allowed to present a social science expert witness to testify to behavioral traits "typically" observed in abused children, traits that were also observed in the child complainant. On appeal, the defendant claimed that admitting such testimony constituted reversible error. Affirming the conviction, however, the Minnesota Supreme Court stated that "[b]ackground data providing a relevant insight into the puzzling aspects of the child's conduct and demeanor which the jury could not otherwise bring to its evaluation of her credibility is helpful and appropriate."

C. Social framework as an organizing concept

Comparison of these four cases with *Leon* makes it immediately clear that social science was not being used to provide "legislative facts." In *Leon*, a change in a legal rule was the express purpose for which the social science research was introduced. In the four cases just presented, however, neither party contemplated a change in any rule of law. Rather, accepting the rules of law governing his or her respective case, the party introducing the research was attempting to demonstrate that the findings would assist the jury to decide the specific factual issues being litigated.

At the same time, comparison of these cases with *Processed Plastic* reveals that social science was not being used to provide "adjudicative facts" either. In *Processed Plastic*, the research was conducted with products manufactured by the immediate parties to the case. In none of the four examples described above, however, were the parties to the case involved in the research at all. The expert witnesses relied heavily—and in some of the cases, exclusively—on "off the rack" research studies published before the events that gave rise to the litigation took place, studies performed by researchers and using subjects with no knowledge of the case at bar.

Yet the way social science was used in these cases—while neither legislative nor adjudicative fact—does have some of the hallmarks of each. In each case, the research being introduced shared the critical characteristic of legislative fact—generality. The studies bore on issues at trial only as those issues were particular instances of larger empirical relationships that had been uncovered. Just as the research used in *Leon* addressed the "collective" costs and benefits of modifying the exclusionary rule, the studies in *Chapple* considered "general factors" affecting all eyewitnesses. Similarly, the data introduced in *Davis* applied to the recidivism rate of all offenders "sharing [the defendant's]...demographic 'features,'" the research proffered in *Kelly* addressed beliefs that were "common" to battered women as a group, and the empirical information in *Myers* concerned "general characteristics" that were "typically observed" in large classes of abused children.

However, as in cases involving the use of social research to determine adjudicative facts, the studies here were introduced solely to help resolve specific factual issues disputed by the immediate parties to the case, issues whose resolution had no substantive significance beyond the case at hand. Just as the research used in *Processed Plastic* addressed only whether consumers were confused when presented with two given products, the studies in *Chapple* were considered solely to rebut the testimony of eyewitnesses to that particular crime. Research data were introduced in *Davis* only for the purpose of assessing Davis' own character, and the studies in *Kelly* were provided exclusively so that inferences might be made about that defendant's state of mind. The empirical information in *Myers* was offered for the sole purpose of determining whether the named victim was, in fact, abused.

The research used in these examples, then, is not pure legislative or adjudicative fact but rather incorporates the essential aspects of both of the established categories. We therefore propose a new category, which we term social framework, to refer to *the use of general conclusions from social science research in determining factual issues in a specific case.....*

II. Substantive concerns about social frameworks

Each use of a social framework raises its own set of issues and can be evaluated only case by case. Yet several concerns recur with such regularity in judicial opinions that the question arises whether there is some categorical reason to bar this use of social science altogether. To address this overarching question, we take as our point of departure the traditional concerns of the law of evidence—concerns that, thus far, have set the agenda for the debate on the introduction of social frameworks. More specifically, we measure social frameworks against the standards of those Federal Rules that are most frequently held germane in deciding on the admissibility of a framework. We are not concerned with the "admissibility" of social frameworks, but rather with the normative question of whether the use of social frameworks is generally prudent. Thus we use evidentiary concerns only to assess controversial policy issues posed by frameworks.

A. The relevance of frameworks

"Relevance" is the fundamental requirement of the Federal Rules of Evidence. Evidence that is not relevant is never admissible. The Rules define relevant evidence as evidence "having any tendency to make the existence of any fact that is of consequence to the determination of the action more probable or less probable than it would be without the evidence." Determining whether material is relevant under this definition, therefore, requires two judgments: whether the information pertains to a fact that is "of consequence," and whether the information renders that fact "more probable or less probable." Social frameworks pose no special problems with regard to the first of these judgments. Deciding whether the issue being framed by the research is one that is "of consequence" to some legal determination is identical to deciding whether any other issue is consequential.

The second judgment, however, poses a more difficult issue: whether the framework makes any fact in the case "more probable or less probable." The source of the difficulty appears to be that social frameworks present information that is not collected from any immediate party to the case. Rather, the information has been derived from studying groups of people who are claimed to be similar in certain key respects to one of the immediate parties. Making inferences about an individual's behavior from the individual's membership in some group or class is something often done in the legal context of predicting an individual's *future* behavior. Since future acts have not yet occurred, it is easy to understand how estimates derived from group data of the likelihood that future acts will occur are acceptable in the law. For example, in estimating how much money a negligently injured or killed individual would have earned in his or her lifetime, courts are quite comfortable in turning to economists to estimate the value of the person's future labor based on statistics derived from groups of people in the same occupation and with the same life expectancy as the injured or deceased person. The same is true with the use of group data to predict individual criminal behavior in bail, sentencing, and parole decisions.

Some courts that are quite willing to countenance the use of group data to infer how an individual member of the group will behave in the future draw a bright line prohibiting the use of such information at trial to assist in determining how an individual has acted in the past. In *State v. Saldana*, for example, the defendant was convicted of rape at a trial at which an expert witness for the prosecution compared the complainant's reactions to the reactions of groups of women who had been raped. The Minnesota Supreme Court, in overturning the conviction, stated that the jury "must not decide this case on the basis of how most people react to rape." Rather, the jury "must decide what happened in *this case.*"

The logic of making inferences about individual behavior from group membership, however, is as applicable to past as to future acts. As Laurence Tribe has noted:

> It is not the future character of an event that induces us to give weight to probabilistic evidence, but the lack of other, more convincing evidence—an absence more common in, but certainly not limited to, future occurrences....Insofar as the relevance of probability concepts is concerned, then, there is simply no inherent distinction between future and past events.

It would appear, therefore, that while social frameworks can never in themselves establish with certainty the existence of any fact that is of consequence to an issue at trial, they are surely capable of providing information regarding the probability that something did or did not occur. This is all that the concept of relevance requires and all that sound policy would seem to demand.

B. Potential for prejudice or confusion

A second point of departure in the generic evaluation of social frameworks is the proposition that relevant evidence may be excluded if its probative value is accompanied by a risk that the evidence will unfairly prejudice one of the parties or will confuse or affirmatively mislead the jury. Any potential to prejudice, confuse, or mislead, must be balanced against probative value, so that the former does not "substantially outweigh" the latter. Otherwise, the material will be excluded.

"Unfair prejudice" reflects two concerns. The first is that decisions not be swayed by appeals to the jurors' emotions. To our knowledge, the charge of playing on the jurors' emotions has never been leveled against the introduction of a social framework. If anything, the occasional complaint has been that empirical data are "cold"—that is, that they lack any emotional impact at all. This should not be surprising. The goal of social science—and of all other types of science as well—is to provide "dispassionate" tests of competing hypotheses to account for observed states of affairs.

The second concern subsumed under the rubric of "unfair prejudice" is not frivolous when applied to social frameworks. The concern is that such information, precisely because it is termed "empirical" and the product of "research," will categorically be accorded undue (and thus "unfair") value by naive jurors who are overly deferential to anything portrayed as "science." As the Minnesota Supreme Court stated, "[p]ermitting a person in the role of an expert" to present information on the reactions that characterize groups of women who have been raped "unfairly prejudices the appellant by creating an aura of special reliability and trustworthiness" and this "danger of unfair prejudice outweighs any probative value" that the framework may possess.

The claim that jurors will be so awed by the scientific "aura" of social frameworks that they will, in effect, accord frameworks a probative value in excess of the probative value to which they are logically entitled, is an empirical claim. Fortunately, it is a claim that has been thoroughly investigated. It appears that aggregate "statistical" information, in actual practice, is likely to be highly *undervalued* by lay decision-makers. Numerous studies have found that when people are presented with social frameworks (often called "base rates" in the research literature) and with factual information specific to the case at issue, they strongly tend to give less weight to the framework than the logic of inference suggests is due.

The introduction of a social framework thus creates little risk of inciting turmoil and appears unlikely to be accorded "excessive" probative value. But might a framework still engender sufficient cognitive confusion or be so likely to mislead the fact finder as to outweigh whatever admittedly probative value it may have? The answer to this question would appear to depend on how the social framework is presented to the trier of fact. It is, of course, possible to present a social framework confusingly. But it is also possible to present a social framework clearly and in perspective. In none of the four framework illustrations presented in Part I, for example, did the courts find the proffered frameworks confusing or distracting. There are "good" and "bad" expert witnesses and "good" and "bad" briefs in terms of their ability to enlighten rather than confuse or distract the trier of fact. Particular witnesses or briefs presenting empirical information may fall into either category. Nothing in the nature of social frameworks, however, suggests that they inevitably, or even often, tax the cognitive capacities of judges or juries. Certainly no categorical exclusion is justified on this ground.

C. Information value

The Federal Rules permit the introduction of "scientific…knowledge," provided that it will "assist the trier of fact to understand the evidence or to determine a fact in issue." This in essence restates earlier formulations that expert scientific testimony must present information that is outside the "common knowledge" of the average lay person. These rules suggest that empirical frameworks must provide fact-finders with information they do not already have.

There is good reason to believe that in many particular situations social science research will provide new insight. Although comparatively young among the sciences, social research has already made important contributions to knowledge. The framework cases that have been adjudicated to date suggest that judges often find that empirical research provides uncommon and otherwise unavailable insights into factual issues at trial.

In *State v. Chapple,* for example, the Arizona Supreme Court stated that it could not "assume that the average juror would be aware" of factors reported by research to affect the accuracy of eyewitness testimony. Two of the factors mentioned by the court were the relationship between stress and eyewitness accuracy and the degree to which the confidence of an eyewitness was related to the accuracy of the identification. Many lay persons, including jurors, appear to believe that high stress increases the accuracy of a witness' memory, and that the more confident a witness is in his or her identification, the more accurate that identification will be. Yet a number of researchers have concluded that high levels of stress cause distortions in recall, and that there is little, if any, association between the confidence and the accuracy of an eyewitness.

Similarly, in *State v. Kelly* the New Jersey Supreme Court found that social research about battered women examined "an area where the purported common knowledge of the jury may be very much mistaken, an area where jurors' logic, drawn from their own experience, may lead to a wholly incorrect conclusion, an area where expert knowledge would enable the jurors to disregard their prior conclusions as being common myths rather than common knowledge." Knowledge of certain topics, therefore, appears not to be common among lay fact-finders, and what passes for knowledge in other areas may be bogus. A growing number of courts have held that the use of social frameworks to correct beliefs that are erroneous does indeed "assist the trier of fact."

D. Character evidence

Finally, the prohibition against character evidence has been a focal point in the debate on the introduction of social frameworks. In a sense, this prohibition is a special case of the more general proposition that relevant evidence may be prohibited if it will unfairly prejudice one of the parties. The rule against character evidence indicates an instance of presumed unfairness. The Federal Rules provide that "[e]vidence of a person's character or a trait of his character is not admissible for the purpose of proving that he acted in conformity therewith on a particular occasion." Strictly speaking, the data offered to create a social framework are not "character evidence," since they do not pertain to "*a person's* character or a trait of *his* character." Rather, the research describes the behavior of *groups* or *other* persons. Yet the purpose of offering character evidence is similar to the purpose of introducing social frameworks: to prove—that is, to make "more probable or less probable"—that an individual acted in conformity with an established pattern. By definition, knowledge of the general pattern of an individual's behavior (i.e., his or her character)—like knowledge of the general pattern of behavior of persons in the groups to which he or she belongs—allows one to recalculate the probabilities that the person acted in a certain way on a given occasion. The policy concern that gave rise to a rule barring the admissibility of evidence of an individual's "characteristic" behavior applies with equal force to the use of information on behavior characteristic of the groups to which he or she belongs: individuals should be accountable for their specific acts and not for their general proclivities. In the context of social frameworks, as in the context of traditional character evidence, the basis of that concern "lies more in history and experience than in logic."

However firm the libertarian values barring the admission of character evidence, modern evidence law, as exemplified by the Federal Rules, contains several important exceptions allowing the introduction of character evidence. In criminal proceedings, the defendant may offer evidence of his or her own character and, if this occurs, the prosecution may offer character evidence in rebuttal. The defendant also may offer evidence of the victim's character, and if this occurs, the prosecution again may offer character evidence in rebuttal. In either civil or criminal proceedings, any party may offer evidence of the character of a witness. In addition, the prohibition against character evidence operates only when that evidence is used to prove that a person "acted" in conformity with his or her character on a particular occasion. Character evidence may be admissible for many other purposes such as proof of knowledge, intent, or preparation.

The rule against character evidence, therefore, suggests a bar to some, but by no means all, applications of social frameworks. Where traditional forms of character evidence are prohibited, social frameworks also should be barred;

where traditional forms of character evidence are allowed, there is no reason to prohibit social frameworks.

E. General conclusions

Measuring social frameworks according to broad evidentiary policy reveals no general bar to this third use of social science in law. Social frameworks can make the existence of a fact at issue in a legal proceeding more probable or less probable than it would otherwise appear. Frameworks run little risk of inflaming a juror's emotions or taking advantage of a juror's credulity. They can, with careful presentation, clarify rather than confuse the issues to be decided at trial. Frameworks often tell jurors something they do not already know, or disabuse them of common but erroneous perceptions. And while the use of frameworks should be constrained by the concerns expressed in the rule against character evidence, numerous exceptions to that rule suggest ample opportunity for the application of frameworks.....

IV. Conclusion

A novel role for empirical research is emerging—a use of general research conclusions to set a background context for deciding crucial factual issues at trial. We see no substantive reason for a categorical bar of this new application of social science in law. Indeed, we see potential benefits from using research in this way. However, each introduction of a social framework must be assessed on its own empirical and legal merits. This requires major changes in procedural mechanisms currently used for dealing with social frameworks. Drawing on the concept of social authority, we have developed a comprehensive set of proposals that includes new procedures for obtaining and evaluating aggregate empirical data, and for communicating the results of this investigation to juries. As social science attends to more aspects of human behavior, and as courts seek to benefit from these advances, the need to adopt such changes will become compelling.

A list of other cases and articles relevant to this topic.

Monahan, J. and L. Walker (1998). *Social Science in Law*. Westbury, NY: Foundation Press.

Saks, M. (1974) Ignorance of science is no excuse. *Trial* 10: 18.

Wrightsman, L. (2001). *Forensic Psychology*. Belmont CA: Wadsworth Publishing.

Discussion and Review Questions

1. Identify the three types of social scientific evidence that may be introduced in court and provide an example of each.
2. Using Findlaw.com or another legal database (e.g., Lexis Nexis), locate recent cases that have introduced social scientific evidence or relied on experts in social science to assist jurors in making determinations about human behavior. What types of evidence did you find, would the evidence or testimony establish an adjudicative, legislative or social framework fact.

References

Articles

Babbie, E. (2002). *The Basics of Social Research*. CA: Wadsworth Publishing.

Clark, J. T. (1993). The "community standard" in the trial of obscenity cases—A mandate for empirical evidence in search of the truth. *Ohio Northern University Law Review* 20: 13.

Davis, K. C. (1942). An approach to problems of evidence in the administrative process. *Harvard Law Review* 55: 364.

Gravetter, F. J. and L. B. Forzano (2003). *Research methods: For the behavioral sciences*. Belmont, CA: Wadsworth Publishing.

Monahan, J. and L. Walker (1987). Social frameworks: A new use of social science in law. *Virginia Law Review* 73: 559.

Monahan, J. and L. Walker (1998). *Social Science in Law*. Westbury, NY: Foundation Press.

Peterson, J. (1998). Comment: Behind the curtain of privacy: How obscenity law inhibits the expression of ideas about sex and gender. *Wisconsin Law Review* 625.

Saks, M. (1974). Ignorance of science is no excuse. *Trial* 10: 18.

Wells, G.L. (1993). What do we know about eyewitness identification? *American Pyschologist* 48: 553–571.

Wrightsman, L. S. (2001). *Forensic Psychology*. Belmont CA: Wadsworth Publishing.

Zeisel, H. and S. S. Diamond (1974). Convincing empirical evidence. *Chicago Law Review* 41: 281–295.

Case Citations

Brown v. Board of Education, 347 U.S. 483 (1954).
Hamling v. United States, 418 U.S. 87 (1974).

Kaplan v. California, 413 U.S. 115 (1973).
Miller v. California, 413 U.S. 15 (1973).
Muller v. Oregon, 208 U.S. 41 (1908).
Paris Adult Theatre I v. Slaton, 413 U.S. 49 (1973).
Plessy v. Ferguson, 163 U.S. 537 (1896)
Pope v. Illinois, 481 U. S. 497 (1987)
United States v. Pryba, 900 F.2d 748 (4th Cir. 1990).
United States v. Various Articles of Merchandise, 750 F.2d 596 (7th Cir. 1984).
Williams v. Florida, 399 U.S. 78 (1970).

CHAPTER 3

THE LEGAL SCIENCE
OF SOCIAL SCIENCE

If scientific, technical, or other specialized knowledge will assist the trier
of fact to understand the evidence or to determine a fact in issue, a witness qualified as an expert by knowledge, skill, experience, training, or
education, may testify thereto in the form of an opinion or otherwise.

–Rule 702, Federal Rules of Evidence

A wife claims to be repeatedly and violently battered by her husband for
years during their marriage. These violent episodes are broken up by periods
of relative calm and harmony. While the wife is pregnant with their second
child, she is battered, accused of carrying another man's child, and threatened
with a fractured skull if she attempts to leave or seek divorce. The wife is aware
of other violent incidents by her husband against his ex-wife and several others. This violence is corroborated by their testimony. The wife is aware that
her husband keeps loaded guns in the house.

One morning, an argument erupts between the wife and the husband. Although she is pregnant and he had promised not to hit her, the husband hits
her over the head with a magazine and his fists. He drags her up to their bedroom and orders her to pack a suitcase and leave. When she objects, he hits
her with his fists and a wooden brush. To protect her abdomen, she turns her
back to his blows and takes most of the attack to her back, buttocks and
thighs. The husband grabs a gun, points it at her face and states "You are going
out of here this morning one way or the other."

The husband leaves the bedroom for his office in the home. The wife pleads
with him to be reasonable from the bedroom where she sits with her daughter. He tells her that he does not want to argue anymore and tells her to pack.
Shortly thereafter he returns to the bedroom and there is a struggle. The wife
claims that she believed the husband was going for the gun, so she grabs it

from the dresser, and she fires one shot to scare him. As she walks down the stairs, the husband jumps out at her and she fires two more shots. She does not realize that one bullet hits him in the abdomen. He goes to his home office, and when the wife follows, she believes he has a gun in his hand and she shoots him in the head, killing him.

The husband's secretary, who arrives at their home shortly before the shooting, claims that she did not see what happened between the husband and wife, but she heard a gunshot three seconds after she saw the husband walk into the room with his wife. She hears a thumping noise as if someone was falling down the stairs, and then hears the husband say "don't shoot me anymore" followed by the second shot. As she reaches the office door, the secretary hears the wife say "I am not going to leave you, I mean it"—then she hears the third and final shot. (*Ibn-Tamas v. United States*)

The wife was charged with second-degree murder while armed, and she wanted to call Dr. Lenore Walker, a clinical psychologist, to testify as an expert on the subject of "battered women" during her trial. She claimed there were two purposes for this testimony—to describe the phenomenon of "wife battering" and to give Walker's opinion that her personality and behavior corresponded with those of other battered women. The defense claimed the evidence was relevant to assist the jury in assessing the wife's credibility and her claim that she believed that she was in imminent danger from her husband and that she acted in self-defense. (*Ibn-Tamas*).

This was the first time any court had confronted the question of the admissibility of this type of evidence. The trial court refused to admit Dr. Walker's testimony at trial, and on appeal the court held that although the evidence was relevant to the issue at trial, the court found that there was insufficient evidence as to the adequacy of the methodology used by Dr. Walker in determining whether an individual suffers from the effects of battering. Dr. Walker based her determinations on her research with 110 battered women, and the court believed that the science was simply too new and there was not general acceptance of her ideas and methodology of study in the scientific community to justify admission. The wife was tried without Dr. Walker's testimony, was found guilty as charged, and sentenced to prison.

Over the next several years, courts refused to admit testimony about battering and its effects for three reasons—they held the evidence was irrelevant, unnecessary, and the methodology was insufficiently developed.(Bjerregaard and Blowers 1996). In the last twenty years, a great deal has changed. All fifty states now allow the introduction of evidence (to varying degrees) concerning battering and its effects at trial. (Raeder 1996; Parrish 1995). What

> **Relevant:** Applying to the matter in question; affording something to the purpose. Fact is relevant to another fact when, according to common course of events, existence of one taken alone or in connection with the other fact renders of the other certain or more probable.... [T]estimony is relevant if reasonable inferences can be drawn therefrom regarding or if any light is shed upon, a contested matter. (Black's Law Dictionary)
> **Reliable:** Trustworthy, worthy of confidence (Black's Law Dictionary).
> **Reliability:** (1) That quality of measurement method that suggests that the same data would have been collected each time in repeated observations of the same phenomenon.....(2) Quality of repeatability in untruths. (Babbie 2002).

changed? By the mid-1980s, many researchers had studied, written about, and discussed the implications of battering and its effects. In other words, courts were persuaded that the testimony was **relevant**, necessary to assist jurors and that the methodology was sufficiently **reliable**.

How do courts determine whether social science evidence is admissible at trial?

For 70 years, the answer to this question was that the *Frye* test was used to determine the admissibility of "science" at trial. In a very short decision, it was only two pages in length and without citing a single authority, the Court of Appeals for the District of Columbia determined that to be admissible the results of a scientific test must be "deduced from a well-recognized scientific principle or discovery" and that the test and results "be sufficiently established to have gained general acceptance in the particular field in which it belongs." In the *Frye* case, the court was deciding whether the results of a polygraph test should be admitted at a defendant's trial. Since the court found the polygraph had not yet gained general acceptance in the scientific community, it was not admissible.

In 1993, the United States Supreme Court modified the *Frye* decision, based on changes to Federal Rule of Evidence 702 (the text of which introduces this chapter), and it removed the "general acceptance" requirement for admissibility of scientific evidence. (*Daubert v. Merrell Dow Pharmaceuticals*).

In making this change, the Court relied on the language of Rule 702:

> If scientific, technical or other specialized knowledge will assist the trier of fact to understand the evidence or to determine a fact in issue,

> **Exculpatory:** Clearing or tending to clear from alleged fault or guilt; excusing. (Black's Law Dictionary)

a witness qualified as an expert by knowledge, skill, experience training or education, may testify thereto in the form of an opinion or otherwise.

By removing the general acceptance requirement as a pre-condition to admissibility in 1993, lawyers argued that polygraph evidence should be admitted as evidence at trial. To date, polygraph evidence has not been admitted at a trial and is a hotly debated topic among scholars. (Gallai 1999). In a recent decision by the Supreme Court, it seems that polygraph evidence will not be admitted at trials anytime soon. In *United States v. Scheffer*, the Court held that Military Rule of Evidence 707 which makes polygraph results *per se* inadmissible in military court-martial proceedings was not unconstitutional as a violation of a defendant's right to present a complete defense and to introduce **exculpatory** evidence. One reason for its exclusion of evidence was given by Justice Thomas when he stated that "there is simply no consensus that polygraph evidence is reliable," and some scientists have noted that its accuracy is " 'little better than could be obtained by the toss of a coin.' "

It is important to remember that under the *Daubert* decision, trial judges must still determine whether scientific testimony and evidence are relevant and reliable. The decision concerning relevance is a legal one; whereas the decision regarding reliability is a mix of legal and scientific issues. To decide reliability, the trial court may, but is not required to consider, the validity of the research **methodology**, whether the theory or technique has been subject to **peer review** and publication, and the general acceptance of the theory, methodology and the technique by the scientific community. Courts may also consider anything else it deems as relevant to the determination of admissibility.

Six years after *Daubert*, the Court in *Kumho Tire Company v. Carmichael et al.* held that Rule 702 and *Daubert* applied to all expert witnesses, testimony and evidence. Thus, testimony based on 'technical' and 'other specialized knowledge', similar to scientific evidence, must be found reliable and relevant by the trial court prior to its use at trial.

Social science evidence has been influential to varying degrees in resolving issues in criminal cases. This book reviews issues where social science has been relied on or rejected in resolving criminal substantive and procedural issues. It also will discuss legal issues that have not relied on social science informa-

> **Methodology:** "the science of finding out"…[i.e.,] how social scientists find out about human social life. (Babbie 2002: 5)
> **Peer Review:** Research that is reviewed by anonymous and confidential evaluators to ensure the quality of the published work.

tion, but raised social science questions. In this chapter, excerpts from *Daubert v. Merrell Dow Pharmaceuticals* and *Kumho Tire Company v. Carmichael* are included.

Daubert v. Merrell Dow Pharmaceuticals,
509 U.S. 579 (1993)

OPINION BY: JUSTICE BLACKMUN

In this case we are called upon to determine the standard for admitting expert scientific testimony in a federal trial.

Petitioners Jason Daubert and Eric Schuller are minor children born with serious birth defects. They and their parents sued respondent in California state court, alleging that the birth defects had been caused by the mothers' ingestion of Bendectin, a prescription antinausea drug marketed by respondent….

After extensive discovery, respondent moved for summary judgment, contending that Bendectin does not cause birth defects in humans and that petitioners would be unable to come forward with any admissible evidence that it does. In support of its motion, respondent submitted an affidavit of Steven H. Lamm, physician and epidemiologist, who is a well-credentialed expert on the risks from exposure to various chemical substances. Doctor Lamm stated that he had reviewed all the literature on Bendectin and human birth defects—more than 30 published studies involving over 130,000 patients. No study had found Bendectin to be a human teratogen (*i.e.*, a substance capable of causing malformations in fetuses). On the basis of this review, Doctor Lamm concluded that maternal use of Bendectin during the first trimester of pregnancy has not been shown to be a risk factor for human birth defects.

Petitioners did not (and do not) contest this characterization of the published record regarding Bendectin. Instead, they responded to respondent's motion with the testimony of eight experts of their own, each of whom also possessed impressive credentials. These experts had concluded that Bendectin can cause birth defects. Their conclusions were based upon "in vitro" (test tube) and "in vivo" (live) animal studies that found a link between Bendectin and malformations; pharmacological studies of the chemical structure of Bendectin that purported to show similarities between the structure of the drug and that of other substances known to cause birth defects; and the "reanalysis" of previously published epidemiological (human statistical) studies....

In the 70 years since its formulation in the *Frye* case, the "general acceptance" test has been the dominant standard for determining the admissibility of novel scientific evidence at trial. See E. Green & C. Nesson, Problems, Cases, and Materials on Evidence 649 (1983). Although under increasing attack of late, the rule continues to be followed by a majority of courts, including the Ninth Circuit.

The *Frye* test has its origin in a short and citation-free 1923 decision concerning the admissibility of evidence derived from a systolic blood pressure deception test, a crude precursor to the polygraph machine. In what has become a famous (perhaps infamous) passage, the then Court of Appeals for the District of Columbia described the device and its operation and declared:

"Just when a scientific principle or discovery crosses the line between the experimental and demonstrable stages is difficult to define. Somewhere in this twilight zone the evidential force of the principle must be recognized, and while courts will go a long way in admitting expert testimony deduced from a well-recognized scientific principle or discovery, *the thing from which the deduction is made must be sufficiently established to have gained general acceptance in the particular field in which it belongs.*" 54 App. D.C. at 47, 293 F. at 1014 (emphasis added).

Because the deception test had "not yet gained such standing and scientific recognition among physiological and psychological authorities as would justify the courts in admitting expert testimony deduced from the discovery, development, and experiments thus far made," evidence of its results was ruled inadmissible. *Ibid.*

The merits of the *Frye* test have been much debated, and scholarship on its proper scope and application is legion.[4] Petitioners' primary attack, however,

---

4. See, *e.g.*, Green, Expert Witnesses and Sufficiency of Evidence in Toxic Substances Litigation: The Legacy of *Agent Orange* and Bendectin Litigation, 86 *NW. U. L. Rev.* 643 (1992) (hereinafter Green); Becker & Orenstein, The Federal Rules of Evidence After Sixteen Years—The Effect of "Plain Meaning" Jurisprudence, the Need for an Advisory Committee on the Rules of Evidence, and Suggestions for Selective Revision of the Rules, 60 *Geo. Wash. L. Rev.* 857, 876–885 (1992); Hanson, James Alphonzo Frye is Sixty-Five Years Old; Should He Retire?, 16 *West. St. U. L. Rev.* 357 (1989); Black, A Unified Theory of Scientific Evidence, 56 Ford. L. Rev. 595 (1988); Imwinkelried, The "Bases" of Expert Testimony: The Syllogistic Structure of Scientific Testimony, 67 *N. C. L. Rev.* 1 (1988); Proposals for a Model Rule on the Admissibility of Scientific Evidence, 26 *Jurimetrics J.* 235

is not on the content but on the continuing authority of the rule. They contend that the *Frye* test was superseded by the adoption of the Federal Rules of Evidence. We agree.

....Here there is a specific Rule that speaks to the contested issue. Rule 702, governing expert testimony, provides:

"If scientific, technical, or other specialized knowledge will assist the trier of fact to understand the evidence or to determine a fact in issue, a witness qualified as an expert by knowledge, skill, experience, training, or education, may testify thereto in the form of an opinion or otherwise."

Nothing in the text of this Rule establishes "general acceptance" as an absolute prerequisite to admissibility. Nor does respondent present any clear indication that Rule 702 or the Rules as a whole were intended to incorporate a "general acceptance" standard. The drafting history makes no mention of *Frye*, and a rigid "general acceptance" requirement would be at odds with the "liberal thrust" of the Federal Rules and their "general approach of relaxing the traditional barriers to 'opinion' testimony."...Given the Rules' permissive backdrop and their inclusion of a specific rule on expert testimony that does not mention "general acceptance," the assertion that the Rules somehow assimilated *Frye* is unconvincing. *Frye* made "general acceptance" the exclusive test for admitting expert scientific testimony. That austere standard, absent from, and incompatible with, the Federal Rules of Evidence, should not be applied in federal trials.

That the *Frye* test was displaced by the Rules of Evidence does not mean however, that the Rules themselves place no limits on the admissibility of purportedly scientific evidence. Nor is the trial judge disabled from screening such evidence. To the contrary, under the Rules the trial judge must ensure that any and all scientific testimony or evidence admitted is not only relevant, but reliable.

The primary locus of this obligation is Rule 702, which clearly contemplates some degree of regulation of the subjects and theories about which an

---

(1986); Giannelli, The Admissibility of Novel Scientific Evidence: *Frye* v. *United States*, a Half-Century Later, 80 *Colum. L. Rev.* 1197 (1980); The Supreme Court, 1986 Term, 101 *Harv. L. Rev.* 7, 119, 125–127 (1987).

Indeed, the debates over *Frye* are such a well-established part of the academic landscape that a distinct term—"*Frye*-ologist"—has been advanced to describe those who take part. See Behringer, Introduction, Proposals for a Model Rule on the Admissibility of Scientific Evidence, 26 *Jurimetrics J.* 237, 239 (1986), quoting Lacey, Scientific Evidence, 24 *Jurimetrics J.* 254, 264 (1984).

expert may testify. "*If scientific,* technical, or other specialized *knowledge will assist the trier of fact* to understand the evidence or to determine a fact in issue" an expert "may testify *thereto.*" (Emphasis added.) The subject of an expert's testimony must be "scientific..knowledge." [8] The adjective "scientific" implies a grounding in the methods and procedures of science. Similarly, the word "knowledge" connotes more than subjective belief or unsupported speculation. The term "applies to any body of known facts or to any body of ideas inferred from such facts or accepted as truths on good grounds." Webster's Third New International Dictionary 1252 (1986). Of course, it would be unreasonable to conclude that the subject of scientific testimony must be "known" to a certainty; arguably, there are no certainties in science. See, *e.g.,* Brief for Nicolaas Bloembergen et al. as *Amici Curiae* 9 ("Indeed, scientists do not assert that they know what is immutably 'true'—they are committed to searching for new, temporary, theories to explain, as best they can, phenomena"); Brief for American Association for the Advancement of Science et al. as *Amici Curiae* 7–8 ("Science is not an encyclopedic body of knowledge about the universe. Instead, it represents a *process* for proposing and refining theoretical explanations about the world that are subject to further testing and refinement" (emphasis in original)). But, in order to qualify as "scientific knowledge," an inference or assertion must be derived by the scientific method. Proposed testimony must be supported by appropriate validation—*i.e.,* "good grounds," based on what is known. In short, the requirement that an expert's testimony pertain to "scientific knowledge" establishes a standard of evidentiary reliability.[9]

---

8. Rule 702 also applies to "technical, or other specialized knowledge." Our discussion is limited to the scientific context because that is the nature of the expertise offered here.

9. We note that scientists typically distinguish between "validity" (does the principle support what it purports to show?) and "reliability" (does application of the principle produce consistent results?). See Black, 56 *Ford. L. Rev.,* at 599. Although "the difference between accuracy, validity, and reliability may be such that each is distinct from the other by no more than a hen's kick," Starrs, *Frye v. United States* Restructured and Revitalized: A Proposal to Amend Federal Evidence Rule 702, 26 *Jurimetrics J.* 249, 256 (1986), our reference here is to *evidentiary* reliability—that is, trustworthiness. Cf., *e.g.,* Advisory Committee's Notes on Fed. Rule Evid. 602, 28 U.S.C. App., p. 755 ("'The rule requiring that a witness who testifies to a fact which can be perceived by the senses must have had an opportunity to observe, and must have actually observed the fact' is a 'most pervasive manifestation' of the common law insistence upon 'the most reliable sources of information'" (citation omitted)); Advisory Committee's Notes on Art. VIII of Rules of Evidence, 28 U.S.C. App., p. 770 (hearsay exceptions will be recognized only "under circumstances sup-

Rule 702 further requires that the evidence or testimony "assist the trier of fact to understand the evidence or to determine a fact in issue." This condition goes primarily to relevance. "Expert testimony which does not relate to any issue in the case is not relevant and, ergo, non-helpful." 3 Weinstein & Berger P702[02], p. 702–18. See also *United States* v. *Downing*, 753 F.2d 1224, 1242 (CA3 1985) ("An additional consideration under Rule 702—and another aspect of relevancy—is whether expert testimony proffered in the case is sufficiently tied to the facts of the case that it will aid the jury in resolving a factual dispute"). The consideration has been aptly described by Judge Becker as one of "fit." *Ibid.* "Fit" is not always obvious and scientific validity for one purpose is not necessarily scientific validity for other, unrelated purposes. See Starrs, *Frye v. United States* Restructured and Revitalized: A Proposal to Amend Federal Evidence Rule 702, 26 Jurimetrics J. 249, 258 (1986). The study of the phases of the moon, for example, may provide valid scientific "knowledge" about whether a certain night was dark, and if darkness is a fact in issue, the knowledge will assist the trier of fact. However (absent creditable grounds supporting such a link), evidence that the moon was full on a certain night will not assist the trier of fact in determining whether an individual was unusually likely to have behaved irrationally on that night. Rule 702's "helpfulness" standard requires a valid scientific connection to the pertinent inquiry as a precondition to admissibility.

That these requirements are embodied in Rule 702 is not surprising. Unlike an ordinary witness, see Rule 701, an expert is permitted wide latitude to offer opinions, including those that are not based on firsthand knowledge or observation. See Rules 702 and 703. Presumably, this relaxation of the usual requirement of firsthand knowledge—a rule which represents "a 'most pervasive manifestation' of the common law insistence upon 'the most reliable sources of information,'" Advisory Committee's Notes on Fed. Rule Evid. 602, 28 U.S.C. App., p. 755 (citation omitted)—is premised on an assumption that the expert's opinion will have a reliable basis in the knowledge and experience of his discipline.

Faced with a proffer of expert scientific testimony, then, the trial judge must determine at the outset....whether the expert is proposing to testify to (1) scientific knowledge that (2) will assist the trier of fact to understand or determine a fact in issue. This entails a preliminary assessment of whether the

---

posed to furnish guarantees of trustworthiness"). In a case involving scientific evidence, *evidentiary reliability* will be based upon *scientific validity*.

reasoning or methodology underlying the testimony is scientifically valid and of whether that reasoning or methodology properly can be applied to the facts in issue. We are confident that federal judges possess the capacity to undertake this review. Many factors will bear on the inquiry, and we do not presume to set out a definitive checklist or test. But some general observations are appropriate.

Ordinarily, a key question to be answered in determining whether a theory or technique is scientific knowledge that will assist the trier of fact will be whether it can be (and has been) tested. "Scientific methodology today is based on generating hypotheses and testing them to see if they can be falsified; indeed, this methodology is what distinguishes science from other fields of human inquiry." Green 645. See also C. Hempel, Philosophy of Natural Science 49 (1966) ("The statements constituting a scientific explanation must be capable of empirical test"); K. Popper, Conjectures and Refutations: The Growth of Scientific Knowledge 37 (5th ed. 1989) ("The criterion of the scientific status of a theory is its falsifiability, or refutability, or testability") (emphasis deleted).

Another pertinent consideration is whether the theory or technique has been subjected to peer review and publication. Publication (which is but one element of peer review) is not a *sine qua non* of admissibility; it does not necessarily correlate with reliability, see S. Jasanoff, The Fifth Branch: Science Advisors as Policymakers 61–76 (1990), and in some instances well-grounded but innovative theories will not have been published, see Horrobin, The Philosophical Basis of Peer Review and the Suppression of Innovation, 263 JAMA 1438 (1990). Some propositions, moreover, are too particular, too new, or of too limited interest to be published. But submission to the scrutiny of the scientific community is a component of "good science," in part because it increases the likelihood that substantive flaws in methodology will be detected. See J. Ziman, Reliable Knowledge: An Exploration of the Grounds for Belief in Science 130–133 (1978); Relman & Angell, How Good Is Peer Review?, 321 New Eng. J. Med. 827 (1989). The fact of publication (or lack thereof) in a peer reviewed journal thus will be a relevant, though not dispositive, consideration in assessing the scientific validity of a particular technique or methodology on which an opinion is premised.

Additionally, in the case of a particular scientific technique, the court ordinarily should consider the known or potential rate of error, see, *e.g., United States* v. *Smith*, 869 F.2d 348, 353–354 (CA7 1989) (surveying studies of the error rate of spectrographic voice identification technique), and the existence and maintenance of standards controlling the technique's operation, see

United States v. *Williams*, 583 F.2d 1194, 1198 (CA2 1978) (noting professional organization's standard governing spectrographic analysis), cert. denied, 439 U.S. 1117, 59 L. Ed. 2d 77, 99 S. Ct. 1025 (1979).

Finally, "general acceptance" can yet have a bearing on the inquiry. A "reliability assessment does not require, although it does permit, explicit identification of a relevant scientific community and an express determination of a particular degree of acceptance within that community." *United States* v. *Downing*, 753 F.2d at 1238. See also 3 Weinstein & Berger P702[03], pp. 702–41 to 702–42. Widespread acceptance can be an important factor in ruling particular evidence admissible, and "a known technique which has been able to attract only minimal support within the community," *Downing*, 753 F.2d at 1238, may properly be viewed with skepticism.

The inquiry envisioned by Rule 702 is, we emphasize, a flexible one. Its overarching subject is the scientific validity—and thus the evidentiary relevance and reliability—of the principles that underlie a proposed submission. The focus, of course, must be solely on principles and methodology, not on the conclusions that they generate.

Throughout, a judge assessing a proffer of expert scientific testimony under Rule 702 should also be mindful of other applicable rules. Rule 703 provides that expert opinions based on otherwise inadmissible hearsay are to be admitted only if the facts or data are "of a type reasonably relied upon by experts in the particular field in forming opinions or inferences upon the subject." Rule 706 allows the court at its discretion to procure the assistance of an expert of its own choosing. Finally, Rule 403 permits the exclusion of relevant evidence "if its probative value is substantially outweighed by the danger of unfair prejudice, confusion of the issues, or misleading the jury...." Judge Weinstein has explained: "Expert evidence can be both powerful and quite misleading because of the difficulty in evaluating it. Because of this risk, the judge in weighing possible prejudice against probative force under Rule 403 of the present rules exercises more control over experts than over lay witnesses." Weinstein, 138 F.R.D. at 632.

We conclude by briefly addressing what appear to be two underlying concerns of the parties and *amici* in this case. Respondent expresses apprehension that abandonment of "general acceptance" as the exclusive requirement for admission will result in a "free-for-all" in which befuddled juries are confounded by absurd and irrational pseudoscientific assertions. In this regard respondent seems to us to be overly pessimistic about the capabilities of the jury and of the adversary system generally. Vigorous cross-examination, presentation of contrary evidence, and careful instruction on the burden of proof are the traditional and appropriate means of attacking shaky but admissible evidence. See *Rock* v. *Arkansas*, 483 U.S. 44, 61, 97 L. Ed. 2d 37, 107 S. Ct. 2704 (1987). Additionally, in the event the trial court concludes that the scintilla of evidence presented supporting a position is insufficient to allow a reasonable juror to conclude that the position more likely than not is true, the court remains free to direct a judgment, Fed. Rule Civ. Proc. 50(a), and likewise to grant summary judgment, Fed. Rule Civ. Proc. 56. Cf., *e.g., Turpin* v. *Merrell Dow Pharmaceuticals, Inc.*, 959 F.2d 1349 (CA6) (holding that scientific evidence that provided foundation for expert testimony, viewed in the light most favorable to plaintiffs, was not sufficient to allow a jury to find it more probable than not that defendant caused plaintiff's injury), cert. denied, 506 U.S. 826, 121 L. Ed. 2d 47, 113 S. Ct. 84 (1992); *Brock* v. *Merrell Dow Pharmaceuticals, Inc.*, 874 F.2d 307 (CA5 1989) (reversing judgment entered on jury verdict for plaintiffs because evidence regarding causation was insufficient), modified, 884 F.2d 166 (CA5 1989), cert. denied, 494 U.S. 1046 (1990); Green 680–681. These conventional devices, rather than wholesale exclusion under an uncompromising "general acceptance" test, are the appropriate safeguards where the basis of scientific testimony meets the standards of Rule 702.

Petitioners and, to a greater extent, their *amici* exhibit a different concern. They suggest that recognition of a screening role for the judge that allows for the exclusion of "invalid" evidence will sanction a stifling and repressive scientific orthodoxy and will be inimical to the search for truth. See, *e.g.*, Brief for Ronald Bayer et al. as *Amici Curiae*. It is true that open debate is an essential part of both legal and scientific analyses. Yet there are important differences between the quest for truth in the courtroom and the quest for truth in the laboratory. Scientific conclusions are subject to perpetual revision. Law, on the other hand, must resolve disputes finally and quickly. The scientific project is advanced by broad and wide-ranging consideration of a multitude of hypotheses, for those that are incorrect will eventually be shown to be so, and that in itself is an advance. Conjectures that are probably wrong are of little use, however, in the project of reaching a quick, final, and binding legal judgment—often of great consequence—about a particular set of events in the past. We recognize that, in practice, a gatekeeping role for the judge, no matter how flexible, inevitably on occasion will prevent the jury from learning of authentic insights and innovations. That, nevertheless, is the balance that is struck by Rules of Evidence designed not for the exhaustive search for cosmic understanding but for the particularized resolution of legal disputes.

To summarize: "General acceptance" is not a necessary precondition to the admissibility of scientific evidence under the Federal Rules of Evidence, but the Rules of Evidence—especially Rule 702—do assign to the trial judge the task of ensuring that an expert's testimony both rests on a reliable foundation and is relevant to the task at hand. Pertinent evidence based on scientifically valid principles will satisfy those demands.

The inquiries of the District Court and the Court of Appeals focused almost exclusively on "general acceptance," as gauged by publication and the decisions of other courts. Accordingly, the judgment of the Court of Appeals is vacated, and the case is remanded for further proceedings consistent with this opinion. *It is so ordered....*

Kumho Tire Co. v. Carmichael
526 U.S. 137 (1999)(Excerpt)

OPINION BY: JUSTICE BREYER

In Daubert v. *Merrell Dow Pharmaceuticals, Inc.,* 509 U.S. 579, 125 L. Ed. 2d 469, 113 S. Ct. 2786 (1993), this Court focused upon the admissibility of scientific expert testimony. It pointed out that such testimony is admissible only if it is both relevant and reliable. And it held that the Federal Rules of Evidence "assign to the trial judge the task of ensuring that an expert's testimony both rests on a reliable foundation and is relevant to the task at hand." Id. at 597. The Court also discussed certain more specific factors, such as testing, peer review, error rates, and "acceptability" in the relevant scientific community, some or all of which might prove helpful in determining the reliability of a particular scientific "theory or technique." 509 U.S. at 593–594.

This case requires us to decide how *Daubert* applies to the testimony of engineers and other experts who are not scientists. We conclude that *Daubert*'s general holding—setting forth the trial judge's general "gatekeeping" obligation—applies not only to testimony based on "scientific" knowledge, but also to testimony based on "technical" and "other specialized" knowledge. See Fed. Rule Evid. 702. We also conclude that a trial court *may* consider one or more of the more specific factors that *Daubert* mentioned when doing so will help determine that testimony's reliability. But, as the Court stated in *Daubert,* the test of reliability is "flexible," and *Daubert*'s list of specific factors neither necessarily nor exclusively applies to all experts or in every case. Rather, the law grants a district court the same broad latitude when it decides *how* to determine reliability as it enjoys in respect to its ultimate reliability determination. See *General Electric Co. v. Joiner*, 522 U.S. 136, 143, 139 L. Ed. 2d 508, 118 S. Ct. 512 (1997) (courts of appeals are to apply "abuse of discretion" standard when reviewing district court's reliability determination). Applying these standards, we determine that the District Court's decision in this case—not to admit certain expert testimony—was within its discretion and therefore lawful....

List of other cases and articles relevant to this topic

Frye v. United States, 293 F. 1013 (1923)

Herzberger, S.D. (1993). Social science contributions to the law: Understanding and predicting behavior. *Connecticut Law Review* 25: 1067.

Roesch, R., S. Golding, V. Hans and D. Reppucci (1991). Social science and the courts: The role of amicus briefs. *Law and Human Behavior* 15: 1–11.

Discussion and Review Questions

1. What scientific evidence was being introduced in *Daubert* and *Kumho*? Was this social scientific evidence? Would you consider the evidence going to prove an adjudicative fact, legislative fact or social framework evidence?

2. How would you apply the *Daubert/Kumho* analysis apply to social science evidence?

References

Articles

Babbie, E. (2002). *The Basics of Social Research*. CA: Wadsworth Publishing.

Bjerregaard, Beth and A. N. Blowers (1996). The appropriateness of the *Frye* test in determining the admissibility of the battered woman syndrome in the courtroom. *University of Louisville Journal of Family Law* 35: 1.

Gallai, D. (1999). Polygraph evidence in federal courts: Should it be admissible? *American Criminal Law Review* 36: 87.

Parrish, J. (1995). *Trend analysis: Expert testimony on battering and its effects in criminal cases*. Washington DC: U.S. Department of Justice.

Raeder, M.S. (1996). Proving the case battered woman and batterer syndrome, the double-edged sword: Admissibility of battered woman syndrome by and against batterers in cases implicating domestic violence. *Colorado Law Review* 67: 789.

Case Citations

Brown v. Board of Education, 347 U.S. 483 (1954).

Daubert v. Merrell Dow Pharmaceuticals, 509 U.S. 579 (1993).

Flynt v. State, 264 S.E. 2d 669 (Ga. Ct. App. 1980).

Frye v. United States, 407 A. 293 F. 1013 (1923)

Ibn-Tamas v. United States, 407 A. 2d 626 (DC 1979)

Kumho Tire Company v. Carmichael, 526 U.S. 137 (1999)

United States v. Scheffer, 118 U.S. 1261 (1998)

Chapter 4

Police Stops and Seizures

In October 2001, a billboard on New Jersey's Turnpike, near Newark airport, read "Stopped or searched by the New Jersey State Police? They admit to racial profiling. You might win money damages. Call the ACLU Hotline...."

The Equal Protection Clause of the United States Constitution prohibits the "selective enforcement of the law based on considerations such as race." *Whren v. United States*, 517 U.S. 806, 813, 116 S. Ct. 1769, 135 L.Ed. 2d 89 (1996). Prior to September 11, 2001, the Supreme Court, as well as federal and state courts across the country, began to address the implications of **racial profiling** and relied on social science information to form the basis of these discussions. It is expected that the Court will be confronted with many more types of racial profiling cases in the wake of the terrorist attacks, the war on terrorism and the adoption of the U.S.A. Patriot Act.

Does racial profiling exist?

Social science has demonstrated that a disproportionate number of black drivers are stopped on the highways in Maryland, New Jersey, Ohio and other states (Lamberth 1996; Lichtenberg 1999; Report of the NJ Senate Judiciary Committee's Investigation of Racial Profiling and the NJ State Police 2001). Based on the Lamberth (1996) research, a federal court in Maryland concluded that racial profiling by state police agencies existed in Maryland.[1] Also relying on this data, Lamberth (1996) found that the rate of stops with searches that resulted in finding drugs was not statistically different for black and white motorists.

---

1. Lamberth was an expert in the litigation in New Jersey in *State v. Soto* (734 A.2d 350, 1996) as well as Maryland in *Wilkins v. Maryland* (No. MJG–93–468, 1996).

> **Racial profiling**: occurs when the police target someone for investigation on the basis of that person's race, national origin, or ethnicity. Examples of profiling are the use of race to determine which drivers to stop for minor traffic violations ("driving while black") and the use of race to determine which motorists or pedestrians to search for contraband. (ACLU).

Since race is an illegal basis to stop a citizen, under what circumstances can a police officer make a stop? How has the Fourth Amendment been interpreted to give direction to the police and limit their discretion?

Despite the language of the Fourth Amendment, the United States Supreme Court has allowed police to search and seize citizens and their effects without warrants and based on less than probable cause. These exceptions to the Fourth Amendment have been set out with a great deal of specificity. One of these exceptions was created in the case of *Terry v. Ohio*, 392 U.S. 1 (1968). In *Terry*, the United States Supreme Court held that it was lawful for a police officer to stop and frisk a person the officer has a "**reasonable suspicion**" to believe was about to engage in, had engaged in or was in the process of engaging in wrong-doing. Reasonable suspicion must be based on specific facts. A mere hunch or gut-feeling is not reasonable suspicion to stop.

Additionally, a *Terry* stop is a temporary, investigatory detention, not a full scale seizure. The Court reasoned that this type of stop does not require the full protection of the Fourth Amendment, i.e., a warrant and probable cause. In other words, this temporary, investigatory detention based on reasonable and articulable suspicion that criminal activity was afoot was not prohibited by the reasonableness clause of the Fourth Amendment. The reasonableness of a stop is examined by the Court using the "totality of the circumstances" test. This test has also been referred to as the "whole picture" test. (*United States v. Cortez*, 449 U.S. 411 (1981); Klotter and Kanovitz 1995). Using this test, the Court has held that the police officers subjective intentions for stopping an individual are not relevant to an evaluation of whether a stop or

> **Reasonable suspicion**: Reasonable suspicion which will justify officer in stopping defendant in public place is quantum knowledge sufficient to induce ordinarily prudent and cautious man under circumstances to believe criminal activity is at hand. (Black's Law Dictionary)

seizure was objectively justified (*Whren v. United States* (1996). The Court has also held that citizens may be arrested for minor traffic violations consistent with the Fourth Amendment (*Atwater v. City of Lago Vista*). The *Atwater* Court upheld the warrantless arrest of a woman for failing to wear her seat-belt, a violation that carried only the penalty of a fine. The court found the arrest based on probable cause consistent with Fourth Amendment principles. Some scholars have suggested that these two decisions—*Whren* and *Atwa-ter*—may "perpetuate the problem of racially discriminatory policing" (Cooper 2001). Cooper argues:

> We already have a situation in the United States where some police officers stop drivers and walkers because of their race or ethnicity. And where a white citizen might be told to slow down or given a warning, a black citizen could be verbally abused or given a ticket. Now with *Atwater* on their side, racist police officers can choose to take blacks, Latinos and other nonwhites into custody and never be required to provide any articulable reason why they choose that course of action over simply giving a citation. (Cooper 2001).

What does the Court say about someone who runs from the police? Why would an innocent person run from the police?

In 1995, Sam Wardlow fled upon seeing police officers patrolling an area known for heavy narcotics trafficking. Two officers chased him, stopped him and conducted a pat-down search for weapons. They found a .38 caliber hand-gun, and he was arrested. The question raised in *Illinois v. Wardlow*, 528 U.S. 119 (2000) was whether the officers' stop of Wardlow violated the Fourth Amendment. In other words, did the officers have reasonable and articulable suspicion to conduct an investigatory stop of Wardlow because he ran from the police?

In a previous decision, the Court held that an individual's presence in a high crime area alone was not sufficient to establish reasonable suspicion to justify a stop. *Brown v. Texas*, 443 U.S. 47 (1979). However, presence in a high crime area could be one factor to consider in raising a reasonable suspicion, and the Court in *Wardlow* found that "it was not merely respondent's pres-ence in an area of heavy narcotics trafficking that aroused the officers' suspi-cion but his unprovoked flight upon noticing the police." In arriving at its holding that this amounted to reasonable suspicion and the police officers were justified in stopping Wardlow, Justice Rhenquist (writing the opinion for the Court) stated:

In reviewing the propriety of an officer's conduct, courts do not have available empirical studies dealing with inferences drawn from suspicious behavior, and we cannot reasonably demand scientific certainty from judges or law enforcement officers when none exists. Thus, the determination of reasonable suspicion must be based on common-sense judgments and inferences about human behavior.

At the oral argument, Justice Scalia asked one of the lawyers whether there was any empirical evidence concerning why, other than wrongdoing, someone would run from the police. The lawyer could not provide any empirical information on this point at the oral argument, however several amicus curaie (friend of the court) briefs filed by interested parties did address this question. Rhenquist noted that in the briefs before the Court, it was argued that "there are innocent reasons for flight from police and that, therefore, flight is not necessarily indicative of ongoing criminal activity." Rhenquist did not doubt the truth of the argument, however, he responded that this fact "does not establish a violation of the Fourth Amendment."

In the concurring opinion, Justice Stevens discusses the reasons, other than involvement in criminal activity, that individuals might have for running upon sight of the police. One concern may be that police presence indicates nearby criminal activity, and the bystander seeks to avoid involvement or injury. In identifying this reason, Justice Stevens notes that although "statistical studies of bystander victimization are rare," one study found that there were "substantial increases in reported bystander killings" in four large cities over an 11-year period. (Sherman, Steele, Laufersweiler, Hooper and Julian (1989).

Justice Stevens made a second observation, based on social science research, about minority groups and the police. He argued that it is plausible that a person running from the police is entirely innocent, but may believe that contact with the police can be dangerous. In making this observation, Justice Stevens cited a series of empirical studies in footnote 7 that demonstrate there is a great deal of distrust of police among African-Americans, that African-Americans perceive police brutality and harassment as a serious problem, and that there is empirical support for the proposition that minorities are disproportionately stopped by the police in various cities. Specifically, Justice Stevens highlighted the mounting data concerning racial profiling and the tensions between minority communities and the police. In footnote 10, Justice Stevens cited the New Jersey's Attorney General Office investigation demonstrating that racial profiling was real and not imagined. This social science evidence is essential to assessments about unprovoked flight from the police.

In fact, there is a great deal of research that demonstrates that young people, African-Americans, Hispanics and residents of lower class neighborhoods hold more negative views of the police (Cheurprakobkit 2000; Hurst and Frank 2000; Weitzer 1999). In each study, the relationship between the police and citizens was negatively impacted by face-to-face encounters as well as vicarious encounters with the police involving brutality, harassment, and unwarranted physical and verbal abuse. Given these findings, it may not be surprising that certain groups within society will run away from the police even when they have nothing to hide. They are fearful of law enforcement.

Despite these observations, Justice Stevens did not advance a rule that would hold all stops based on unprovoked flight as *per se* violations of the Fourth Amendment. Contrary to the majority opinion, Justice Stevens did not believe that there was reasonable suspicion, under the 'totality of the circumstances' test, to justify Wardlow's detention. Among other missing information, the officer did not remember whether the van was marked or unmarked, he was not asked whether the other vans were marked or unmarked, or whether any of the other seven officers involved were in uniform. In fact, there was little information in the record that established that this was a "high crime area." Based on the missing information, Justice Stevens disagreed with the Court's holding that the state produced articulate facts sufficient to support reasonable suspicion.

In assessing whether facts are sufficient to establish reasonable suspicion, the Court does take into consideration the officers experiences and their assessments of facts based on those experiences. Likewise, the Court in *United States v. Sokolow*, 490 U.S. 1 (1989) upheld the detention of an individual suspected of trafficking in narcotics based on a 'drug courier' profile.

The Court found that although the individual factors may be consistent with innocent activity, taken together as a whole they amounted to reasonable suspicion of wrong-doing. The Court stated that the individual factors as observed by the officers and in their experience lent reasonable suspicion to the belief that Sokolow was engaged in drug trafficking in the airport.

The factors in *Sokolow* were as follows:

(1) Sokolow paid $2,100 for two airplane tickets from a roll of $20 bills; (2) he traveled under a name that did not match the name under which his telephone was listed; (3) his original destination was Miami, a source city for illicit drugs; (4) he stayed in Miami for only 48 hours, even though a round-trip flight from Honolulu to Miami

takes 20 hours; (5) he appeared nervous during his trip; and (6) he checked none of his luggage.

In two other cases, the court also upheld the use of a 'drug courier' profile. In *Florida v. Royer*, 460 U.S. 491 (1983), the Court, in a footnote, stated:

> The "drug courier profile" is an abstract of characteristics found to be typical of persons transporting illegal drugs. In Royer's case, the detectives attention was attracted by the following facts which were considered to be within the profile: (a) Royer was carrying American Tourister luggage, which appeared to be heavy, (b) he was young, apparently between 25–35, (c) he was casually dressed, (d) he appeared pale and nervous, looking around at other people, (e) he paid for his ticket in cash with a large number of bills, and (f) rather than completing the airline identification tag to be attached to checked baggage, which had space for a name, address, and telephone number, he wrote only a name and the destination.

Similarly, the Court in *U.S. v. Mendenhall*, 446 U.S. 544 (1980) found the following facts amounted to reasonable suspicion:

> The agent testified that the respondent's behavior fit the so-called "drug courier profile"—an informally compiled abstract of characteristics thought typical of persons carrying illicit drugs. In this case the agents thought it relevant that (1) the respondent was arriving on a flight from Los Angeles, a city believed by the agents to be the place of origin for much of the heroin brought to Detroit; (2) the respondent was the last person to leave the plane, "appeared to be very nervous," and "completely scanned the whole area where [the agents] were standing"; (3) after leaving the plane the respondent proceeded past the baggage area without claiming any luggage; and (4) the respondent changed airlines for her flight out of Detroit.

Although the Court has not explicitly approved of the 'drug courier' profile, its failure to find the profiles unconstitutional has resulted in its widespread use. From 1976 to 1992, appellate courts used the drug courier profile or relied on it as an analogy in deciding 568 cases (Ryan 1994). "[C]ourts have assumed that use of the profile as a trigger for investigative stops by law enforcement agents is constitutionally permissible." (Ryan 1994: 219, fn 1). No reference whatsoever is found in the *Sokolow* decision concerning empirical support for defining "reasonable suspicion" or the use of the profile. Similar to Rhenquist's decision in *Wardlow*, the Court relies on "commonsense."

Although the *Sokolow* Court did not countenance the use of profiling, the use of drug courier profiles proliferated during the 1980s and there was not a single standard, the profiles varied based on location, situation and law enforcement experience (Ryan 1994). Despite the proliferation of these profiles, there is not social scientific evidence that demonstrates their validity, accuracy and usefulness (Ryan 1994). In fact, many of the profiles are contradictory (Ryan 1994). In light of the terrorist attacks on the World Trade Center and Pentagon, the Federal Bureau of Investigation along with other police agencies may be relying on profiles that include ethnicity to justify the stop and detention of many middle-eastern men. In August 2002, a convention with attorneys, scholars, civil authorities and community members discussed the "de facto nation security policy" to race profile Arab and Muslim individuals. (*PR Newswire* July 18, 2002). Challenges to the actions of law enforcement will begin to percolate through the criminal justice system and the United States Supreme Court may need to balance issues of racial profiling and national security.

What can be done to limit the use of racial profiling by the police?

In response to the national attention given to the racial profiling of black and Hispanic drivers, the police executive research forum (PERF) in Washington DC conducted extensive research and made numerous recommendations for addressing this problem. In 2001, PERF published "Racially Biased Policing: A Principled Response" by Lorie Fridell, Robert Lunney, Drew Diamond and Bruce Kubu. Fridell et al. (2001) made several important recommendations to address the problem of racial profiling in Chapter 4 of their report. The policy they propose:

1. emphasizes that arrests, traffic stops, investigative detentions, searches, and property seizures must be based on reasonable suspicion or probable cause;
2. restricts officers' ability to use race/ethnicity in establishing reasonable suspicion or probable cause to those situations in which trustworthy, locally relevant information links a person or persons of a specific race/ethnicity to a particular unlawful incident(s);
3. applies the restrictions above to requests for consent searches and even those "non-consensual encounters" that do not amount to legal detentions;
4. articulates that the use of race and ethnicity must be in accordance with the equal protection clause of the Fourteenth Amendment; and

5. includes provisions related to officer behavior during encounters that can serve to prevent perceptions of racially biased policing.
(Fridell, et al 2001: 49–50).

In this chapter, excerpts from the New Jersey Supreme Court's decision in *State v. Soto*, and the United States Department of Justice study entitled *Criminal victimization and perceptions of community safety in 12 cities* are included.

State v. Soto
734 A. 2d 350 (NJ Super. 1996) (Excerpt)

OPINION BY: R.E. FRANCIS

These are consolidated motions to suppress under the equal protection and due process clauses of the Fourteenth Amendment. Seventeen defendants of African ancestry claim that their arrests on the New Jersey Turnpike south of exit 3 between 1988 and 1991 result from discriminatory enforcement of the traffic laws by the New Jersey State Police. After a lengthy hearing, I find defendants have established a prima facie case of selective enforcement which the State has failed to rebut requiring suppression of all contraband and evidence seized.

Defendants base their claim of institutional racism primarily on statistics. During discovery, each side created a database of all stops and arrests by State Police members patrolling the Turnpike between exits 1 and 7A out of the Moorestown Station for thirty-five randomly selected days between April 1988 and May 1991 from arrest reports, patrol charts, radio logs and traffic tickets. The databases are essentially the same. Both sides counted 3060 stops which the State found to include 1212 race identified stops (39.6%), the defense 1146 (37.4%).

To establish a standard against which to compare the stop data, the defense conducted a traffic survey and a violator survey. Dr. John Lamberth, Chairman of the Psychology Department at Temple University who I found is qualified as an expert in statistics and social psychology, designed both surveys.

The traffic survey was conducted over twenty-one randomly selected two and one-half hour sessions between June 11 and June 24, 1993 and between 8:00 a.m. and 8:00 p.m. at four sites, two northbound and two southbound, between exits 1 and 3 of the Turnpike. Teams supervised by Fred Last, Esq., of the Office of the Public Defender observed and recorded the number of vehicles that passed them except for large trucks, tractortrailers, buses and government vehicles, how many contained a "black" occupant and the state of origin of each vehicle. Of the 42,706 vehicles counted, 13.5% had a black occupant. Dr. Lamberth testified that this percentage is consistent with the 1990 Census figures for the eleven states from where almost 90% of the observed vehicles were registered. He said it is also consistent with a study done by the Triangle Group for the U.S. Department of Transportation with which he was familiar.

The violator survey was conducted over ten sessions in four days in July 1993 by Mr. Last traveling between exits 1 and 3 in his vehicle at sixty miles per hour on cruise control after the speedometer had been calibrated and observing and recording the number of vehicles that passed him, the number of vehicles he passed and how many had a black occupant. Mr. Last counted a total of 2096 vehicles other than large trucks, tractortrailers, buses and government vehicles of which 2062 or 98.1% passed him going in excess of sixty miles per hour including 306 with a black occupant equaling about 15% of those vehicles clearly speeding. Multiple violators, that is those violating the speed limit and committing some other moving violation like tailgating, also equaled about 15% black. Dr. Lamberth testified that the difference between the percentage of black violators and the percentage of black travelers from the surveys is statistically insignificant and that there is no evidence traffic patterns changed between the period April 1988 to May 1991 in the databases and June–July 1993 when the surveys were done.

Using 13.5% as the standard or benchmark against which to compare the stop data, Dr. Lamberth found that 127 or 46.2% of the race identified stops between exits 1 and 3 were of blacks constituting an absolute disparity of 32.7%, a comparative disparity of 242% (32.7% divided by 13.5%) and 16.35 standard deviations. By convention, something is considered statistically significant if it would occur by chance fewer than five times in a hundred (over two standard deviations). In case I were to determine that the appropriate stop data for comparison with the standard is the stop data for the entire portion of the Turnpike patrolled by the Moorestown Station in recognition of the fact that the same troopers patrol between exits 3 and 7A as patrol between exits 1 and 3, Dr. Lamberth found that 408 or 35.6% of the race identified stops between exits 1 and 7A were of blacks constituting an absolute disparity of 22.1%, a comparative disparity of 164% and 22.1 standard deviations.[3.] He

---

3.. Dr. Lamberth erred in using 13.5% as the standard for comparison with the stop data. The violator survey indicates that 14.8%, rounded to 15%, of those observed speeding were black. This percentage is the percentage Dr. Lamberth should have used in mak-

opined it is highly unlikely such statistics could have occurred randomly or by chance.[4]

Defendants also presented the testimony of Dr. Joseph B. Kadane, an eminently qualified statistician.....Dr. Kadane testified that in his opinion both the traffic and violator surveys were well designed, carefully performed and statistically reliable for analysis. From the surveys and the defense database, he calculated that a black was 4.85 times as likely as a white to be stopped between exits 1 and 3. This calculation led him to "suspect" a racially non-neutral stopping policy. While he noted that the surveys were done in 1993 and compared to data from 1988 to 1991, he was nevertheless satisfied that the comparisons were useable and accurate within a few percent. He was not concerned that the violator survey failed to count cars going less than sixty miles per hour and traveling behind Mr. Last when he started a session. He was concerned, however, with the fact that only 37.4% of the stops in the defense database were race identified.[5] In order to determine if the comparisons were sensitive to the missing racial data, he did calculations performed on the log odds of being stopped. Whether he assumed the probability of having one's race recorded if black and stopped is the same as if white and stopped or two or three times as likely, the log odds were still greater than .99 that blacks were stopped at higher rates than whites on the Turnpike between exits 1 and 3 during the period April 1988 to May 1991. He therefore concluded that the comparisons were not sensitive to the missing racial data.

Supposing that the disproportionate stopping of blacks was related to police discretion, the defense studied the traffic tickets issued by State Police members between exits 1 and 7A on the thirty-five randomly selected days

---

ing statistical comparisons with the stop data in the databases. Nonetheless, it would appear that whatever the correctly calculated disparities and standard deviations are, they would be nearly equal to those calculated by Dr. Lamberth.

4. In this opinion I am ignoring the arrest data in the databases and Dr. Lamberth's analysis thereof since neither side produced any evidence identifying the Turnpike population between exits 1 and 3 or 1 and 7A eligible to be arrested for drug offenses or otherwise. See *Wards Cove Packing Co. v. Atonio*, 490 U.S. 642, 109 S. Ct. 2115, 104 L. Ed. 2d 733 (1989).

5. That 62.6 percent of the stops in the defense database are not race identified is a consequence of both the destruction of the radio logs for ten of the thirty-five randomly selected days in accordance with the State Police document retention policy and the frequent dereliction of State Police members to comply with S.O.P. F3 effective July 13, 1984 requiring them to communicate by radio to their respective stations the race of all occupants of vehicles stopped prior to any contact.

broken down by State Police unit.[6] There are 533 racially identified tickets in the databases issued by either the now disbanded Radar Unit, the Tactical Patrol Unit or general road troopers ("Patrol Unit"). The testimony indicates that the Radar Unit focused mainly on speeders using a radar van and chase cars and exercised limited discretion regarding which vehicles to stop. The Tac-Pac concentrates on traffic problems at specific locations and exercises somewhat more discretion as regards which vehicles to stop. Responsible to provide general law enforcement, the Patrol Unit exercises by far the most discretion among the three units. From Mr. Last's count, Dr. Lamberth computed that 18% of the tickets issued by the Radar Unit were to blacks, 23.8% of the tickets issued by the Tac-Pac were to blacks while 34.2% of the tickets issued by the Patrol Unit were to blacks. South of exit 3, Dr. Lamberth computed that 19.4% of the tickets issued by the Radar Unit were to blacks, 0.0% of the tickets issued by the Tac-Pac were to blacks while 43.8% of the tickets issued by the Patrol Unit were to blacks. In his opinion, the Radar Unit percentages are statistically consistent with the standard established by the violator survey, but the differences between the Radar Unit and the Patrol Unit between both exits 1 and 3 and 1 and 7A are statistically significant or well in excess of two standard deviations.

The State presented the testimony of Dr. Leonard Cupingood to challenge or refute the statistical evidence offered by the defense. I found Dr. Cupingood is qualified to give expert testimony in the field of statistics....Dr. Cupingood had no genuine criticism of the defense traffic survey. Rather, he centered his criticism of the defense statistical evidence on the violator survey. Throughout his testimony he maintained that the violator survey failed to capture the relevant data which he opined was the racial mix of those speeders most likely to be stopped or the "tail of the distribution." He even recommended the State authorize him to design a study to collect this data, but the State declined. He was unclear, though, how he would design a study to ascertain in a safe way the vehicle going the fastest above the speed limit at a given time at a given location and the race of its occupants without involving the credibility of State Police members. In any event, his supposition that maybe blacks drive faster than whites above the speed limit was repudiated by all State Police members called by the State who were questioned about it. Colonel Clinton Pagano, Trooper Donald Nemeth, Trooper Stephen Baumann

---

6. Of the 3060 stops in the databases, 1292 are ticketed stops. Hence, no tickets were issued for nearly 60% of the stops

and Detective Timothy Grant each testified that blacks drive indistinguishably from whites. Moreover, Dr. Cupingood acknowledged that he knew of no study indicating that blacks drive worse than whites. Nor could he reconcile the notion with the evidence that 37% of the unticketed stops between exits 1 and 7A in his database were black and 63% of those between exits 1 and 3. Dr. James Fyfe, a criminal justice professor at Temple who the defense called in its rebuttal case and who I found is qualified as an expert in police science and police procedures, also testified that there is nothing in the literature or in his personal experience to support the theory that blacks drive differently from whites....

The defense did not rest on its statistical evidence alone. Along with the testimony of former troopers Kenneth Ruff and Kenneth Wilson about having been trained and coached to make race based profile stops but whose testimony is weakened by bias related to their not having been reappointed at the end of their terms, the defense elicited evidence through cross-examination of State witnesses and a rebuttal witness, Dr. James Fyfe, that the State Police hierarchy allowed, condoned, cultivated and tolerated discrimination between 1988 and 1991 in its crusade to rid New Jersey of the scourge of drugs.....

Despite the paucity of training materials and lack of periodic and complete impact evaluations and studies, a glimpse of the work of DITU emerges from the preserved checklists and the testimony of Sergeants Brian Caffrey and David Cobb. Sergeant Caffrey was the original assistant supervisor of DITU and became the supervisor in 1989. Sergeant Cobb was an original member of DITU and became the assistant supervisor in 1989. Sergeant Caffrey left DITU sometime in 1992, Sergeant Cobb sometime in 1991. Both testified that a major purpose of DITU was to teach trainees tip-offs and techniques about what to look for and do to talk or "dig" their way into a vehicle after, not before, a motor vehicle stop to effectuate patrol related arrests. Both denied teaching or using race as a tip-off either before or after a stop. Nevertheless, Sergeant Caffrey condoned a comment by a DITU trainer during the time he was the supervisor of DITU stating:

> "Trooper Fash previously had DITU training, and it showed in the way he worked. He has become a little reluctant to stop cars in lieu [sic] of the Channel 9 News Report. He was told as long as he uses Title 39 he can stop any car he wants.   He enjoys DITU and would like to ride again."

As the defense observes in its closing brief, "Why would a trooper who is acting in a racially neutral fashion become reluctant to stop cars as a result of a news story charging that racial minorities were being targeted [by the New Jersey State Police]?" Even A.A.G. Ronald Susswein, Deputy Director of the Division of Criminal Justice, acknowledged that this comment is incomplete because it fails to add the caveat, "as long as he doesn't also use race or ethnicity." Further, Sergeant Caffrey testified that "ethnicity is something to keep in mind" albeit not a tip-off and that he taught attendees at both the annual State Police in-service training session in March 1987 and the special State Police in-service training sessions in July and August 1987 that Hispanics are mainly involved in drug trafficking and showed them the film Operation Pipeline wherein the ethnicity of those arrested, mostly Hispanics, is prominently depicted. Dr. Fyfe criticized Sergeant Caffrey's teaching Hispanics are mainly involved and his showing Operation Pipeline as well as the showing of the Jamaican Posse film wherein only blacks are depicted as drug traffickers at the 1989 annual State Police inservice training session saying trainers should not teach what they do not intend their trainees to act upon. At a minimum, teaching Hispanics are mainly involved in drug trafficking and showing films depicting mostly Hispanics and blacks trafficking in drugs at training sessions worked at cross-purposes with concomitant instruction pointing out that neither race nor ethnicity may be considered in making traffic stops.

Key corroboration for finding the State Police hierarchy allowed and tolerated discrimination came from Colonel Pagano. Colonel Pagano was Superintendent of the State Police from 1975 to February 1990. He testified there was a noisy demand in the 1980s to get drugs off the streets. In accord, Attorney General Cary Edwards and he made drug interdiction the number one priority of law enforcement. He helped formulate the Attorney General's Statewide Action Plan for Narcotics Enforcement and established DITU within the State Police. He kept an eye on DITU through conversations with staff officers and Sergeants Mastella and Caffrey and review of reports generated under the traditional reporting system and D-62 in evidence. He had no thought DITU would engage in constitutional violations. He knew all State Police members were taught that they were guardians of the Constitution and that targeting any race was unconstitutional and poor police practice to boot. He recognized it was his responsibility to see that race was not a factor in who was stopped, searched and arrested. When he became Superintendent, he formed the Internal Affairs Bureau to investigate citizen complaints against State Police members to maintain the integrity of the Division. Substantiated deviations from regulations resulted in sanctions, additional training or counseling.

More telling, however, is what Colonel Pagano said and did, or did not do, in response to the Channel 9 expose entitled "Without Just Cause" which aired in 1989 and which troubled Trooper Fash and what he did not do in response to complaints of profiling from the NAACP and ACLU and these consolidated motions to suppress and similar motions in Warren and Middlesex Counties. He said to Joe Collum of Channel 9 that "[violating rights of motorists was] of serious concern [to him], but no where near the concern that I think we have got to look to in trying to correct some of the problems we find with the criminal element in this State" and "the bottom line is that those stops were not made on the basis of race alone." (emphasis added) Since perhaps these isolated comments were said inadvertently or edited out of context, a truer reflection of his attitude about claims of racism would appear to be his videotaped remarks shown all members of the State Police at roll call in conjunction with the WOR series. Thereon he clearly said that he did not want targeting or discriminatory enforcement and that "when you put on this uniform, you leave your biases and your prejudices behind." But he also said as regarded the charge of a Trenton school principal named Jones that he had been stopped on the Turnpike and threatened, intimidated and assaulted by a trooper, "We know that the teacher assaulted the trooper. He didn't have a driver's license or a registration for his fancy new Mercedes." (emphasis added) And he called Paul McLemore, the first African-American trooper in New Jersey and now a practicing attorney and who spoke of discrimination within the ranks of the State Police, "an ingrate." And he told the members to "keep the heat on" and then assured them:

"...Here at Division Headquarters we'll make sure that when the wheels start to squeak, we'll do whatever we can to make sure that you're supported out in the field....Anything that goes toward implementing the Drug Reform Act is important. And, we'll handle the squeaky wheels here."

He admitted the Internal Affairs Bureau was not designed to investigate general complaints, so he could not refer the general complaints of discrimination to it for scrutiny. Yet he never requested the Analytical Unit to investigate stop data from radio logs, patrol charts and tickets or search and seizure data from arrest reports, operations reports, investigation reports and consent to search forms, not even after the Analytical Unit informed him in a report on arrests by region, race and crime that he had requested from it for his use in the WOR series that "...arrests are not a valid reflection of stops (data relative to stops with respect to race is not compiled)." The databases compiled for these motions attest, of course, to the fact that race identified stop data could have been compiled. He testified he could not launch an investigation into every general complaint because of limited resources and that there was insufficient evidence of discrimination in the Channel 9 series, the

NAACP and ACLU complaints and the various motions to suppress for him to spend his "precious" resources. In short, he left the issue of discrimination up to the courts and months of testimony in this and other counties at State expense.

The right to be free from discrimination is firmly supported by the Fourteenth Amendment to the United States Constitution and the protections of Article I, paragraphs 1 and 5 of the New Jersey Constitution of 1947. To be sure, "the eradication of the 'cancer of discrimination' has long been one of our State's highest priorities." *Dixon v. Rutgers, The State University of N.J.*, 110 N.J. 432, 451, 541 A.2d 1046 (1988). It is indisputable, therefore, that the police may not stop a motorist based on race or any other invidious classification. See *State v. Kuhn*, 213 N.J. Super. 275, 517 A.2d 162 (1986).

Generally, however, the inquiry for determining the constitutionality of a stop or a search and seizure is limited to "whether the conduct of the law enforcement officer who undertook the [stop or] search was objectively reasonable, without regard to his or her underlying motives or intent." *State v. Bruzzese*, 94 N.J. 210, 463 A.2d 320 (1983). Thus, it has been said that the courts will not inquire into the motivation of a police officer whose stop of a vehicle was based upon a traffic violation committed in his presence. See *United States v. Smith*, 799 F.2d 704, 708–709 (11th Cir. 1986); *United States v. Hollman*, 541 F.2d 196, 198 (8th Cir. 1976); cf. *United States v. Villamonte-Marquez*, 462 U.S. 579, 103 S. Ct. 2573, 77 L. Ed. 2d 22 (1983). But where objective evidence establishes "that a police agency has embarked upon an officially sanctioned or de facto policy of targeting minorities for investigation and arrest," any evidence seized will be suppressed to deter future insolence in office by those charged with enforcement of the law and to maintain judicial integrity. *State v. Kennedy*, 247 N.J. Super. 21, 588 A.2d 834 (App. Div. 1991).

Statistics may be used to make out a case of targeting minorities for prosecution of traffic offenses provided the comparison is between the racial composition of the motorist population violating the traffic laws and the racial composition of those arrested for traffic infractions on the relevant roadway patrolled by the police agency. *Wards Cove Packing Co. v. Atonio, supra*; *State v. Kennedy*, 247 N.J. Super. at 33–34. While defendants have the burden of proving "the existence of purposeful discrimination," discriminatory intent may be inferred from statistical proof presenting a stark pattern or an even less extreme pattern in certain limited contexts. *McCleskey v. Kemp*, 481 U.S. 279, 107 S. Ct. 1756, 95 L. Ed. 2d 262 (1987). Kennedy, supra, implies that discriminatory intent may be inferred from statistical proof in a traffic stop context probably because only uniform variables (Title 39 violations) are relevant to the challenged stops and the State has an opportunity to explain the statistical disparity. "[A] selection procedure that is susceptible of abuse…supports the presumption of discrimination raised by the statistical showing." *Castaneda v. Partida*, 430 U.S. 482, 494, 97 S. Ct. 1272, 51 L. Ed. 2d 498 (1977).

Once defendants expose a prima facie case of selective enforcement, the State generally cannot rebut it by merely calling attention to possible flaws or unmeasured variables in defendants' statistics. Rather, the State must introduce specific evidence showing that either there actually are defects which bias the results or the missing factors, when properly organized and accounted for, eliminate or explain the disparity. *Bazemore v. Friday*, 478 U.S. 385, 106 S. Ct. 3000, 92 L. Ed. 2d 315 (1986); *EEOC v. General Telephone Co. of Northwest, Inc.*, 885 F.2d 575 (9th Cir. 1989). Nor will mere denials or reliance on the good faith of the officers suffice. *Castaneda v. Partida*, 430 U.S. at 498 n. 19.

Here, defendants have proven at least a de facto policy on the part of the State Police out of the Moorestown Station of targeting blacks for investigation and arrest between April 1988 and May 1991 both south of exit 3 and between exits 1 and 7A of the Turnpike. Their surveys satisfy Wards Cove, supra. The statistical disparities and standard deviations revealed are indeed stark. The discretion devolved upon general road troopers to stop any car they want as long as Title 39 is used evinces a selection process that is susceptible of abuse. The utter failure of the State Police hierarchy to monitor and control a crackdown program like DITU or investigate the many claims of institutional discrimination manifests its indifference if not acceptance. Against all this, the State submits only denials and the conjecture and flawed studies of Dr. Cupingood.

The eradication of illegal drugs from our State is an obviously worthy goal, but not at the expense of individual rights. As Justice Brandeis so wisely said dissenting in *Olmstead v. United States*, 277 U.S. 438, 479, 72 L. Ed. 944, 48 S. Ct. 564 (1928):

"Experience should teach us to be most on our guard to protect liberty when the government's purposes are beneficent. Men born to freedom are naturally alert to repel invasion of their liberty by evil-minded rulers. The greatest dangers to liberty lurk in insidious encroachment by men of zeal, well-meaning but without understanding." Motions granted.

Smith S.K., G.W. Steadman, T.D. Minton and M. Townsend (May 1999), *Criminal victimization and perceptions of community safety in 12 cities*, Washington DC: U. S. Depart. of Justice. (Excerpt) 1998.

Introduction

For the first time in 20 years, the Bureau of Justice Statistics(BJS) and the Office of Community Oriented Policing Services(COPS) sponsored city-level crime victimization surveys. The Census Bureau conducted the surveys. The National Institute of Justice provided funding for the city survey in Washington, DC, as part of its research support to the District of Columbia Revitalization Initiative.

The 12 cities are listed below:

- Chicago, Illinois
- Kansas City, Missouri
- Knoxville, Tennessee
- Los Angeles, California
- Madison, Wisconsin
- New York, New York
- San Diego, California
- Savannah, Georgia
- Spokane, Washington
- Springfield, Massachusetts
- Tucson, Arizona
- Washington, D.C.

Cities selected for the survey project had police departments that represented varying stages in the development of community policing. The project surveyed sampled house-holds residing within the selected cities' jurisdictional limits to account for the area served by the local police department. The survey did not capture victimizations experienced by those who lived outside the city limits but that may have occurred within the city. It does include victimizations reported by city residents which may have occurred outside the city limits. Respondents were asked about their experiences with crime over the past 12 months.

The Nation's law enforcement community has increasingly requested city-level information regarding crime victimizations and citizen attitudes. BJS and COPS undertook this study to examine how NCVS questions could be administered at a local level using the RDD methodology. The purposes of the project were to collect baseline data on city-level violent crime, to measure fear of crime and community attitudes toward neighborhoods and police, and to test the RDD methodology.

Community attitudes

The neighborhood

About 80% or more of the residents in each of the 12 cities said they were satisfied with the quality of life in their neighborhood. Few residents, 6% or less in any of the 12 cities, were "very dissatisfied" with their neighborhood. (Table 8 omitted) Less than half the residents in each of the cities were fearful of crime in their neighborhood (table 9 omitted). Fewer than 1 in 10 in each of the cities said they were "very fearful."

Residents who said they were very or somewhat fearful of crime in their neighborhood were asked if their level of fear had changed at all over the past 12 months (table 10 omitted). The majority of residents who were fearful of crime said their fear of neighborhood crime had not changed over the past 12 months. Each of the 12 cities generally had few residents (10% or less) who thought their fear of crime had decreased over the past year....

Attitudes toward the local police

Residents in each of the 12 cities were asked if they had been in contact with the local police for any reason over the past 12 months. About 3 in 10 residents or more in each city—ranging from 29% in New York to 44% in Savannah and Tucson—said they had contact of some kind with the police over the past 12 months (Table 29 omitted).

Overall, 8% of the residents had contact with the police because they reported a crime; 6% called for police service; 6% had a casual conversation with the police; and 6% said they had provided information to the police (table 30 omitted).

A majority of respondents across all 12 cities said they had not noticed a change in police presence in the past 12 months (table 31 omitted). Twenty-three percent of all respondents reported an increase in police presence. In two of the largest cities, New York (26%) and Los Angeles (23%), about a quarter of the residents reported increases in police presence.

Residents were asked what kind of activities they saw police doing in their neighborhood. Thirty-seven percent of respondents reported seeing police talking to residents (table 32, omitted). Recreational and school activities with

Table 33. Residents in 12 cities, by degree of satisfaction with local police, 1998

| | Estimated number of residents age 16 or older | Percent of Residents | | | | | |
| | | Satisfied | | | Dissatisfied | | |
		Total	Very satisfied	Satisfied	Total	Dissat-isfied	Very dis-satisfied
Total	11,913,071	85%	18%	66%	15%	12%	3%
Chicago	1,901,575	80	16	64	20	15	4
Kansas City	330,761	89	24	65	11	7	4
Knoxville	116,356	89	22	66	11	9	2
Los Angeles	2,557,680	86	20	66	14	12	3
Madison	147,236	97	31	66	3	3	—
New York	4,973,711	84	16	67	16	13	4
San Diego	848,531	93	25	68	7	6	1
Savannah	93,110	86	21	65	15	10	4
Spokane	133,288	87	19	68	13	11	2
Springfield	102,609	87	23	64	13	10	3
Tucson	336,711	87	19	68	13	10	3
Washington DC	371,503	78	14	63	22	17	6

Note: Don't know responses and refusals to answer are excluded from table. Details may not add to total because of rounding. Zero indicates no cases in sample. Includes Asian, Pacific Islander and American Indian, Aleut, and Eskimo.

Question: "In general, how satisfied are you with the police who serve your neighborhood? Are you very satisfied, satisfied, dissatisfied, or very dissatisfied?"

children (30%) and facilitating crime watch and prevention activities (27%) were other commonly reported police activities.

Satisfaction with local police

The household telephone survey asked residents age 16 or older about their level of satisfaction with the police who served their neighborhood. The vast majority of residents in each of the 12 cities were "satisfied" or "very satisfied" with the local police.

The level of satisfaction with the police ranged from 97% of residents in Madison reporting being "satisfied" or "very satisfied" to 78% in Washington, D.C. (table 33). Few residents in the 12 cities, 6% or less, said they were "very dissatisfied" with the police. In total, white residents in the 12 cities were more likely than black residents to have said they were satisfied with the police who

Table 34. Residents in 12 cities, by degree of satisfaction with local police, by race, 1998

	Estimated number of residents age or older	Percent of residents satisfied or dissatisfied with police					
		White		Black		Other*	
		Satisfied	Dis-satisfied	Satisfied	Dis-satisfied	Satisfied	Dis-satisfied
Total	11,913,070	90%	10%	76%	24%	78%	22%
Chicago	1,901,575	89	11	69	31	67	33
Kansas City	330,762	90	10	86	14	84	16
Knoxville	116,355	91	9	63	37	100	0
Los Angeles	2,557,679	89	11	82	18	80	20
Madison	147,236	97	3	97	3	98	2
New York	4,973,710	89	11	77	23	77	23
San Diego	848,530	95	5	89	11	87	13
Savannah	93,110	88	12	81	19	92	8
Spokane	133,289	88	12	79	21	73	27
Springfield	102,609	90	10	76	24	82	18
Tucson	336,713	88	12	91	9	76	24
Washington DC	371,502	81	19	75	25	83	17

Note: Don't know responses and refusals to answer are excluded from table. Details may not add to total because of rounding. Zero indicates no cases in sample.

*Includes Asian, Pacific Islander and American Indian, Aleut, and Eskimo.

Question: "In general, how satisfied are you with the police who serve your neighborhood? Are you very satisfied, satisfied, dissatisfied, or very dissatisfied?"

served their neighborhood (table 34). The proportion of black residents who said they were satisfied with the police ranged from 63% in Knoxville to 97% in Madison.

For each of the 12 cities, residents who had been a victim of violent crime were less likely than others to say they were satisfied with the local police (table 35 omitted).

Likewise, compared to those who were not fearful of neighborhood crime, persons who were fearful of crime in their neighborhood were somewhat less likely to be satisfied with the local police (table 36 omitted)....

List of other cases and articles relevant to this topic

Atwater v. City of Lago Vista, 532 U.S. 318 (2001).

Cheurprakobkit, S. (2000). Police-citizen contact and police performance: Attitudinal difference between Hispanics and non-Hispanics. *Journal of Criminal Justice* 28: 325–336.

Sherman, L. W., L. Steele and S.A. Julian (1989). Stray bullets and "mushrooms": Random shootings in four cities, 1977–1988. *Journal of Quantitative Criminology* 5: 297.

Smith and Alpert (2002). Searching for direction: Courts, social science, and the adjudication of racial profiling claims. *Justice Quarterly* 19: 673–703

Terry v. Ohio, 392 U.S. 1 (1968)

Discussion and Review Questions

1   Many individuals are stopped at our borders, including our airports, based on the suspicion of drug trafficking and terrorism. Do you think it is possible to develop an empirically valid "profile" to justify the stopping of individuals at our borders? How would you determine its validity and accuracy? Do you think that a single profile could meet the needs of law enforcement?

2   Distrust of the police by segments of society has remained the "norm" for decades, why do you think that little has improved concerning this issue? Several government publications have addressed the problem of community-law enforcement tensions. Find one of the articles and examine the recommendations to improve these relations. Do you think that the recommendations, if implemented, would work? Why or why not?

3. In light of the racial profiling findings of *State v. Soto,* do you think that certain segments of society may be justified in "running" away from the police? Find the United States Supreme Court decision in *Illinois v. Wardlow*, 528 U.S. 119 (2000). If you were a defense lawyer in the *Wardlow* case and had unlimited funds, what kind of study do you think might have persuaded Justice Rhenquist that the inference of suspicious behavior does not naturally flow from running away from the police?

4. Examine the factors relied on by the United States Supreme Court in finding reasonable suspicion to stop individuals at airports for drug trafficking as discussed in this chapter (*Sokolow, Royer,* and *Mendenhall*). Do you think these factors amount to a reasonable suspicion that crim-

inal activity is at hand? In other words, do you agree or disagree with the Court's assessment? Why or why not?

References

Articles

Cheurprakobkit, S. (2000). Police-citizen contact and police performance: Attitudinal differences between Hispanics and non-Hispanics. *Journal of Criminal Justice* 28: 325–336.

Cooper, C. (2001). Driving scared. *New Jersey Law Journal.*

Fridell, L., R. Lunney, D. Diamond and B. Kabu (2001). *Racially biased policing: A principled response.* Washington DC: Police Executive Research Forum.

Hurst, F. and S.L. Browning (2000). The attitudes of juveniles toward the police: A comparison of black and white youth. *Policing: An International Journal of Police Strategies and Management* 23: 37–53.

Klotter, J. C. and J. R. Kanovitz (1995). *Constitutional Law*, Seventh Edition. Cincinnati, Ohio: Anderson Publishing.

Lamberth, J. (1996). *Report in the Wilkins v. Maryland State Police case, Plaintiff's Expert* at 9.

Lichtenberg, I. (1999). *Voluntary Consent or Obedience to Authority: An Inquiry into the 'Voluntary' Police-Citizen Interaction.* Dissertation Abstracts.

PR Newswire (July 18, 2002). Racial profiling post September 11. PR Newswire Association.

Report of the New Jersey Senate Judiciary Committee's Investigation of Racial Profiling and the New Jersey State Police (2001).

Ryan, K. (1994). Technicians and interpreters in moral crusades: The case of the drug courier profile. *Deviant Behavior* 15: 217–240.

Sherman, L.W., L. Steele and S.A. Julian (1989). *Stray bullets and "mushrooms': Random shootings in four cities, 1977–1988.* Washington, D.C.: Crime Control Institute

Weitzer, R. (1999). Citizens' perceptions of police misconduct: Race and neighborhood context. *Justice Quarterly* 16: 819–846.

Case Citations

Atwater v. City of Lago Vista, 532 U.S. 318 (2001).

Brown v. Texas, 443 U.S. 47 (1979)

Florida v. Royer, 460 U.S. 491 (1983).

Illinois v. Wardlow, 528 U.S. 119 (2000)
State v. Soto, 734 A. 2d 350 (1996)
Terry v. Ohio, 392 U.S. 1 (1968).
Whren v. United States, 517 U.S. 806 (1996).
United States v. Cortez, 449 U.S. 411 (1981).
United States v. Mendenhall, 446 U.S. 544 (1980).
United States v. Sokolow, 490 U.S. 1 (1989)

CHAPTER 5

THE EXCLUSIONARY RULE

The poorest man may in his cottage bid defiance to all the forces of the Crown. It may be frail; its roof may shake; the wind may blow through it; the storm may enter; the rain may enter; but the King of England cannot enter—all his force dares not cross the threshold of the ruined tenement!

–William Pitt, the Earl of Chatham (1763) speech during a Parliamentary debate on privacy in the home. *Miller v. United States*, 357 U.S. 301, 307, 78 S. Ct. 1190, 2 L. Ed. 2d 1332 (1958).

In the last chapter, the Fourth Amendment protection against unreasonable **searches** and **seizures** was discussed. What happens when law enforcement violates the Fourth Amendment? Since the language of the Fourth Amendment does not provide a remedy for its violation, the United States Supreme Court created a rule that prohibits the use of illegally obtained evidence at trial. This is called the **exclusionary rule**.

What is the legal history of the exclusionary rule and under what circumstances does it apply?

The application of this rule to all law enforcement and criminal prosecutions was a slow process. In 1914, the United States Supreme Court announced for the first time that evidence obtained in violation of the Fourth Amendment (illegal search or seizure) would not be admissible in federal criminal prosecutions (*Weeks v. United States*, 232 U.S. 383 (1914). This decision did not disallow, however, the use of illegally seized evidence in state prosecutions or in federal prosecutions if seized by state officers. The practice of state police illegally seizing evidence for use in federal prosecutions became known as the "silver platter" doctrine. State law enforcement officers handed the evidence over to federal prosecutors on a 'silver platter.'

> **Search:** An examination of a [person]'s house or other buildings or premises, or of his person, or of his vehicle, aircraft etc....(Black's law dictionary).
>
> **Seizure:**....connotes the taking of one physically or constructively into custody and detaining him, thus causing a deprivation of his freedom in a significant way, with real interruption of his liberty of movement. (Black's Law Dictionary)
>
> **Exclusionary rule:** This rule commands that where evidence has been obtained in violation of the privileges guaranteed by the U.S. Constitution, the evidence must be excluded at the trial. Evidence which is obtained by an unreasonable search and seizure is excluded from evidence under the Fourth Amendment, U.S. Constitution and this rule is applicable to the States. (Black's Law Dictionary)

In 1949, the United States Supreme Court was asked to apply the exclusionary rule to the states, but it refused to do so. In *Wolf v. Colorado*, 338 U.S. 25 (1949), the Court acknowledged that the Fourth Amendment proscription of unreasonable searches and seizures applied to the states, however, the Court held that the exclusionary rule was not an "essential ingredient" of the Fourth Amendment guarantee. The Court encouraged state courts to adopt the exclusionary rule, and some did, but it refused to require its adoption as part of the Fourth Amendment. It was not until 1960, in *Elkins v. United States*, 364 U.S. 206 (1960) that the Court struck down the 'silver platter' doctrine. In *Elkins*, the Court held that evidence illegally seized by state law enforcement was not admissible in federal criminal prosecutions.

A year later, the Court rendered its decision in *Mapp v. Ohio*, 367 U.S. 643 (1961) holding that 'the exclusionary rule is an essential part of both the Fourth and Fourteenth Amendments is not only the logical dictate of prior cases, but it also makes very good sense.' The Court found that it was contrary to commonsense to disallow a federal prosecutor from making use of illegally seized evidence, but allowing the state prosecutor to use this evidence. In addition, the Court relied on two reasons for its decision. First, the exclusionary rule provides a judicially created safeguard for the Fourth Amendment and will act as a deterrent against illegal searches and seizures by law enforcement. In other words, the Court believed that the exclusionary rule would deter police misconduct. Second, the Court believed that it was necessary to apply the exclusionary rule for the preservation of "judicial integrity." The courts should not be complicit in violating the Constitution by admitting and countenancing illegally seized evidence.

> **Search warrant:** An order in writing, issued by a justice or other magistrate, in the name of the state, directed to…[an] officer, authorizing him to search or seize any property that constitutes evidence of the commission of a crime, contraband, the fruits of crime, or things otherwise criminally possessed; or, property designed or intended…as the means of committing a crime. (Black's Law Dictionary)

More than two decades later, the United States Supreme Court was confronted with the question: 'whether the Fourth Amendment exclusionary rule should be modified so as not to bar the use in the prosecution's case in chief of evidence obtained by officers acting in reasonable reliance on a search warrant issued by a detached and neutral magistrate but ultimately found to be unsupported by probable cause.' In *United States v. Leon*, 468 U.S. 897 (1984), the police had information about drug dealing from a confidential informant. Based on this information, the police undertook an investigation and applied for a **search warrant**. The application was reviewed by several district attorneys and approved by a Superior Court Judge. The warrant was facially valid, the police executed it, and found large quantities of drugs.

At a suppression hearing, the trial judge found that there was insufficient evidence of **probable cause** and excluded the drug evidence from trial. The prosecutor argued that the Fourth Amendment exclusionary rule should not apply where evidence is seized in reasonable, good-faith reliance on a search warrant. In other words, the police officers did everything they thought that they should to conduct a lawful search and seizure, and therefore the exclusionary rule should not apply. Although the trial judge rejected this argument, the United States Supreme Court held that it would modify the exclusionary rule to accommodate this situation.

The Court held that the exclusionary rule could be modified without jeopardizing its ability to perform its intended function. In developing this exception to the exclusionary rule, the Court found that in assessing the costs

> **Probable cause:** Reasonable cause; having more evidence for than against.…Probable cause for search and seizure with or without search warrant involves probablities which are not technical but factual and practical considerations of every day life upon which reasonable and prudent men act, and essence of probable cause is reasonable ground for belief of guilt. Black's Law Dictonary.

and benefits of the rule, the rule's purpose would not be served under these circumstances. Specifically, the Court stated: "Under these circumstances, the officers' reliance on the magistrate's determination of probable cause was objectively reasonable, and application of the extreme sanction of exclusion is inappropriate." The Court did not modify the exclusionary rule; nor did it sanction situations where the police misinform a magistrate or a judge becomes a rubber-stamp for all police warrants. In arriving at this decision, the Court examined existing social science research on the impact of the exclusionary rule that found its impact negligible and insubstantial and that any deterrent effect would not be served under these circumstances.

Since *Leon*, the United States Supreme Court has extended the application of the exclusionary rule to situations where the police have relied on a statute later determined to be invalid (*Illinois v. Krull*, 480 U.S. 340 (1987) and when the police rely on information given to them from a computer later determined to be in error (*Arizona v. Evans*, 514 U.S. 1 (1995). In *Evans*, the police officer made an arrest for an outstanding warrant and it was later determined that the warrant remained in the computer due to a clerical error. In other words, there was not an active warrant for Evans. During his arrest, Evans was found in the possession of marijuana. The Court extended the *Leon* good faith exception to this situation and reasoned that the ends of the exclusionary rule, i.e. deterrence of future police misconduct, would not be served by extending it to this circumstance.

In arriving at these decisions, the Court is engaging in a balancing test. It is balancing the interests served by suppressing evidence obtained in contravention of the Fourth Amendment and the costs associated with that suppression (the loss of a case). In *Evans*, similar to its decision in *Leon* and *Krull*, the Court found that the purpose of the exclusionary rule (to deter police misconduct) would not be served by suppressing evidence obtained through the mistake of the court clerk. In coming to this conclusion the Court did not examine social science evidence or information concerning how often this type of error is made, the relationship between law enforcement with the clerk's office or the impact or cost associated with suppression on society.

How has the exclusionary rule impacted the police, criminal justice system and society?

The cost/benefit debate on the exclusionary rule continues. Since the Court's decision in 1984, legal scholars have engaged in unabated discussions about the impact of the exclusionary rule, the effectiveness of the rule in deterring police misconduct and the impact of the *Leon* 'good faith exception.' There exist two distinct camps in terms of the exclusionary rule—those that advance its virtues in deterring police misconduct and others who argue that Congress should pass legislation to overrule the rule. According to Christopher Slobogin (1999), behavioral and motivational theories demonstrate that the rule is unable to deter individual police officers from engaging in illegal searches and seizures. Slobogin argues that an administrative damages system that allows actions to be brought directly against the police and hold the police personally responsible would be more effective. Timothy Lynch (1998) argues, however, the exclusionary rule can be justified on separation-of-powers principles. According to Lynch, it is the obligation of the courts to monitor misbehavior on the part of the executive branch (e.g., police agents who subvert the use of warrants in conducting searches).

Although the exclusionary rule debate is more than four decades old, little social scientific research has been conducted that examines police conduct, the warrant process and the application of the exclusionary rule. Only a handful of studies have been conducted that explore several aspects of the implementation of the exclusionary rule. One of these few studies provides insight into the search warrant process (Van Duizend, Sutton and Carter 1984). This study examined police preparation of an application, a warrant and an affidavit for judicial approval. In some jurisdictions, they found that prosecutors work closely with police officers and assist them in preparing these documents or actually review them prior to submission for judicial approval. In some rural areas, warrants may be obtained by getting prosecutorial approval over the telephone, and officers get judicial approval thereafter. During office hours (9a.m. to 5p.m.), the police may go to the courthouse, after hours the police must take warrants to the homes of judges for review and authorizing signatures. In the Van Duizend et al (1984) study, few warrant applications were ever refused by the judge. After judicial approval is obtained, police officers are free to execute the warrants. However, these warrants must be served within a short period of time—usually ten days—to prevent the information from becoming stale. In a recent decision, the Court held it was a violation of the Fourth Amendment for law enforcement to bring the media on a "ride-a-long" during the execution of a warrant because the media served no law enforcement purpose and did not assist in anyway in the execution of the warrant (*Wilson v. Layne*, 526 U.S. 603 (1999).

After the *Leon* decision, some researchers examined the impact of the exclusionary rule on "lost cases" (Uchida and Bynum 1991), police compliance with the law (Hefferman and Lovely 1991) and the impact of the *Leon* decision

(Uchida, Bynum, Rogan et al 1988). In a study of 2,115 search warrant applications and interviews with 187 individuals from seven criminal justice systems, Uchida and Bynum (1991) found that motions to suppress were only successful 0.9% of the primary warrants (15 of 1,748). According to the researchers, "[f]ew cases were "lost" as a result of the exclusionary rule in seven jurisdictions when police used search warrants." In the seven jurisdictions, police officers demonstrated a willingness to work with prosecutors and insure that their warrants met standards of probable cause. Additionally, there was a much lower rate of successful motions to suppress when police worked closely with prosecutors. In summary, Uchida and Bynum (1991: 1055) conclude

> the 'cost' of the exclusionary rule in lost cases is slight when the police obtain a search warrant. While critics of the exclusionary rule argue that it imposes a high cost on society by depriving the courts of reliable evidence and allowing criminals freedom, we have found that, in fact, few criminals are freed, and when they are, their crimes are not serious. Thus, the cost to society is limited.

A similar finding emerged in a study by Uchida, Bynum, Rogan et al. (1988). Uchida et al. found the empirical effects of the *Leon* decision were minimal. After *Leon*, police practices in terms of getting search warrants—the number of warrants, the content of the warrants, and the quality of the search warrants—were unaffected by the decision. Similarly, the trial court practices in disposing of motions to suppress did not change. The numbers of motions filed and the success rate remained unchanged. Despite the amount of time that legal scholars and others spend on the exclusionary rule, these initial studies seem to raise the question "what is all the fuss about?" The Court may have made a substantial legal ruling in *Mapp* and *Leon*, however, the practical implications of these decisions may be minimal.

In another study by Heffernan and Lovely (1991), researchers examined the knowledge of police officers, defense attorneys and prosecutors involving Fourth Amendment fact scenarios. They found that officers frequently were uncertain about the "rules" applicable to search and seizure situations; and in fact, that twenty-five percent of the situations, police officers, defense attorneys and prosecutors made mistakes about the legality of hypothetical intrusions. Heffernan and Lovely (1991) argued the purpose of the exclusionary rule would best be carried out by encouraging police (and other criminal justice personnel) training on the Fourth Amendment. One weakness of the exclusionary rule is that it does not address inadvertent or unknowing violations of the Fourth Amendment. Since the law changes so rapidly, it is necessary as pointed out by Heffernan and Lovely (1991) that police officers be educated about the evolving rules of search and seizure. In addition, more long-term studies on the impact of the exclusionary rule and the 'good faith exception' are necessary for an adequate assessment of its effect. In this chapter, an excerpt from *United States v. Leon* is included.

United States v. Leon
468 U.S. 897 (1984)(Excerpt)

OPINION BY: WHITE

This case presents the question whether the Fourth Amendment exclusionary rule should be modified so as not to bar the use in the prosecution's case in chief of evidence obtained by officers acting in reasonable reliance on a search warrant issued by a detached and neutral magistrate but ultimately found to be unsupported by probable cause. To resolve this question, we must consider once again the tension between the sometimes competing goals of, on the one hand, deterring official misconduct and removing inducements to unreasonable invasions of privacy and, on the other, establishing procedures under which criminal defendants are "acquitted or convicted on the basis of all the evidence which exposes the truth." *Alderman v. United States*, 394 U.S. 165, 175 (1969).

In August 1981, a confidential informant of unproven reliability [provided information to an officer about the sale of drugs by a couple in two locations in Burbank, California].... On the basis of this information, the Burbank police initiated an extensive investigation focusing [on those locations].... [Based on their observations, an officer drafted an] extensive application [which] was reviewed by several Deputy District Attorneys. A facially valid search warrant was issued in September 1981 by a State Superior Court Judge. The ensuing searches produced large quantities of drugs.... [Defendants were charged with several drug related crimes, and they subsequently,] filed motions to suppress the evidence seized pursuant to the warrant. The District Court held an evidentiary hearing and, while recognizing that the case was a close one, see *id.*, at 131, granted the motions to suppress in part. It concluded that the affidavit was insufficient to establish probable cause...In response to a request from the Government, the court made clear that Officer Rombach had acted in good faith, but it rejected the Government's suggestion that the Fourth Amendment exclusionary rule should not apply where evidence is seized in reasonable, good-faith reliance on a search warrant....

The Government's petition...presented only the question "[whether] the Fourth Amendment exclusionary rule should be modified so as not to bar the admission of evidence seized in reasonable, good-faith reliance on a search warrant that is subsequently held to be defective."...We have concluded that, in the Fourth Amendment context, the exclusionary rule can be modified somewhat without jeopardizing its ability to perform its intended functions....

The Fourth Amendment contains no provision expressly precluding the use of evidence obtained in violation of its commands, and an examination of its origin and purposes makes clear that the use of fruits of a past unlawful search or seizure "[works] no new Fourth Amendment wrong." *United States* v. *Calandra*, 414 U.S. 338, 354 (1974). The wrong condemned by the Amendment is "fully accomplished" by the unlawful search or seizure itself, *ibid.*, and the exclusionary rule is neither intended nor able to "cure the invasion of the defendant's rights which he has already suffered." *Stone* v. *Powell, supra*, at 540 (WHITE, J., dissenting). The rule thus operates as "a judicially created remedy designed to safeguard Fourth Amendment rights generally through its deterrent effect, rather than a personal constitutional right of the party aggrieved." *United States* v. *Calandra, supra*, at 348.

Whether the exclusionary sanction is appropriately imposed in a particular case, our decisions make clear, is "an issue separate from the question whether the Fourth Amendment rights of the party seeking to invoke the rule were violated by police conduct." *Illinois* v. *Gates, supra*, at 223. Only the former question is currently before us, and it must be resolved by weighing the costs and benefits of preventing the use in the prosecution's case in chief of inherently trustworthy tangible evidence obtained in reliance on a search warrant issued by a detached and neutral magistrate that ultimately is found to be defective.

The substantial social costs exacted by the exclusionary rule for the vindication of Fourth Amendment rights have long been a source of concern. "Our cases have consistently recognized that unbending application of the exclusionary sanction to enforce ideals of governmental rectitude would impede unacceptably the truth-finding functions of judge and jury." *United States* v. *Payner*, 447 U.S. 727, 734 (1980). An objectionable collateral consequence of this interference with the criminal justice system's truth-finding function is that some guilty defendants may go free or receive reduced sentences as a result of favorable plea bargains.[6] Particularly when law enforcement officers

---

6. Researchers have only recently begun to study extensively the effects of the exclusionary rule on the disposition of felony arrests. One study suggests that the rule results in the nonprosecution or nonconviction of between 0.6% and 2.35% of individuals arrested

have acted in objective good faith or their transgressions have been minor, the magnitude of the benefit conferred on such guilty defendants offends basic concepts of the criminal justice system. *Stone* v. *Powell*, 428 U.S., at 490. Indiscriminate application of the exclusionary rule, therefore, may well "[generate] disrespect for the law and administration of justice." *Id.*, at 491. Accordingly, "[as] with any remedial device, the application of the rule has been restricted to those areas where its remedial objectives are thought most efficaciously served." *United States* v. *Calandra, supra*, at 348; see *Stone* v. *Powell, supra*, at 486–487; *United States* v. *Janis*, 428 U.S. 433, 447 (1976)....

As yet, we have not recognized any form of good-faith exception to the Fourth Amendment exclusionary rule. But the balancing approach that has evolved during the years of experience with the rule provides strong support for the modification currently urged upon us. As we discuss below, our eval-

---

for felonies. Davies, A Hard Look at What We Know (and Still Need to Learn) About the "Costs" of the Exclusionary Rule: The NIJ Study and Other Studies of "Lost" Arrests, 1983 A. B. F. Res. J. 611, 621. The estimates are higher for particular crimes the prosecution of which depends heavily on physical evidence. Thus, the cumulative loss due to nonprosecution or nonconviction of individuals arrested on felony drug charges is probably in the range of 2.8% to 7.1%. *Id.*, at 680. Davies' analysis of California data suggests that screening by police and prosecutors results in the release because of illegal searches or seizures of as many as 1.4% of all felony arrestees, *id.*, at 650, that 0.9% of felony arrestees are released, because of illegal searches or seizures, at the preliminary hearing or after trial, *id.*, at 653, and that roughly 0.05% of all felony arrestees benefit from reversals on appeal because of illegal searches. *Id.*, at 654. See also K. Brosi, *A Cross-City Comparison of Felony Case Processing* 16, 18–19 (1979); U.S. General Accounting Office, Report of the Comptroller General of the United States, *Impact of the Exclusionary Rule on Federal Criminal Prosecutions* 10–11, 14 (1979); F. Feeney, F. Dill, & A. Weir, *Arrests Without Convictions: How Often They Occur and Why* 203–206 (National Institute of Justice 1983); National Institute of Justice, *The Effects of the Exclusionary Rule: A Study in California* 1–2 (1982); Nardulli, The Societal Cost of the Exclusionary Rule: An Empirical Assessment, 1983 A. B. F. Res. J. 585, 600. The exclusionary rule also has been found to affect the plea-bargaining process. S. Schlesinger, *Exclusionary Injustice: The Problem of Illegally Obtained Evidence* 63 (1977). But see Davies, *supra*, at 668–669; Nardulli, *supra*, at 604–606.

Many of these researchers have concluded that the impact of the exclusionary rule is insubstantial, but the small percentages with which they deal mask a large absolute number of felons who are released because the cases against them were based in part on illegal searches or seizures. "[Any] rule of evidence that denies the jury access to clearly probative and reliable evidence must bear a heavy burden of justification, and must be carefully limited to the circumstances in which it will pay its way by deterring official unlawfulness." *Illinois* v. *Gates*, 462 U.S., at 257–258 (WHITE, J., concurring in judgment). Because we find that the rule can have no substantial deterrent effect in the sorts of situations under consideration in this case, see *infra*, at 916–921, we conclude that it cannot pay its way in those situations.

uation of the costs and benefits of suppressing reliable physical evidence seized by officers reasonably relying on a warrant issued by a detached and neutral magistrate leads to the conclusion that such evidence should be admissible in the prosecution's case in chief.

Because a search warrant "provides the detached scrutiny of a neutral magistrate, which is a more reliable safeguard against improper searches than the hurried judgment of a law enforcement officer 'engaged in the often competitive enterprise of ferreting out crime,'" *United States* v. *Chadwick*, 433 U.S. 1, 9 (1977) (quoting *Johnson* v. *United States*, 333 U.S. 10, 14 (1948)), we have expressed a strong preference for warrants and declared that "in a doubtful or marginal case a search under a warrant may be sustainable where without one it would fall." *United States* v. *Ventresca*, 380 U.S. 102, 106 (1965). See *Aguilar* v. *Texas*, 378 U.S., at 111. Reasonable minds frequently may differ on the question whether a particular affidavit establishes probable cause, and we have thus concluded that the preference for warrants is most appropriately effectuated by according "great deference" to a magistrate's determination. *Spinelli* v. *United States*, 393 U.S., at 419. See *Illinois* v. *Gates*, 462 U.S., at 236; *United States* v. *Ventresca*, *supra*, at 108–109.

Deference to the magistrate, however, is not boundless. It is clear, first, that the deference accorded to a magistrate's finding of probable cause does not preclude inquiry into the knowing or reckless falsity of the affidavit on which that determination was based. *Franks* v. *Delaware*, 438 U.S. 154 (1978). Second, the courts must also insist that the magistrate purport to "perform his 'neutral and detached' function and not serve merely as a rubber stamp for the police." *Aguilar* v. *Texas*, *supra*, at 111. See *Illinois* v. *Gates*, *supra*, at 239. A magistrate failing to "manifest that neutrality and detachment demanded of a judicial officer when presented with a warrant application" and who acts instead as "an adjunct law enforcement officer" cannot provide valid authorization for an otherwise unconstitutional search. *Lo-Ji Sales, Inc.* v. *New York*, 442 U.S. 319, 326–327 (1979).

Third, reviewing courts will not defer to a warrant based on an affidavit that does not "provide the magistrate with a substantial basis for determining the existence of probable cause." *Illinois* v. *Gates*, 462 U.S., at 239. "Sufficient information must be presented to the magistrate to allow that official to determine probable cause; his action cannot be a mere ratification of the bare conclusions of others." *Ibid.* See *Aguilar* v. *Texas*, *supra*, at 114–115; *Giordenello* v. *United States*, 357 U.S. 480 (1958); *Nathanson* v. *United States*, 290 U.S. 41 (1933). Even if the warrant application was supported by more than a "bare bones" affidavit, a reviewing court may properly conclude that, notwithstanding the deference that magistrates deserve, the warrant was invalid because the magistrate's probable-cause determination reflected an improper analysis of the totality of the circumstances, *Illinois* v. *Gates, supra,* at 238–239, or because the form of the warrant was improper in some respect.

Only in the first of these three situations, however, has the Court set forth a rationale for suppressing evidence obtained pursuant to a search warrant; in the other areas, it has simply excluded such evidence without considering whether Fourth Amendment interests will be advanced. To the extent that proponents of exclusion rely on its behavioral effects on judges and magistrates in these areas, their reliance is misplaced. First, the exclusionary rule is designed to deter police misconduct rather than to punish the errors of judges and magistrates. Second, there exists no evidence suggesting that judges and magistrates are inclined to ignore or subvert the Fourth Amendment or that lawlessness among these actors requires application of the extreme sanction of exclusion.[14]

Third, and most important, we discern no basis, and are offered none, for believing that exclusion of evidence seized pursuant to a warrant will have a significant deterrent effect on the issuing judge or magistrate. Many of the factors that indicate that the exclusionary rule cannot provide an effective "special" or "general" deterrent for individual offending law enforcement officers apply as well to judges or magistrates. And, to the extent that the rule is thought to operate as a "systemic" deterrent on a wider audience, it clearly can have no such effect on individuals empowered to issue search warrants. Judges and magistrates are not adjuncts to the law enforcement team; as neutral judicial officers, they have no stake in the outcome of particular criminal prosecutions. The threat of exclusion thus cannot be expected significantly to deter

---

14. Although there are assertions that some magistrates become rubber stamps for the police and others may be unable effectively to screen police conduct, see, *e. g.*, 2 W. LaFave, *Search and Seizure* § 4.1 (1978); Kamisar, Does (Did) (Should) The Exclusionary Rule Rest on a "Principled Basis" Rather than an "Empirical Proposition"?, 16 *Creighton L. Rev.* 565, 569–571 (1983); Schroeder, Deterring Fourth Amendment Violations: Alternatives to the Exclusionary Rule, 69 *Geo. L. J.* 1361, 1412 (1981), we are not convinced that this is a problem of major proportions. See L. Tiffany, D. McIntyre, & D. Rotenberg, *Detection of Crime* 119 (1967); Israel, Criminal Procedure, the Burger Court, and the Legacy of the Warren Court, 75 *Mich. L. Rev.* 1319, 1414, n. 396 (1977); P. Johnson, *New Approaches to Enforcing the Fourth Amendment* 8–10 (Working Paper, Sept. 1978), quoted in Y. Kamisar, W. LaFave, & J. Israel, *Modern Criminal Procedure* 229–230 (5th ed. 1980); R. Van Duizend, L. Sutton, & C. Carter, *The Search Warrant Process,* ch. 7 (Review Draft, National Center for State Courts, 1983).

them. Imposition of the exclusionary sanction is not necessary meaningfully to inform judicial officers of their errors, and we cannot conclude that admitting evidence obtained pursuant to a warrant while at the same time declaring that the warrant was somehow defective will in any way reduce judicial officers' professional incentives to comply with the Fourth Amendment, encourage them to repeat their mistakes, or lead to the granting of all colorable warrant requests.

If exclusion of evidence obtained pursuant to a subsequently invalidated warrant is to have any deterrent effect, therefore, it must alter the behavior of individual law enforcement officers or the policies of their departments. One could argue that applying the exclusionary rule in cases where the police failed to demonstrate probable cause in the warrant application deters future inadequate presentations or "magistrate shopping" and thus promotes the ends of the Fourth Amendment. Suppressing evidence obtained pursuant to a technically defective warrant supported by probable cause also might encourage officers to scrutinize more closley the form of the warrant and to point out suspected judicial errors. We find such arguments speculative and conclude that suppression of evidence obtained pursuant to a warrant should be ordered only on a case-by-case basis and only in those unusual cases in which exclusion will further the purposes of the exclusionary rule.

We have frequently questioned whether the exclusionary rule can have any deterrent effect when the offending officers acted in the objectively reasonable belief that their conduct did not violate the Fourth Amendment. "No empirical researcher, proponent or opponent of the rule, has yet been able to establish with any assurance whether the rule has a deterrent effect...." *United States* v. *Janis*, 428 U.S., at 452, n. 22. But even assuming that the rule effectively deters some police misconduct and provides incentives for the law enforcement profession as a whole to conduct itself in accord with the Fourth Amendment, it cannot be expected, and should not be applied, to deter objectively reasonable law enforcement activity....

This is particularly true, we believe, when an officer acting with objective good faith has obtained a search warrant from a judge or magistrate and acted within its scope. In most such cases, there is no police illegality and thus nothing to deter. It is the magistrate's responsibility to determine whether the officer's allegations establish probable cause and, if so, to issue a warrant comporting in form with the requirements of the Fourth Amendment. In the ordinary case, an officer cannot be expected to question the magistrate's probable-cause determination or his judgment that the form of the warrant is technically sufficient. "[Once] the warrant issues, there is literally nothing more the policeman can do in seeking to comply with the law." *Id.*, at 498 (BURGER, C. J., concurring). Penalizing the officer for the magistrate's error, rather than his own, cannot logically contribute to the deterrence of Fourth Amendment violations....

Suppression therefore remains an appropriate remedy if the magistrate or judge in issuing a warrant was misled by information in an affidavit that the affiant knew was false or would have known was false except for his reckless disregard of the truth. *Franks* v. *Delaware*, 438 U.S. 154 (1978). The exception we recognize today will also not apply in cases where the issuing magistrate wholly abandoned his judicial role in the manner condemned in *Lo-Ji Sales, Inc.* v. *New York*, 442 U.S. 319 (1979); in such circumstances, no reasonably well trained officer should rely on the warrant....

Finally, depending on the circumstances of the particular case, a warrant may be so facially deficient—*i. e.*, in failing to particularize the place to be searched or the things to be seized—that the executing officers cannot reasonably presume it to be valid. Cf. *Massachusetts* v. *Sheppard*, *post*, at 988–991....

When the principles we have enunciated today are applied to the facts of this case, it is apparent that the judgment of the Court of Appeals cannot stand....We have now reexamined the purposes of the exclusionary rule and the propriety of its application in cases where officers have relied on a subsequently invalidated search warrant. Our conclusion is that the rule's purposes will only rarely be served by applying it in such circumstances.

In the absence of an allegation that the magistrate abandoned his detached and neutral role, suppression is appropriate only if the officers were dishonest or reckless in preparing their affidavit or could not have harbored an objectively reasonable belief in the existence of probable cause. Only respondent Leon has contended that no reasonably well trained police officer could have believed that there existed probable cause to search his house; significantly, the other respondents advance no comparable argument. Officer Rombach's application for a warrant clearly was supported by much more than a "bare bones" affidavit. The affidavit related the results of an extensive investigation and, as the opinions of the divided panel of the Court of Appeals make clear, provided evidence sufficient to create disagreement among thoughtful and competent judges as to the existence of probable cause. Under these circumstances, the officers' reliance on the magistrate's determination of probable cause was objectively reasonable, and application of the extreme sanction of exclusion is inappropriate.

Accordingly, the judgment of the Court of Appeals is *Reversed.*

DISSENT: JUSTICE BRENNAN, with whom JUSTICE MARSHALL joins, dissenting.

Ten years ago in *United States* v. *Calandra*, 414 U.S. 338 (1974), I expressed the fear that the Court's decision "may signal that a majority of my colleagues have positioned themselves to reopen the door [to evidence secured by official lawlessness] still further and abandon altogether the exclusionary rule in search-and-seizure cases." *Id.*, at 365 (dissenting opinion). Since then, in case after case, I have witnessed the Court's gradual but determined strangulation of the rule. It now appears that the Court's victory over the Fourth Amendment is complete. That today's decisions represent the *piece de resistance* of the Court's past efforts cannot be doubted, for today the Court sanctions the use in the prosecution's case in chief of illegally obtained evidence against the individual whose rights have been violated—a result that had previously been thought to be foreclosed.

The Court seeks to justify this result on the ground that the "costs" of adhering to the exclusionary rule in cases like those before us exceed the "benefits." But the language of deterrence and of cost/benefit analysis, if used indiscriminately, can have a narcotic effect. It creates an illusion of technical precision and ineluctability. It suggests that not only constitutional principle but also empirical data support the majority's result. When the Court's analysis is examined carefully, however, it is clear that we have not been treated to an honest assessment of the merits of the exclusionary rule, but have instead been drawn into a curious world where the "costs" of excluding illegally obtained evidence loom to exaggerated heights and where the "benefits" of such exclusion are made to disappear with a mere wave of the hand.

The majority ignores the fundamental constitutional importance of what is at stake here. While the machinery of law enforcement and indeed the nature of crime itself have changed dramatically since the Fourth Amendment became part of the Nation's fundamental law in 1791, what the Framers understood then remains true today—that the task of combating crime and convicting the guilty will in every era seem of such critical and pressing concern that we may be lured by the temptations of expediency into forsaking our commitment to protecting individual liberty and privacy. It was for that very reason that the Framers of the Bill of Rights insisted that law enforcement efforts be permanently and unambiguously restricted in order to preserve personal freedoms. In the constitutional scheme they ordained, the sometimes unpopular task of ensuring that the government's enforcement efforts remain within the strict boundaries fixed by the Fourth Amendment was entrusted to the courts. As James Madison predicted in his address to the First Congress on June 8, 1789:

> "If [these rights] are incorporated into the Constitution, independent tribunals of justice will consider themselves in a peculiar manner the guardians of those rights; they will be an impenetrable bulwark against every assumption of power in the Legislative or Executive; they will be naturally led to resist every encroachment upon rights expressly stipulated for in the Constitution by the declaration of rights." 1 Annals of Cong. 439.

If those independent tribunals lose their resolve, however, as the Court has done today, and give way to the seductive call of expediency, the vital guarantees of the Fourth Amendment are reduced to nothing more than a "form of words." *Silverthorne Lumber Co.* v. United States, 251 U.S. 385, 392 (1920).

A proper understanding of the broad purposes sought to be served by the Fourth Amendment demonstrates that the principles embodied in the exclusionary rule rest upon a far firmer constitutional foundation than the shifting sands of the Court's deterrence rationale. But even if I were to accept the Court's chosen method of analyzing the question posed by these cases, I would still conclude that the Court's decision cannot be justified.

... [I]t is clear why the question whether the exclusion of evidence would deter future police misconduct was never considered a relevant concern in the early cases from *Weeks* to *Olmstead*.[16] In those formative decisions, the Court plainly understood that the exclusion of illegally obtained evidence was compelled not by judicially fashioned remedial purposes, but rather by a direct constitutional command. A new phase in the history of the rule, however, opened with the Court's decision in *Wolf* v. *Colorado*, 338 U.S. 25 (1949). Although that decision held that the security of one's person and privacy protected by the Fourth Amendment was "implicit in 'the concept of ordered liberty' and as such enforceable against the States through the Due Process Clause" of the Fourteenth Amendment, *id.*, at 27–28, quoting *Palko* v. *Connecticut*, 302 U.S. 319, 325 (1937), the Court went on, in what can only be

---

16. See generally Kamisar, Does (Did) (Should) The Exclusionary Rule Rest on a "Principled Basis" Rather than an "Empirical Proposition"?, 16 *Creighton L. Rev.* 565, 598–599 (1983); Mertens & Wasserstrom, The Good Faith Exception to the Exclusionary Rule: Deregulating the Police and Derailing the Law, 70 *Geo. L. J.* 365, 379–380 (1981)

regarded as a *tour de force* of constitutional obfuscation, to say that the "ways of enforcing such a basic right raise questions of a different order," 338 U.S., at 28. Notwithstanding the force of the *Weeks* doctrine that the Fourth Amendment required exclusion, a state court was free to admit illegally seized evidence, according to the Court in *Wolf*, so long as the State had devised some other "effective" means of vindicating a defendant's Fourth Amendment rights. 338 U.S., at 31.

Twelve years later, in *Mapp* v. *Ohio*, 367 U.S. 643 (1961), however, the Court restored the original understanding of the *Weeks* case by overruling the holding of *Wolf* and repudiating its rationale. Although in the course of reaching this conclusion the Court in *Mapp* responded at certain points to the question, first raised in *Wolf*, of whether the exclusionary rule was an "effective" remedy compared to alternative means of enforcing the right, see 367 U.S., at 651–653, it nevertheless expressly held that "all evidence obtained by searches and seizures in violation of the Constitution is, *by that same authority*, inadmissible in a state court." *Id.*, at 655 (emphasis added). In the Court's view, the exclusionary rule was not one among a range of options to be selected at the discretion of judges; it was "an essential part of both the Fourth and Fourteenth Amendments." *Id.*, at 657....

Despite this clear pronouncement, however, the Court since *Calandra* has gradually pressed the deterrence rationale for the rule back to center stage. See, e. g., *United States* v. *Peltier*, 422 U.S. 531 (1975); *United States* v. *Janis*, 428 U.S. 433 (1976); *Stone* v. *Powell*, 428 U.S. 465 (1976). The various arguments advanced by the Court in this campaign have only strengthened my conviction that the deterrence theory is both misguided and unworkable. First, the Court has frequently bewailed the "cost" of excluding reliable evidence. In large part, this criticism rests upon a refusal to acknowledge the function of the Fourth Amendment itself. If nothing else, the Amendment plainly operates to disable the government from gathering information and securing evidence in certain ways. In practical terms, of course, this restriction of official power means that some incriminating evidence inevitably will go undetected if the government obeys these constitutional restraints. It is the loss of that evidence that is the "price" our society pays for enjoying the freedom and privacy safeguarded by the Fourth Amendment. Thus, some criminals will go free *not*, in Justice (then Judge) Cardozo's misleading epigram, "because the constable has blundered," *People* v. *Defore*, 242 N. Y. 13, 21, 150 N. E. 585, 587 (1926), but rather because official compliance with Fourth Amendment requirements makes it more difficult to catch criminals. Understood in this way, the Amendment directly contemplates that some reliable and incriminating evidence will be lost to the government; therefore, it is not the exclusionary rule, but the Amendment itself that has imposed this cost.[8]

In addition, the Court's decisions over the past decade have made plain that the entire enterprise of attempting to assess the benefits and costs of the exclusionary rule in various contexts is a virtually impossible task for the judiciary to perform honestly or accurately. Although the Court's language in those cases suggests that some specific empirical basis may support its analyses, the reality is that the Court's opinions represent inherently unstable compounds of intuition, hunches, and occasional pieces of partial and often inconclusive data.... To the extent empirical data are available regarding the general costs and benefits of the exclusionary rule, such data have shown, on the one hand, as the Court acknowledges today, that the costs are not as substantial as critics have asserted in the past, see *ante*, at 907–908, n. 6, and, on the other hand, that while the exclusionary rule may well have certain deterrent effects, it is extremely difficult to determine with any degree of precision whether the incidence of unlawful conduct by police is now lower than it was prior to *Mapp*. See *United States* v. *Janis*, 428 U.S., at 449–453, and n. 22; *Stone* v. *Powell*, 428 U.S., at 492, n. 32.[9] The Court has sought to turn this uncertainty to its advantage by casting the burden of proof upon proponents of

---

8. Justice Stewart has explained this point in detail in a recent article: "Much of the criticism leveled at the exclusionary rule is misdirected; it is more properly directed at the Fourth Amendment itself. It is true that, as many observers have charged, the effect of the rule is to deprive the courts of extremely relevant, often direct evidence of the guilt of the defendant. But these same critics fail to acknowledge that, in many instances, the same extremely relevant evidence would not have been obtained had the police officer complied with the commands of the fourth amendment in the first place...."... The exclusionary rule places no limitations on the actions of the police. The fourth amendment does. The inevitable result of the Constitution's prohibition against unreasonable searches and seizures and its requirement that no warrant shall issue but upon probable cause is that police officers who obey its strictures will catch fewer criminals.... [That] is the price the framers anticipated and were willing to pay to ensure the sanctity of the person, the home, and property against unrestrained governmental power." Stewart, 83 *Colum. L. Rev.*, at 1392–1393.

See also Dellinger, Of Rights and Remedies: The Constitution as a Sword, 85 *Harv. L. Rev.* 1532, 1563 (1972) ("Under the exclusionary rule a court attempts to maintain the status quo that would have prevailed if the constitutional requirement had been obeyed").

9. See generally on this point, Davies, A Hard Look at What We Know (and Still Need to Learn) About the "Costs" of the Exclusionary Rule: The NIJ Study and Other Studies of "Lost" Arrests, 1983 *A. B. F. Res. J.* 611, 627–629; Canon, Ideology and Reality in the Debate over the Exclusionary Rule: A Conservative Argument for its Retention, 23 *S. Tex. L. J.* 559, 561–563 (1982); Critique, On the Limitations of Empirical Evaluations of the Exclusionary Rule: A Critique of the Spiotto Research and *United States v. Calandra*, 69 *NW.*

the rule, see, *e. g., United States* v. *Janis, supra,* at 453–454. "Obviously," however, "the assignment of the burden of proof on an issue where evidence does not exist and cannot be obtained is outcome determinative. [The] assignment of the burden is merely a way of announcing a predetermined conclusion."[10]

By remaining within its redoubt of empiricism and by basing the rule solely on the deterrence rationale, the Court has robbed the rule of legitimacy. A doctrine that is explained as if it were an empirical proposition but for which there is only limited empirical support is both inherently unstable and an easy mark for critics. The extent of this Court's fidelity to Fourth Amendment requirements, however, should not turn on such statistical uncertainties. I share the view, expressed by Justice Stewart for the Court in *Faretta* v. *California,* 422 U.S. 806 (1975), that "[personal[liberties are not rooted in the law of averages." *Id.,* at 834. Rather than seeking to give effect to the liberties secured by the Fourth Amendment through guesswork about deterrence, the Court should restore to its proper place the principle framed 70 years ago in *Weeks* that an individual whose privacy has been invaded in violation of the Fourth Amendment has a right grounded in that Amendment to prevent the government from subsequently making use of any evidence so obtained....

Even if I were to accept the Court's general approach to the exclusionary rule, I could not agree with today's result. There is no question that in the hands of the present Court the deterrence rationale has proved to be a powerful tool for confining the scope of the rule....Thus, in this bit of judicial stagecraft, while the sets sometimes change, the actors always have the same lines. Given this well–rehearsed pattern, one might have predicted with some assurance how the present case would unfold. First there is the ritual incantation of the "substantial social costs" exacted by the exclusionary rule, followed by the virtually foreordained conclusion that, given the marginal benefits, application of the rule in the circumstances of these cases is not warranted. Upon analysis, however, such a result cannot be justified even on the Court's own terms.

U. L. Rev. 740 (1974).

10. Dworkin, Fact Style Adjudication and the Fourth Amendment: The Limits of Lawyering, 48 Ind. L. J. 329, 332–333 (1973). See also White, Forgotten Points in the "Exclusionary Rule" Debate, 81 Mich. L. Rev. 1273, 1281–1282 (1983) (balancing of deterrent benefits and costs is an "inquiry [that] can never be performed in an adequate way and the reality is thus that the decision must rest not upon those grounds, but upon prior dispositions or unarticulated intuitions that are never justified"); Canon, *supra,* at 564; Kamisar, 16 *Creighton L. Rev.,* at 646.

At the outset, the Court suggests that society has been asked to pay a high price—in terms either of setting guilty persons free or of impeding the proper functioning of trials—as a result of excluding relevant physical evidence in cases where the police, in conducting searches and seizing evidence, have made only an "objectively reasonable" mistake concerning the constitutionality of their actions. See *ante*, at 907–908. But what evidence is there to support such a claim?

Significantly, the Court points to none, and, indeed, as the Court acknowledges, see *ante*, at 907–908, n. 6, recent studies have demonstrated that the "costs" of the exclusionary rule—calculated in terms of dropped prosecutions and lost convictions—are quite low. Contrary to the claims of the rule's critics that exclusion leads to "the release of countless guilty criminals," *Bivens* v. *Six Unknown Federal Narcotics Agents*, 403 U.S. 388, 416 (1971) (BURGER, C. J., dissenting), these studies have demonstrated that federal and state prosecutors very rarely drop cases because of potential search and seizure problems. For example, a 1979 study prepared at the request of Congress by the General Accounting Office reported that only 0.4% of all cases actually declined for prosecution by federal prosecutors were declined primarily because of illegal search problems. Report of the Comptroller General of the United States, Impact of the Exclusionary Rule on Federal Criminal Prosecutions 14 (1979). If the GAO data are restated as a percentage of *all* arrests, the study shows that only 0.2% of all felony arrests are declined for prosecution because of potential exclusionary rule problems. See Davies, A Hard Look at What We Know (and Still Need to Learn) About the "Costs" of the Exclusionary Rule: The NIJ Study and Other Studies of "Lost" Arrests, 1983 A. B. F. Res. J. 611, 635.[11] Of course, these data describe only the costs attributable to the exclu-

---

11. In a series of recent studies, researchers have attempted to quantify the actual costs of the rule. A recent National Institute of Justice study based on data for the 4-year period 1976–1979 gathered by the California Bureau of Criminal Statistics showed that 4.8% of all cases that were declined for prosecution by California prosecutors were rejected because of illegally seized evidence. National Institute of Justice, *Criminal Justice Research Report— The Effects of the Exclusionary Rule: A Study in California* 1 (1982). However, if these data are calculated as a percentage of all arrests, they show that only 0.8% of all arrests were rejected for prosecution because of illegally seized evidence. See Davies, 1983 *A. B. F. Res. J.,* at 619.

In another measure of the rule's impact—the number of prosecutions that are dismissed or result in acquittals in cases where evidence has been excluded—the available data again show that the Court's past assessment of the rule's costs has generally been exaggerated. For example, a study based on data from nine midsized counties in Illinois, Michigan, and Pennsylvania reveals that motions to suppress physical evidence were filed in approximately

sion of evidence in all cases; the costs due to the exclusion of evidence in the narrower category of cases where police have made objectively reasonable mistakes must necessarily be even smaller. The Court, however, ignores this distinction and mistakenly weighs the aggregated costs of exclusion in *all* cases, irrespective of the circumstances that led to exclusion, see *ante*, at 907, against the potential benefits associated with only those cases in which evidence is excluded because police reasonably but mistakenly believe that their conduct does not violate the Fourth Amendment, see *ante*, at 915–921. When such faulty scales are used, it is little wonder that the balance tips in favor of restricting the application of the rule.

What then supports the Court's insistence that this evidence be admitted? Apparently, the Court's only answer is that even though the costs of exclusion are not very substantial, the potential deterrent effect in these circumstances is so marginal that exclusion cannot be justified. The key to the Court's conclusion in this respect is its belief that the prospective deterrent effect of the exclusionary rule operates only in those situations in which police officers, when deciding whether to go forward with some particular search, have reason to know that their planned conduct will violate the requirements of the Fourth Amendment. See *ante*, at 919–921. If these officers in fact understand (or reasonably should understand because the law is well settled) that their proposed conduct will offend the Fourth Amendment and that, consequently, any evidence they seize will be suppressed in court, they will refrain from conducting the planned search. In those circumstances, the incentive system created by the exclusionary rule will have the hoped-for deterrent effect. But in situations where police officers reasonably (but mistakenly) believe that their planned conduct satisfies Fourth Amendment requirements—presumably either (a) because they are acting on the basis of an apparently valid warrant,

---

5% of the 7,500 cases studied, but that such motions were successful in only 0.7% of all these cases. Nardulli, The Societal Cost of the Exclusionary Rule: An Empirical Assessment, 1983 *A. B. F. Res. J.* 585, 596. The study also shows that only 0.6% of all cases resulted in acquittals because evidence had been excluded. *Id.*, at 600. In the GAO study, suppression motions were filed in 10.5% of all federal criminal cases surveyed, but of the motions filed, approximately 80–90% were denied. GAO Report, at 8, 10. Evidence was actually excluded in only 1.3% of the cases studied, and only 0.7% of all cases resulted in acquittals or dismissals after evidence was excluded. *Id.*, at 9–11. See Davies, *supra*, at 660. And in another study based on data from cases during 1978 and 1979 in San Diego and Jacksonville, it was shown that only 1% of all cases resulting in nonconviction were caused by illegal searches. F. Feeney, F. Dill, & A. Weir, *Arrests Without Conviction: How Often They Occur and Why* (National Institute of Justice 1983). See generally Davies, *supra*, at 663.

or (b) because their conduct is only later determined to be invalid as a result of a subsequent change in the law or the resolution of an unsettled question of law—then such officers will have no reason to refrain from conducting the search and the exclusionary rule will have no effect.

At first blush, there is some logic to this position. Undoubtedly, in the situation hypothesized by the Court, the existence of the exclusionary rule cannot be expected to have any deterrent effect on the particular officers at the moment they are deciding whether to go forward with the search. Indeed, the subsequent exclusion of any evidence seized under such circumstances appears somehow "unfair" to the particular officers involved. As the Court suggests, these officers have acted in what they thought was an appropriate and constitutionally authorized manner, but then the fruit of their efforts is nullified by the application of the exclusionary rule. *Ante*, at 920–921.

The flaw in the Court's argument, however, is that its logic captures only one comparatively minor element of the generally acknowledged deterrent purposes of the exclusionary rule. To be sure, the rule operates to some extent to deter future misconduct by individual officers who have had evidence suppressed in their own cases. But what the Court overlooks is that the deterrence rationale for the rule is not designed to be, nor should it be thought of as, a form of "punishment" of individual police officers for their failures to obey the restraints imposed by the Fourth Amendment. See *United States* v. *Peltier*, 422 U.S., at 556–557 (BRENNAN, J., dissenting). Instead, the chief deterrent function of the rule is its tendency to promote institutional compliance with Fourth Amendment requirements on the part of law enforcement agencies generally.[12] Thus, as the Court has previously recognized, "over the long term, [the] demonstration [provided by the exclusionary rule] that our

---

12. As Justice Stewart has observed: "[The] exclusionary rule is not designed to serve a specific deterrence function; that is, it is not designed to punish the particular police officer for violating a person's fourth amendment rights. Instead, the rule is designed to produce a 'systematic deterrence': the exclusionary rule is intended to create an incentive for law enforcement officials to establish procedures by which police officers are trained to comply with the fourth amendment because the purpose of the criminal justice system—bringing criminals to justice—can be achieved only when evidence of guilt may be used against defendants." Stewart, 83 *Colum. L. Rev.*, at 1400.   See also Oaks, Studying the Exclusionary Rule in Search and Seizure, 37 *U. Chi. L. Rev.* 665, 709–710 (1970) ("The exclusionary rule is not aimed at special deterrence since it does not impose any direct punishment on a law enforcement official who has broken the rule.... The exclusionary rule is aimed at affecting the wider audience of all law enforcement officials and society at large. It is meant to discourage violations by individuals who have never experienced any sanc-

society attaches serious consequences to violation of constitutional rights is thought to encourage those who formulate law enforcement policies, and the officers who implement them, to incorporate Fourth Amendment ideals into their value system." *Stone* v. *Powell*, 428 U.S., at 492. It is only through such an institutionwide mechanism that information concerning Fourth Amendment standards can be effectively communicated to rank-and-file officers.[13]

If the overall educational effect of the exclusionary rule is considered, application of the rule to even those situations in which individual police officers have acted on the basis of a reasonable but mistaken belief that their conduct was authorized can still be expected to have a considerable long-term deterrent effect. If evidence is consistently excluded in these circumstances,

---

tion for them"); Mertens & Wasserstrom, 70 *Geo. L. J.*, at 399–401; Kamisar, 16 *Creighton L. Rev., at 597*, n. 204.

13. Although specific empirical data on the systemic deterrent effect of the rule are not conclusive, the testimony of those actually involved in law enforcement suggests that, at the very least, the *Mapp* decision had the effect of increasing police awareness of Fourth Amendment requirements and of prompting prosecutors and police commanders to work towards educating rank-and-file officers. For example, as former New York Police Commissioner Murphy explained the impact of the *Mapp* decision: "I can think of no decision in recent times in the field of law enforcement which had such a dramatic and traumatic effect....I was immediately caught up in the entire program of reevaluating our procedures, which had followed the *Defore* rule, and modifying, amending, and creating new policies and new instructions for the implementation of *Mapp*....Retraining sessions had to be held from the very top administrators down to each of the thousands of foot patrolmen." Murphy, Judicial Review of Police Methods in Law Enforcement: The Problem of Compliance by Police Departments, 44 *Texas L. Rev.* 939, 941 (1966).

Further testimony about the impact of the *Mapp* decision can be found in the statement of Deputy Commissioner Reisman: "The *Mapp* case was a shock to us. We had to reorganize our thinking, frankly. Before this, nobody bothered to take out search warrants. Although the U.S. Constitution requires warrants in most cases, the U.S. Supreme Court had ruled that evidence obtained without a warrant—illegally, if you will—was admissible in state courts. So the feeling was, why bother? Well, once that rule was changed we knew we had better start teaching our men about it." N. Y. Times, Apr. 28, 1965, p. 50, col. 1. A former United States Attorney and now Attorney General of Maryland, Stephen Sachs, has described the impact of the rule on police practices in similar terms: "I have watched the rule deter, routinely, throughout my years as a prosecutor....[Police-prosecutor] consultation is customary in all our cases when Fourth Amendment concerns arise....In at least three Maryland jurisdictions, for example, prosecutors are on twenty-four hour call to field search and seizure questions presented by police officers." Sachs, The Exclusionary Rule: A Prosecutor's Defense, 1 *Crim. Justice Ethics* 28, 30 (Summer/Fall 1982). See also LaFave, The Fourth Amendment in an Imperfect World: On Drawing "Bright Lines" and "Good Faith," 43 *U. Pitt. L. Rev.* 307, 319 (1982); Mertens & Wasserstrom, *supra*, at 394–401.

police departments will surely be prompted to instruct their officers to devote greater care and attention to providing sufficient information to establish probable cause when applying for a warrant, and to review with some attention the form of the warrant that they have been issued, rather than automatically assuming that whatever document the magistrate has signed will necessarily comport with Fourth Amendment requirements.

After today's decisions, however, that institutional incentive will be lost. Indeed, the Court's "reasonable mistake" exception to the exclusionary rule will tend to put a premium on police ignorance of the law. Armed with the assurance provided by today's decisions that evidence will always be admissible whenever an officer has "reasonably" relied upon a warrant, police departments will be encouraged to train officers that if a warrant has simply been signed, it is reasonable, without more, to rely on it. Since in close cases there will no longer be any incentive to error on the side of constitutional behavior, police would have every reason to adopt a "let's-wait-until-it's-decided" approach in situations in which there is a question about a warrant's validity or the basis for its issuance. Cf. *United States* v. *Johnson*, 457 U.S. 537, 561 (1982).[14]

Although the Court brushes these concerns aside, a host of grave consequences can be expected to result from its decision to carve this new exception out of the exclusionary rule. A chief consequence of today's decisions will be to convey a clear and unambiguous message to magistrates that their decisions to issue warrants are now insulated from subsequent judicial review. Creation of this new exception for good-faith reliance upon a warrant implicitly tells magistrates that they need not take much care in reviewing warrant applications, since their mistakes will from now on have virtually no consequence: If their decision to issue a warrant was correct, the evidence will be admitted; if their decision was incorrect but the police relied in good faith on the warrant, the evidence will also be admitted. Inevitably, the care and at-

---

14. The authors of a recent study of the warrant process in seven cities concluded that application of a good-faith exception where an officer relies upon a warrant "would further encourage police officers to seek out the less inquisitive magistrates and to rely on boilerplate formulae, thereby lessening the value of search warrants overall. Consequently, the benefits of adoption of a broad good faith exception in terms of a few additional prosecutions appears to be outweighed by the harm to the quality of the entire search warrant process and the criminal justice system in general." R. Van Duizend, L. Sutton, & C. Carter, *The Search Warrant Process: Preconceptions, Perceptions, and Practices* 8–12 (Review Draft, National Center for State Courts, 1983). See also Stewart, 83 Colum. L. Rev., at 1403.

tention devoted to such an inconsequential chore will dwindle. Although the Court is correct to note that magistrates do not share the same stake in the outcome of a criminal case as the police, they nevertheless need to appreciate that their role is of some moment in order to continue performing the important task of carefully reviewing warrant applications. Today's decisions effectively remove that incentive.

Moreover, the good-faith exception will encourage police to provide only the bare minimum of information in future warrant applications. The police will now know that if they can secure a warrant, so long as the circumstances of its issuance are not "entirely unreasonable," *ante*, at 923, all police conduct pursuant to that warrant will be protected from further judicial review. The clear incentive that operated in the past to establish probable cause adequately because reviewing courts would examine the magistrate's judgment carefully, see, *e. g., Franks* v. *Delaware*, 438 U.S. 154, 169–170 (1978); *Jones* v. *United States*, 362 U.S. 257, 271–272 (1960); *Giordenello* v. *United States*, 357 U.S. 480, 483 (1958), has now been so completely vitiated that the police need only show that it was not "entirely unreasonable" under the circumstances of a particular case for them to believe that the warrant they were issued was valid. See *ante*, at 923. The long-run effect unquestionably will be to undermine the integrity of the warrant process.

Finally, even if one were to believe, as the Court apparently does, that police are hobbled by inflexible and hypertechnical warrant procedures, today's decisions cannot be justified. This is because, given the relaxed standard for assessing probable cause established just last Term in *Illinois* v. *Gates*, 462 U.S. 213 (1983), the Court's newly fashioned good-faith exception, when applied in the warrant context, will rarely, if ever, offer any greater flexibility for police than the *Gates* standard already supplies. In *Gates*, the Court held that "[the] task of the issuing magistrate is simply to make a practical, common-sense decision whether, given all the circumstances set forth in the affidavit before him, ... there is a fair probability that contraband or evidence of a crime will be found in a particular place." *Id.*, at 238. The task of a reviewing court is confined to determining whether "the magistrate had a 'substantial basis for ... [concluding]' that probable cause existed." *Ibid.* Given such a relaxed standard, it is virtually inconceivable that a reviewing court, when faced with a defendant's motion to suppress, could first find that a warrant was invalid under the new *Gates* standard, but then, at the same time, find that a police officer's reliance on such an invalid warrant was nevertheless "objectively reasonable" under the test announced today.[17] Because the two standards overlap so completely, it is unlikely that a warrant could be found invalid under *Gates* and yet the police reliance upon it could be seen as objectively reasonable; otherwise, we would have to entertain the mind-boggling concept of objectively reasonable reliance upon an objectively unreasonable warrant.…

When the public, as it quite properly has done in the past as well as in the present, demands that those in government increase their efforts to combat crime, it is all too easy for those government officials to seek expedient solutions. In contrast to such costly and difficult measures as building more prisons, improving law enforcement methods, or hiring more prosecutors and judges to relieve the overburdened court systems in the country's metropolitan areas, the relaxation of Fourth Amendment standards seems a tempting, costless means of meeting the public's demand for better law enforcement. In the long run, however, we as a society pay a heavy price for such expediency, because as Justice Jackson observed, the rights guaranteed in the Fourth Amendment "are not mere second-class rights but belong in the catalog of indispensable freedoms." *Brinegar* v. *United States*, 338 U.S. 160, 180 (1949) (dissenting opinion). Once lost, such rights are difficult to recover. There is hope, however, that in time this or some later Court will restore these precious freedoms to their rightful place as a primary protection for our citizens against overreaching officialdom.

I dissent.

List of other cases and articles relevant to this topic.

Mapp v. Ohio, 367 U.S. 643 (1961)

Illinois v. Krull, 480 U.S. 340 (1987)

Uchida, C.D., T.S. Bynum, D. Rogan, and D. Murasky. (1988) Acting in good faith: The effects of *United States v. Leon* on the police and courts. *Arizona Law Review* 30: 467–495.

Discussion and Review Questions

1. Using Lexis-Nexis or Findlaw.com, find a recent court decision concerning the exclusionary rule. Review the decision and answer the following questions:

---

17. See Kamisar, *Gates*, "Probable Cause," "Good Faith," and Beyond, 69 *Iowa L. Rev.* 551, 588–589 (1984); Wasserstrom, The Incredible Shrinking Fourth Amendment, 21 *Am. Crim. L. Rev.* 257 (1984); LaFave, 43 *U. Pitt. L. Rev.*, at 307.

    a. Was this a case where the police officer had a warrant?

    b. If the officer had a warrant, did the court examine whether an exception to the exclusionary rule was applicable?

    c. If the officer did not have a warrant, did the court examine whether the officer should have gotten a warrant?

    d. Was the evidence excluded from trial? Was there an exception to the exclusionary rule that allowed the introduction of the evidence at trial.

2. Using Lexis-Nexis, Findlaw or some other legal database, identify how many cases for the past five years have been decided by the appellate courts in your state and involve issues concerning the Fourth Amendment and the exclusionary rule. In these cases, who won more often the prosecutor (the evidence was found to be admissible) or the defense (the evidence was found to be inadmissible)?

3. Based on the Court's discussion in *Leon*, is there support to demonstrate the usefulness of the exclusionary rule as a remedial measure? What other alternative measures might be more effective in reducing the incidence of Fourth Amendment violations by law enforcement?

References

Articles

Heffernan, W.C. and R.W. Lovely (1991). Evaluating the Fourth Amendment exclusionary rule: The problem of police compliance with the law. *University of Michigan Journal of Law Reform* 24(2): 311–369.

Lynch, T. (1998). *Policy analysis: In Defense of the exclusionary rule*. Washington DC: Cato Institute.

Slobogin, C. (1999). 'Why liberals should chuck the exclusionary rule.' *University of Illinois Law Review* 2: 363–446.

Uchida, C. and T. Bynum (1991). Search warrants, motions to suppress and 'lost cases': The effects of the exclusionary rule in seven jurisdictions. *Journal of Criminal Law and Criminology* 81: 1034–1066.

Uchida, C., T. Bynum, D. Rogan, and D. Murasky (1988). Acting in good faith: The effects of United States v. Leon on the police and courts. *Arizona Law Review* 30: 467–495.

Van Duizend, R., P. Sutton, and C. Carter (1984). *The search warrant process*. Williamsburg, VA: National Center for State Courts.

Case Citations

Arizona v. Evans, 514 U.S. 1 (1995).
Elkins v. United States, 364 U.S. 206 (1960).
Illinois v. Krull, 480 U.S. 340 (1987)
Mapp v. Ohio, 367 U.S. 643 (1961).
Miller v. United States, 357 U.S. 301 (1958)
United States v. Leon, 468 U.S. 897 (1984).
Weeks v. United States, 232 U.S. 383 (1914).
Wilson v. Layne, 526 U.S. 603 (1999).
Wolf v. Colorado, 338 U.S. 25 (1949).

CHAPTER 6

PRETRIAL PUBLICITY AND CAMERAS IN THE COURTROOM

Upholding the Law as Pretrial Publicity Goes Global.

–Headline in the New York Times (April 27, 2003) following the arrest of Scott Peterson for killing his wife, Laci.

"Pretrial publicity" and cameras in the courtroom raise controversial issues regarding the **First Amendment** right of the press to report information to the public and defendants' **Sixth Amendment** right to a fair trial. The United States Supreme Court, in attempting to balance these two seemingly significant, but conflicting rights, has generally supported the press except under the most egregious circumstances (Fisher 1999). In the 21st Century, however, the Supreme Court guidelines may be put to a real test. In this day and age, the availability of information on the Internet and vast news coverage has created a situation where we are inundated by up-to-the minute details about current events, especially crimes. Technological advancements have allowed 'gavel to gavel' coverage of criminal trials as well as instantaneous reports concerning global events. The case of O.J. Simpson engendered a great deal of debate and criticism about the propriety and impact of allowing news cameras to broadcast the daily events of the trial. People from around the world watched the terrorist attacks against the United States. Nations were glued to their televisions and watched in horror as the World Trade Center towers crumbled to earth. Minute by minute reports about pending investigations by probing reporters (e.g., the Kobe Bryant case) and the use of the media by criminals (e.g., Bin Laden's direct messages to the world via video camera) and victims or their families to generate information (e.g., Laci Peterson's family) will challenge the Court to address these intricate and complex matters as they impact the fairness of judicial proceedings.

Pretrial publicity effects more and more cases each year. In 1988, a study estimated that more than 12,000 cases per year in the United States were af-

> **First Amendment:** Congress shall make no law…abridging the freedom of speech, or of the press.…
>
> **Sixth Amendment:** In all criminal prosecutions, the accused shall enjoy the right to a speedy and public trial, by an impartial jury of the State and district wherein the crime shall have been committed.…

fected by pretrial publicity. (Frasca 1988). One may presume that today, many more cases are impacted by the attention of the media and that the widespread publication of information may diminish the effectiveness of current remedies to neutralize the impact of pretrial publicity on defendants' right to an impartial jury.

The primary concerns about pretrial publicity involve the impact that this information has on jurors, the type of information that creates bias, and the effectiveness of current judicial remedies to neutralize the effect of pretrial publicity on petit juries (Kerr 1994). These questions are legal as well as social scientific. Trial judges must make decisions about whether pretrial publicity will thwart or has thwarted the chance of a fair trial for the defendant in the district where the crime was committed as well as make determinations concerning the appropriate remedy to address the effects from the exposure (Beisecker 1995).

Does pretrial publicity impact jurors?

"The results of social scientific research on pretrial publicity effects justify the courts' concern about prejudicial pretrial publicity. Prejudicial pretrial publicity has been found to influence evaluations of the defendant's likability, sympathy for the defendant, perceptions of the defendant as a typical criminal, pretrial judgments of the defendant's guilt, and final verdicts" (Studebaker and Penrod 1997: 433 citations omitted). In the 1980s, there was a debate about the state of empirical research on the impact of pretrial publicity. Carroll et al. (1986) and Fulero (1987) disagreed on the state of the findings. Carroll et al. (1986) argued that there was insufficient information on the effects of pretrial publicity to make policy recommendations. Fulero (1987) disagreed. Fulero believed that the empirical evidence demonstrated that pretrial publicity had substantial, negative effects on jury verdicts. Today, there seems to be widespread acceptance by social scientists that prejudicial pretrial publicity biases jurors.

In a review of the literature, Kerr (1994) suggests that pretrial publicity can result in biased jury verdicts. In addition, juror attitudes may also be influenced

> **Fair and impartial trial:** One where accused's legal rights are safeguarded and respected. (Black's Law Dictionary).

by the type of information being disseminated to the public, including depictions of unrelated cases in the news or portrayed by the entertainment media. A recent study examined the specific question of whether pretrial publicity has an effect on juror judgment (guilty or not guilty) of a defendant (Steblay et al. 1999). In examining this question, the researchers examined the findings from twenty-three previous studies on pretrial publicity and juror verdicts. The examination included laboratory studies as well as community survey research. They found that individuals exposed to negative publicity were more likely to find defendants guilty than individuals exposed to less or no negative publicity (Steblay et al. 1999: 223). In fact, pretrial publicity was found to impact juror decision-making at three stages of the proceedings—pretrial, post-trial but before deliberations, and the final, post-deliberation verdict. The strongest effect of pretrial publicity was found in communities where real crimes and a great deal of publicity had occurred. The studies found these individuals more likely to be influenced by the publicity.

How do judges determine whether pretrial publicity is problematic in a particular trial?

The burden of proving that pretrial publicity warrants a judicial remedy is on the defendant. Specifically, a defendant must demonstrate that there is a "reasonable likelihood" that s/he will not get a trial before an impartial jury as required by the Sixth Amendment (*Patton v. Yount*). In 1966, the United States Supreme Court found that the massive, pervasive, and prejudicial publicity surrounding the prosecution of Dr. Sam Sheppard[1] for killing his pregnant wife Marilyn by bludgeoning her to death in the upstairs bedroom of their home prevented him from receiving a **fair trial**. The media attention given to this case was pervasive and lasted throughout Sheppard's criminal trial. Each juror except one testified during voir dire (jury selection) that they had either read or heard news broadcasts about the case. In its decision, the United States Supreme Court details the extent of the pretrial publicity that impacted this case both prior to the trial and during the trial itself. The jurors

---

1. This 1954 homicide case continues to generate widespread publicity. It has been the basis of several motion pictures and made-for-television dramas.

were continually exposed to media publicity about Sheppard and were themselves the subject of media attention. The Court compared the atmosphere surrounding the trial to that of a carnival. In light of the extent of the press involvement, the Court held that the inherently prejudicial publicity that saturated the community and disrupted the courtroom proceedings denied Sheppard a fair trial.

That same year, the body of Pamela Rimer, an 18 year-old high school student, was found in a wooded area near her home. There were numerous wounds about her head and cuts on her throat and neck. An autopsy revealed that she died of strangulation when blood from her wounds was drawn into her lungs. The autopsy showed no signs that she had been sexually assaulted. The following morning, Yount, the victim's high school math teacher, gave the police oral and written confessions. At Yount's arraignment (three days after his arrest) his confession was read in open court and later published by the local press. At his trial in 1966, he was convicted after his confessions were admitted into evidence. However, the Pennsylvania Supreme Court reversed the conviction because Yount had inadequate notice of his right to an attorney prior to his confession as required by *Miranda v. Arizona*. Prior to his second trial, in 1970, the trial judge suppressed as evidence his written confession and the portions of his oral confession obtained after he was in custody. The voir dire (selection of the jury) took 10 days for this second trial. Defense counsel moved for a change of venue several times before and during jury selection because the widespread dissemination of prejudicial information about Yount's confession. The trial court denied these motions and the motions for a new trial following Yount's conviction. The trial court found that there was little publicity about the case in between the two trials (1966 to 1970), there was little public interest in the trial, and that the jury was not biased.

The United States Supreme Court accepted this case for review to examine, in the context of this case, the problem of pervasive media publicity that now arises so frequently in the trial of sensational criminal cases. Unlike in the Sheppard case, the Court held that the trial court did not commit **manifest error** in finding that the jury as a whole was impartial. In arriving at this decision, the Court reviewed the amount of publicity the case received. It was noted that most of the publicity, about this crime, occurred in 1966 prior to the first trial. In the two years prior to the second trial, two county newspapers published an average of less than one article per month and most of these reports were brief announcements about trial dates. According to the Court, prior to the second trial there was not a "'barrage of inflammatory publicity

> **Manifest:** Evident to the senses, especially to the sight, obvious to the understanding, evident to the mind, not obscure or hidden, and is synonymous with open, clear, visible, unmistakable, indubitable, indisputable, evident and self-evident. (Black's Law Dictionary).
>
> **Error:** A mistaken judgment or incorrect belief as to the existence or effect of matters of fact, or a false or mistaken conception or application of the law. (Black's Law Dictionary)

immediately prior to trial'...amounting to a 'huge...wave of public passion" (*Yount* at 855). In examining the jury voir dire, the Court found that the time lapse between the initial crime and second trial had a profound effect on the community and jury in softening or effacing opinion. Few jurors remembered the details of the case, that they may have had opinions at one time, but that they no longer held strong views about the case. Thus, in this case, the Court examined the media publicity and the juror testimony during voir dire to determine that there was not a "wave of publicity that would have made a fair trial unlikely by the jury that was empaneled as a whole."

In addition to compilations of written and broadcast publicity prior to trial and jury voir dire questioning to assess the impact of pretrial publicity, three other methods to establish the potentiality of an unfair trial exist: the collection of affidavits from community leaders or others knowledgeable about attitudes toward a defendant, testimony of expert witnesses on community knowledge and attitudes, and public opinion polling about community views and the affect of pretrial publicity.

The United States Supreme Court has not considered a case where community leader affidavits, expert witness testimony or public opinion polling have been used to establish the affect of pretrial publicity. The Court has also not reviewed a case raising questions about national, media and Internet publicity. Affidavits from community leaders and expert witness testimony are commonly introduced in conjunction with compilations of pretrial publicity or public opinion polling (Beseicker 1995). Public opinion polling, however, is a much more recent tool used by defendants to establish prejudicial pretrial publicity (Beseiker 1995). Some have argued that public opinion polls are very useful in distilling the impact of pretrial publicity on a community by asking individuals questions without the pressure of jury selection and the courtroom atmosphere (Beseicker 1995; O'Connell 1988). Opinion polls, however, must be scientific in nature and meet standards within the scientific community to be introduced in court (See chapter 3) (Beseicker 1995).

What are the current remedies to address pretrial publicity, and are they effective?

There are several remedies currently used by trial judges to address issues of pretrial publicity—brief continuances, expanded juror questioning, judicial instructions to the jury, jury sequestration, gag orders and changes of venue. In the *Yount* case discussed previously, the Court noted that the time delay between the first and second trial had dissipated the media attention, public interest and publication of prejudicial information. Brief continuances are based on the assumption that pretrial publicity diminishes over time. (Studebaker and Penrod 1997). The Court apparently believed this to be the case in *Yount*, however this delay was four years. Most cases may not be delayed for that long.

Questioning jurors to assess the influence of pretrial publicity is perhaps the most commonly used remedy (Kerr 1994). In cases with a great deal of publicity, judges may allow extended voir dire to thoroughly question potential jurors about the effect of the publicity. (Kerr 1994). This procedure allows attorneys to excuse from jury service individuals who have been exposed to pretrial publicity or have been unduly influenced by information disseminated by the media. The remedy is based on "the assumptions that (a) jurors will report bias or provide responses that are indicative of bias resulting from exposure to pretrial publicity and (b) attorneys and judges can detect bias in jurors when it is present" (Studebaker and Penrod 1997: 439; Kerr 1994). In addition, this method presupposes that a jury that has either not been exposed to the publicity or not effected by the publicity could be empanelled. In high profile cases (O.J. Simpson's trial, for example), it would have been impossible to find jurors (anywhere) who had not heard about the case.

Judges may admonish jurors, in high publicity cases, to avoid reading about the case in the newspaper or listening to radio and television broadcasts. Prior to deliberation of the case, jurors may also be cautioned against discussing or considering pretrial publicity in rendering a verdict.(Studebaker and Penrod 1997; Kerr 1994). "This judicial admonition is based on the assumptions that (a) jurors are aware of how pretrial publicity has influenced their opinions about the case and (b) they can intentionally disregard that influence when instructed to do so." (Studebaker and Penrod 1997: 439).

Jury sequestration limits jurors, in high publicity cases, access to media sources. Jurors are required to live in hotels, with no contact from family or friends, censured access to newspapers, mail and television broadcasts for the duration of the trial (Neubauer 1999). Sequestration is very debilitating for jurors and extremely costly for the judicial system. The State of New York had a mandatory felony sequestration law until 1996. The state spent more than $ 4 million a year to house and supervise sequestered jurors in criminal cases. (See The Jury Project, Report to the Chief Judge of the State of New York 13 (1994).

Participant gag orders are another method of restricting the release of information to the press. Although courts in most circumstances may not prevent the press from reporting information obtained during judicial proceedings, (*Nebraska v. Press Association v. Stuart*, 427 U.S. 539 (1976), the First Amendment does not prohibit courts from restricting the release of information about a criminal case to the press by police, prosecutors, defense attorneys, defendant and other courtroom members (bailiffs, clerks etc.).(Yaun 1998). Limited or participant gag orders have been issued in many high profile cases. (Wetherington et al. 1999). Such orders have been in place during the Oklahoma City bombing trial of Timothy McVeigh as well as the civil trial of O.J. Simpson. (Wetherington et al. 1999). For example, in the O.J. Simpson case, the trial judge entered the following order:

> No counsel, party or witnesses under the control of counsel may discuss or state any opinions concerning evaluation of evidence, including any witness whether called to testify or not, whether offered, received, excluded, purported to exist but not tendered or not available, the jury or any juror, the Court, including the trial proceedings, or whether the defendant did or did not commit the homicides, outside of the trial proceedings with the media or in public places within hearing of the general public. This order extends to employees and agents or representatives, whether paid or unpaid, of the attorneys. This order does not apply to private discussions by and among the attorneys in preparation of their case, with their clients, staff, investigators and witnesses.... (Wetherington et al. 1999: 460–1).

The final current method available to remedy pretrial publicity is the change of venire or venue for the trial. This method either moves the case to a new jurisdiction or to bring in a panel of jurors from a different locale to hear the case. (Studebaker and Penrod 1997). "Both change of **venire** and change of **venue** are based on the idea that the way to decrease the influence of pretrial publicity on juror and jury decision making is to select jurors who have been exposed to less pretrial publicity" (Studebaker and Penrod 1997: 439). It is the defendant's burden to demonstrate the need for a change of

> **Venire:** ... The list of jurors summoned to serve as jurors for a particular term. (Black's Law Dictionary)
> **Venue:** ... The particular county, or geographical area, in which a court with jurisdiction may hear and determine a case. (Black's Law Dictionary)

venire or venue due to pretrial publicity. The trial court evaluates the need for a change against other considerations, e.g., the expense of moving the trial, the defendant's right to a speedy trial, the inconvenience associated with a move, potential bias in the new jurisdiction, and the demographic composition of the new jurisdiction. (Beseicker 1995: 82). To justify a change of venue, the defendant must demonstrate either "actual juror prejudice" (*Irwin v. Dowd*) or raise the presumption of prejudice by showing that "the setting of the trial is inherently prejudicial" (*Patton v. Yount*). This is a heavy burden for the defendant, and there are few instances where trial courts use this remedy.

How effective are judicial remedies to address pretrial publicity?

Unlike studies on the impact of pretrial publicity on juror's attitudes and verdicts, less data exists on the effectiveness on the judicial remedies available to address this publicity. In one review of the remediation studies, Studebaker and Penrod (1997) found that jury selection measures, continuances, and judicial instructions fail to neutralize the effect of pretrial publicity on jurors. In summary, Studebaker and Penrod (1997: 445) state: "it appears that the effects of pretrial publicity can find their way to the courtroom, can survive the jury selection process, can survive the presentation of trial evidence, can endure the limiting effects of judicial instructions, and cannot only persevere through deliberation, but may actually intensify." In other research, Steblay et al. (1999) suggest that changes in venue appear to be the most productive solutions to publicity impacting jurors.

As pointed out in the beginning of this chapter in the headline from the New York Times, 21st Century technology allows global access to information. Changes in venue and the other remedies may not adequately address the influence of the national and international media coverage of criminal events and allow for a fair trial of accused criminal defendants. It is unlikely that judges will readily adopt the expense and complexities associated with changes in venue and most of the media attention precedes arrest or accusation, thus muting the effect of other judicial remedies to pretrial publicity.

Should cameras in the courtroom be permitted?

Like pretrial publicity, cameras in the courtroom is a very controversial topic and few studies have explored whether cameras have a positive or negative effect. In this chapter an excerpt from *The appearance of justice: TV or not TV— That is the question* reviews the arguments for and against television in the courtroom and an excerpt from the *Sheppard v. Maxwell* case are included.

Sheppard v. Maxwell
384 U.S. 333 (1966) (Excerpt)

OPINION BY: CLARK

This federal habeas corpus application involves the question whether Sheppard was deprived of a fair trial in his state conviction for the second-degree murder of his wife because of the trial judge's failure to protect Sheppard sufficiently from the massive, pervasive and prejudicial publicity that attended his prosecution....We have concluded that Sheppard did not receive a fair trial consistent with the Due Process Clause of the Fourteenth Amendment and, therefore, reverse the judgment.

Marilyn Sheppard, petitioner's pregnant wife, was bludgeoned to death in the upstairs bedroom of their lakeshore home in Bay Village, Ohio, a suburb of Cleveland. On the day of the tragedy, July 4, 1954, Sheppard pieced together for several local officials the following story: He and his wife had entertained neighborhood friends, the Aherns, on the previous evening at their home. After dinner they watched television in the living room. Sheppard became drowsy and dozed off to sleep on a couch. Later, Marilyn partially awoke him saying that she was going to bed. The next thing he remembered was hearing his wife cry out in the early morning hours. He hurried upstairs and in the dim light from the hall saw a "form" standing next to his wife's bed. As he struggled with the "form" he was struck on the back of the neck and rendered unconscious. On regaining his senses he found himself on the floor next to his wife's bed. He rose, looked at her, took her pulse and "felt that she was gone." He then went to his son's room and found him unmolested. Hearing a noise he hurried downstairs. He saw a "form" running out the door and pursued it to the lake shore. He grappled with it on the beach and again lost consciousness. Upon his recovery he was lying face down with the lower portion of his body in the water. He returned to his home, checked the pulse on his wife's neck, and "determined or thought that she was gone." He then went downstairs and called a neighbor, Mayor Houk of Bay Village. The Mayor and his wife came over at once, found Sheppard slumped in an easy chair downstairs and asked, "What happened?" Sheppard replied: "I don't know but somebody ought to try to do something for Marilyn." Mrs. Houk immediately went up to the bedroom. The Mayor told Sheppard, "Get hold of yourself. Can you tell me what happened?" Sheppard then related the above-outlined events. After Mrs. Houk discovered the body, the Mayor called the local police, Dr. Richard Sheppard, petitioner's brother, and the Aherns. The local police were the first to arrive. They in turn notified the Coroner and Cleveland police. Richard Sheppard then arrived, determined that Marilyn was dead, examined his brother's injuries, and removed him to the nearby clinic operated by the Sheppard family. When the Coroner, the Cleveland police and other officials arrived, the house and surrounding area were thoroughly searched, the rooms of the house were photographed, and many persons, including the Houks and the Aherns, were interrogated. The Sheppard home and premises were taken into "protective custody" and remained so until after the trial.[4]

From the outset officials focused suspicion on Sheppard. After a search of the house and premises on the morning of the tragedy, Dr. Gerber, the Coroner, is reported—and it is undenied—to have told his men, "Well, it is evident the doctor did this, so let's go get the confession out of him." He proceeded to interrogate and examine Sheppard while the latter was under sedation in his hospital room. On the same occasion, the Coroner was given the clothes Sheppard wore at the time of the tragedy together with the personal items in them. Later that afternoon Chief Eaton and two Cleveland police officers interrogated Sheppard at some length, confronting him with evidence and demanding explanations. Asked by Officer Shotke to take a lie detector test, Sheppard said he would if it were reliable. Shotke replied that it was "infallible" and "you might as well tell us all about it now." At the end of the interrogation Shotke told Sheppard: "I think you killed your wife." Still later in the same afternoon a physician sent by the Coroner was permitted to make a detailed examination of Sheppard. Until the Coroner's inquest on July 22, at which time he was subpoenaed, Sheppard made himself available for frequent and extended questioning without the presence of an attorney.

On July 7, the day of Marilyn Sheppard's funeral, a newspaper story appeared in which Assistant County Attorney Mahon—later the chief prosecu-

---

4. But newspaper photographers and reporters were permitted access to Sheppard's home from time to time and took pictures throughout the premises.

tor of Sheppard—sharply criticized the refusal of the Sheppard family to permit his immediate questioning. From there on headline stories repeatedly stressed Sheppard's lack of cooperation with the police and other officials. Under the headline "Testify Now In Death, Bay Doctor Is Ordered," one story described a visit by Coroner Gerber and four police officers to the hospital on July 8. When Sheppard insisted that his lawyer be present, the Coroner wrote out a subpoena and served it on him. Sheppard then agreed to submit to questioning without counsel and the subpoena was torn up. The officers questioned him for several hours. On July 9, Sheppard, at the request of the Coroner, re-enacted the tragedy at his home before the Coroner, police officers, and a group of newsmen, who apparently were invited by the Coroner. The home was locked so that Sheppard was obliged to wait outside until the Coroner arrived. Sheppard's performance was reported in detail by the news media along with photographs. The newspapers also played up Sheppard's refusal to take a lie detector test and "the protective ring" thrown up by his family. Front-page newspaper headlines announced on the same day that "Doctor Balks At Lie Test; Retells Story." A column opposite that story contained an "exclusive" interview with Sheppard headlined: "'Loved My Wife, She Loved Me,' Sheppard Tells News Reporter." The next day, another headline story disclosed that Sheppard had "again late yesterday refused to take a lie detector test" and quoted an Assistant County Attorney as saying that "at the end of a nine hour questioning of Dr. Sheppard, I felt he was now ruling [a test] out completely." But subsequent newspaper articles reported that the Coroner was still pushing Sheppard for a lie detector test. More stories appeared when Sheppard would not allow authorities to inject him with "truth serum."[5]

On the 20th, the "editorial artillery" opened fire with a front-page charge that somebody is "getting away with murder." The editorial attributed the ineptness of the investigation to "friendships, relationships, hired lawyers, a husband who ought to have been subjected instantly to the same third-degree to which any other person under similar circumstances is subjected...." The following day, July 21, another page-one editorial was headed: "Why No Inquest? Do It Now, Dr. Gerber." The Coroner called an inquest the same day and subpoenaed Sheppard. It was staged the next day in a school gymnasium; the Coroner presided with the County Prosecutor as his advisor and two detec-

---

5. At the same time, the newspapers reported that other possible suspects had been "cleared" by lie detector tests. One of these persons was quoted as saying that he could not understand why an innocent man would refuse to take such a test.

tives as bailiffs. In the front of the room was a long table occupied by reporters, television and radio personnel, and broadcasting equipment. The hearing was broadcast with live microphones placed at the Coroner's seat and the witness stand. A swarm of reporters and photographers attended. Sheppard was brought into the room by police who searched him in full view of several hundred spectators. Sheppard's counsel were present during the three-day inquest but were not permitted to participate. When Sheppard's chief counsel attempted to place some documents in the record, he was forcibly ejected from the room by the Coroner, who received cheers, hugs, and kisses from ladies in the audience. Sheppard was questioned for five and one-half hours about his actions on the night of the murder, his married life, and a love affair with Susan Hayes.[6] At the end of the hearing the Coroner announced that he "could" order Sheppard held for the grand jury, but did not do so.

Throughout this period the newspapers emphasized evidence that tended to incriminate Sheppard and pointed out discrepancies in his statements to authorities. At the same time, Sheppard made many public statements to the press and wrote feature articles asserting his innocence.[7] During the inquest on July 26, a headline in large type stated: "Kerr [Captain of the Cleveland Police] Urges Sheppard's Arrest." In the story, Detective McArthur "disclosed that scientific tests at the Sheppard home have definitely established that the killer washed off a trail of blood from the murder bedroom to the downstairs section," a circumstance casting doubt on Sheppard's accounts of the murder. No such evidence was produced at trial. The newspapers also delved into Sheppard's personal life. Articles stressed his extramarital love affairs as a motive for the crime. The newspapers portrayed Sheppard as a Lothario, fully explored his relationship with Susan Hayes, and named a number of other women who were allegedly involved with him. The testimony at trial never showed that Sheppard had any illicit relationships besides the one with Susan Hayes.

On July 28, an editorial entitled "Why Don't Police Quiz Top Suspect" demanded that Sheppard be taken to police headquarters. It described him in the following language:

---

6. The newspapers had heavily emphasized Sheppard's illicit affair with Susan Hayes, and the fact that he had initially lied about it.

7. A number of articles calculated to evoke sympathy for Sheppard were printed, such as the letters Sheppard wrote to his son while in jail. These stories often appeared together with news coverage which was unfavorable to him.

"Now proved under oath to be a liar, still free to go about his business, shielded by his family, protected by a smart lawyer who has made monkeys of the police and authorities, carrying a gun part of the time, left free to do whatever he pleases...."

A front-page editorial on July 30 asked: "Why Isn't Sam Sheppard in Jail?" It was later titled "Quit Stalling—Bring Him In." After calling Sheppard "the most unusual murder suspect ever seen around these parts" the article said that "except for some superficial questioning during Coroner Sam Gerber's inquest he has been scot-free of any official grilling...." It asserted that he was "surrounded by an iron curtain of protection [and] concealment."

That night at 10 o'clock Sheppard was arrested at his father's home on a charge of murder. He was taken to the Bay Village City Hall where hundreds of people, newscasters, photographers and reporters were awaiting his arrival. He was immediately arraigned—having been denied a temporary delay to secure the presence of counsel—and bound over to the grand jury.

The publicity then grew in intensity until his indictment on August 17. Typical of the coverage during this period is a front-page interview entitled: "DR. SAM: 'I Wish There Was Something I Could Get Off My Chest—but There Isn't.'" Unfavorable publicity included items such as a cartoon of the body of a sphinx with Sheppard's head and the legend below: "'I Will Do Everything In My Power to Help Solve This Terrible Murder.'—Dr. Sam Sheppard." Headlines announced, *inter alia*, that: "Doctor Evidence is Ready for Jury," "Corrigan Tactics Stall Quizzing," "Sheppard 'Gay Set' Is Revealed By Houk," "Blood Is Found In Garage," "New Murder Evidence Is Found, Police Claim," "Dr. Sam Faces Quiz At Jail On Marilyn's Fear Of Him." On August 18, an article appeared under the headline "Dr. Sam Writes His Own Story." And reproduced across the entire front page was a portion of the typed statement signed by Sheppard: "I am not guilty of the murder of my wife, Marilyn. How could I, who have been trained to help people and devoted my life to saving life, commit such a terrible and revolting crime?" We do not detail the coverage further. There are five volumes filled with similar clippings from each of the three Cleveland newspapers covering the period from the murder until Sheppard's conviction in December 1954. The record includes no excerpts from newscasts on radio and television but since space was reserved in the courtroom for these media we assume that their coverage was equally large.

With this background the case came on for trial two weeks before the November general election at which the chief prosecutor was a candidate for common pleas judge and the trial judge, Judge Blythin, was a candidate to succeed himself. Twenty-five days before the case was set, 75 veniremen were called as prospective jurors. All three Cleveland newspapers published the names and addresses of the veniremen. As a consequence, anonymous letters and telephone calls, as well as calls from friends, regarding the impending prosecution were received by all of the prospective jurors. The selection of the jury began on October 18, 1954.

The courtroom in which the trial was held measured 26 by 48 feet. A long temporary table was set up inside the bar, in back of the single counsel table. It ran the width of the courtroom, parallel to the bar railing, with one end less than three feet from the jury box. Approximately 20 representatives of newspapers and wire services were assigned seats at this table by the court. Behind the bar railing there were four rows of benches. These seats were likewise assigned by the court for the entire trial. The first row was occupied by representatives of television and radio stations, and the second and third rows by reporters from out-of-town newspapers and magazines. One side of the last row, which accommodated 14 people, was assigned to Sheppard's family and the other to Marilyn's. The public was permitted to fill vacancies in this row on special passes only. Representatives of the news media also used all the rooms on the courtroom floor, including the room where cases were ordinarily called and assigned for trial. Private telephone lines and telegraphic equipment were installed in these rooms so that reports from the trial could be speeded to the papers. Station WSRS was permitted to set up broadcasting facilities on the third floor of the courthouse next door to the jury room, where the jury rested during recesses in the trial and deliberated. Newscasts were made from this room throughout the trial, and while the jury reached its verdict.

On the sidewalk and steps in front of the courthouse, television and newsreel cameras were occasionally used to take motion pictures of the participants in the trial, including the jury and the judge. Indeed, one television broadcast carried a staged interview of the judge as he entered the courthouse. In the corridors outside the courtroom there was a host of photographers and television personnel with flash cameras, portable lights and motion picture cameras. This group photographed the prospective jurors during selection of the jury. After the trial opened, the witnesses, counsel, and jurors were photographed and televised whenever they entered or left the courtroom. Sheppard was brought to the courtroom about 10 minutes before each session began; he was surrounded by reporters and extensively photographed for the newspapers and television. A rule of court prohibited picture-taking in the courtroom during the actual sessions of the court, but no restraints were put on photographers during recesses, which were taken once each morning and afternoon, with a longer period for lunch.

All of these arrangements with the news media and their massive coverage of the trial continued during the entire nine weeks of the trial. The courtroom remained crowded to capacity with representatives of news media. Their movement in and out of the courtroom often caused so much confusion that, despite the loud-speaker system installed in the courtroom, it was difficult for the witnesses and counsel to be heard. Furthermore, the reporters clustered within the bar of the small courtroom made confidential talk among Sheppard and his counsel almost impossible during the proceedings. They frequently had to leave the courtroom to obtain privacy. And many times when counsel wished to raise a point with the judge out of the hearing of the jury it was necessary to move to the judge's chambers. Even then, news media representatives so packed the judge's anteroom that counsel could hardly return from the chambers to the courtroom. The reporters vied with each other to find out what counsel and the judge had discussed, and often these matters later appeared in newspapers accessible to the jury.

The daily record of the proceedings was made available to the newspapers and the testimony of each witness was printed verbatim in the local editions, along with objections of counsel, and rulings by the judge. Pictures of Sheppard, the judge, counsel, pertinent witnesses, and the jury often accompanied the daily newspaper and television accounts. At times the newspapers published photographs of exhibits introduced at the trial, and the rooms of Sheppard's house were featured along with relevant testimony. The jurors themselves were constantly exposed to the news media. Every juror, except one, testified at *voir dire* to reading about the case in the Cleveland papers or to having heard broadcasts about it. Seven of the 12 jurors who rendered the verdict had one or more Cleveland papers delivered in their home; the remaining jurors were not interrogated on the point. Nor were there questions as to radios or television sets in the jurors' homes, but we must assume that most of them owned such conveniences. As the selection of the jury progressed, individual pictures of prospective members appeared daily. During the trial, pictures of the jury appeared over 40 times in the Cleveland papers alone. The court permitted photographers to take pictures of the jury in the box, and individual pictures of the members in the jury room. One newspaper ran pictures of the jurors at the Sheppard home when they went there to view the scene of the murder. Another paper featured the home life of an alternate juror. The day before the verdict was rendered—while the jurors were at lunch and sequestered by two bailiffs—the jury was separated into two groups to pose for photographs which appeared in the newspapers.

We now reach the conduct of the trial. While the intense publicity continued unabated, it is sufficient to relate only the more flagrant episodes:

1. On October 9, 1954, nine days before the case went to trial, an editorial in one of the newspapers criticized defense counsel's random poll of people on the streets as to their opinion of Sheppard's guilt or innocence in an effort to use the resulting statistics to show the necessity for change of venue. The article said the survey "smacks of mass jury tampering," called on defense counsel to drop it, and stated that the bar association should do something about it. It characterized the poll as "non-judicial, non-legal, and non-sense." The article was called to the attention of the court but no action was taken.

2. On the second day of *voir dire* examination a debate was staged and broadcast live over WHK radio. The participants, newspaper reporters, accused Sheppard's counsel of throwing roadblocks in the way of the prosecution and asserted that Sheppard conceded his guilt by hiring a prominent criminal lawyer. Sheppard's counsel objected to this broadcast and requested a continuance, but the judge denied the motion. When counsel asked the court to give some protection from such events, the judge replied that "WHK doesn't have much coverage," and that "after all, we are not trying this case by radio or in newspapers or any other means. We confine ourselves seriously to it in this courtroom and do the very best we can."

3. While the jury was being selected, a two-inch headline asked: "But Who Will Speak for Marilyn?" The front-page story spoke of the "perfect face" of the accused. "Study that face as long as you want. Never will you get from it a hint of what might be the answer…." The two brothers of the accused were described as "Prosperous, poised. His two sisters-in law. Smart, chic, well-groomed. His elderly father. Courtly, reserved. A perfect type for the patriarch of a staunch clan." The author then noted Marilyn Sheppard was "still off stage," and that she was an only child whose mother died when she was very young and whose father had no interest in the case. But the author—through quotes from Detective Chief James McArthur—assured readers that the prosecution's exhibits would speak for Marilyn. "Her story," McArthur stated, "will come into this courtroom through our witnesses." The article ends: "Then you realize how what and who is missing from the perfect setting will be supplied. "How in the Big Case justice will be done. "Justice to Sam Sheppard.

"And to Marilyn Sheppard."

4. As has been mentioned, the jury viewed the scene of the murder on the first day of the trial. Hundreds of reporters, cameramen and onlookers were there, and one representative of the news media was permitted to accompany

the jury while it inspected the Sheppard home. The time of the jury's visit was revealed so far in advance that one of the newspapers was able to rent a helicopter and fly over the house taking pictures of the jurors on their tour.

5. On November 19, a Cleveland police officer gave testimony that tended to contradict details in the written statement Sheppard made to the Cleveland police. Two days later, in a broadcast heard over Station WHK in Cleveland, Robert Considine likened Sheppard to a perjurer and compared the episode to Alger Hiss' confrontation with Whittaker Chambers. Though defense counsel asked the judge to question the jury to ascertain how many heard the broadcast, the court refused to do so. The judge also overruled the motion for continuance based on the same ground, saying:

"Well, I don't know, we can't stop people, in any event, listening to it. It is a matter of free speech, and the court can't control everybody....We are not going to harass the jury every morning....It is getting to the point where if we do it every morning, we are suspecting the jury. I have confidence in this jury...."

6. On November 24, a story appeared under an eight-column headline: "Sam Called A 'Jekyll-Hyde' By Marilyn, Cousin To Testify." It related that Marilyn had recently told friends that Sheppard was a "Dr. Jekyll and Mr. Hyde" character. No such testimony was ever produced at the trial. The story went on to announce: "The prosecution has a 'bombshell witness' on tap who will testify to Dr. Sam's display of fiery temper—countering the defense claim that the defendant is a gentle physician with an even disposition." Defense counsel made motions for change of venue, continuance and mistrial, but they were denied. No action was taken by the court.

7. When the trial was in its seventh week, Walter Winchell broadcast over WXEL television and WJW radio that Carole Beasley, who was under arrest in New York City for robbery, had stated that, as Sheppard's mistress, she had borne him a child. The defense asked that the jury be queried on the broadcast. Two jurors admitted in open court that they had heard it. The judge asked each: "Would that have any effect upon your judgment?" Both replied, "No." This was accepted by the judge as sufficient; he merely asked the jury to "pay no attention whatever to that type of scavenging....Let's confine ourselves to this courtroom, if you please." In answer to the motion for mistrial, the judge said:

"Well, even, so, Mr. Corrigan, how are you ever going to prevent those things, in any event? I don't justify them at all. I think it is outrageous, but in a sense, it is outrageous even if there were no trial here. The trial has nothing to do with it in the Court's mind, as far as its outrage is concerned, but—

"Mr. CORRIGAN: I don't know what effect it had on the mind of any of these jurors, and I can't find out unless inquiry is made.

"The COURT: How would you ever, in any jury, avoid that kind of a thing?"

8. On December 9, while Sheppard was on the witness stand he testified that he had been mistreated by Cleveland detectives after his arrest. Although he was not at the trial, Captain Kerr of the Homicide Bureau issued a press statement denying Sheppard's allegations which appeared under the headline: "'Bare-faced Liar,' Kerr Says of Sam." Captain Kerr never appeared as a witness at the trial.

9. After the case was submitted to the jury, it was sequestered for its deliberations, which took five days and four nights. After the verdict, defense counsel ascertained that the jurors had been allowed to make telephone calls to their homes every day while they were sequestered at the hotel. Although the telephones had been removed from the jurors' rooms, the jurors were permitted to use the phones in the bailiffs' rooms. The calls were placed by the jurors themselves; no record was kept of the jurors who made calls, the telephone numbers or the parties called. The bailiffs sat in the room where they could hear only the jurors' end of the conversation. The court had not instructed the bailiffs to prevent such calls. By a subsequent motion, defense counsel urged that this ground alone warranted a new trial, but the motion was overruled and no evidence was taken on the question.

The principle that justice cannot survive behind walls of silence has long been reflected in the "Anglo-American distrust for secret trials." *In re Oliver*, 333 U.S. 257, 268 (1948). A responsible press has always been regarded as the handmaiden of effective judicial administration, especially in the criminal field. Its function in this regard is documented by an impressive record of service over several centuries. The press does not simply publish information about trials but guards against the miscarriage of justice by subjecting the police, prosecutors, and judicial processes to extensive public scrutiny and criticism. This Court has, therefore, been unwilling to place any direct limitations on the freedom traditionally exercised by the news media for "what transpires in the court room is public property." *Craig* v. *Harney*, 331 U.S. 367, 374 (1947). The "unqualified prohibitions laid down by the framers were intended to give to liberty of the press…the broadest scope that could be countenanced in an orderly society." *Bridges* v. *California*, 314 U.S. 252, 265 (1941). And where there was "no threat or menace to the integrity of the trial," *Craig* v. *Harney, supra*, at 377, we have consistently required that the press have a free hand, even though we sometimes deplored its sensationalism.

But the Court has also pointed out that "legal trials are not like elections, to be won through the use of the meeting-hall, the radio, and the newspaper." *Bridges* v. *California, supra*, at 271. And the Court has insisted that no one be punished for a crime without "a charge fairly made and fairly tried in a public tribunal free of prejudice, passion, excitement, and tyrannical power." *Chambers* v. *Florida*, 309 U.S. 227, 236–237 (1940). "Freedom of discussion should be given the widest range compatible with the essential requirement of the fair and orderly administration of justice." *Pennekamp* v. *Florida*, 328 U.S. 331, 347 (1946). But it must not be allowed to divert the trial from the "very purpose of a court system...to adjudicate controversies, both criminal and civil, in the calmness and solemnity of the courtroom according to legal procedures." *Cox* v. *Louisiana*, 379 U.S. 559, 583 (1965) (BLACK, J., dissenting). Among these "legal procedures" is the requirement that the jury's verdict be based on evidence received in open court, not from outside sources. Thus, in *Marshall* v. *United States*, 360 U.S. 310 (1959), we set aside a federal conviction where the jurors were exposed "through news accounts" to information that was not admitted at trial. We held that the prejudice from such material "may indeed be greater" than when it is part of the prosecution's evidence "for it is then not tempered by protective procedures." At 313. At the same time, we did not consider dispositive the statement of each juror "that he would not be influenced by the news articles, that he could decide the case only on the evidence of record, and that he felt no prejudice against petitioner as a result of the articles." At 312. Likewise, in *Irvin* v. *Dowd*, 366 U.S. 717 (1961), even though each juror indicated that he could render an impartial verdict despite exposure to prejudicial newspaper articles, we set aside the conviction holding:

"With his life at stake, it is not requiring too much that petitioner be tried in an atmosphere undisturbed by so huge a wave of public passion...." At 728. The undeviating rule of this Court was expressed by Mr. Justice Holmes over half a century ago in *Patterson* v. *Colorado*, 205 U.S. 454, 462 (1907):

"The theory of our system is that the conclusions to be reached in a case will be induced only by evidence and argument in open court, and not by any outside influence, whether of private talk or public print."

Moreover, "the burden of showing essential unfairness...as a demonstrable reality," *Adams* v. *United States ex rel. McCann*, 317 U.S. 269, 281 (1942), need not be undertaken when television has exposed the community "repeatedly and in depth to the spectacle of [the accused] personally confessing in detail to the crimes with which he was later to be charged." *Rideau* v. *Louisiana*, 373 U.S. 723, 726 (1963). In *Turner* v. *Louisiana*, 379 U.S. 466 (1965), two key witnesses were deputy sheriffs who doubled as jury shepherds during the trial. The deputies swore that they had not talked to the jurors about the case, but the Court nonetheless held that, "even if it could be assumed that the deputies never did discuss the case directly with any members of the jury, it would be blinking reality not to recognize the extreme prejudice inherent in this continual association...."

While we cannot say that Sheppard was denied due process by the judge's refusal to take precautions against the influence of pretrial publicity alone, the court's later rulings must be considered against the setting in which the trial was held. In light of this background, we believe that the arrangements made by the judge with the news media caused Sheppard to be deprived of that "judicial serenity and calm to which [he] was entitled." *Estes* v. *Texas, supra,* at 536. The fact is that bedlam reigned at the courthouse during the trial and newsmen took over practically the entire courtroom, hounding most of the participants in the trial, especially Sheppard. At a temporary table within a few feet of the jury box and counsel table sat some 20 reporters staring at Sheppard and taking notes. The erection of a press table for reporters inside the bar is unprecedented. The bar of the court is reserved for counsel, providing them a safe place in which to keep papers and exhibits, and to confer privately with client and co-counsel. It is designed to protect the witness and the jury from any distractions, intrusions or influences, and to permit bench discussions of the judge's rulings away from the hearing of the public and the jury. Having assigned almost all of the available seats in the courtroom to the news media the judge lost his ability to supervise that environment. The movement of the reporters in and out of the courtroom caused frequent confusion and disruption of the trial. And the record reveals constant commotion within the bar. Moreover, the judge gave the throng of newsmen gathered in the corridors of the courthouse absolute free rein. Participants in the trial, including the jury, were forced to run a gantlet of reporters and photographers each time they entered or left the courtroom. The total lack of consideration for the privacy of the jury was demonstrated by the assignment to a broadcasting station of space next to the jury room on the floor above the courtroom, as well as the fact that jurors were allowed to make telephone calls during their five-day deliberation.

There can be no question about the nature of the publicity which surrounded Sheppard's trial. We agree, as did the Court of Appeals, with the findings in Judge Bell's opinion for the Ohio Supreme Court:

"Murder and mystery, society, sex and suspense were combined in this case in such a manner as to intrigue and captivate the public fancy to a degree perhaps unparalleled in recent annals. Throughout the preindictment investigation, the subsequent legal skirmishes and the nine-week trial, circulation-conscious editors catered to the insatiable interest of the American public in the bizarre....In this atmosphere of a 'Roman holiday' for the news media, Sam Sheppard stood trial for his life." 165 Ohio St., at 294, 135 N. E. 2d, at 342.

Indeed, every court that has considered this case, save the court that tried it, has deplored the manner in which the news media inflamed and prejudiced the public.[10]

Much of the material printed or broadcast during the trial was never heard from the witness stand, such as the charges that Sheppard had purposely impeded the murder investigation and must be guilty since he had hired a prominent criminal lawyer; that Sheppard was a perjurer; that he had sexual relations with numerous women; that his slain wife had characterized him as a "Jekyll-Hyde"; that he was "a bare-faced liar" because of his testimony as to police treatment; and, finally, that a woman convict claimed Sheppard to be the father of her illegitimate child. As the trial progressed, the newspapers summarized and interpreted the evidence, devoting particular attention to the material that incriminated Sheppard, and often drew unwarranted inferences from testimony. At one point, a front-page picture of Mrs. Sheppard's bloodstained pillow was published after being "doctored" to show more clearly an alleged imprint of a surgical instrument.

Nor is there doubt that this deluge of publicity reached at least some of the jury. On the only occasion that the jury was queried, two jurors admitted in open court to hearing the highly inflammatory charge that a prison inmate claimed Sheppard as the father of her illegitimate child. Despite the extent and nature of the publicity to which the jury was exposed during trial, the judge refused defense counsel's other requests that the jurors be asked whether they had read or heard specific prejudicial comment about the case, including the incidents we have previously summarized. In these circumstances, we can assume that some of this material reached members of the jury. See *Commonwealth* v. *Crehan*, 345 Mass. 609, 188 N. E. 2d 923 (1963).

---

10 Typical comments on the trial by the press itself include:

"The question of Dr. Sheppard's guilt or innocence still is before the courts. Those who have examined the trial record carefully are divided as to the propriety of the verdict. But almost everyone who watched the performance of the Cleveland press agrees that a fair hearing for the defendant, in that area, would be a modern miracle." Harrison, "The Press vs. the Courts," The Saturday Review (Oct. 15, 1955).

"At this distance, some 100 miles from Cleveland, it looks to us as though the Sheppard murder case was sensationalized to the point at which the press must ask itself if its freedom, carried to excess, doesn't interfere with the conduct of fair trials." Editorial, The Toledo Blade (Dec. 22, 1954).

The court's fundamental error is compounded by the holding that it lacked power to control the publicity about the trial. From the very inception of the proceedings the judge announced that neither he nor anyone else could restrict prejudicial news accounts. And he reiterated this view on numerous occasions. Since he viewed the news media as his target, the judge never considered other means that are often utilized to reduce the appearance of prejudicial material and to protect the jury from outside influence. We conclude that these procedures would have been sufficient to guarantee Sheppard a fair trial....

The carnival atmosphere at trial could easily have been avoided since the courtroom and courthouse premises are subject to the control of the court. As we stressed in *Estes*, the presence of the press at judicial proceedings must be limited when it is apparent that the accused might otherwise be prejudiced or disadvantaged. Bearing in mind the massive pretrial publicity, the judge should have adopted stricter rules governing the use of the courtroom by newsmen, as Sheppard's counsel requested. The number of reporters in the courtroom itself could have been limited at the first sign that their presence would disrupt the trial. They certainly should not have been placed inside the bar. Furthermore, the judge should have more closely regulated the conduct of newsmen in the courtroom. For instance, the judge belatedly asked them not to handle and photograph trial exhibits lying on the counsel table during recesses.

Secondly, the court should have insulated the witnesses. All of the newspapers and radio stations apparently interviewed prospective witnesses at will, and in many instances disclosed their testimony. A typical example was the publication of numerous statements by Susan Hayes, before her appearance in court, regarding her love affair with Sheppard. Although the witnesses were barred from the courtroom during the trial the full verbatim testimony was available to them in the press. This completely nullified the judge's imposition of the rule. See *Estes v. Texas, supra*, at 547.

Thirdly, the court should have made some effort to control the release of leads, information, and gossip to the press by police officers, witnesses, and the counsel for both sides. Much of the information thus disclosed was inaccurate, leading to groundless rumors and confusion.[13] That the judge was

---

13. The problem here was further complicated by the independent action of the newspapers in reporting "evidence" and gossip which they uncovered. The press not only inferred that Sheppard was guilty because he "stalled" the investigation, hid behind his family, and hired a prominent criminal lawyer, but denounced as "mass jury tampering" his efforts to gather evidence of community prejudice caused by such publications. Sheppard's counterattacks added some fuel but, in these circumstances, cannot preclude him from as-

aware of his responsibility in this respect may be seen from his warning to Steve Sheppard, the accused's brother, who had apparently made public statements in an attempt to discredit testimony for the prosecution. The judge made this statement in the presence of the jury:

"Now, the Court wants to say a word. That he was told—he has not read anything about it at all—but he was informed that Dr. Steve Sheppard, who has been granted the privilege of remaining in the court room during the trial, has been trying the case in the newspapers and making rather uncomplimentary comments about the testimony of the witnesses for the State.

"Let it be now understood that if Dr. Steve Sheppard wishes to use the newspapers to try his case while we are trying it here, he will be barred from remaining in the court room during the progress of the trial if he is to be a witness in the case.

"The Court appreciates he cannot deny Steve Sheppard the right of free speech, but he can deny him the...privilege of being in the court room, if he wants to avail himself of that method during the progress of the trial."

Defense counsel immediately brought to the court's attention the tremendous amount of publicity in the Cleveland press that "misrepresented entirely the testimony" in the case. Under such circumstances, the judge should have at least warned the newspapers to check the accuracy of their accounts. And it is obvious that the judge should have further sought to alleviate this problem by imposing control over the statements made to the news media by counsel, witnesses, and especially the Coroner and police officers. The prosecution repeatedly made evidence available to the news media which was never offered in the trial. Much of the "evidence" disseminated in this fashion was clearly inadmissible. The exclusion of such evidence in court is rendered meaningless when news media make it available to the public. For example, the publicity about Sheppard's refusal to take a lie detector test came directly from police officers and the Coroner.[14] The story that Sheppard had been called a "Jekyll-Hyde" personality by his wife was attributed to a prosecution witness.

---

serting his right to a fair trial. Putting to one side news stories attributed to police officials, prospective witnesses, the Sheppards, and the lawyers, it is possible that the other publicity "would itself have had a prejudicial effect." Cf. Report of the President's Commission on the Assassination of President Kennedy, at 239.

14. When two police officers testified at trial that Sheppard refused to take a lie detector test, the judge declined to give a requested instruction that the results of such a test would be inadmissible in any event. He simply told the jury that no person has an obligation "to take any lie detector test."

No such testimony was given. The further report that there was "a 'bombshell witness' on tap" who would testify as to Sheppard's "fiery temper" could only have emanated from the prosecution. Moreover, the newspapers described in detail clues that had been found by the police, but not put into the record.[15]

The fact that many of the prejudicial news items can be traced to the prosecution, as well as the defense, aggravates the judge's failure to take any action. See *Stroble v. California*, 343 U.S. 181, 201 (1952) (Frankfurter, J., dissenting). Effective control of these sources—concededly within the court's power—might well have prevented the divulgence of inaccurate information, rumors, and accusations that made up much of the inflammatory publicity, at least after Sheppard's indictment.

More specifically, the trial court might well have proscribed extrajudicial statements by any lawyer, party, witness, or court official which divulged prejudicial matters, such as the refusal of Sheppard to submit to interrogation or take any lie detector tests; any statement made by Sheppard to officials; the identity of prospective witnesses or their probable testimony; any belief in guilt or innocence; or like statements concerning the merits of the case. See *State v. Van Duyne*, 43 N. J. 369, 389, 204 A. 2d 841, 852 (1964), in which the court interpreted Canon 20 of the American Bar Association's Canons of Professional Ethics to prohibit such statements. Being advised of the great public interest in the case, the mass coverage of the press, and the potential prejudicial impact of publicity, the court could also have requested the appropriate city and county officials to promulgate a regulation with respect to dissemination of information about the case by their employees.[16] In addition, reporters who wrote or broadcast prejudicial stories, could have been warned as to the impropriety of publishing material not introduced in the proceedings. The judge was put on notice of such events by defense counsel's complaint about the WHK broadcast on the second day of trial. See p. 346, *supra*. In this manner, Sheppard's right to a trial free from outside interference would have been given added protection without corresponding curtailment of the news media. Had

---

15. Such "premature disclosure and weighing of the evidence" may seriously jeopardize a defendant's right to an impartial jury. "Neither the press nor the public had a right to be contemporaneously informed by the police or prosecuting authorities of the details of the evidence being accumulated against [Sheppard]." Cf. Report of the President's Commission, *supra*, at 239, 240.

16. The Department of Justice, the City of New York, and other governmental agencies have issued such regulations. E. g., 28 CFR § 50.2 (1966). For general information on this topic see periodic publications (e. g., Nos. 71, 124, and 158) by the Freedom of Information Center, School of Journalism, University of Missouri.

the judge, the other officers of the court, and the police placed the interest of justice first, the news media would have soon learned to be content with the task of reporting the case as it unfolded in the courtroom—not pieced together from extrajudicial statements.

From the cases coming here we note that unfair and prejudicial news comment on pending trials has become increasingly prevalent. Due process requires that the accused receive a trial by an impartial jury free from outside influences. Given the pervasiveness of modern communications and the difficulty of effacing prejudicial publicity from the minds of the jurors, the trial courts must take strong measures to ensure that the balance is never weighed against the accused. And appellate tribunals have the duty to make an independent evaluation of the circumstances. Of course, there is nothing that proscribes the press from reporting events that transpire in the courtroom. But where there is a reasonable likelihood that prejudicial news prior to trial will prevent a fair trial, the judge should continue the case until the threat abates, or transfer it to another county not so permeated with publicity. In addition, sequestration of the jury was something the judge should have raised *sua sponte* with counsel. If publicity during the proceedings threatens the fairness of the trial, a new trial should be ordered. But we must remember that reversals are but palliatives; the cure lies in those remedial measures that will prevent the prejudice at its inception. The courts must take such steps by rule and regulation that will protect their processes from prejudicial outside interferences. Neither prosecutors, counsel for defense, the accused, witnesses, court staff nor enforcement officers coming under the jurisdiction of the court should be permitted to frustrate its function. Collaboration between counsel and the press as to information affecting the fairness of a criminal trial is not only subject to regulation, but is highly censurable and worthy of disciplinary measures.

Since the state trial judge did not fulfill his duty to protect Sheppard from the inherently prejudicial publicity which saturated the community and to control disruptive influences in the courtroom, we must reverse the denial of the habeas petition. The case is remanded to the District Court with instructions to issue the writ and order that Sheppard be released from custody unless the State puts him to its charges again within a reasonable time. *It is so ordered.*

C. Lassiter. The appearance of justice: TV or not TV—That is the question. *
Journal of Criminal Law and Criminology
volume 86, page 928 (Excerpt) (1996)

Introduction

The Courtroom Television Network…is the first serious commercial effort to televise selected trials nationally and to provide expert commentary on what happens in America's courtrooms. More than twenty million viewers have access to the Court TV network. Court TV has televised more than 340 trials. Apart from its entrepreneurial aspirations, Court TV hopes to permit the American public to see the inner workings of a trial courtroom.

Televised coverage of trials is a growth industry, fueled by an oversupply of lawyers competing for clients in an information-intensive free market economy as well by a public eager for courtroom drama. Forty-seven states have adopted legislation which allow television cameras in the courtroom in some form, subject to the judge's discretion. However, the exercise of this discretion may yield to the siren call of the media. Only Indiana, Mississippi, South Dakota and the District of Columbia impose an absolute ban against in-court cameras.

Despite the surge in popularity of televised court proceedings, the bar has always, at best, been ambivalent about embracing cameras in the courtroom. Television coverage of a high profile criminal case such as the O.J. Simpson trial—the new "trial of the century" and perhaps the most watched event in history—has by its very success or excess renewed interest in the wisdom of allowing cameras in court.

Contemporaneous with the excesses of television coverage, a discernible tide has risen against cameras in court, especially in simulcasts of high profile cases. It is not yet determined how state courts will cope with the problems of televisions' impact on trials in the aftermath of the O.J. Simpson trial. This question is already under review in a number of influential jurisdictions. For example, the New York State legislature recently rejected a bill to continue its experiment with cameras in the state trial level courts. The state legislatures

---

* reprinted with the permission of C. Lassiter, author.

from California to Georgia have re-examined or adopted more restrictive measures designed to limit cameras in court, while Tennessee has become less restrictive in allowing camera coverage since the O.J. Simpson trial. In-court camera coverage has only on-again/off-again appeal in federal courts, where judges are appointed with life tenure and do not depend on high visibility for re-election. In the 1994 U.S. Judicial Conference, the policy-makers for the federal courts rejected a proposal to allow television cameras in federal courts on a permanent basis, effectively banning cameras from the federal courtrooms. In 1996, the U.S. Judicial Commission reversed that absolute position by a fourteen to twelve vote to allow cameras in federal court rooms if the individual judge chooses to do so. The United States Supreme Court has not formally considered, nor appears likely to approve, any request to televise oral arguments before the Supreme Court. Other countries also hesitate to permit cameras in the courtroom. Reported resistance includes courts in Canada, England, Ireland, Scotland, and Italy.

This Article discusses the prejudicial impact of cameras in the courtroom. At the outset, it is important to distinguish between the effect of cameras in the courtroom and cameras outside of the courtroom. Likewise, it is important to distinguish between pretrial television publicity and television publicity occurring during the trial. This Article focuses on the impact of in-court cameras on the judicial process; it explores the ways that merely adding a camera to the reporter's arsenal of media tools significantly alters the judicial process in ways which pad and pen never did. The wisdom of hindsight presages reconsideration of current practices permitting cameras in the courtroom. TV or not TV in the courtroom is indeed the question. The answer is worth reconsideration starting from first principles.

The lens cap should be put back on cameras in the courtroom. Why not televised trials? The answer in a word is that television makes trials more political and less judicial. In the Anglo-American legal tradition, ideally, courts are elevated above the morass of public clamor, political crassness, personal bias, and petty idiosyncracies to perform the solemn task of deciding competing factual claims in accordance with objectively neutral law. The high mark of secular justice in the advanced stage of modern nations is the separation of justice from general politics. Television is the newest of technology, but it takes us back to the oldest problem for jurisprudence, the merging of justice and politics. Here is how the eye of a camera brings a political focus to a trial process which is designed to minimize political considerations. To begin, court television viewers are not screened by voir dire, their consideration of matters are not limited by the strict laws of evidence, nor are they

sworn to follow court instructions for evaluating the case under consideration. Somewhat like a boxing match, the television public emotes politically
at what it sees in a free consciousness form round-by-round. The public reaction becomes the media's recognized perception of the trial—and just as
frequently the media creates the news it wants to report. This political, non-
deliberative reaction becomes known to the parties at trial via cameras outside of the courtroom through nightly analysis and investigative journalism.
Knowledge of the public's reaction in the minds of the trial participants becomes a form of technological tampering that taints the proceedings with political input from the sidelines. Although the rights of a free press and the educational and inspirational potential of television are not easily denied, these
considerations must be balanced against the infusion of general politics which
television introduces to any process or event it showcases.

Television coverage of a trial would be worthwhile where major issues of
law having societal significance were under discussion. And therein lies an
argument for using the television as communicator and educator. But in the
vast majority of cases there is little in the way of precedent-setting issues. In
the main, courts adjudicate highly personal disputes involving intimate details amassed from the personal lives of people and comprising nothing of
interest to the general public beyond that of prurient voyeurism. The trial
process represents the best possible human effort to do justice in an imperfect world. In-court camera coverage, which in the words of Steve Brill "gives
people a feeling that we're doing this together," can be prejudicial to the very
judicial process it seeks to showcase by infecting it with political bias of all
kinds, petty, personal and demographic. Television cameras do so by creating a comprehensive and instantaneous feedback loop between the trial participants and the television audience. This feedback loop provides a medium
by which the reactions of a remote public to the ongoings at trial become
known to the trial actors. When the trial actors respond to public reaction,
the trial loses its judicial character and becomes a bully pulpit for the reign-
ing political concerns as orchestrated by the media. There are three prejudicial effects of cameras in the courtroom. First, the trial, in reality, operates
on a larger theme than the matter under charge; the judicial process is corrupted by a substitution of the solemn, calm, deliberate judgment of the
finder of fact for the outrage of an inflamed public. Second, the adversarial
system, designed for neutral and dispassionate judicial prosecution, transforms into an instrument of a politically motivated persecution. Third, the
public outcry leads to a political vice of judicial disposition against a disfa-
vored minority....

Arguments favoring television in the courtroom

Television inspires public confidence in the trial process

In addition to the First and Sixth Amendment arguments...proponents of televised trial coverage increasingly argue the educational potential of television as a basis for the inclusion of cameras in the courtroom. It is well established as a matter of federal constitutional law that the public has a right of access to judicial proceedings, which has historically been considered vital not only to protect the rights of the parties, but also to increase public confidence by ensuring that the proceedings are conducted fairly.

As the United States Supreme Court recognized in *Press-Enterprise v. Superior Court:*

The value of openness lies in the fact that people not actually attending trials can have confidence that standards of fairness are being observed; the sure knowledge that anyone is free to attend gives assurance that established procedures are being followed and that deviations will become known. Openness thus enhances both the basic fairness of the criminal trial and the appearance of fairness so essential to public confidence in the system.

The Court continued: "people in an open society do not demand infallibility from their institutions, but it is difficult for them to accept what they are prohibited from observing."

The ability to observe the conduct of judicial proceedings becomes particularly important in cases where there are highly charged public issues involved, including claims of prejudice, favoritism, and official misconduct. It may be argued that in high profile cases, it is even more critical that the public receive the maximum amount of information about the process by which a particular result has been achieved:

When a shocking crime occurs, a community reaction of outrage and public protest often follows....Thereafter the open processes of justice serve an important prophylactic purpose, providing an outlet for community concern, hostility and emotion. Without an awareness that society's responses to criminal conduct are underway, natural human reactions of outrage and protest are frustrated and may manifest themselves in some form of vengeful "self-help," as indeed they did regularly in the activities of vigilante "committees" on our frontiers....It is not enough to say that results alone will satiate the natural community desire for "satisfaction." A result considered untoward may undermine public confidence, and where the trial has been concealed from public view an unexpected outcome can cause a reaction that the system at best has failed and at worst has been corrupted. To work effectively, it is important that society's criminal process "satisfy the appearance of justice"…and the appearance of justice can best be provided by allowing people to observe it.

In modern times, the press has played an ever-increasing role in providing valuable information to the public regarding the conduct of judicial proceedings. In cases where physical access to the courtroom is extremely limited, the public's right of access truly becomes viable only through the surrogate media. To enable the media to most effectively perform that function, the maximum amount of information must be available to pass on to the interested public, and the most effective means of making that information available in its truest form is through courtroom cameras.

As Justices Brennan and Marshall observed in Richmond Newspapers: In advancing these purposes [of open judicial proceedings], the availability of a trial transcript is no substitute for a public presence at the trial itself. As any experienced appellate judge can attest, the "cold" record is a very imperfect reproduction of events that transpire in the courtroom. Indeed, to the extent that publicity serves as a check upon trial officials, "[recordation]…would be found to operate rather as [cloak] than [check]; as [cloak] in reality, as [check] only in appearance."

Similarly, the importance of the public's "attendance" at courtroom proceedings is best served by the availability of contemporaneous, complete audio and video accounts of the trial, which can only occur if cameras are present in the courtroom. Through electronic coverage, members of the public can observe for themselves the demeanor, tone, contentiousness and perhaps even competency and veracity of the trial participants. Moreover, the ability of the press to accurately and completely report on proceedings that the public may choose not to attend or watch in their entirety is immeasurably enhanced by their own access to video footage of the proceedings themselves.

In the absence of television broadcast, the public and members of the press not fortunate enough or able to obtain permanent seats in the courtroom will be relegated to relying upon the eyes and ears of others, or upon a "cold" transcript, for information about trials. In an age when the public increasingly relies on television technology, it may seem strange to limit trial coverage to fifteenth century technology. Indeed, if the vast majority of people receive news through the electronic media, excluding cameras from the courtroom might be unacceptable when the trial at issue appears to be newsworthy, volatile and complex. Arguably, complete broadcast coverage of the trial is important to achieve the valuable ends served by increasing public access to judicial proceedings.

Television as educator

It is axiomatic that an educated citizenry is essential to a healthy and functioning democracy. Only an informed public can know, observe and, when necessary, change the laws and procedures that provide the structure of any democracy. Only an informed public can work to ensure that those laws and procedures are fairly and lawfully implemented by government officials, including judges, law enforcement officers, prosecutors, and others. Television broadcasts of trial proceedings would also provide a unique and powerful educational opportunity both in the United States and abroad for the public to learn about courts and court proceedings. Further, students, educators, and lawyers would additionally benefit by being able to observe "firsthand," via the broadcast and videotape, the trial and its participants.

It is well recognized that education of citizens regarding the legal system is one of the primary benefits of media coverage of trials. It is undeniably good and right that the public knows the workings of one of the most essential aspects of government, namely, the courts.

That televised court proceedings can be an immensely important and powerful educational tool is widely recognized. Indeed, in his concurring opinion in Estes, Justice Harlan recognized that "television is capable of performing an educational function by acquainting the public with the judicial process in action." The majority opinion in Richmond Newspapers agreed:

When a criminal trial is conducted in the open, there is at least an opportunity both for understanding the system in general and its workings in a particular case: "The educative effect of public attendance is a material advantage. Not only is respect for the law increased and intelligent acquaintance acquired with the methods of government, but a strong confidence in judicial remedies is secured which could never have been inspired by a system of secrecy."

Undoubtably the public has a need for such education. As one commentator noted, television access to trials is essential to "educate a public largely ignorant about the conduct of state and federal trials...There is no field of governmental activity about which the people are so poorly informed as the judicial branch."

Through televised coverage, millions of television viewers can be reached worldwide. In the United States, for example, ""television is our...most common and constant learning environment, the mainstream of our culture. In a typical American home, the set is on for more than seven hours each day, engaging its audience in a ritual most people perform with great regularity.'" Furthermore, students in elementary schools, high schools, colleges, law schools, and even practicing lawyers, can learn much from watching videotapes of these proceedings long after the trial has been completed. As Justice Frankfurter expressed several years ago, he longed for the day when "the news media would cover the Supreme Court as thoroughly as it did the World Series," believing that "the public confidence in the judiciary hinges on the public's perception of it, and that perception necessarily hinges on the media's portrayal of the legal system." In addition, camera coverage of judicial proceedings leads to heightened public awareness of societal problems such as domestic abuse, date rape, sexual harassment and violent crimes.

Empirical surveys indicate that cameras in the courtroom do not have any negative effect on the proceedings

Several states[209] have conducted studies on the potential impact of electronic media coverage on courtroom proceedings, particularly focusing on the effect cameras have upon courtroom decorum and upon witnesses, jurors, attorneys and judges.[210] In all of these states, the courts permitted electronic

---

209. Among them Arizona, California, Florida, Hawaii, Kansas, Louisiana, Maine, Massachusetts, Minnesota, Nevada, New Jersey, New York, Ohio, Virginia, and Washington.

210. Arizona—Untitled [hereinafter The Arizona Study], which is at handwritten page 39 of the Information Service Memorandum IS 88.002, TV Cameras In the Courts, Evaluation of Experiments) (with Attachments) (Sample Survey); California—Evaluation of California's Experiment With Extended Media Coverage of Courts, Submitted by Ernst H. Short and Associates, Inc. (Sept. 1981) [hereinafter The California Study]; see also Cameras In Court, 1983 Report To The Governor And Legislature; Florida—Untitled [hereinafter The Florida Study]; Louisiana—Report On Pilot Project On The Presence Of Cameras And Electronic Equipment In The Courtroom (undated) [hereinafter The Louisiana Study]; Minnesota—Report Of The Minnesota Advisory Commission On Cameras In The Courtroom To The Supreme Court (Jan. 1982) [hereinafter The Minnesota Study]; Nevada—Final Statistical Report Cameras In The Courtroom In Nevada (1980) [hereinafter The Nevada Study]; New York—Report Of The Chief Administrator To The New York State Legislature The Governor And Chief Judge On The Effect Of Audio-Visual Coverage On The Conduct Of Judicial Proceedings, Matthew T. Crosson (March 1991) [hereinafter The 1991 New York Study]; Report of The Committee On Audio-Visual Coverage Of Court Proceedings, Hon. Burton B. Roberts, Chair (May 1994) [hereinafter The 1994 New York Study]; Washington—Cameras In the Courtroom—A Two-Year Review In The State Of Washington, A Project Of The Washington State Superior Court Judges' Association Committee On Courts and Community (Sept. 1978) [hereinafter The Washington Study].

Most of these state studies, and studies from Hawaii, Kansas, Maine, Massachusetts, New Jersey, Ohio and Virginia, are described in Electronic Media Coverage of Courtroom

media coverage in both civil and criminal proceedings, although the majority of coverage was in criminal cases.[211] The results from the state studies were unanimous: the impact of electronic media coverage of courtroom proceedings, whether civil or criminal, shows few side effects.[212]

In September 1990, the Judicial Conference of the United States implemented what was to be a three year pilot program that permitted electronic media coverage in civil proceedings in six federal district courts and two circuit courts. The Federal Evaluation indicated, among other things, that:

* overall, attitudes of judges towards electronic media were neutral and became more favorable after experience under the experimental program;

* generally, judges and attorneys who had experience with electronic media coverage reported observing small or no effects on camera presence on proceeding participants, courtroom decorum, or the administration of justice;

* overall, judges and court personnel reported that the media were very cooperative and complied with program guidelines and other restrictions that were imposed.

Indeed, the Federal Judicial Center's "Summary of Findings" concluded that no negative impact resulted from having cameras in the courtroom. In 1994, the Federal Judicial Center specifically found that results from state

---

Proceedings: Effects On Witnesses And Jurors, Supplement Report Of The Federal Judicial Center To The Judicial Conference Committee On Court Administration And Case Management (1994).

211. California's report on the effect of electronic coverage of court proceedings is probably the most comprehensive of the state evaluations that have been completed. In addition to evaluating the impact of cameras on jurors and witnesses through surveys, as many other states have done, the researchers involved in the California evaluation also observed the jurors' behavior. In addition, the California study included observations and comparisons of proceedings that were covered by the electronic media, and proceedings that were not. See generally The California Study at 20, 55–67, 82–98. The California results were favorable to including cameras in the court room. For example, after systematically observing proceedings where cameras were and were not present, consultants who conducted California's study concluded that witnesses were equally effective at communicating in both sets of circumstances. The California Study at 103–04. Furthermore, the behavior observations in California also reinforced survey results from California and other state and federal courts, which had found that jurors in proceedings where electronic media were present were equally attentive to testimony as jurors in proceedings without such coverage. Id. at 86–88, 105–06, 111. The California Study also revealed that there was no, or only minimal, impact upon courtroom decorum from the presence of cameras. Id. at 78–79.

212. J. Stratton Shartel, Cameras in the Courts: Early Returns Show Few Side Effects, Inside Litig., at 1, 19 (1993).

court evaluations of the effects of electronic media on jurors and witnesses indicate that most respondents believe electronic media presence has minimal or no detrimental effects on jurors or witnesses. As with the handful of state surveys, the federal survey found that "most participants [say] electronic media presence has no or minimal detrimental effects on jurors or witnesses."

Arguments opposing cameras in the courtroom

Although the generation following the 1981 Supreme Court decision in Chandler has seen the proliferation of televised criminal trials with Court TV, CNN and E! leading the way, there is no constitutional right to introduce cameras in the courtroom. The rise of cameras in the courtroom has seen the federal judiciary, a significant minority of states, and media scholars oppose cameras in the courtroom. Moreover, a growing number of witnesses, jurors, and lawyers have grown weary of the lure of television coverage and more sensitive to its distorting impact on justice.

Surveys on cameras in the courtroom lack reliability

While subjective surveys invariably report that a majority of those responding indicate that cameras in court had no substantial impact on the proceedings, real cases prove that cameras do have a substantial impact. The studies, which invariably purport to demonstrate that television coverage of trials was innocuous, rely exclusively on the subjective self-report responses of participants in the judicial process. There is one main problem with self-reporting data as compiled by these studies: the very nature of self-reporting creates a bias favoring those who respond, and what they choose to report. Since judges and jurors are supposed to be impartial, lawyers business-like, and witnesses truthful, it is possible that those who believed themselves compromised by the improper influence of television coverage might be disinclined to acknowledge their partiality. The possible bias due to non-response is particularly acute when it is recognized that many of the state studies rely on a very small sample. The Virginia study surveyed only fifty-seven respondents, California relied on only fifty-six respondents, Nevada only thirty-one respondents and New Jersey's study noted only a "relatively small number of respondents surveyed." However, even with the bias of self-reporting, each of these studies reveal that a significant minority of jurors, attorneys, and witnesses reported that cameras in the courtroom significantly affected their role in the trial. It seems fairly uncontrovertible that a fair trial cannot be held unless all of the participants properly perform their roles.

Cameras are distinct from the press

Max Frankel, a lifelong newspaper reporter and editor of the New York Times heads the list of responsible journalists who have soured on the basic media position that rights enjoyed by the written press necessarily belong to television cameras. Frankel states:

I am certain now that the camera is not just another incarnation of "press," entitled to the unabridged freedom thereof. It's a different beast that should enter a court by a different door, under different rules....Reporters and spectators must attend trials to guard against a star chamber proceeding. But no camera should come into court without the defendant's consent. I would let a prosecutor and judge object as well. Though there is no proof that television coverage alters the conduct of a case, [because no serious methodological research has been done], the suspicion that it does inevitably grows as the camera magnifies the din and compounds the stakes, in fame and fortune, for every participant. Justice may not often be compromised, but society's sense of it can certainly be demeaned.

The reality seems clear that the use of a camera to record courtroom proceedings transforms the courtroom to a potentially global village that permits nearly instantaneous feedback of a remote public to prejudice the trial. To the same effect, nationally syndicated columnist Anthony Lewis wrote in an Op-Ed piece:

Television has an emotional power, an immediacy that the written word can hardly match. As a student at Columbia University's Graduate School of Journalism put it to me the other day: "It's harder to filter television, to screen it. With print you have to reason. Television goes right through to your emotions."

Prejudicial impact

Televising trials may negatively affect the performance of many jurors, witnesses, lawyers and judges. On April 13, 1991, the Criminal Justice Section of the New York Bar Association presented a fact sheet which demonstrated that even the New York Office of Court Administration's limited self-reported survey data supported a conclusion that a substantial minority of courtroom participants reported that television cameras had a prejudicial impact on the trial. The New York study, which suffers from the same methodological self-reporting flaws as the other state and federal surveys, nevertheless bears detailed review, because New York remains unsold on a permanent rule authorizing cameras in the courtroom.

The New York study broke down reporting by attorneys, defense attorneys, prosecutors, jurors, and witnesses. In summary form, results were as follows:

Attorneys Reported:

* Thirty-seven percent of attorneys reported that the atmosphere in the courtroom was tense and 35% stated that the atmosphere was uneasy as a result of audio-visual coverage. Thirty-seven percent of the attorney respondents reported that they were more self-conscious as a result of audio-visual coverage.

* Thirty-eight percent of attorney respondents stated that the testimony of witnesses was affected by audio-visual coverage. Among those who said that witnesses were affected by audio-visual coverage, 28% of the attorney-respondents stated that witnesses had a reluctance to be identified or broadcasted; 14% said that audio-visual coverage places pressure on the witnesses; 10% believed that witnesses appeared nervous and/or anxious; 7% reported that witnesses appeared to be putting on an act and/or looking for public exposure, and an additional 7% felt that witnesses did not concentrate on the testimony as a result of the presence of the media.

* Thirty-four percent of attorney-respondents were concerned that audio-visual coverage would affect the security of their witnesses and clients.

* Twenty-three percent of the attorney-respondents found the presence of cameras distracting.

* Twenty-seven percent of attorney-respondents believed that the procedures leading to the decision to permit audio-visual coverage did not allow them sufficient time to ascertain the views of their clients or witnesses.

* Five percent of the attorneys who had one or more of their witnesses receive audio-visual coverage stated that one or more of their witnesses refused to and did not testify because of audio-visual coverage. Fifteen percent of attorneys whose witnesses experienced audio-visual coverage stated that one or more of their witnesses initially declined to testify because of audio-visual coverage, but nonetheless did testify. Finally 3% of attorneys stated that the court compelled one or more of their witnesses to testify.

* Forty-six percent of attorneys believe that audio-visual coverage of arraignments negatively affects fairness.

* Forty-four percent of attorneys stated that audio-visual coverage of trials negatively affects fairness.

* With regard to suppression hearings and sentencings, 64% and 34%, respectively, believe that audio-visual coverage affects these proceedings negatively.

Defense Attorneys Reported:

* Fifty-six percent of defense attorneys felt that the fairness of trials was negatively affected by audio-visual coverage.

* Sixty-seven percent of defense attorneys felt that the fairness of arraignments was negatively affected by audio-visual coverage.

* Eighty percent of defense attorneys felt that the fairness of suppression hearings was negatively affected by audio-visual coverage.

* Fifty-four percent of defense attorneys felt that the fairness of sentencings was negatively affected by audio-visual coverage.

Prosecutors Reported:

* Twenty-six percent of prosecutors felt that the fairness of trials was negatively affected by audio-visual coverage.

* Overall, 18% of prosecutors reported being opposed to audio-visual coverage in the courtroom.

* Twenty-three percent of prosecutors felt that the fairness of arraignments was negatively affected by audio-visual coverage.

* Fifty-three percent of prosecutors felt that the fairness of suppression hearings was negatively affected by audio-visual coverage.

* Ten percent of prosecutors felt that the fairness of sentencings was negatively affected by audio-visual coverage.

Jurors Reported:

* Nineteen percent of the jurors thought that the fairness of trials would be negatively affected.

* The presence of cameras made 28% of juror respondents think the [*970] proceeding was more important.

Witnesses Reported:

* In the prior experiment, 27% of witnesses reported feeling either anxious or nervous as a result of the presence of cameras. In the current experiment, 30% of witnesses reported feeling somewhat uneasy, and 39% felt either tense or somewhat tense.

* Of the sixty-four witnesses surveyed, twenty-five or 39% reported that the presence of cameras had some effect on them. Of these twenty-five respondents, 39% indicated that they were tense or somewhat tense; 30% felt somewhat uneasy; 44% felt somewhat more self-conscious; 16% felt somewhat insecure; 10% were reluctant to participate; 21% felt that the case was more serious, and 19% of the witnesses reported being distracted.

The courts have long recognized that as society becomes more experienced with cameras in the courtroom, the novelty will wear off and cameras will fade into the background as in other areas (banks, airports, convenience stores, high security areas, sporting events, weddings, etc.). Perhaps the day will come to pass that cameras are too common-place to cause concern, but for now the evidence tends to rebut this notion. While lawyers, judges, jurors, and even witnesses may be loath to admit in a self-reporting survey that the presence of cameras had a detrimental impact on their participation in the trial, the difference is not hidden to court watchers, especially those who seek justice in the proceedings.

Dignity and decorum

In the early years of televised trial proceedings, the courts frequently found inter alia that the physical presence of cameras could have a prejudicial impact on courtroom decorum and the dignity of the proceedings. However, the advance of technology has mostly overcome the bulky camera problem dating back to the *Hauptmann* case. Moreover, states have adopted many rules aimed at reducing disruptions and distractions caused by cameras in the courtroom. Nevertheless, courts have recognized that the physical presence of camera equipment alone could substantially interfere with dignity and decorum. This is so simply because of the awareness that the proceedings are televised.

With the advent of technology to minimize the physical presence of cameras and the various rules to facilitate courtroom administration, the more refined battleground over televised coverage of trial proceedings on the dignity and decorum front deals with the possible psychological impact on the trial proceedings. While courts which have been asked to examine the impact of television coverage on the participants in particular trials have long concluded that such coverage did not have a sufficiently adverse impact on the trial participants to constitute a denial of due process on a per se basis, at least one appellate court has upheld the declination of television coverage of trial proceedings because of the adverse impact on dignity and decorum in the courtroom.

Measuring psychological impact may well require more than simplistic, and perhaps self-serving, surveys. It requires an understanding of how knowledge of cameras broadcasting to a remote public of local, state, national, and even worldwide dimension in some cases may affect the psychology of the participants through subtle and not so subtle nuances. As media scholar Richard D. Heffner said:

I don't like [cameras in the courts]. I don't believe that a free press requires them. And I don't believe that in our best understanding of the phrase, due process can over time truly tolerate them. For I share the concerns (undocumented to be sure) of many thoughtful professionals that what happens in the view of courtroom cameras will inevitably and increasingly be molded by trial participants' awareness of what will "play" on the 6 or the 11 o'clock news! Can we realistically expect that they alone in American life will resist the Lorelei call of mass media?

The plain truth is that no matter how much the camera blends into the background, and no matter how unobtrusive is the camera operator, the mere knowledge that the courtroom is converted to a world stage changes the dynamic. Change the audience and you change the message.

Only cameras outside of the courtroom educate

When considering the important, solemn, and personal nature of the work of courtrooms, the trade-off of a lower quality of justice in exchange for a speculative claim to achieving general education seems dubious at best. Court TV makes two educational claims: first, that gavel-to-gavel coverage inspires confidence in the result of the specific trial viewed and; second, that its overall programming helps to educate the American public about the legal process. There are several counterpoints to these arguments. First, the claims made for confidence-inspiring and general education-building can be served without sacrificing courtroom autonomy by providing extensive news coverage, expert commentary, and panel discussions outside the courtroom. Indeed Court TV has made an extraordinary, credible effort to educate the public on the law by expert commentary and panel discussions outside of the courtroom.

Second, it is by no means certain that actual viewing of courtroom performance gavel-to-gavel has achieved substantial educational or confidence-inspiring results. Experienced legal educators know that high profile cases are of mixed pedagogical worth: they excite student interest, but the student interest fixates on the political lure of the trial and not the legal issue implicated in the discussion. While there remains the potential for learning by watching trials, even those selected by Court TV for commercial appeal, there has yet to surface a study testing viewers to see if their actual knowledge of the legal system has improved as a result of cameras inside the courtroom. It may well be that interest is peaked and viewers may subjectively believe their knowledge is enhanced by hours of television, but like Colin Ferguson, who unsuccessfully defended himself in the New York subway shooting case, must now know, there is more to criminal justice than superficially mimicking legal phrases.

The argument that live in-court camera coverage inspires confidence in the criminal justice system and jury verdicts in particular by showing the public the evidence presented at trial has its greatest merit from the perspective of the parties. Defendants acquitted at trial have long been heard to complain about tarnished reputations in the press. Gavel-to-gavel coverage explains the trial results to the public. During the O.J. Simpson trial, lead defense counsel Johnnie Cochran, pursuant to his co-counsel's wishes, took the microphone at a spare moment to quell rumors of a possible plea agreement. The perverse impact of the media in the O.J. Simpson case, both from in- as well as out-of-court cameras of panel discussions during breaks in the trial, was that the overall effect tended to persecute Simpson even as his trial found him not guilty. The media instigated and maintained racial overtones to the trial by tracking the racial composition of the jury and the prosecution and defense teams. Despite the acquittal, the media generally pronounced O.J. Simpson guilty.

There are other more general downsides to television attention to the parties at trial. The need to gain public support while simultaneously trying the case creates concerns for litigation. The concern for appearance dogged the O.J. Simpson trial from the beginning and created one its most bizarre controversies: the Time magazine retouched "mugshot" photograph of O.J. Simpson as the cover feature announcing O.J. Simpson's arrest. Critics charged that the darkened photograph made O.J. Simpson appear more sinister. Because of the bright lighting necessary for television cameras and the shadowy effect over the natural curvature of the face, television too tends to make a face appear somewhat sinister. Perhaps the most famous example of this phenomenon was the first televised presidential debate between a youthful made-up John F. Kennedy, the eventual winner, and the seasoned Richard M. Nixon who due to illness, a lack of make-up, and without a fresh shave appeared sinister and murky. At least one study shows that people more accurately perceive truth from the written word than from the televised word.[264]

In short, the confidence-inspiring aspects of television coverage are speculative. Judge Ito intended to make the O.J. Simpson case a lesson on the criminal justice system for the television public. To that end, he allowed lawyers to air lengthy arguments, to comment directly to the public. It may be speculated that Judge Ito even set early adjournment each day (3:00 pm. Pacific Time) so as to not overrun prime time network news beginning on the East

---

264. See Richard Wiseman, The Megalab Truth Test, 373 Nature 391 (1995). This article reports a study purporting to demonstrate that the public discerns falsehoods better when receiving news through the printed media versus either radio or television. This study has been criticized for limited sample size. Oliver Braddick, Distinguishing Truth From Lies, 374 Nature 315 (1995).

Coast at the same time. However, if media reports are reliable, there were few viewers of the O.J. Simpson verdict who did not come away disillusioned. Lawyers, judges, and the press, increasingly embarrassed at the spectacle, began open and stinging criticism of Judge Ito. Even the sequestered O.J. Simpson jury was disillusioned with the trial, evidenced by their refusal to come to the trial one day in a sort of mini-revolt.

Third, television seeks its own low level of entertainment. High profile cases seem to be chosen for their salacious detail rather than for a salutary concern to inspire confidence in results or provide legal education in general. Regardless of today's attempts at professionalism, when rating wars for televised trials commence, commercial television inevitably slides toward the tabloid marketing lure of sex, power, and the perverse. As bad as its influence on the remote public, television has a unique capacity to compound public clamor over lurid details by bringing the public's reaction to these features of the case back into the case it seeks to showcase and to prejudice the result thereby....

List of other cases and articles relevant to this topic

Murphy v. *Florida*, 421 U.S. 794 (1975)

Nebraska v. *Press Association*, 427 U.S. 539 (1976)

Irwin v. *Dowd*, 366 U.S. 717 (1961)

Studebaker, C.A. and S.D. Penrod (1997) Pretrial publicity: The media, the law and common sense *Psychology, Public Policy and Law* 3: 428–460.

Otto, A.L., S. Penrod, and H.R. Dexter (1994) The biasing impact of pretrial publicity on juror judgments. *Law and Human Behavior* 18(4): 453–469.

Discussion and Review Questions

1. Do you think it is possible for any high profile criminal defendant to get a fair trial in the United States?
2. In light of technological advances, what type of accommodations or restrictions do you think the courts must undertake to ensure defendants get a fair trial?
3. Which of the remedies or combination of remedies do you think show the greatest promise for protecting defendant's rights to a fair and impartial jury?
4. What limitations on the press and their ability to publish information do you think the Court may be willing to impose?
5. Why are the remedial measures, currently available, inadequate to address the effect of pretrial publicity?

References

Articles

Beisecker, T. (1995). Court system panel: The role of change of venue in an electronic age. *Kansas Journal of Law and Public Policy* 81–94.

Carroll, J.S. et al. (1986). Free press and fair trial: The role of behavioral research. *Law and Human Behavior* 11: 259–264.

Fisher, L. (1999). *American Constitutional Law, Third Edition*. Durham, NC: Carolina Academic Press.

Frasca, R. (1988). Estimating the occurrence of trials prejudiced by press coverage. *Judicature* 72: 162–169.

Fulero, S.M. (1987). The role of behavioral research in the free press/fair trial controversy: Another view. *Law and Human Behavior* 11: 259–264.

Kerr, N. (Nov./Dec.1994). The effects of pretrial publicity on jurors. *Judicature* 120–127.

Neubauer, D. (1999). *America's Courts and the Criminal Justice System*. CA: Wadsworth.

O'Connell, P. D. (1988). Pretrial publicity, change of venue, public opinion polls—A theory of procedural justice. *University of Detroit Law Review* 169–183.

Steblay, N.M., J. Besirevic, S.M. Fulero, et al. (1999). The effects of pretrial publicity on juror verdicts: A meta–analytic review. *Law and Human Behavior* 23: 219–235.

Studebaker, C.A. and S.D. Penrod (1997). Pretrial publicity: The media, the law and common sense. *Psychology, Public Policy and Law* 3: 428–460.

The Jury Project (1994). Report to the Chief Judge of the State of New York.

Wetherington, G. T., H. Lawton, and D. I. Pollock (1999). Preparing for the high profile cases: An omnibus treatment for judges and lawyers. *Florida Law Review* 51: 425.

Yuan, L.S. (1998). Comment: Gag orders and the ultimate sanction. *Loyola of Los Angeles Entertainment Law Journal* 18: 629.

Case Citations

Irwin v. Dowd, 366 U.S. 717 (1961)

Miranda v. Arizona, 384 U.S. 436 (1966)

Nebraska v. Press Association v. Stuart, 427 U.S. 539 (1976).

Patton v. Yount, 467 U.S. 1025 (1984)

Sheppard v. Maxwell, 384 U.S. 333 (1966)

CHAPTER 7

RIGHT TO COUNSEL

The right to be heard would be, in many cases, of little avail if it did not comprehend the right to be heard by counsel. Even the intelligent and educated layman has small and sometimes no skill in the science of law. If charged with crime, he is incapable, generally, of determining for himself whether the indictment is good or bad. He is unfamiliar with the rules of evidence. Left without the aid of counsel he may be put on trial without a proper charge, and convicted upon incompetent evidence, or evidence irrelevant to the issue or otherwise inadmissible....He requires the guiding hand of counsel at every step in the proceedings against him. Without it, though he be not guilty, he faces the danger of conviction because he does not know how to establish his innocence.

–*Powell v. Alabama*, 287 U.S. 45 (1932)(Justice Sutherland)

In a hand-written note to the United States Supreme Court, Clarence Earl Gideon asked to have his conviction for burglary reversed because he was forced to appear in court without a lawyer. 372 U.S. 335 (1963) Today, we take for granted that people accused of crimes are provided counsel to assist them in their defense. However, until 1960, that was not the case. Although the Sixth Amendment to the United States Constitution (1791) states, in pertinent part: "In all criminal prosecutions, the accused shall enjoy the right...to have the Assistance of Counsel for his defense," the United States Supreme Court initially held that this Amendment only applied to prosecutions in federal court and to defendants charged with capital crimes in state court. *Powell v. Alabama*, 287 U.S. 45 (1932); *Johnson v. Zerbst*, 304 U.S. 458 (1938). In 1942, the Court held that **indigent defendants** in state prosecutions for non-capital crimes were not entitled to appointed counsel. *Betts v. Brady*, 316 U.S. 455 (1942). Gideon was charged with a non-capital felony in state court and had no funds to hire a lawyer. When he asked for appointed counsel, the trial judge responded:

> **Indigent defendant:** A person indicted or complained of who is without funds or the ability to hire a lawyer to defend him and who, in most instances, is entitled to appointed counsel, consistent with the protection of the Sixth and Fourteenth Amendments to the United States Constitution. (Black's Law Dictionary).

> Mr. Gideon, I am sorry, but I cannot appoint counsel to represent you in this case. Under the laws of the state of Florida, the only time the Court can appoint Counsel to represent a defendant is when that person is charged with a capital offense. I am sorry, but I will have to deny your request to appoint Counsel to defend you in this case.

Gideon defended himself before the jury, was found guilty and sentenced to five years in prison. On appeal to the United States Supreme Court, Gideon argued that he was denied his Sixth Amendment right to counsel as provided in the United States Constitution. The Court appointed counsel to represent Gideon and asked each attorney to address the following question: "Should this Court's holding in *Betts v. Brady,* 316 U.S. 455, be reconsidered?"

The United States Supreme Court had previously held that Betts, convicted before a Maryland jury on robbery charges and refused appointed counsel, had not had his due process rights under the Fourteenth Amendment violated. The Due Process Clause of the Fourteenth Amendment was not found to be applicable to state prosecutions (counsel was necessary in federal prosecutions) because the refusal to appoint counsel was not so offensive to the common and fundamental ideas of fairness as to amount to a denial of due process.

The *Gideon* Court overruled its decision in *Betts v. Brady.* The Court held that the *Betts* decision was wrong to assert that the Sixth Amendment right to counsel was not a fundamental one. The language in *Powell v. Alabama,* 287 U.S. 45 (1932), which introduces this chapter, holding that indigent defendants charged with capital crimes were entitled to the appointment of counsel under the **Fourteenth Amendment Due Process Clause** was used to support the extension of this ruling to those charged with felonies.

Several legal and social science questions have arisen concerning the right to counsel since the Court's decision in *Gideon v. Wainwright.* The legal ques-

> **Fourteenth Amendment Due Process Clause:**....nor shall any state deprive any person of life, liberty, or property, without due process of law....

> **Arraignment:** Procedure whereby the accused is brought before the court to plead to the criminal charge in the indictment or information. The charge is read to him and he is asked to plead "guilty" or "not guilty" or, where permitted, "nolo contendere." (Black's Law Dictionary).
> **Bail:** The surety or sureties who procure the release of a person under arrest, by becoming responsible for his appearance at the time and place designated. Those persons who become sureties for the appearance of the defendant in court. (Black's Law Dictionary).

tions concern "when" the right to counsel attaches? In other words, at what stage in the process are individuals accused of crimes entitled to a lawyer? Are they entitled to have legal representation upon arrest, custodial interrogations, line-ups, at first appearance, during bail hearings, grand jury hearings, plea-bargaining, sentencing and appeal? Another legal question is whether an accused is entitled to "effective" representation? There has been a great deal of scholarly debate concerning this latter question. Whether indigent clients receive adequate and effective representation as compared to those who can afford to hire a private attorney? Whether there are significant difference in the effectiveness in representation across the type of indigent defense provided— public defender, contract system and assigned counsel system? These latter questions can be and have been addressed using social science.

When does the right to counsel attach?

In a series of cases following *Gideon* and extending through the 1970s, the Court hammered out the parameters of the Sixth Amendment right to counsel. These decisions impact every stage of the criminal justice process from police investigations through the appellate process after conviction. The Court has reasoned, in a wide range of cases, that accused individuals are entitled to counsel at "critical stages" in the criminal justice process. This analysis has its root in a case that pre-dates *Gideon* and involved the state prosecution of an Alabama man for homicide. The Alabama man was entitled to counsel under *Powell v. Alabama*, 287 U.S. 45 (1932)(holding that indigent defendants in state court prosecutions for capital crimes are entitled to legal representation). The question in *Hamilton v. Alabama*, 368 U.S. 52 (1961) was whether an indigent accused is entitled to counsel during his arraignment. An **arraignment** is generally the stage where the accused is informed of the official charges, **bail** may be considered and a plea entered.

In 1961, Alabama law provided that at arraignment:

It is then that the defense of insanity must be pleaded (15 Ala. Code §423), or the opportunity is lost. *Morrell v. State*, 136 Ala. 44, 34 So. 208. Thereafter that plea may not be made except in the discretion of the trial judge, and his refusal to accept it is "not revisable" on appeal. *Rohn v. State*, 186 Ala. 5, 8, 65 So. 42, 43. Cf. *Garrett v. State*, 248 Ala. 612, 614–615, 29 So. 2d 8, 9. Pleas in abatement must also be made at the time of arraignment. 15 Ala. Code §279. It is then that motions to quash based on systematic exclusion of one race from grand juries (*Reeves v. State*, 264 Ala. 476, 88 So. 2d 561), or on the ground that the grand jury was otherwise improperly drawn (*Whitehead v. State*, 206 Ala. 288, 90 So. 351), must be made.

Hamilton v. Alabama, 368 U.S. 52 (1961) Under these circumstances, the United States Supreme Court held that this was a "critical stage in a criminal proceeding," and therefore Hamilton was entitled to counsel at this proceeding. Although the *Hamilton* Court made a fact-specific ruling concerning the arraignment procedures in Alabama, this decision has been cited for the broader proposition that counsel is necessary at arraignments in state court proceedings (Klotter and Kanovitz 1995). This "critical stage" analysis has been used to determine whether counsel is necessary for the preservation of the Sixth Amendment at all stages of the criminal court process. This right to counsel has been held to extend to post-indictment line-ups (*United States v. Wade*, 388 U.S. 218 (1967), preliminary hearings (*Coleman v. Alabama*, 399 U.S. 1 (1970), post-trial proceedings, such as sentencing (*Mempa v. Rhay*, 389 U.S. 128 (1967), and for an indigents first appeal from conviction (*Douglas v. California*, 372 U.S. 353 (1963). Assistance of counsel is provided for anyone charged with an offense (felony, misdemeanor or petty) that may involve some incarceration (*Argersinger v. Hamilton*, 407 U.S. 25 (1972); *Scott v. Illinois*, 440 U.S. 367 (1979). The assistance of counsel has not been deemed a matter of right for all aspects of the legal process. Indigents are not entitled to counsel for any appeals following the first one (*Ross v. Moffitt*, 417 U.S. 600 (1974), defendant's seeking post-conviction relief (*Murray v. Giarrantano*, 492 U.S. 1 (1989), and post-indictment photographic displays for identification of offender (*United States v. Ash*, 413 U.S. 300 (1973). (Spangenberg et al. 1986).

Defendants are entitled to counsel unless they voluntarily waive this right (*Johnson v. Zerbst*, 304 U.S. 458 (1938). The waiver of this right must be an intelligent and informed choice. To be valid, the trial judge must determine that the waiver of counsel was voluntary, knowing and intelligent as determined by the totality of the circumstances. The factors that should be considered by the trial judge in making this decision include the age of the defendant, the experience of the defendant, the defendant's education, background, intelligence and emotional state. In addition, the trial judge must assess whether there has been intimidation, coercion, or deception (*Johnson v. Zerbst*; *Patterson v. Illinois*, 487 U.S. 285 (1988). Specifically, the waiver must reflect an "intentional relinquishment or abandonment of a known right or privilege," "the accused must know what he is doing, so that the choice is made with eyes open," and "the key inquiry regarding the validity of the purported waiver of the Sixth Amendment right to the assistance of counsel is whether the accused has been made sufficiently aware of his right to have counsel present during the pre-indictment questioning" (*Patterson v. Illinois*).

So, Gideon required that indigents accused of crimes had to be represented by counsel... how did states go about doing that?

The decision in *Gideon* was 'legally' profound, however the Court gave no direction to the states as to how to provide this representation to the poor. Several methods of court appointment of counsel for indigent criminal defense are used in the United States. These approaches are not mutually exclusive and in fact, most states (and counties) incorporate more than one method of representation. The three primary types of representation in state court prosecutions are: public defender, contract attorneys and assigned counsel (Bureau of Justice Statistics 1999). In the federal system, there are three types of programs providing indigent defense: public defender organizations, community defender organizations, and panel attorneys (Bureau of Justice Statistics 1999). Public defender systems comprise public and private organizations that hire attorneys on a full- and part-time basis to provide representation to indigent individuals accused of crimes. These lawyers are employed by the government and given a salary with benefits (Neubauer 1999). Contract systems provide representation to indigents through governmental contracts given to law firms expected to provide representation on a yearly basis for a set fee (Neubauer 1999). The federal community defender organizations are similar to the contract systems. Assigned counsel systems provide representation on a case-by-case basis. In other words, private lawyers are appointed by judges to represent individual defendants (Neubauer 1999). Panel attorneys in federal court accept case appointments by judges on a case-by-case basis as well. Essentially, public defender offices are most often found in larger, urban communities; assigned counsel systems are the most prevalent type of indigent defense; and contract counsel systems are most commonly found in smaller, rural areas.

Does counsel have to be effective? How is effectiveness measured? What is the legal standard?

In 1984, the United States Supreme Court held that criminal defendants have a Sixth Amendment right to "reasonably effective" legal assistance (*Strickland v. Washington*, 466 U.S. 668 (1984). The Court announced a two-prong test to determine whether representation exceeds or falls below reasonable effectiveness: "A defendant claiming ineffective assistance of counsel must show (1) that counsel's representation 'fell below an objective standard of reasonableness,' and (2) that counsel's deficient performance prejudiced the defendant" (*Roe v. Flores-Ortega*, 528 U.S. 470 (2000). This is a relatively high burden of proof and the determination is a very fact-specific one. To demonstrate ineffectiveness, defendants must show that there is a reasonable probability that, but for counsel's unprofessional errors, the result of the proceeding would have been different. Courts make these determinations on a case-by-case basis. The United States Supreme Court has found ineffective assistance of counsel when defense counsel fails to file a notice of appeal without the client's consent (*Roe v. Flores-Ortega*, 528 U.S. 470 (2000) and when defense counsel fails to discover and present mitigating evidence during the death penalty phase of a trial (*Williams v. Taylor*, 529 U.S. 362 (2000). The Fifth Circuit Court of Appeal held in *Burdine v. Johnson*, 262 F. 3d 336 (5th Cir. 2001) that a defendant is denied the effective assistance of counsel when counsel repeatedly slept during portions of his trial. The *Burdine* Court found that prejudice to the defendant could be presumed in this circumstance.

Many scholars, however, argue that the burden of proving ineffective counsel is too high, and many indigent defendants are not provided competent representation. This is born out by the lack of reversals on appeal for ineffective assistance of counsel. Of 103 cases of ineffective assistance on appeal in the State of California from 1989 through 1996, the California Supreme Court denied 94 claims, remanded 3 for further factual development and granted six. (Cole 1999). In his book, *No equal justice: race and class in the American criminal justice system*, David Cole summarizes the impossibility of getting a new trial under the *Strickland* standard:

> Courts have declined to find ineffective assistance where defense counsel slept during portions of the trial, where counsel used heroin and cocaine throughout the trial, where counsel allowed his client to wear the same sweatshirt and shoes in court that the perpetrator was

alleged to have worn on the day of the crime, where counsel stated prior to trial that he was not prepared on the law or facts of the case, and where counsel appointed in a capital case could not name a single Supreme Court decision on the death penalty. (Cole 1999: 78–9).

I don't want a public defender...I want a "real" lawyer. Are there differences in the quality of representation by court appointed and private counsels?

A recent note in the prestigious Harvard Law Review (2000) is critical of the state of indigent defense in the United States. Citing to several studies,[1] the note suggests "there is broad consensus that criminal defense systems are in "a state of perpetual crisis." Specifically, it is argued that:

> The evidence is unambiguous and telling. Lawyers representing indigent defendants often have unmanageable caseloads that frequently run into the hundreds, far exceeding professional guidelines. These same lawyers typically receive compensation at the lowest end of the professional pay scale. Stories of intoxicated, sleeping, and otherwise incompetent public defenders are legion, such that it has become trite to lament the sometimes shockingly incompetent quality of indigent defense counsel in America today.

The adequacy of the legal representation of indigent criminal defendants affects a large number of individuals. The Bureau of Justice Statistics (BJS) study (1999) of the nation's 75 most populous counties reported that 66% of felony defendants in 1998 and 82% in 1996 had publicly financed defense attorneys. By race/ethnicity, 69% of white, 77% of black and 73% of Hispanic state prison inmates had publicly financed attorneys. In this study, BJS compared conviction rates and sentence length by privately or publicly funded criminal defense. Conviction rates were essentially the same for indigent and privately retained defense counsel in both State and Federal courts—90% of

---

1. Stephen J. Schulhofer and David D. Friedman (1993), Rethinking indigent defense: Promoting effective representation through consumer sovereignty and freedom of choice for all criminal defendants, *Am. Crim. L. Rev.* 31, 96–122 (1993) (advocating free-market reforms to the provision of indigent defense counsel), and Frank H. Easterbrook, Plea bargaining as compromise, *Yale Law Journal* 101: 1969, 1974 (1992) (advocating fee awards for defendants who prevail in criminal cases as a means of attracting more highly qualified counsel).

federal defendants and 75% of state defendants (in the most populous counties) were found guilty.

However, guilty defendants represented by publicly financed attorneys were more likely to be incarcerated than defendants who hired private attorneys. Eighty-eight percent of indigent defendants were incarcerated compared to 77% of those with private counsel in Federal courts and 71% of indigent defendants compared to 54% of defendants with private counsel in the most populous counties in state courts were incarcerated. This same study found that defendants with publicly financed attorneys went to jail or prison for shorter periods of time than those with private representation. On average, in Federal court those with publicly financed attorneys received sentences of less than five years whereas those with private lawyers were sentenced to just over five years. In state court, indigent defendants received sentences on average of 2 1/2 years compared to defendants with private counsel who received on average 3 years.

Several weaknesses plague the statistics reported in the BJS study. The simple comparison between outcomes is insufficient to assess differences in the quality of representation. It is important in assessing the adequacy of counsel to identify how "effectiveness" is being measured. In other words, what is being compared to examine whether defendants are getting effective representation? The BJS study simply looked at three possible outcomes—conviction rates, incarceration rates and sentence length. Moreover, a variety of factors—in which type of legal representation is only one—may affect the outcome of a case. This study did not examine the influence of strength of evidence, seriousness of crime, and availability of witnesses on conviction rates. Similarly, the BJS study did not control for several important factors that influence incarceration and sentence. For example, the study failed to examine the seriousness of the crime, the number of crimes charged, prior histories of criminal convictions, as well as other mitigating and aggravating circumstances.

In a seminal article examining the role of the criminal defense attorney, Abraham Blumberg discussed the difference between the social expectations and beliefs about how the criminal defense attorney operates and social reality. He found the expectation and representations of criminal defense lawyers on television are inconsistent with reality. The expectation that criminal defense attorneys are bull dogs who zealously advocate for criminal defendants in a harsh, adversarial setting is inconsistent with the realities of everyday life in the courthouse. In fact, as found by Blumberg (and subsequent others), few cases are resolved at trial, most defendants enter into plea bargains with the prosecutor. Defense lawyers are members of a courtroom workgroup.

Courtroom workgroups essentially comprise the judge, prosecutor and defense lawyers. The group works together, not as adversaries but operate on the basis of shared norms. In a critique of the role of criminal defense lawyers, Rodney Uphoff suggests that the effectiveness as well as the zealousness of criminal defense attorneys varied by jurisdiction. The organizational structure of the criminal defense system influenced behavior. Delay in the appointment of counsel, organizational pressure to plea bargain, availability of resources for indigent defense, and caseload pressure were influential in determining the effectiveness of criminal defense representation. Uphoff suggests improving the delivery of indigent defense services is the best way to improve overall quality of criminal representation by a justice system. In one study comparing the three indigent defense systems, Worden (1991) found that each has merit and vary in effectiveness based upon the individual needs of the communities. For example, she found that full-time public defender's offices are ill-suited for sparsely populated and isolated rural counties (1991: 413).

Several studies have examined the role of the criminal defense lawyer or compared the adequacy of representation between privately retained counsel and the various types of indigent defense using more sophisticated analyses.[2] In an examination of the role of criminal defense and plea-bargaining, Dean Champion (1989) noted the high rate at which cases are disposed of by plea rather than by trial. In plea bargaining, Champion found that prosecutors were more likely to drop criminal charges when defendants were represented by private attorneys as opposed to publicly funded attorneys. Punishments or sentence were more harsh and fewer cases went to jury trial for defendants with publicly-funded attorneys. In a study comparing retained and appointed counsel in death penalty cases, Beck and Shumsky (1997) found that defendants with appointed counsel were more likely to get the death penalty than

---

2. Blumberg, Abraham (1967). The practice of law as a confidence game: Organizational Co-Optation of a Profession. *Law and Society Review* 15: 28–31; Hanson, Roger A. and Brian J. Ostrom (1992). *Indigent Defenders Get the Job Done and Done Well*. Williamsburg, VA: National Center for State Courts; Champion, Dean (1989). Private Counsels and Public Defenders: A Look at Weak Cases, Prior Records and Leniency in Plea Bargaining. *Journal of Criminal Justice* 17: 253–263; Worden, Alissa Pollitz (1991). Privatizing Due Process: Issues in the Comparison of Assigned Counsel, Public Defender, and Contracted Indigent Defense Systems. *The Justice System Journal* 14: 390–418; Uphoff, Rodney J. (1992). The Criminal Defense Lawyer: Zealous Advocate, Double Agent, or Beleaguered Dealer? *Criminal Law Bulletin* 28: 419–456; Beck, James C. and Robert Shumsky (1997). A Comparison of Retained and Appointed Counsel in Cases of Capital Murder. *Law and Human Behavior* 21: 525–538.

those with privately retained counsel. Contrary to Beck and Shumsky, Hanson, Ostrom, Hewitt et al. (1992) found, in looking at felony dispositions, that indigent defenders were generally as successful as privately retained counsel. Success was defined on the basis of conviction rates, charge reductions, and incarceration rates. On each of these comparisons, indigent defense counsels did as well as privately retained lawyers. These findings were consistent across the three types of indigent representation as well.

According to Champion, one explanation for these differences may concern the defendants, as opposed to who is representing them. Champion notes that much research suggests that the system discriminates against those of lower socio-economic status, thus their inability to afford private counsel may affect the outcome of their cases. David Cole in his assessment of the entire system suggested that race also plays a significant role in this discriminatory effect. However and contrary to these assertions, Beck and Shumsky found that "the system was, and is, working to the detriment of many convicted murderers independent of the character and record of the defendant and of the circumstances of the crime." Beck and Shumsky urge more research be conducted on the influence of hiring a private attorney versus appointed counsel on variations in punishment, particularly the death penalty.

This chapter includes an excerpt from the case of *Strickland v. Washington* and the Bureau of Justice Statistics article entitled *Defense Counsel in Criminal Cases*, 2000.

Strickland v. Washington,
466 U.S. 668 (1984)(Excerpt)

OPINION BY: O'CONNOR

This case requires us to consider the proper standards for judging a criminal defendant's contention that the Constitution requires a conviction or death sentence to be set aside because counsel's assistance at the trial or sentencing was ineffective.

During a 10-day period in September 1976, respondent planned and committed three groups of crimes, which included three brutal stabbing murders, torture, kidnaping, severe assaults, attempted murders, attempted extortion, and theft. After his two accomplices were arrested, respondent surrendered to police and voluntarily gave a lengthy statement confessing to the third of the criminal episodes. The State of Florida indicted respondent for kidnaping and murder and appointed an experienced criminal lawyer to represent him.

Counsel actively pursued pretrial motions and discovery. He cut his efforts short, however, and he experienced a sense of hopelessness about the case, when he learned that, against his specific advice, respondent had also confessed to the first two murders. By the date set for trial, respondent was subject to indictment for three counts of first-degree murder and multiple counts of robbery, kidnaping for ransom, breaking and entering and assault, attempted murder, and conspiracy to commit robbery. Respondent waived his right to a jury trial, again acting against counsel's advice, and pleaded guilty to all charges, including the three capital murder charges.

In the plea colloquy, respondent told the trial judge that, although he had committed a string of burglaries, he had no significant prior criminal record and that at the time of his criminal spree he was under extreme stress caused by his inability to support his family. App. 50–53. He also stated, however, that he accepted responsibility for the crimes. E. g., id., at 54, 57. The trial judge told respondent that he had "a great deal of respect for people who are willing to step forward and admit their responsibility" but that he was making no statement at all about his likely sentencing decision. Id., at 62.

Counsel advised respondent to invoke his right under Florida law to an advisory jury at his capital sentencing hearing. Respondent rejected the advice and waived the right. He chose instead to be sentenced by the trial judge without a jury recommendation.

In preparing for the sentencing hearing, counsel spoke with respondent about his background. He also spoke on the telephone with respondent's wife and mother, though he did not follow up on the one unsuccessful effort to meet with them. He did not otherwise seek out character witnesses for respondent. App. to Pet. for Cert. A265. Nor did he request a psychiatric examination, since his conversations with his client gave no indication that respondent had psychological problems. Id., at A266.

Counsel decided not to present and hence not to look further for evidence concerning respondent's character and emotional state....Counsel also excluded from the sentencing hearing other evidence he thought was potentially damaging. He successfully moved to exclude respondent's "rap sheet." Id., at A227; App. 311. Because he judged that a presentence report might prove more detrimental than helpful, as it would have included respondent's criminal history and thereby would have undermined the claim of no significant history of criminal activity, he did not request that one be prepared. App. to Pet. for Cert. A227–A228, A265–A266.

At the sentencing hearing, counsel's strategy was based primarily on the trial judge's remarks at the plea colloquy as well as on his reputation as a sentencing judge who thought it important for a convicted defendant to own up to his crime. Counsel argued that respondent's remorse and acceptance of responsibility justified sparing him from the death penalty. *Id.*, at A265–A266. Counsel also argued that respondent had no history of criminal activity and that respondent committed the crimes under extreme mental or emotional disturbance, thus coming within the statutory list of mitigating circumstances. He further argued that respondent should be spared death because he had surrendered, confessed, and offered to testify against a codefendant and because respondent was fundamentally a good person who had briefly gone badly wrong in extremely stressful circumstances. The State put on evidence and witnesses largely for the purpose of describing the details of the crimes. Counsel did not cross-examine the medical experts who testified about the manner of death of respondent's victims....

In short, the trial judge found numerous aggravating circumstances and no (or a single comparatively insignificant) mitigating circumstance. With respect to each of the three convictions for capital murder, the trial judge concluded: "A careful consideration of all matters presented to the court impels the conclusion that there are insufficient mitigating circumstances...to outweigh the aggravating circumstances." See *Washington* v. *State*, 362 So. 2d 658, 663–664 (Fla. 1978) (quoting trial court findings), cert. denied, 441 U.S. 937 (1979). He therefore sentenced respondent to death on each of the three counts of murder and to prison terms for the other crimes. The Florida Supreme Court upheld the convictions and sentences on direct appeal.....

[W]e granted certiorari to consider the standards by which to judge a contention that the Constitution requires that a criminal judgment be overturned because of the actual ineffective assistance of counsel. 462 U.S. 1105 (1983)....

In a long line of cases that includes *Powell* v. *Alabama*, 287 U.S. 45 (1932), *Johnson* v. *Zerbst*, 304 U.S. 458 (1938), and *Gideon* v. *Wainwright*, 372 U.S. 335 (1963), this Court has recognized that the Sixth Amendment right to counsel exists, and is needed, in order to protect the fundamental right to a fair trial.... [A] fair trial is one in which evidence subject to adversarial testing is presented to an impartial tribunal for resolution of issues defined in advance of the proceeding. The right to counsel plays a crucial role in the adversarial system embodied in the Sixth Amendment, since access to counsel's skill and knowledge is necessary to accord defendants the "ample opportunity to meet the case of the prosecution" to which they are entitled. *Adams* v. *United States ex rel. McCann*, 317 U.S. 269, 275, 276 (1942); see *Powell* v. *Alabama, supra*, at 68–69....

A convicted defendant's claim that counsel's assistance was so defective as to require reversal of a conviction or death sentence has two components.

First, the defendant must show that counsel's performance was deficient. This requires showing that counsel made errors so serious that counsel was not functioning as the "counsel" guaranteed the defendant by the Sixth Amendment. Second, the defendant must show that the deficient performance prejudiced the defense. This requires showing that counsel's errors were so serious as to deprive the defendant of a fair trial, a trial whose result is reliable. Unless a defendant makes both showings, it cannot be said that the conviction or death sentence resulted from a breakdown in the adversary process that renders the result unreliable.... When a convicted defendant complains of the ineffectiveness of counsel's assistance, the defendant must show that counsel's representation fell below an objective standard of reasonableness.

More specific guidelines are not appropriate. The Sixth Amendment refers simply to "counsel," not specifying particular requirements of effective assistance. It relies instead on the legal profession's maintenance of standards sufficient to justify the law's presumption that counsel will fulfill the role in the adversary process that the Amendment envisions. See *Michel v. Louisiana*, 350 U.S. 91, 100–101 (1955). The proper measure of attorney performance remains simply reasonableness under prevailing professional norms.

Representation of a criminal defendant entails certain basic duties. Counsel's function is to assist the defendant, and hence counsel owes the client a duty of loyalty, a duty to avoid conflicts of interest. See *Cuyler v. Sullivan, supra*, at 346. From counsel's function as assistant to the defendant derive the overarching duty to advocate the defendant's cause and the more particular duties to consult with the defendant on important decisions and to keep the defendant informed of important developments in the course of the prosecution. Counsel also has a duty to bring to bear such skill and knowledge as will render the trial a reliable adversarial testing process. See *Powell v. Alabama*, 287 U.S., at 68–69.

These basic duties neither exhaustively define the obligations of counsel nor form a checklist for judicial evaluation of attorney performance. In any case presenting an ineffectiveness claim, the performance inquiry must be whether counsel's assistance was reasonable considering all the circumstances. Prevailing norms of practice as reflected in American Bar Association standards and the like, *e. g.*, ABA Standards for Criminal Justice 4–1.1 to 4–8.6 (2d ed. 1980) ("The Defense Function"), are guides to determining what is reasonable, but they are only guides. No particular set of detailed rules for counsel's conduct can satisfactorily take account of the variety of circumstances faced by defense counsel or the range of legitimate decisions regarding how best to represent a criminal defendant. Any such set of rules would interfere with the

constitutionally protected independence of counsel and restrict the wide latitude counsel must have in making tactical decisions. See *United States* v. *Decoster,* 199 U. S. App. D. C., at 371, 624 F.2d, at 208. Indeed, the existence of
detailed guidelines for representation could distract counsel from the over-
riding mission of vigorous advocacy of the defendant's cause. Moreover, the
purpose of the effective assistance guarantee of the Sixth Amendment is not
to improve the quality of legal representation, although that is a goal of considerable importance to the legal system. The purpose is simply to ensure that
criminal defendants receive a fair trial.

Judicial scrutiny of counsel's performance must be highly deferential. It is all
too tempting for a defendant to second-guess counsel's assistance after conviction or adverse sentence, and it is all too easy for a court, examining counsel's
defense after it has proved unsuccessful, to conclude that a particular act or omission of counsel was unreasonable. Cf. *Engle* v. *Isaac,* 456 U.S. 107, 133–134
(1982). A fair assessment of attorney performance requires that every effort be
made to eliminate the distorting effects of hindsight, to reconstruct the circumstances of counsel's challenged conduct, and to evaluate the conduct from counsel's perspective at the time. Because of the difficulties inherent in making the
evaluation, a court must indulge a strong presumption that counsel's conduct
falls within the wide range of reasonable professional assistance; that is, the defendant must overcome the presumption that, under the circumstances, the challenged action "might be considered sound trial strategy." See *Michel* v. *Louisiana,*
supra, at 101. There are countless ways to provide effective assistance in any given
case. Even the best criminal defense attorneys would not defend a particular
client in the same way. See Goodpaster, The Trial for Life: Effective Assistance of
Counsel in Death Penalty Cases, 58 *N. Y. U. L. Rev.* 299, 343 (1983).

The availability of intrusive post-trial inquiry into attorney performance or
of detailed guidelines for its evaluation would encourage the proliferation of
ineffectiveness challenges. Criminal trials resolved unfavorably to the defendant would increasingly come to be followed by a second trial, this one of
counsel's unsuccessful defense. Counsel's performance and even willingness
to serve could be adversely affected. Intensive scrutiny of counsel and rigid requirements for acceptable assistance could dampen the ardor and impair the
independence of defense counsel, discourage the acceptance of assigned cases,
and undermine the trust between attorney and client.

Thus, a court deciding an actual ineffectiveness claim must judge the reasonableness of counsel's challenged conduct on the facts of the particular case,
viewed as of the time of counsel's conduct. A convicted defendant making a
claim of ineffective assistance must identify the acts or omissions of counsel

that are alleged not to have been the result of reasonable professional judgment. The court must then determine whether, in light of all the circumstances, the identified acts or omissions were outside the wide range of professionally competent assistance. In making that determination, the court should keep in mind that counsel's function, as elaborated in prevailing professional norms, is to make the adversarial testing process work in the particular case. At the same time, the court should recognize that counsel is strongly presumed to have rendered adequate assistance and made all significant decisions in the exercise of reasonable professional judgment.

These standards require no special amplification in order to define counsel's duty to investigate, the duty at issue in this case. As the Court of Appeals concluded, strategic choices made after thorough investigation of law and facts relevant to plausible options are virtually unchallengeable; and strategic choices made after less than complete investigation are reasonable precisely to the extent that reasonable professional judgments support the limitations on investigation. In other words, counsel has a duty to make reasonable investigations or to make a reasonable decision that makes particular investigations unnecessary. In any ineffectiveness case, a particular decision not to investigate must be directly assessed for reasonableness in all the circumstances, applying a heavy measure of deference to counsel's judgments.

The reasonableness of counsel's actions may be determined or substantially influenced by the defendant's own statements or actions. Counsel's actions are usually based, quite properly, on informed strategic choices made by the defendant and on information supplied by the defendant. In particular, what investigation decisions are reasonable depends critically on such information. For example, when the facts that support a certain potential line of defense are generally known to counsel because of what the defendant has said, the need for further investigation may be considerably diminished or eliminated altogether. And when a defendant has given counsel reason to believe that pursuing certain investigations would be fruitless or even harmful, counsel's failure to pursue those investigations may not later be challenged as unreasonable. In short, inquiry into counsel's conversations with the defendant may be critical to a proper assessment of counsel's investigation decisions, just as it may be critical to a proper assessment of counsel's other litigation decisions. See *United States* v. *Decoster, supra*, at 372–373, 624 F.2d, at 209–210.

An error by counsel, even if professionally unreasonable, does not warrant setting aside the judgment of a criminal proceeding if the error had no effect on the judgment. Cf. *United States* v. *Morrison*, 449 U.S. 361, 364–365 (1981). The purpose of the Sixth Amendment guarantee of counsel is to ensure that a defendant has the assistance necessary to justify reliance on the outcome of the proceeding. Accordingly, any deficiencies in counsel's performance must be prejudicial to the defense in order to constitute ineffective assistance under the Constitution.

In certain Sixth Amendment contexts, prejudice is presumed. Actual or constructive denial of the assistance of counsel altogether is legally presumed to result in prejudice. So are various kinds of state interference with counsel's assistance. See *United States* v. *Cronic, ante,* at 659, and n. 25. Prejudice in these circumstances is so likely that case-by-case inquiry into prejudice is not worth the cost. *Ante,* at 658. Moreover, such circumstances involve impairments of the Sixth Amendment right that are easy to identify and, for that reason and because the prosecution is directly responsible, easy for the government to prevent.

One type of actual ineffectiveness claim warrants a similar, though more limited, presumption of prejudice. In *Cuyler* v. *Sullivan,* 446 U.S., at 345–350, the Court held that prejudice is presumed when counsel is burdened by an actual conflict of interest. In those circumstances, counsel breaches the duty of loyalty, perhaps the most basic of counsel's duties. Moreover, it is difficult to measure the precise effect on the defense of representation corrupted by conflicting interests. Given the obligation of counsel to avoid conflicts of interest and the ability of trial courts to make early inquiry in certain situations likely to give rise to conflicts, see, *e. g.,* Fed. Rule Crim. Proc. 44(c), it is reasonable for the criminal justice system to maintain a fairly rigid rule of presumed prejudice for conflicts of interest. Even so, the rule is not quite the *per se* rule of prejudice that exists for the Sixth Amendment claims mentioned above. Prejudice is presumed only if the defendant demonstrates that counsel "actively represented conflicting interests" and that "an actual conflict of interest adversely affected his lawyer's performance." *Cuyler* v. *Sullivan, supra,* at 350, 348 (footnote omitted).

Conflict of interest claims aside, actual ineffectiveness claims alleging a deficiency in attorney performance are subject to a general requirement that the defendant affirmatively prove prejudice. The government is not responsible for, and hence not able to prevent, attorney errors that will result in reversal of a conviction or sentence. Attorney errors come in an infinite variety and are as likely to be utterly harmless in a particular case as they are to be prejudicial. They cannot be classified according to likelihood of causing prejudice. Nor can they be defined with sufficient precision to inform defense attorneys correctly just what conduct to avoid. Representation is an art, and an act or omission that is unprofessional in one case may be sound or even brilliant in another. Even if a defendant shows that particular errors of counsel were unreasonable, therefore, the defendant must show that they actually had an adverse effect on the defense.

It is not enough for the defendant to show that the errors had some conceivable effect on the outcome of the proceeding. Virtually every act or omission of counsel would meet that test, cf. *United States* v. *Valenzuela-Bernal*, 458 U.S. 858, 866–867 (1982), and not every error that conceivably could have influenced the outcome undermines the reliability of the result of the proceeding. Respondent suggests requiring a showing that the errors "impaired the presentation of the defense." Brief for Respondent 58. That standard, however, provides no workable principle. Since any error, if it is indeed an error, "impairs" the presentation of the defense, the proposed standard is inadequate because it provides no way of deciding what impairments are sufficiently serious to warrant setting aside the outcome of the proceeding.

On the other hand, we believe that a defendant need not show that counsel's deficient conduct more likely than not altered the outcome in the case. This outcome-determinative standard has several strengths. It defines the relevant inquiry in a way familiar to courts, though the inquiry, as is inevitable, is anything but precise. The standard also reflects the profound importance of finality in criminal proceedings. Moreover, it comports with the widely used standard for assessing motions for new trial based on newly discovered evidence. See Brief for United States as *Amicus Curiae* 19–20, and nn. 10, 11. Nevertheless, the standard is not quite appropriate.

Even when the specified attorney error results in the omission of certain evidence, the newly discovered evidence standard is not an apt source from which to draw a prejudice standard for ineffectiveness claims. The high standard for newly discovered evidence claims presupposes that all the essential elements of a presumptively accurate and fair proceeding were present in the proceeding whose result is challenged. Cf. *United States* v. *Johnson*, 327 U.S. 106, 112 (1946). An ineffective assistance claim asserts the absence of one of the crucial assurances that the result of the proceeding is reliable, so finality concerns are somewhat weaker and the appropriate standard of prejudice should be somewhat lower. The result of a proceeding can be rendered unreliable, and hence the proceeding itself unfair, even if the errors of counsel cannot be shown by a preponderance of the evidence to have determined the outcome.

Accordingly, the appropriate test for prejudice finds its roots in the test for materiality of exculpatory information not disclosed to the defense by the prosecution, *United States* v. *Agurs*, 427 U.S., at 104, 112–113, and in the test for materiality of testimony made unavailable to the defense by Government deportation of a witness, *United States* v. *Valenzuela-Bernal, supra*, at 872–874. The defendant must show that there is a reasonable probability that, but for counsel's unprofessional errors, the result of the proceeding would have been different. A reasonable probability is a probability sufficient to undermine confidence in the outcome.

In making the determination whether the specified errors resulted in the required prejudice, a court should presume, absent challenge to the judgment on grounds of evidentiary insufficiency, that the judge or jury acted according to law. An assessment of the likelihood of a result more favorable to the defendant must exclude the possibility of arbitrariness, whimsy, caprice, "nullification," and the like. A defendant has no entitlement to the luck of a lawless decision-maker, even if a lawless decision cannot be reviewed. The assessment of prejudice should proceed on the assumption that the decision-maker is reasonably, conscientiously, and impartially applying the standards that govern the decision. It should not depend on the idiosyncracies of the particular decision-maker, such as unusual propensities toward harshness or leniency. Although these factors may actually have entered into counsel's selection of strategies and, to that limited extent, may thus affect the performance inquiry, they are irrelevant to the prejudice inquiry. Thus, evidence about the actual process of decision, if not part of the record of the proceeding under review, and evidence about, for example, a particular judge's sentencing practices, should not be considered in the prejudice determination.

The governing legal standard plays a critical role in defining the question to be asked in assessing the prejudice from counsel's errors. When a defendant challenges a conviction, the question is whether there is a reasonable probability that, absent the errors, the fact-finder would have had a reasonable doubt respecting guilt. When a defendant challenges a death sentence such as the one at issue in this case, the question is whether there is a reasonable probability that, absent the errors, the sentencer—including an appellate court, to the extent it independently reweighs the evidence—would have concluded that the balance of aggravating and mitigating circumstances did not warrant death.

In making this determination, a court hearing an ineffectiveness claim must consider the totality of the evidence before the judge or jury. Some of the factual findings will have been unaffected by the errors, and factual findings that were affected will have been affected in different ways. Some errors will have had a pervasive effect on the inferences to be drawn from the evidence, altering the entire evidentiary picture, and some will have had an isolated, trivial effect. Moreover, a verdict or conclusion only weakly supported by the record is more likely to have been affected by errors than one with overwhelming record support. Taking the unaffected findings as a given, and taking due account of the effect of the errors on the remaining findings, a court making the prejudice inquiry must ask if the defendant has met the burden of showing that the decision reached would reasonably likely have been different absent the errors....

Having articulated general standards for judging ineffectiveness claims, we think it useful to apply those standards to the facts of this case in order to illustrate the meaning of the general principles.....Application of the governing principles is not difficult in this case. The facts as described above, see *supra*, at 671–678, make clear that the conduct of respondent's counsel at and before respondent's sentencing proceeding cannot be found unreasonable. They also make clear that, even assuming the challenged conduct of counsel was unreasonable, respondent suffered insufficient prejudice to warrant setting aside his death sentence.

With respect to the performance component, the record shows that respondent's counsel made a strategic choice to argue for the extreme emotional distress mitigating circumstance and to rely as fully as possible on respondent's acceptance of responsibility for his crimes....Counsel's strategy choice was well within the range of professionally reasonable judgments, and the decision not to seek more character or psychological evidence than was already in hand was likewise reasonable.

The trial judge's views on the importance of owning up to one's crimes were well known to counsel. The aggravating circumstances were utterly overwhelming. Trial counsel could reasonably surmise from his conversations with respondent that character and psychological evidence would be of little help. Respondent had already been able to mention at the plea colloquy the substance of what there was to know about his financial and emotional troubles. Restricting testimony on respondent's character to what had come in at the plea colloquy ensured that contrary character and psychological evidence and respondent's criminal history, which counsel had successfully moved to exclude, would not come in. On these facts, there can be little question, even without application of the presumption of adequate performance, that trial counsel's defense, though unsuccessful, was the result of reasonable professional judgment.

With respect to the prejudice component, the lack of merit of respondent's claim is even more stark. The evidence that respondent says his trial counsel should have offered at the sentencing hearing would barely have altered the sentencing profile presented to the sentencing judge....Given the overwhelming aggravating factors, there is no reasonable probability that the omitted evidence would have changed the conclusion that the aggravating circumstances outweighed the mitigating circumstances and, hence, the sentence imposed.... We conclude, therefore, that the District Court properly declined to issue a writ of habeas corpus. The judgment of the Court of Appeals is accordingly *Reversed.*

C.W. Harlow, *Defense Counsel in Criminal Cases.*
Washington DC: United States Justice Department (Excerpt)(2000)[3]

Highlights

At felony case termination, court-appointed counsel represented 82% of State defendants in the 75 largest counties in 1996 and 66% of Federal defendants in 1998.

Defendants with publicly financed or private attorneys had the same conviction rates.

Almost all persons charged with a felony in Federal and large State courts were represented by counsel, either hired or appointed. But over a third of persons charged with a misdemeanor in cases terminated in Federal court represented themselves (pro se) in court proceedings prior to conviction, as did almost a third of those in local jails. Indigent defense involves the use of publicly financed counsel to represent criminal defendants who are unable to afford private counsel. At the end of their case approximately 66% of felony Federal defendants and 82% of felony defendants in large State courts were represented by public defenders or assigned counsel.

In both Federal and large State courts, conviction rates were the same for defendants represented by publicly financed and private attorneys. Approximately 9 in 10 Federal defendants and 3 in 4 State defendants in the 75 largest counties were found guilty, regardless of type of attorney. However, of those found guilty, higher percentages of defendants with publicly financed counsel were sentenced to incarceration. Of defendants found guilty in Federal district courts, 88% with publicly financed counsel and 77% with private coun-

---

3. The tables and graphics found in this report are not included here. Some footnotes and text have also been omitted. The complete report may be viewed on line at http://www.ojp.usdoj.gov/bjs/. Also, bolding was added to the report to differentiate topics that were not in the original text-version of the reports.

| | Percent of defendants | |
	Felons	Misdemeanants
75 largest counties		
Public defender	68.3%	—
Assigned counsel	13.7	—
Private attorney	17.6	—
Self (pro se)/other	0.4	—
U.S. district courts		
Federal Defender Organization	30.1%	25.5%
Panel attorney	36.3	17.4
Private attorney	33.4	18.7
Self representation	0.3	38.4

Note: These data reflect use of defense counsel at termination of the case.

—Not available.

* Over 80% of felony defendants charged with a violent crime in the country's largest counties and 66% in U.S. district courts had publicly financed attorneys.

* About half of large county felony defendants with a public defender or assigned counsel and three-quarters with a private lawyer were released from jail pending trial.

sel received jail or prison sentences; in large State courts 71% with public counsel and 54% with private counsel received jail or prison sentences.....

In this report the type of counsel for Federal and State defendants was the type at case termination. Other counsel may have represented the defendant earlier. Data describing counsel at filing or initiation were not used because they were incomplete or unavailable. The terms "publicly financed attorneys," "public attorney," and "appointed attorney" used in this report include public defenders, panel attorneys, assigned counsel, contract attorneys, and any other government-funded attorney programs for those unable to provide their own attorney....

Two types of programs provide indigent representation in Federal cases

Pursuant to the Criminal Justice Act of 1964 (18 USC 3006 A), the Defender Services Division of the Administrative Office of the U.S. Courts oversees spending for Federal defendants through two types of programs:

* Panel attorneys, appointed by the court from a list of private attorneys on a case-by-case basis. At the end of 1998 all 94 U.S. district courts used such panels, including 20 districts in which only panel attorneys were used.

Case disposition	Public counsel	Private counsel
75 largest counties		
Guilty by plea	71.0%	72.8%
Guilty by trial	4.4	4.3
Case dismissal	23.0	21.2
Acquittal	1.3	1.6
U.S. district courts		
Guilty by plea	87.1%	84.6%
Guilty by trial	5.2	6.4
Case dismissal	6.7	7.4
Acquittal	1.0	1.6

* In State courts in the largest counties, 3 in 4 defendants with either court-appointed or private counsel were convicted; in Federal courts 9 in 10 felony defendants with public or private attorneys were found guilty.

* In Federal court 88% of felony defendants with publicly financed attorneys and 77% with private lawyers received a prison sentence. Except for State drug offenders, Federal and State inmates received about the same sentence on average with appointed or private legal counsel.

* Federal defender organizations (FDO's), take one of two forms:—Federal public defender organizations staffed with Federal Government employees and headed by a public defender appointed by the court of appeals

or

—Community defender organizations that are incorporated, nonprofit legal service organizations receiving grants from the Administrative Office of

	State prison inmates		Federal prison inmates	
	Public counsel	Private counsel	Public counsel	Private counsel
Offenses				
Total	155 mo	179 mo	126 mo	126 mo
Violent	223	231	164	162
Property	118	128	59	59
Drug	97	140	126	132

* Three-fourths of State and Federal inmates with an appointed counsel and two-thirds with a hired counsel had pleaded guilty.

the U.S. Courts.At the end of 1998, 63 Federal or community defender or-ganizations served 74 of the 94 U.S. district courts.

Workloads rose more than spending for the Defender Services Division

The panel attorney and FDO programs can represent defendants at any time from arraignment through appeal and during supervised release. The Defender Services Division counts use of these publicly financed attorneys in terms of representations.

Total representations by panel attorneys and FDO's rose 26% from 80,200 in fiscal year 1994 to 101,200 in fiscal 1998. The number of criminal repre-sentations grew substantially during the period (25%), with the FDO work-load increasing 35% and the panel attorney workload 17%. The Defender Ser-vices Division estimates that court-appointed counsel represent 85% of criminal defendants at some time during the conduct of their case (unpub-lished correspondence).

From fiscal year 1994 through fiscal year 1998, spending grew 20% in con-stant 1998 dollars from $293 million to $353 million. Criminal Justice Act ob-ligations, 1994–98 (in 1998 dollars):

1994	$293,342,000
1995	$296,794,000
1996	$316,884,000
1997	$338,028,000
1998	$352,837,000

Note: An obligation is generally defined as a legal commitment for goods or services ordered or received by the government. Source: Un-published data, Administrative Office of the U.S. Courts, Defender Ser-vices Division.

All felony defendants in cases terminated in U.S. district court had an attorney in 1998

Nearly all defendants facing a felony charge terminated in U.S. district court in 1998 and almost two-thirds with a misdemeanor charge had lawyers to rep-resent them in court. Felony defendants were more likely than misdemeanants to have publicly financed counsel. Sixty-six percent of those facing a felony charge and 43% with a misdemeanor charge had used either a FDO or panel attorney. Defendants charged with a felony (33%) were also more likely than those charged with a misdemeanor (19%) to have private representation. About a third of misdemeanants represented themselves during judicial proceedings.

	Type of counsel	
Disposition	Public*	Private
Guilty by plea	87.1%	84.6 %
By trial	5.2	6.4
Acquittal	1.0	1.6
Dismissal	6.7	7.4
Number of defendants	37,188	18,709

* Includes Federal Defender Organizations (FDO's) and panel attorneys.
Source: Administrative Office of the U.S. Courts, Criminal Master File, FY 1998.

White collar Federal defendants most likely to use private counsel.

Most likely to have a private attorney were defendants charged with a white collar offense, primarily fraud or a regulatory offense. Having private counsel were 43% of fraud defendants and 63% of those charged with a regulatory offense—violations of laws pertaining to agriculture, antitrust, food and drug, transportation, civil rights, communications, customs, and postal delivery. By contrast, about 2 in 10 defendants charged with a violent crime used private attorneys.

9 in 10 Federal defendants found guilty regardless of type of attorney

In 1998, 92% of defendants with public counsel and 91% with private counsel either pleaded guilty or were found guilty at trial.

Incarceration more likely for Federal defendants with public counsel than for those with private attorneys

Defendants found guilty after using a FDO or panel attorney were more likely to be sentenced to prison (about 88% of defendants found guilty) than

	Type of counsel	
Sentence	Public*	Private
Incarceration	87.6%	76.5%
Probation only	12.1	22.4
Fine only	0.3	1.1
Number of defendants	33,068	16,622

*Includes Federal Defender Organization (FDO's) and panel attorneys.
Source: Administrative Office of the U.S. Courts, Criminal Master File, FY 1998.

those with private attorneys (77%). The difference in incarceration rates is explained in part by the likelihood of prison after conviction for different types of offenses. As has been shown, public counsel represented a higher percentage of violent, drug, and public-order (excluding regulatory crimes) offenders, who were very likely to receive a sentence to serve time, and private counsel represented a higher percentage of white collar defendants, who are not as likely to receive incarceration sentences.

Federal defendants with private attorneys had longer average sentences than defendants with publicly financed attorneys

Defendants with private attorneys were sentenced to an average of 62 months in prison, and those with publicly financed attorneys, to 58 months. The primary differences in average sentence length were between offenses, not between the types of attorney. Other factors not shown may also have had a role. Among those sentenced to incarceration, drug offenders who used publicly financed counsel had shorter sentences on average than those who used private attorneys—an average of 75 months compared to 84 months.

Among Federal violent and regulatory offenders, those with private attorneys received shorter sentences than those with public lawyers. Violent offenders who used private attorneys were given 74 months on average, and those with public counsel, 84 months. Similarly, those sentenced for a regulatory offense with a private lawyer had an average sentence of 23 months, and those with a public attorney, 33 months.

Most criminal defendants are tried in State courts

The bulk of the task of providing counsel for the indigent has fallen to lawyers working in State courts. Approximately 95% of criminal defendants are charged in State courts, with the remainder tried in Federal courts.

Two-thirds of State prosecutors reported that their courts used public defenders

Three systems now serve as the primary means for providing defense services to indigent criminal defendants charged in State court.

* Under a public defender system, salaried staff attorneys render criminal indigent defense services through a public or private non-profit organization or as direct government employees. In 1994, 68% of State court prosecutors

reported that a public defender program was used to defend indigents in cases they prosecuted.

* In an assigned counsel system, courts appoint attorneys from a list of private bar members who accept cases on a judge-by-judge, court-by-court, or case-by-case basis. About 63% of prosecutors in State criminal courts reported an assigned counsel program in their jurisdiction.

* In contract attorney systems, private attorneys, bar associations, law firms, groups of attorneys, and nonprofit corporations provide indigent services based on legal agreements with State, county, or other local governmental units. Approximately 29% of prosecutors indicated that in their jurisdiction contracts were awarded to attorney groups to provide indigents with legal representation.

Although the Supreme Court in Gideon mandated that the States must provide counsel for indigents accused of serious crimes, the court did not specify how such services were to be provided. State court prosecutors increasingly report that their jurisdictions use more than one type of program to defend indigents. In 1990, 31% of prosecutors' offices reported that their courts used a combination of public defenders, assigned counsel, and contract attorneys; in 1994—the last time BJS asked prosecutors about their indigent defense systems—53% of the courts relied on more than one program.

In 1994 about 6% of prosecutors reported the court of their jurisdiction using all three systems: public defenders, assigned counsel, and contract attorneys. The most prevalent combination of two programs was public defenders and assigned counsel—indicated by almost a third of prosecutors' offices.

8 in 10 felony defendants in large State courts used publicly financed attorneys

In 1992 and 1996 about 80% of defendants charged with a felony in the Nation's 75 most populous counties reported having public defenders or assigned counsel while nearly 20% hired an attorney. Between 1992 and 1996 the percentage of felons in large counties using public defenders increased from 59% to 68% and the percentage with assigned counsel decreased from 21% to 14%. Defendants charged with violent, property, and drug crimes were more likely to have been represented by public defenders or assigned counsel (81%–84%) than those charged with public-order offenses (73%). Public-order offenses include weapons, driving-related, flight/escape, parole or probation, prison contraband, habitual offender, obstruction of justice, rioting, libel, slander, treason, perjury, prostitution/pandering, bribery, and tax law violations.

State defendants with a criminal record more likely than other defendants to use public counsel

Felony defendants with prior convictions were more likely than those without a criminal record to have used a publicly financed lawyer. According to criminal history records available to the court, 86% with a previous conviction and 77% without had public defenders or assigned counsel. When arrested for their current charge, about 86% of those already on criminal justice status—for example, on pretrial release, probation, or parole and 79% not on criminal justice status used appointed counsel.

Pretrial release less common for State defendants with public attorneys

About half of defendants using a public defender or assigned counsel, compared with over three-quarters employing a private attorney, were released from jail prior to trial. Release on bail, a payment to a court to guarantee the defendant's appearance at subsequent court dates, was awarded to 57% of defendants with public counsel and to 65% with a private lawyer. Of those allowed bail, about a third with a public attorney and three-quarters with a hired attorney were released before adjudication.

About 3 in 4 State defendants with public or private attorneys were found guilty

Conviction rates were about the same for defendants with court-appointed attorneys (75%) and for those who hired private counsel (77%). Of those convicted, about 8 in 10 were convicted of a felony and the remainder of a misdemeanor, regardless of type of attorney. Almost a quarter of defendants with publicly financed or private attorneys had their cases dismissed or were acquitted. Just over a fifth had charges dismissed and around 2% were acquitted.

State defendants with public counsel sentenced more often to prison or jail but for shorter terms than those with private lawyers

Convicted defendants represented by publicly financed counsel were more likely than those who hired a private attorney to be sentenced to incarceration. About 7 in 10 with appointed counsel and 5 in 10 with a private attorney were sentenced to a prison or jail term.

Of defendants sentenced to serve time, those using publicly financed attorneys had shorter sentences than those with private counsel.

Those with publicly financed attorneys were sentenced to an average of 2 1/2 years of incarceration and those with private counsel to 3 years. Similar to drug offenders convicted in Federal court, those sentenced for drug offenses with court-appointed attorneys had shorter sentences (2 years) than those who hired their attorneys (3 years). For other offense categories, sentences were about the same for defendants with public and private attorneys.

Local jail inmates described their experiences with the criminal justice system

In addition to gathering information on defendants in Federal and State courts, BJS sponsors interviews of inmates in local jails and State and Federal prisons. Nationally representative samples of inmates describe their personal experiences with the criminal justice system. Jail inmates either may be awaiting trial or sentencing or may be serving their sentence; prison inmates are serving a sentence. In the 1996 Survey of Inmates in Local Jails, most inmates charged with a felony reported they were represented by counsel; 97% had an attorney—77% a court-appointed counsel and 20% a private attorney. Over a quarter of jail inmates charged with a misdemeanor had no attorney, and over half used public counsel. The percent of all jail inmates who had been represented by a publicly financed attorney rose from 64% in 1989 to 68% in 1996.

Defendants in jail for homicide most likely to hire their own attorneys

About 40% of jail inmates charged with homicide hired their own attorney, as did 25% charged with rape or sexual assault, 28% driving while intoxicated, and 25% weapons offenses. Public-order defendants were more likely than other defendants to represent themselves in legal proceedings. About 4 in 10 charged with a public-order offense such as obstruction of justice, a traffic violation, drunkenness, or a violation of probation or parole represented themselves. Two in ten charged with driving while intoxicated reported that they had no lawyer.

**1 in 4 convicted jail inmates with public counsel and
with bail set were released before trial**

Whether their attorney was appointed or hired, about three-quarters of convicted jail inmates charged with a felony had bail or bond set for them. Of inmates with bail set, a quarter with a court-appointed attorney and two-thirds with hired attorneys were released on bond before their trial. The lack of financial assets that prevented hiring a private attorney may have also impeded posting bond.

Convicted jail inmates with a public attorney were more likely than those with private counsel to have entered a guilty plea after reaching an agreement with the prosecutor to plead guilty to a lesser charge or fewer counts. An estimated 54% with a publicly financed attorney and 49% with a hired attorney plea bargained.

**Prison inmates—those already convicted—reported
their experience with their attorneys**

In 1997 publicly financed attorneys had represented in court proceedings 3 in 4 inmates in State prison and 6 in 10 in Federal prison. About 1%–2% represented themselves rather than using a lawyer. From 1991 to 1997 the percentage of State inmates with appointed counsel remained the same, while that of sentenced Federal inmates increased from 54% to 60%.

**Prison inmates spoke to court-appointed lawyers later
and less often than to private attorneys**

Of inmates with court-appointed counsel, 37% of State inmates and 54% of Federal inmates spoke with their attorneys within the first week. In contrast, of those with hired counsel, about 60% of State inmates and 75% of Federal inmates had contact with their attorneys within a week of arrest. Few inmates said they never spoke to their attorneys. Of those with appointed counsel, about 5% of State inmates and 2% of Federal inmates did not discuss their cases with an attorney; of those with hired attorneys, 1–2% never spoke to them. Inmates with appointed lawyers spoke to them less frequently than inmates with private lawyers. About 26% of State inmates and 46% of Federal inmates with court-appointed attorneys discussed their cases with counsel at least four times. An estimated 58% of State inmates and 65% of Federal inmates who employed their own attorneys talked with them four or more times about their charges. Inmates who used public counsel were less likely to proceed to trial than those employing private attorneys.

A quarter of both State and Federal inmates with public counsel pleaded not guilty, as did about a third of those with hired attorneys.

In an Alford plea the defendant agrees to plead guilty because he or she realizes that there is little chance to win acquittal because of the strong evidence of guilt. About 17% of State inmates and 5% of Federal inmates submitted either an Alford plea or a no contest plea, regardless of the type of attorney. This difference reflects the relative readiness of State courts, compared to Federal courts, to accept an alternative plea.

State and Federal inmates who used public attorneys were less likely than those with private attorneys to have been tried by jury. Among State inmates 17% who used appointed counsel and 22% who employed a private lawyer were tried before a jury. Among Federal inmates 21% of those with appointed lawyers and 27% with privately hired counsel had jury trials.

State and Federal inmates with public attorneys and those with private lawyers were equally likely to have pleaded guilty to a lesser offense or fewer counts than originally charged. About half had plea bargained, regardless of the type of attorney or the jurisdiction of the court.

State inmates with public attorneys had shorter sentences than inmates with private counsel

On average State inmates who used appointed counsel expected to serve over 7 years on sentences of 13 years, while those who hired their attorneys expected to remain in prison 8 years on sentences of 15 years. Federal inmates expected to serve an average of almost 9 years for sentences of 10 1/2 years, whether they had appointed attorneys or hired their own. Drug offenders in State prison who had appointed counsel expected shorter prison stays on shorter sentences than those who hired their own lawyers. The average length of stay expected by State drug offenders who used appointed counsel was 4 years while that expected by those who employed their own lawyers was almost 5 years. Federal public-order offenders with appointed counsel had on average shorter sentence lengths than those with private counsel (9 versus 10 years).

Minority inmates were more likely than whites
to have appointed counsel

In State prisons, while 69% of white inmates reported they had lawyers appointed by the court, 77% of blacks and 73% of Hispanics had public defenders or assigned counsel. In the Federal system, blacks also were more likely to have public defenders or panel attorneys than other inmates; 65% of blacks had publicly financed attorneys. About the same percentage of whites and Hispanics used publicly financed attorneys (57% of whites and 56% of Hispanics).

Lower educational attainment among inmates was associated with higher use of court appointed attorneys. Over 7 in 10 with less than a high school diploma or GED used government financed attorneys. Sixty-one percent of State inmates and 50% of Federal inmates who had attended at least some college also had appointed lawyers.

Inmates who were unemployed were more likely than other inmates to use court-appointed attorneys

About 8 in 10 State inmates without a job before their most recent arrest, compared to 7 in 10 employed full time, had appointed counsel. Among Federal inmates two-thirds who were not employed and half who were employed full time had publicly financed attorneys. Over three-quarters of State inmates with monthly personal incomes of less than $1,000 had publicly financed defenders. Less than two-thirds of those with incomes of $2,000 or more per month had publicly financed lawyers. Over two-thirds of Federal inmates with incomes less than $1,000 and nearly half with incomes of $2,000 or more per month had publicly supported attorneys. For both State and Federal inmates, 9 in 10 who were homeless at any time in the year before their most recent arrest had court-appointed counsel.

Type of counsel for prison inmates varied by conviction offense

Among State offenders, those serving sentences for burglary, larceny, fraud, or robbery had relatively high rates of court appointed attorneys; about 8 in 10 had publicly financed counsel. Similarly in the Federal system, 8 in 10 robbery or burglary offenders used public defenders or panel attorneys. State inmates convicted of serious violent and drug offenses made less use of publicly financed attorneys. Approximately two-thirds of those convicted of homicide, sexual offenses, drug trafficking, and drug possession reported using public defenders or assigned counsel.

Among Federal offenders about half convicted of fraud (46%), drug trafficking (55%), or drug possession (56%) reported using public defenders or panel attorneys. Over 8 in 10 sentenced for rape or other sexual crime, robbery, and burglary used publicly financed attorneys.[4]

List of other cases and articles relevant to this topic.

Beck, J. C. and R. Shumsky (1997). A comparison of retained and appointed counsel in cases of capital murder. *Law and Human Behavior* 21 (5): 525–538.

Uphoff, R. (1992). The criminal defense lawyer: Zealous advocate, double agent, or beleaguered dealer? *Criminal Law Bulletin* 28(5): 419–456.

Hanson, R.A., B. J. Ostrom, and W.E. Hewitt et al (1992). *Indigent defenders get the job done and done well.* Williamsburg Va: National Center for State Courts.

Discussion and Review Questions

1. In 1942, the United States Supreme Court held that felony defendants were not entitled to counsel, what changed by the year 1960 when the Court in *Gideon* held that indigent defendants were entitled to legal counsel.

2. What is effective assistance of counsel according to the Court, and is this an adequate definition? Critique the Court's decision in *Strickland v. Washington.*

---

4. Caroline Wolf Harlow wrote this report under the supervision of Allen J. Beck.

In BJS, Carol DeFrances consulted extensively on research approaches and reviewed the State prosecutor data analysis; John Scalia provided numbers and reviewed the items dealing with Federal defendants; Tim Hart reviewed the section from State Court processing Statistics; David Levin assisted in accessing the SCPS dataset; Tracy Snell provided a statistical review of material from the surveys of inmates in State or Federal prisons or local jails; and Greg Steadman reviewed the standard error calculations.

William Sabol, formerly of Urban Institute, verified the Federal data from the Criminal Master File. Staff of the Administrative Office of the U.S. Courts, Steven R. Schlesinger and Catherine Whitaker of the Statistical Division, and Theodore J. Lidz, Steven G. Asin, George M. Drakalich, and Stephan C. Macartney of the Defender Services Division, provided and verified data and reviewed text. Tom Hester and Ellen Goldberg produced and edited the report. Jayne Robinson prepared the report for final printing.

November 2000 NCJ 179023

3. Identify the three primary types of indigent defense and assess under what circumstances each program may be most effective, and why.

4. Did the Bureau of Justice Statistics improve its evaluation of publicly financed defense attorneys and privately retained defense attorneys in its 2000 report excerpted in your readings? If you were to establish criteria and an instrument to measure effectiveness of counsel, what would you include, and why?

References

Articles

Beck, J.C. and R. Shumsky (1997). A comparison of retained and appointed counsel in cases of capital murder. *Law and Human Behavior* 21: 525–538.

Blumberg, A. (1967). The practice of law as a confidence game: Organizational co-optation of a profession. *Law and Society Review* 15: 28–31.

Bureau of Justice Statistics (1999). *Indigent Defense Statistics: A Summary of Findings*. Washington DC: National Institute of Justice.

Champion, D. (1989). Private counsels and public defenders: A look at weak cases,prior records and leniency in plea bargaining. *Journal of Criminal Justice* 17: 253–263.

Cole, D. (1999). *No Equal Justice: Race and Class in the American Criminal Justice System*. New York: The New Press.

Easterbrook, F. H. (1992). Plea bargaining as compromise. *Yale Law Journal* 101, 1969.

Hanson, R.A., B.J. Ostrom, W.E.Hewitt et al. (1992). *Indigent defenders get the job done and done well*. Williamsburg, Va: National Center for State Courts.

Harvard Law Review (2000). Note: Gideon's promise unfullfilled. *Harvard Law Review* 113: 2062.

Klotter, J.C. and J.R. Kanovitz (1995). *Constitutional Law*, Seventh Edition. Cincinnati, OH: Anderson Publishing.

Neubauer, D. (1999). *America's Courts and the Criminal Justice System*. CA: Wadsworth.

Schulhofer, S.J. and D.D. Friedman (1993). Rethinking indigent defense: Promoting effective representation through consumer sovereignty and freedom of choice for all criminal defendants. *American Criminal Law Review* 73: 96–122.

Spangenberg, R.L., B. Lee, M. Batlaglia, P. Smith, and A.D. Davis (1986). *National Criminal Defense System Study: Final Report*. Washington DC: U.S. Department of Justice.

Uphoff, R.J. (1992). The criminal defense lawyer: Zealous advocate, double agent, or beleaguered dealer? *Criminal Law Bulletin* 28: 419–456.

Worden, A.P. (1991). Privatizing due process: Issues in the comparison of assigned counsel, public defender and contracted indigent defense systems. *The Justice System Journal* 14: 390–418.

Case Citations

Argersinger v. Hamilton, 407 U.S. 25 (1972)
Betts v. Brady, 316 U.S. 455 (1942)
Burdine v. Johnson, 262 F. 3d 336 (5th Cir. 2001)
Coleman v. Alabama, 399 U.S. 1 (1970)
Douglas v. California, 372 U.S. 353 (1963)
Gideon v. Wainwright, 372 U.S. 335 (1963)
Hamilton v. Alabama, 368 U.S. 52 (1961)
Johnson v. Zerbst, 304 U.S. 458 (1938)
Mempa v. Rhay, 389 U.S. 128 (1967)
Murray v. Giarrantano, 492 U.S. 1 (1989)
Patterson v. Illinois, 487 U.S. 285 (1988)
Powell v. Alabama, 287 U.S. 45 (1932)
Roe v. Flores-Ortega, 528 U.S. 470 (2000)
Ross v. Moffit, 417 U.S. 600 (1974)
Scott v. Illinois, 440 U.S. 367 (1979)
Strickland v. Washington, 466 U.S. 668 (1984)
United States v. Ash, 413 U.S. 300 (1973)
United States v. Wade, 388 U.S. 218 (1967)
Williams v. Taylor, 529 U.S. 362 (2000)

CHAPTER 8

SIX PERSONS, A FAIR CROSS-SECTION, AND NULLIFICATION— THE RIGHT TO A JURY TRIAL.

A right to jury trial is granted to criminal defendants in order to prevent oppression by the government. Those who wrote our constitution knew from history and experience that it was necessary to protect against unfounded criminal charges brought to eliminate enemies and against judges too responsive to the voice of higher authority....Providing an accused with the right to be tried by a jury of his peers gave him an inestimable safeguard against the corrupt or overzealous prosecutor and against the complacent, biased, or eccentric judge....

–*Duncan v. Louisiana*, 391 U.S. 145 (1968) (Justice White).

In the previous chapter, the right to the effective assistance of counsel was deemed necessary by the Court to ensure that a defendant is given a fair trial. This chapter discusses the meaning of a trial, the history of jury trials, jury size, composition, and nullification.

What is a trial?

Seems like a very easy question, right? The answer, however, has varied over time. Centuries ago, trials by ordeal were held to determine the guilt or innocence of the criminally accused. Trials by ordeal subjected the accused to drowning, fire or hot rock. In each of these trials, the instruments of the ordeal were blessed by the church, and the accused would be placed in water (sinking meant guilt), burned at a stake (burning meant guilt) or their hand burned with a hot rock, the hand wrapped and three days later the injury viewed for healing (infection meant guilt). It was presumed that divine intervention would assist the innocent and they would not drown, burn or they would heal. In 1215, the church objected to these practices and put an end to its participation in trials by ordeal. Without the participation of a priest to bless the instruments, the trials were no longer considered 'trustworthy.'

From the demise of trials by ordeal emerged the trial by jury. However, the trials we know today took some time to develop. Few rights—e.g., the right against self-incrimination and the right to confront witnesses—were available to defendants. Moreover, many defendants refused the jury trial option and remained in prison, which at the time was very harsh. Why? During the thirteenth century, if convicted by a jury, a defendant had to give all his property to the king. If however, defendants died in prison waiting for trial without conviction, their property passed to their heirs. Thus, many men subjected themselves to the tortures of confinement for the benefit of their families. Over time, the jury process changed, defendants were afforded many more rights and trials became more fair.

The writings of the Magna Carta of 1215 were influential in the development of our jury system. The Magna Carta stated that persons could not be imprisoned or put to death unless judged guilty of a crime by their peers. In 1789, Article III, of the Constitution included that "the trial of all crimes, except cases of impeachment, shall be by jury." The Sixth Amendment to the United States Constitution adopted two years later guarantees the right to a trial by jury: "In all criminal prosecutions, the accused shall enjoy the right to [trial] by an impartial jury...."

In *Duncan v. Louisiana*, 391 U.S. 145 (1968), the Court held that the right to a trial by jury was fundamental to due process and therefore state court prosecutions must afford accuseds the right to a jury trial. Although this language is sweeping, there are exceptions. In *Baldwin v. New York*, 399 U.S. 66 (1970), the Court held that defendants facing less than six months in prison may not be entitled to a jury trial. The Court recognized that a person facing incarceration for six months may not consider this punishment "petty" or "trivial" and there may be "repercussions affecting...career[s] and...reputation[s]," however these effects from six-months incarceration are outweighed by the need for "speedy and inexpensive nonjury adjudications." The administrative inconveniences do not, however, outweigh the costs to an accused facing more than six months imprisonment. *Baldwin v. New York*.

In a footnote to this holding, the Court cited H. Kalven & H. Zeisel, *The American Jury* (1966) to support its position by noting that in California, where all cases were entitled to a jury trial, most individuals charged with 'petty' crimes waived this right.[1]

Although in deciding this fundamental issue of when an accused is entitled to a jury trial the Court did not rely heavily on social science evidence, there are three other issues where social science has played a much larger role—the size of the jury, the composition of the jury and the power of jury nullification.

Is there a magic number of persons for a jury?

Most people think that juries *must* consist of twelve people. At common law this was the case, and federal courts and most state courts use twelve-person juries. However, the United States Supreme Court has held that twelve-person juries are not guaranteed by the Constitution. In *Williams v. Florida*, 399 U.S. 78 (1970), the Court was confronted with the issue of whether a six-person jury was constitutional under the Sixth Amendment. In the *Williams* case the Court ignored history and found that there was nothing magical about the number twelve.

In *Williams*, the defendant was charged with robbery and in a pretrial motion demanded a jury of twelve persons instead of the six-person jury provided by Florida law in all cases but capital crimes. His request was denied and he was found guilty as charged before a jury of six. The issue before the Court was whether: "the constitutional guarantee of a trial by jury necessarily requires trial by exactly twelve persons, rather than some lesser number". In holding that a twelve-person jury was not a necessary ingredient of the constitutional guarantee of "trial by jury," the Court reviewed the history of the Sixth Amendment and found little support for the twelve-person jury standard. The Court also examined the argument that a twelve-person jury may provide defendants with a greater chance of acquittal than a six-person jury. In rejecting this argument the Court cited a number of empirical studies and experiments (in footnotes 48 and 49) that examined jury deliberations based on differing numbers of jurors and small group decision-making to support their view that "there is no discernable difference between the results reached by the two different-sized juries."

The Court, in 1978, was confronted with the question: "whether a state criminal trial to a jury of only five persons deprives the accused of the right to trial by jury guaranteed...by the Sixth and Fourteenth Amendments." In *Ballew v. Georgia*, 435 U.S. 223 (1978), the defendant was charged with mis-

---

1. In addition to these exceptions to the right to a jury trial, juveniles are also not guaranteed by the Constitution the right to a trial by jury (*McKeiver v. Pennsylvania*, 403 U.S. 528 (1971) and trials before a military tribunal need not have juries (*Ex parte Milligan*, 71 U.S. 2 (1886).

demeanor distribution of obscene materials. After a jury of five persons was sworn, the defendant asked that the trial court impanel a jury of twelve. The request for a twelve-person jury was denied, and the defendant was tried and convicted by five people. Ballew was sentenced to one year in prison. This case made its way to the United States Supreme Court and it held that five-member juries do not satisfy the jury trial guarantee under the Sixth and Fourteenth Amendments.

In arriving at this conclusion, the Court noted that a great deal of scholarly research on jury size was undertaken following their decisions in *Williams v. Florida* (holding six person juries in criminal cases constitutional) and *Colgrove v. Battin*, 413 U.S. 149 (1973) (holding six person juries in civil cases constitutional). The functioning of twelve, six or fewer member juries was the focus of the research. In footnote 10 of *Ballew*, the court listed a number of published studies on the topic as examples of this scholarly work. The Court stated that they reviewed these studies carefully "because they provide the only basis, besides judicial hunch, for a decision about whether smaller and smaller juries will be able to fulfill the purpose and functions of the Sixth Amendment" (*Ballew* at footnote 10). In summarizing the findings from the empirical studies, the Court concluded that smaller than six-member juries are less likely to "foster effective group deliberation," decrease quality of group performance and productivity, increase inconsistencies in verdicts and increase the likelihood of convicting an innocent person. In addition, the Court found that the scholarly research demonstrated that smaller juries were less representative of their communities. Thus, the Court held fewer than six-person juries unconstitutional.

Since the Court's 1978 ruling in *Ballew*, scholars have continued to study the affect of jury size on the constitutionality of their decision-making based on the criteria as set forth by the Court. Saks and Marti (1997) conducted a meta-analysis of all studies that compared differences between six- and twelve-person juries. They found, among other things, that larger juries are more likely to consist of members from minority populations, deliberate longer, result in hung juries more often, and demonstrate a more accurate memory of trial testimony.

Are there rules of jury selection?

There are two types of challenges to prospective jurors—**challenges for cause** and **peremptory challenges**. Striking a juror for cause requires some rational basis to disqualify a juror from service, e.g., an inability to understand the proceedings or to render a fair and impartial decision. Peremptory challenges ostensibly allow parties to eliminate, for any reason or no reason at all,

> **Challenge for Cause:** A request from a party to a judge that a certain prospective juror not be allowed to be a member of the jury because of specified causes or reasons. (Black's Law Dictionary).
>
> **Peremptory Challenge:** A request from a party that a judge not allow a certain prospective juror to be a member of the jury. No reason or "cause" need be stated for this type of challenge. The number of peremptory challenges afforded each party is normally set by statute or court rule. (Black's Law Dictionary)

individuals from sitting on the jury. However the Court has restricted the use of the peremptory challenge. Jurors may not be eliminated from service based on their race, ethnicity or gender. *Batson v. Kentucky*, 476 U.S. 79 (1986); *J.E.B v. Alabama*, 511 U.S. 127 (1994). Initially, the Court's decisions focused on race-based challenges to jurors. It wasn't until 1994 that the Court extended this proscription to gender-based challenges (*J.E.B v. Alabama*, 511 U.S. 127 (1994).

There are several grounds for the Court's reasoning that exclusion from jury service based on these factors is unconstitutional. In *Peters v. Kiff*, 407 U.S. 493 (1972), a case dealing with race-based exclusions, the Court outlined the constitutional principles thwarted by discrimination in the jury system. The *Kiff* case concerned the exclusion of black jurors from service, and the Court found that this type of discrimination offended the **14th Amendment Equal Protection Clause**, an essential feature of the Sixth Amendment which guarantees the fair possibility of obtaining a representative, cross-section of the community on the jury panel, and the 14th and 5th Amendment due process of law protection by undermining the entire system of justice predicated upon the fairness of the system. In a more recent case, the Court acknowledged that discrimination in the selection of juries reduces public confidence in the entire legal system (*Georgia v. McCollum*, 505 U.S. 42 (1992).

In the seminal case of *Batson v. Kentucky*, 476 U.S. 79 (1986), the United States Supreme Court developed the procedure and burden of proof currently employed to assess the discriminatory nature of peremptory challenges during voir dire. In *Batson*, the Court reaffirmed the decision in *Strauder v. West Virginia*, 100 U.S. 303 (1880) that equal protection is violated when a state prosecutes a black defendant and purposefully excludes members of his race from the jury. Although a defendant does not have the constitutional right to a particular racial composition on the jury panel, the state may not constitutionally deprive the potential for fair representation (*Batson*). The Court also reversed its decision in *Swain v. Alabama*, 380 U.S. 202 (1965) which placed a heavy evidentiary burden of proving equal protection violation claims on the defendant. In *Batson*, the Court held that a defendant may establish a prima facie case of purposeful discrimination based solely on evidence concerning the prosecutor's exercise of peremptory challenges at the defendant's trial. To make a viable claim, the defendant must show that the prosecutor exercised peremptory challenges against a member of a protected group and show facts that raise an inference that the challenges were made based on a discriminatory reason (e.g., the race of the veniremen). At this juncture, the burden shifts to the prosecutor to demonstrate that there exists a race-neutral (or ethnic- and gender-neutral) basis for the challenge.

In *Batson*, the Court also required the defendant to show she or he was a member of the group discriminated against, this part of the decision was later reversed. In *Powers v. Ohio*, 499 U.S. 400 (1991), the Court held that under the equal protection clause and to ensure the integrity of the legal system, anyone can raise a challenge to discrimination in the selection of jurors. In *Powers*, a white defendant challenged that he was deprived a jury comprised of a fair-cross section of the community due to the exclusion of black members from the venire. This decision was affirmed in *Campbell v. Louisiana*, 523 U.S. 392 (1998) where the Court held that a white defendant had standing to raise a challenge to the exclusion of black individuals from appointment to grand jury foreperson.

The Court has extended the application of the *Batson* rule. In 1992, the Court held that the decision in *Batson* prohibiting race-based peremptory challenges applies to criminal defendants as well as well as prosecutors. In other words, criminal defendants may not exclude jurors for a discriminatory purpose. In 1994, the Court held that the Equal Protection Clause also prohibits discrimination in jury selection on the basis of gender, or on the assumption that an individual will be biased in a particular case solely because that person happens to be a woman or a man.

Despite the legal restrictions, some have argued that the 'neutral' bases for peremptory challenges are making a farce out of the legal system. (See Melilli 1996 for a review of the reasons given by lawyers to justify juror challenges on neutral grounds). Some argue that peremptory challenges should be eliminated altogether. These debates, however, have been conducted in a virtual empirical vacuum (Rose 1999). Only a few studies have examined the impact of *Batson* (e.g., Kerr, Kramer, Carroll, and Alfini 1991), and only one study has examined actual jury selection data. Rose (1999) investigated the use of peremptory challenges in North Carolina jury trials, the affect of peremptory challenges on racial and gender composition of the juries, and its comparison to the venire. Overall, she found that there was no association between race and jury selection and only a slight relationship with gender. However, she did identify a pattern to the striking of jurors for individual panels. Defense attorneys were more likely to dismiss white jurors and prosecutors were more likely to dismiss black jurors. More research must be conducted to examine whether peremptory challenges continue to be used to discriminate by eliminating individuals from jury service based on race, ethnicity or gender and whether *Batson* and progeny are having the intended effect.

Can juries disregard the law?

"Jury nullification refers to the idea that juries have the right to refuse to apply the law in criminal cases despite facts that leave no reasonable doubt that the law was violated" (Neubauer 2001). Juror nullification is not something new, nor is it uncontroversial. The first and only United States Supreme Court case to discuss jury nullification was *Sparf and Hansen v. United States* (1895). In a prosecution of two men for a homicide on the "high seas," the trial judge instructed the jury that the men were either guilty or not guilty of murder and that manslaughter was not, as a matter of law, a possibility under the facts. The United States Supreme Court provided a lengthy, historical discussion of the division that judges determine law and jurors determine facts. The Court held that jurors were not permitted to disregard the law and that to allow jurors to make determinations of law would imperil the criminal court system by creating instability of its decisions. The *Sparf and Hansen* anti-nullification decision has been universally followed by the lower courts. Two more recent Circuit Court decisions—*United States v. Dougherty*[2] and *United States v. Thomas* reiterate the anti-nullification sentiments of the Court. In *Dougherty*, the DC Circuit Court was presented with the questions of whether defendants had the right to an instruction about "its right to acquit...without regard to the law and the evidence" and lawyers the permission to argue this right to the jury. In its decision, the court conceded that there has "evolved in the Anglo-American system an undoubted jury prerogative-in-fact, derived from its power to bring in a general verdict of not guilty in a criminal case,

---

2. 473 F.2d 1113 (DC Cir. 1972)(however holding that the trial judge erred when it removed a deliberating juror for failing to follow the law when the record demonstrated that there was a distinct possibility that the juror was simply not persuaded by the prosecutor's case).

> **Seditious Libel:** A communication written with the intent to incite the people to change the government otherwise than by lawful means, or to advocate the overthrow of the government by force or violence. (Black's Law Dictionary)

that is not reversible by the court." Numerous instances of nullification can be identified as examples of this prerogative—the 18th Century acquittal of Peter Zenger of **seditious libel**, the 19th Century acquittals of violators of the fugitive slave law and the acquittals of those charged with violating alcohol laws during the Prohibition. Despite these flagrant examples of nullification, the *Dougherty* Court and others will not formalize "jury lawlessness."[3] In citing to several authorities, including H. Kalven and H. Zeisel's book—*The American Jury*—a composite study of 3,576 criminal jury trials, the *Dougherty* Court found that citizens are aware of their power to nullify and need not be informed of this right because to do so would place "untoward strains on the jury system."

With this back-drop of anti-judicial sentiment for nullification instructions, only two states provide any information to juries regarding this power—Maryland and Indiana. (Horowitz 1985). Although there are some proponents of informed-juries, the debate and judicial decisions on nullification are conducted with little empirical support to examine the many assumptions concerning this power. There is, however, some empirical evidence that exists and it does suggest that jurors do engage in some nullification. In an experiment comparing the jury verdicts in a case where a physician provided unscreened blood to a patient, mock jurors were more likely to find the doctor not guilty when the penalty for the crime was severe (twenty-five years in prison) versus non-severe (a monetary fine). (Niedermeier et al. 1999). However, another study, which examined whether citizens were even aware of the power to nullify or not follow the law, found that only five percent knew of this power. (Brody and Rivera 1997). Finally, some studies have found that the presumption that jurors will arbitrarily and capriciously employ the power to nullify if they are instructed that they have the power and cause "chaos" in the court

---

3. R. Pound (1910), Law in Books and Law in Action, *American Law Review* 44, 12 ("Jury lawlessness is the greatest corrective of law in its actual administration. The will of the state at large imposed on a reluctant community, the will of a majority imposed on a vigorous and determined minority, find the same obstacle in the local jury that formerly confronted kings and ministers.")

is not supported. But, variation in instructions does have some effect on jury outcomes. For example, in an experimental comparison of two cases (a murder-robbery scenario and a euthanasia scenario) and three sets of jury instructions (standard instructions, one that allows for jury nullification,[4] and a third, more radical, instruction on juror power to nullify the law), jurors with the standard instruction discussed the evidence produced at the trial whereas the jurors with the radical instruction were more likely to discuss their personal life experiences and "individual notions of justice." (Horowitz 1985; Horowitz et al. 2001). In addition, jurors who received the muted nullification instruction (the Maryland instruction) did not differ significantly from those given the standard jury instruction. (Horowitz 1985; Horowitz et al. 2001).

In *Jury nullification: Legal and psychological perspectives*, Horowitz, Kerr and Niedermeier outline the arguments for and against jury nullification, and discuss much of the empirical evidence available concerning nullification issues—e.g., whether juries are engaging in the act of nullification, whether individuals are aware of their power to nullify, and what the actual impact of instructing jurors about this power would be. In addition, they identify "open empirical questions" where there has been little study, e.g., how widespread nullification is among contemporary (as opposed to historical) American juries, when nullification occurs, and what types of nullification instructions impact juror deliberations? In this chapter, *Ballew v. Georgia*, 435 U.S. 223 (1978)(holding five-person juries unconstitutional), *Batson v. Kentucky*, 476 U.S. 79 (1986)(holding discrimination in the selection of jurors unconstitutional), *United States v. Dougherty*, 473 F. 2d 1113 (DC Cir. 1972)(discussing the history of jury nullification and holding that it is inconsistent with the law to instruct jurors on their power to nullify) and Irwin A. Horowitz, Norbert L. Kerr and Keith E. Niedermeier's law review article *Jury nullification: Legal and psychological perspectives* are included.

Ballew v. Georgia,
435 U.S. 223 (1978)(Excerpt)

OPINION BY: BLACKMUN

This case presents the issue whether a state criminal trial to a jury of only five persons deprives the accused of the right to trial by jury guaranteed to

---

4. The instruction was based on the Maryland instruction which provides that the law "is not binding upon you" and "you may accept or reject it...."

him by the Sixth and Fourteenth Amendments. Our resolution of the issue requires an application of principles enunciated in *Williams v. Florida*, 399 U.S. 78 (1970), where the use of a six-person jury in a state criminal trial was upheld against similar constitutional attack.

In November 1973 petitioner Claude Davis Ballew was the manager of the Paris Adult Theatre at 320 Peachtree Street, Atlanta, Ga. On November 9 two investigators from the Fulton County Solicitor General's office viewed at the theater a motion picture film entitled "Behind the Green Door." Record 46–48, 90. After they had seen the film, they obtained a warrant for its seizure, returned to the theater, viewed the film once again, and seized it. Id., at 48–50, 91. Petitioner and a cashier were arrested. Investigators returned to the theater on November 26, viewed the film in its entirety, secured still another warrant, and on November 27 once again viewed the motion picture and seized a second copy of the film. Id., at 53–55. On September 14, 1974, petitioner was charged in a two-count misdemeanor accusation with [exhibiting an obscene movie].

Petitioner was brought to trial in the Criminal Court of Fulton County. After a jury of 5 persons had been selected and sworn, petitioner moved that the court impanel a jury of 12 persons. Record 37–38. That court, however, tried its misdemeanor cases before juries of five persons pursuant to Ga. Const., Art. 6. § 16, P1, codified as Ga. Code § 2–5101 (1975), and to 1890–1891 Ga. Laws, No. 278, pp. 937–938, and 1935 Ga. Laws, No. 38, p. 498. Petitioner contended that for an obscenity trial, a jury of only five was constitutionally inadequate to assess the contemporary standards of the community. Record 13, 38. He also argued that the Sixth and Fourteenth Amendments required a jury of at least six members in criminal cases. Id., at 38.

The motion for a 12-person jury was overruled, and the trial went on to its conclusion before the 5-person jury that had been impaneled. At the conclusion of the trial, the jury deliberated for 38 minutes and returned a verdict of guilty on both counts of the accusation. Id., at 205–208....Petitioner took an appeal to the Court of Appeals of the State of Georgia. There he argued....the use of the five-member jury deprived him of his Sixth and Fourteenth Amendment right to a trial by jury. Id., at 222–224.

In its consideration of the five-person-jury issue, the court noted that *Williams v. Florida* had not established a constitutional minimum number of jurors. Absent a holding by this Court that a five-person jury was constitutionally inadequate, the Court of Appeals considered itself bound by *Sanders v. State*, 234 Ga. 586, 216 S.E. 2d 838 (1975), cert. denied, 424 U.S. 931 (1976), over the constitutionality of the five-person jury had been upheld. The court also cited the earlier case of *McIntyre v. State*, 190 Ga. 872, 11 S.E. 2d 5 (1940), a holding to the same general effect but without elaboration.

The Supreme Court of Georgia denied certiorari. App. 26.

In his petition for certiorari here, petitioner raised…the unconstitutionality of the five-person jury.…We granted certiorari. 429 U.S. 1071 (1977). [W]e now hold that the five member jury does not satisfy the jury trial guarantee of the Sixth Amendment, as applied to the States through the Fourteenth.…

The Fourteenth Amendment guarantees the right of trial by jury in all state nonpetty criminal cases. *Duncan v. Louisiana*, 391 U.S. 145, 159–162 (1968). The Court in *Duncan* applied this Sixth Amendment right to the States because "trial by jury in criminal cases is fundamental to the American scheme of justice." Id., at 149. The right attaches in the present case because the maximum penalty for violating §26–2101, as it existed at the time of the alleged offenses, exceeded six months' imprisonment. See *Baldwin v. New York*, 399 U.S. 66, 68–69 (1970) (opinion of WHITE, J.).

In *Williams v. Florida*, 399 U.S., at 100, the Court reaffirmed that the "purpose of the jury trial, as we noted in *Duncan*, is to prevent oppression by the Government. 'Providing an accused with the right to be tried by a jury of his peers gave him an inestimable safeguard against the corrupt or overzealous prosecutor and against the compliant, biased, or eccentric judge.' *Duncan v. Louisiana*." See *Apodaca v. Oregon*, 406 U.S. 404, 410 (1972) (opinion of WHITE, J.). This purpose is attained by the participation of the community in determinations of guilt and by the application of the common sense of laymen who, as jurors, consider the case. *Williams v. Florida*, 399 U.S., at 100.…

When the Court in *Williams* permitted the reduction in jury size—or, to put it another way, when it held that a jury of six was not unconstitutional—it expressly reserved ruling on the issue whether a number smaller than six passed constitutional scrutiny. Id., at 91 n. 28. See *Johnson v. Louisiana*, 406 U.S. 356, 365–366 (1972) (concurring opinion). The Court refused to speculate when this so-called "slippery slope" would become too steep. We face now, however, the two-fold question whether a further reduction in the size of the state criminal trial jury does make the grade too dangerous, that is, whether it inhibits the functioning of the jury as an institution to a significant degree, and, if so, whether any state interest counterbalances and justifies the disruption so as to preserve its constitutionality.

Williams v. Florida and *Colgrove v. Battin*, 413 U.S. 149 (1973) (where the Court held that a jury of six members did not violate the Seventh Amendment right to a jury trial in a civil case), generated a quantity of scholarly work on jury size. [omitted note 10 provides a lengthy list of empirical studies considered by the court]. These writings do not draw or identify a bright line below which the number of jurors would not be able to function as required by the standards enunciated in *Williams*. On the other hand, they raise significant questions about the wisdom and constitutionality of a reduction below six. We examine these concerns:

First, recent empirical data suggest that progressively smaller juries are less likely to foster effective group deliberation. At some point, this decline leads to inaccurate fact-finding and incorrect application of the common sense of the community to the facts. Generally, a positive correlation exists between group size and the quality of both group performance and group productivity. A variety of explanations have been offered for this conclusion. Several are particularly applicable in the jury setting. The smaller the group, the less likely are members to make critical contributions necessary for the solution of a given problem. Because most juries are not permitted to take notes, see Forston, Sense and Non-Sense: Jury Trial Communication, 1975 B.Y.U.L. Rev. 601, 631–633, memory is important for accurate jury deliberations. As juries decrease in size, then, they are less likely to have members who remember each of the important pieces of evidence or argument. Furthermore, the smaller the group, the less likely it is to overcome the biases of its members to obtain an accurate result. When individual and group decision-making were compared, it was seen that groups performed better because prejudices of individuals were frequently counterbalanced, and objectivity resulted. Groups also exhibited increased motivation and self-criticism. All these advantages, except, perhaps, self-motivation, tend to diminish as the size of the group diminishes. Because juries frequently face complex problems laden with value choices, the benefits are important and should be retained. In particular, the counterbalancing of various biases is critical to the accurate application of the common sense of the community to the facts of any given case.

Second, the data now raise doubts about the accuracy of the results achieved by smaller and smaller panels. Statistical studies suggest that the risk of convicting an innocent person (Type I error) rises as the size of the jury diminishes. Because the risk of not convicting a guilty person (Type II error) increases with the size of the panel, an optimal jury size can be selected as a function of the interaction between the two risks. Nagel and Neef concluded that the optimal size, for the purpose of minimizing errors, should vary with the importance attached to the two types of mistakes. After weighting Type I error as 10 times more significant than Type II, perhaps not an unreasonable assumption, they concluded that the optimal jury size was between six and eight. As the size diminished to five and below, the weighted sum of errors increased because of the enlarging risk of the conviction of innocent defendants.

Another doubt about progressively smaller juries arises from the increasing inconsistency that results from the decreases. Saks argued that the "more a jury type fosters consistency, the greater will be the proportion of juries which select the correct (i.e., the same) verdict and the fewer 'errors' will be made." Saks 86–87. From his mock trials held before undergraduates and former jurors, he computed the percentage of "correct" decisions rendered by 12-person and 6-person panels. In the student experiment, 12-person groups reached correct verdicts 83% of the time; 6-person panels reached correct verdicts 69% of the time. The results for the former-juror study were 71% for the 12-person groups and 57% for the 6-person groups. Ibid. Working with statistics described in H. Kalven & H. Zeisel, The American Jury 460 (1966), Nagel and Neef tested the average conviction propensity of juries, that is, the likelihood that any given jury of a set would convict the defendant. They found that half of all 12-person juries would have average conviction propensities that varied by no more than 20 points. Half of all six-person juries, on the other hand, had average conviction propensities varying by 30 points, a difference they found significant in both real and percentage terms. Lempert reached similar results when he considered the likelihood of juries to compromise over the various views of their members, an important phenomenon for the fulfillment of the commonsense function. In civil trials averaging occurs with respect to damages amounts. In criminal trials it relates to numbers of counts and lesser included offenses. And he predicted that compromises would be more consistent when larger juries were employed. For example, 12-person juries could be expected to reach extreme compromises in 4% of the cases, while 6-person panels would reach extreme results in 16%. All three of these post-*Williams* studies, therefore, raise significant doubts about the consistency and reliability of the decisions of smaller juries.

Third, the data suggest that the verdicts of jury deliberation in criminal cases will vary as juries become smaller, and that the variance amounts to an imbalance to the detriment of one side, the defense. Both Lempert and Zeisel found that the number of hung juries would diminish as the panels decreased in size. Zeisel said that the number would be cut in half—from 5% to 2.4% with a decrease from 12 to 6 members. Both studies emphasized that juries in criminal cases generally hang with only one, or more likely two, jurors remaining unconvinced of guilt. Also, group theory suggests that a person in the minority will adhere to his position more frequently when he has at least one other person supporting his argument. In the jury setting the significance of this tendency is demonstrated by the following figures: If a minority viewpoint is shared by 10% of the community, 28.2% of 12-member juries may be expected to have no minority representation, but 53.1% of 6-member juries would have none. Thirty-four percent of 12-member panels could be expected to have two minority members, while only 11% of six-member panels would have two. As the numbers diminish below six, even fewer panels would have one member with the minority viewpoint and still fewer would have two. The chance for hung juries would decline accordingly.

Fourth, what has just been said about the presence of minority viewpoint as juries decrease in size foretells problems not only for jury decision-making, but also for the representation of minority groups in the community. The Court repeatedly has held that meaningful community participation cannot be attained with the exclusion of minorities or other identifiable groups from jury service. "It is part of the established tradition in the use of juries as instruments of public justice that the jury be a body truly representative of the community." *Smith v. Texas*, 311 U.S. 128, 130 (1940). The exclusion of elements of the community from participation "contravenes the very idea of a jury...composed of 'the peers or equals of the person whose rights it is selected or summoned to determine.'" *Carter v. Jury Comm'n*, 396 U.S. 320, 330 (1970), quoting *Strauder v. West Virginia*, 100 U.S. 303, 308 (1880). Although the Court in *Williams* concluded that the six-person jury did not fail to represent adequately a cross-section of the community, the opportunity for meaningful and appropriate representation does decrease with the size of the panels. Thus, if a minority group constitutes 10% of the community, 53.1% of randomly selected six-member juries could be expected to have no minority representative among their members, and 89% not to have two. Further reduction in size will erect additional barriers to representation.

Fifth, several authors have identified in jury research methodological problems tending to mask differences in the operation of smaller and larger juries. For example, because the judicial system handles so many clear cases, decision-makers will reach similar results through similar analyses most of the time. One study concluded that smaller and larger juries could disagree in their verdicts in no more than 14% of the cases. Disparities, therefore, appear in only small percentages. Nationwide, however, these small percentages will represent a large number of cases. And it is with respect to those cases that the jury trial right has its greatest value. When the case is close, and the guilt or innocence of the defendant is not readily apparent, a properly functioning jury system will insure evaluation by the sense of the community and will also tend to insure accurate fact-finding.

Studies that aggregate data also risk masking case-by-case differences in jury deliberations. The authors, H. Kalven and H. Zeisel, of *The American Jury* (1966), examined the judge jury disagreement. They found that judges held for plaintiffs 57% of the time and that juries held for plaintiffs 59%, an insignificant difference. Yet case-by-case comparison revealed judge-jury disagreement in 22% of the cases. Id., at 63, cited in Lempert 656. This casts doubt on the conclusion of another study that compared the aggregate results of civil cases tried before 6-member juries with those of 12-member jury trials. The investigator in that study had claimed support for his hypothesis that damages awards did not vary with the reduction in jury size. Although some might say that figures in the aggregate may have supported this conclusion, a closer view of the cases reveals greater variation in the results of the smaller panels, i.e., a standard deviation of $58,335 for the 6-member juries, and of $24,834 for the 12-member juries. Again, the averages masked significant case-by-case differences that must be considered when evaluating jury function and performance.

While we adhere to, and reaffirm our holding in *Williams v. Florida*, these studies, most of which have been made since *Williams* was decided in 1970, lead us to conclude that the purpose and functioning of the jury in a criminal trial is seriously impaired, and to a constitutional degree, by a reduction in size to below six members. We readily admit that we do not pretend to discern a clear line between six members and five. But the assembled data raise substantial doubt about the reliability and appropriate representation of panels smaller than six. Because of the fundamental importance of the jury trial to the American system of criminal justice, any further reduction that promotes inaccurate and possibly biased decision-making, that causes untoward differences in verdicts, and that prevents juries from truly representing their communities, attains constitutional significance.....

With the reduction in the number of jurors below six creating a substantial threat to Sixth and Fourteenth Amendment guarantees, we must consider whether any interest of the State justifies the reduction. We find no significant state advantage in reducing the number of jurors from six to five.

The States utilize juries of less than 12 primarily for administrative reasons. Savings in court time and in financial costs are claimed to justify the reductions. The financial benefits of the reduction from 12 to 6 are substantial; this is mainly because fewer jurors draw daily allowances as they hear cases. On the other hand, the asserted saving in judicial time is not so clear. Pabst in his study found little reduction in the time for voir dire with the six-person jury because many questions were directed at the veniremen as a group. Total trial time did not diminish, and court delays and backlogs improved very little. The point that is to be made, of course, is that a reduction in size from six to five or four or even three would save the States little. They could reduce slightly the daily allowances, but with a reduction from six to five the saving would be minimal. If little time is gained by the reduction from 12 to 6, less will be gained with a reduction from 6 to 5. Perhaps this explains why only two States, Georgia and Virginia, have reduced the size of juries in certain nonpetty criminal cases to five. Other States appear content with six members or more. In short, the State has offered little or no justification for its reduction to five members.

Petitioner, therefore, has established that his trial on criminal charges before a five-member jury deprived him of the right to trial by jury guaranteed by the Sixth and Fourteenth Amendments.

The judgment of the Court of Appeals is reversed, and the case is remanded for further proceedings not inconsistent with this opinion. It is so ordered.

Batson v. Kentucky
476 U.S. 79 (1986)(Excerpt)

OPINION BY: POWELL

This case requires us to reexamine that portion of *Swain* v. *Alabama*, 380 U.S. 202 (1965), concerning the evidentiary burden placed on a criminal defendant who claims that he has been denied equal protection through the State's use of peremptory challenges to exclude members of his race from the petit jury.

Petitioner, a black man, was indicted in Kentucky on charges of second-degree burglary and receipt of stolen goods. On the first day of trial in Jefferson Circuit Court, the judge conducted *voir dire* examination of the venire, excused certain jurors for cause, and permitted the parties to exercise peremptory challenges. The prosecutor used his peremptory challenges to strike all four black persons on the venire, and a jury composed only of white persons was selected. Defense counsel moved to discharge the jury before it was sworn on the ground that the prosecutor's removal of the black veniremen violated petitioner's rights under the Sixth and Fourteenth Amendments to a jury drawn from a cross section of the community, and under the Fourteenth Amendment to equal protection of the laws. Counsel requested a hearing on his motion. Without expressly ruling on the request for a hearing, the trial judge observed that the parties were entitled to use their peremptory challenges to "strike anybody they want to." The judge then denied petitioner's motion, reasoning that the cross-section requirement applies only to selection of the venire and not to selection of the petit jury itself.

The jury convicted petitioner on both counts. On appeal to the Supreme Court of Kentucky, petitioner pressed, among other claims, the argument concerning the prosecutor's use of peremptory challenges. Conceding that *Swain* v. *Alabama, supra,* apparently foreclosed an equal protection claim based solely on the prosecutor's conduct in this case, petitioner urged the court to follow decisions of other States, *People* v. *Wheeler,* 22 Cal. 3d 258, 583 P. 2d 748 (1978); *Commonwealth* v. *Soares,* 377 Mass. 461, 387 N. E. 2d 499, cert. denied, 444 U.S. 881 (1979), and to hold that such conduct violated his rights under the Sixth Amendment and §11 of the Kentucky Constitution to a jury drawn from a cross section of the community. Petitioner also contended that the facts showed that the prosecutor had engaged in a "pattern" of discriminatory challenges in this case and established an equal protection violation under *Swain.*

The Supreme Court of Kentucky affirmed. In a single paragraph, the court declined petitioner's invitation to adopt the reasoning of *People* v. *Wheeler, supra,* and *Commonwealth* v. *Soares, supra.* The court observed that it recently had reaffirmed its reliance on *Swain,* and had held that a defendant alleging lack of a fair cross section must demonstrate systematic exclusion of a group of jurors from the venire. See *Commonwealth* v. *McFerron,* 680 S. W. 2d 924 (1984). We granted certiorari, 471 U.S. 1052 (1985), and now reverse.

In *Swain* v. *Alabama,* this Court recognized that a "State's purposeful or deliberate denial to Negroes on account of race of participation as jurors in the administration of justice violates the Equal Protection Clause." 380 U.S., at 203–204. This principle has been "consistently and repeatedly" reaffirmed, *id.,* at 204, in numerous decisions of this Court both preceding and following *Swain.* We reaffirm the principle today.

More than a century ago, the Court decided that the State denies a black defendant equal protection of the laws when it puts him on trial before a jury from which members of his race have been purposefully excluded. *Strauder* v. *West Virginia,* 100 U.S. 303 (1880). That decision laid the foundation for the Court's unceasing efforts to eradicate racial discrimination in the procedures used to select the venire from which individual jurors are drawn. In *Strauder,* the Court explained that the central concern of the recently ratified Fourteenth Amendment was to put an end to governmental discrimination on account of race. *Id.,* at 306–307. Exclusion of black citizens from service as jurors constitutes a primary example of the evil the Fourteenth Amendment was designed to cure.

In holding that racial discrimination in jury selection offends the Equal Protection Clause, the Court in *Strauder* recognized, however, that a defendant has no right to a "petit jury composed in whole or in part of persons of his own race." *Id.*, at 305. "The number of our races and nationalities stands in the way of evolution of such a conception" of the demand of equal protection. *Akins* v. *Texas*, 325 U.S. 398, 403 (1945). But the defendant does have the right to be tried by a jury whose members are selected pursuant to nondiscriminatory criteria. *Martin* v. *Texas*, 200 U.S. 316, 321 (1906); *Ex parte Virginia*, 100 U.S. 339, 345 (1880). The Equal Protection Clause guarantees the defendant that the State will not exclude members of his race from the jury venire on account of race, *Strauder, supra,* at 305, or on the false assumption that members of his race as a group are not qualified to serve as jurors, see *Norris* v. *Alabama*, 294 U.S. 587, 599 (1935); *Neal* v. *Delaware*, 103 U.S. 370, 397 (1881)....

Racial discrimination in selection of jurors harms not only the accused whose life or liberty they are summoned to try. Competence to serve as a juror ultimately depends on an assessment of individual qualifications and ability impartially to consider evidence presented at a trial. See *Thiel* v. *Southern Pacific Co.*, 328 U.S. 217, 223–224 (1946). A person's race simply "is unrelated to his fitness as a juror." *Id.*, at 227 (Frankfurter, J., dissenting). As long ago as *Strauder*, therefore, the Court recognized that by denying a person participation in jury service on account of his race, the State unconstitutionally discriminated against the excluded juror. 100 U.S., at 308; see *Carter* v. *Jury Comm'n of Greene County, supra,* at 329–330; *Neal* v. *Delaware, supra,* at 386.

The harm from discriminatory jury selection extends beyond that inflicted on the defendant and the excluded juror to touch the entire community. Selection procedures that purposefully exclude black persons from juries undermine public confidence in the fairness of our system of justice. See *Ballard* v. *United States*, 329 U.S. 187, 195 (1946); *McCray* v. *New York*, 461 U.S. 961, 968 (1983) (MARSHALL, J., dissenting from denial of certiorari). Discrimination within the judicial system is most pernicious because it is "a stimulant to that race prejudice which is an impediment to securing to [black citizens] that equal justice which the law aims to secure to all others." *Strauder*, 100 U.S., at 308.

In *Strauder*, the Court invalidated a state statute that provided that only white men could serve as jurors. *Id.*, at 305. We can be confident that no State now has such a law. The Constitution requires, however, that we look beyond the face of the statute defining juror qualifications and also consider challenged selection practices to afford "protection against action of the State through its administrative officers in effecting the prohibited discrimination." *Norris* v. *Alabama, supra,* at 589; see *Hernandez* v. *Texas,* 347 U.S. 475, 478–479 (1954); *Ex parte Virginia, supra,* at 346–347. Thus, the Court has found a denial of equal protection where the procedures implementing a neutral statute operated to exclude persons from the venire on racial grounds, n10 and has made clear that the Constitution prohibits all forms of purposeful racial discrimination in selection of jurors. While decisions of this Court have been concerned largely with discrimination during selection of the venire, the principles announced there also forbid discrimination on account of race in selection of the petit jury. Since the Fourteenth Amendment protects an accused throughout the proceedings bringing him to justice, *Hill* v. *Texas,* 316 U.S. 400, 406 (1942), the State may not draw up its jury lists pursuant to neutral procedures but then resort to discrimination at "other stages in the selection process," *Avery* v. *Georgia,* 345 U.S. 559, 562 (1953); see *McCray* v. *New York, supra,* at 965, 968 (MARSHALL, J., dissenting from denial of certiorari); see also *Alexander* v. *Louisiana,* 405 U.S. 625, 632 (1972).

Accordingly, the component of the jury selection process at issue here, the State's privilege to strike individual jurors through peremptory challenges, is subject to the commands of the Equal Protection Clause. Although a prosecutor ordinarily is entitled to exercise permitted peremptory challenges "for any reason at all, as long as that reason is related to his view concerning the outcome" of the case to be tried, *United States* v. *Robinson,* 421 F.Supp. 467, 473 (Conn. 1976), mandamus granted *sub nom. United States* v. *Newman,* 549 F.2d 240 (CA2 1977), the Equal Protection Clause forbids the prosecutor to challenge potential jurors solely on account of their race or on the assumption that black jurors as a group will be unable impartially to consider the State's case against a black defendant.

The principles announced in *Strauder* never have been questioned in any subsequent decision of this Court. Rather, the Court has been called upon repeatedly to review the application of those principles to particular facts. A recurring question in these cases, as in any case alleging a violation of the Equal Protection Clause, was whether the defendant had met his burden of proving purposeful discrimination on the part of the State. *Whitus* v. *Georgia,* 385 U.S. 545, 550 (1967); *Hernandez* v. *Texas, supra,* at 478–481; *Akins* v. *Texas,* 325 U.S., at 403–404; *Martin* v. *Texas,* 200 U.S. 316 (1906). That question also was at the heart of the portion of *Swain* v. *Alabama* we reexamine today....

The showing necessary to establish a prima facie case of purposeful discrimination in selection of the venire may be discerned in this Court's decisions. *E. g., Castaneda* v. *Partida,* 430 U.S. 482, 494–495 (1977); *Alexander* v. *Louisiana, supra,* at 631–632. The defendant initially must show that he is a member of a racial group capable of being singled out for differential treatment. *Castaneda* v. *Partida, supra,* at 494. In combination with that evidence, a defendant may then make a prima facie case by proving that in the particular jurisdiction members of his race have not been summoned for jury service over an extended period of time. *Id.,* at 494. Proof of systematic exclusion from the venire raises an inference of purposeful discrimination because the "result bespeaks discrimination." *Hernandez* v. *Texas,* 347 U.S., at 482; see *Arlington Heights* v. *Metropolitan Housing Development Corp., supra,* at 266.

Since the ultimate issue is whether the State has discriminated in selecting the defendant's venire, however, the defendant may establish a prima facie case "in other ways than by evidence of long-continued unexplained absence" of members of his race "from many panels." *Cassell* v. *Texas,* 339 U.S. 282, 290 (1950) (plurality opinion). In cases involving the venire, this Court has found a prima facie case on proof that members of the defendant's race were substantially underrepresented on the venire from which his jury was drawn, and that the venire was selected under a practice providing "the opportunity for discrimination." *Whitus* v. *Georgia, supra,* at 552; see *Castaneda* v. *Partida, supra,* at 494; *Washington* v. *Davis, supra,* at 241; *Alexander* v. *Louisiana, supra,* at 629–631. This combination of factors raises the necessary inference of purposeful discrimination because the Court has declined to attribute to chance the absence of black citizens on a particular jury array where the selection mechanism is subject to abuse. When circumstances suggest the need, the trial court must undertake a "factual inquiry" that "takes into account all possible explanatory factors" in the particular case. *Alexander* v. *Louisiana, supra,* at 630.

Thus, since the decision in *Swain,* this Court has recognized that a defendant may make a prima facie showing of purposeful racial discrimination in selection of the venire by relying solely on the facts concerning its selection *in his case.* These decisions are in accordance with the proposition, articulated in *Arlington Heights* v. *Metropolitan Housing Development Corp.,* that "a consistent pattern of official racial discrimination" is not "a necessary predicate to a violation of the Equal Protection Clause. A single invidiously discriminatory governmental act" is not "immunized by the absence of such discrimination in the making of other comparable decisions." 429 U.S., at 266, n. 14. For evidentiary requirements to dictate that "several must suffer discrimination" before one could object, *McCray* v. *New York,* 461 U.S., at 965 (MARSHALL, J., dissenting from denial of certiorari), would be inconsistent with the promise of equal protection to all.

The standards for assessing a prima facie case in the context of discriminatory selection of the venire have been fully articulated since *Swain*. See *Castaneda* v. *Partida, supra*, at 494–495; *Washington* v. *Davis*, 426 U.S., at 241–242; *Alexander* v. *Louisiana, supra*, at 629–631. These principles support our conclusion that a defendant may establish a prima facie case of purposeful discrimination in selection of the petit jury solely on evidence concerning the prosecutor's exercise of peremptory challenges at the defendant's trial. To establish such a case, the defendant first must show that he is a member of a cognizable racial group, *Castaneda* v. *Partida, supra*, at 494, and that the prosecutor has exercised peremptory challenges to remove from the venire members of the defendant's race. Second, the defendant is entitled to rely on the fact, as to which there can be no dispute, that peremptory challenges constitute a jury selection practice that permits "those to discriminate who are of a mind to discriminate." *Avery* v. *Georgia*, 345 U.S., at 562. Finally, the defendant must show that these facts and any other relevant circumstances raise an inference that the prosecutor used that practice to exclude the veniremen from the petit jury on account of their race. This combination of factors in the empaneling of the petit jury, as in the selection of the venire, raises the necessary inference of purposeful discrimination.

In deciding whether the defendant has made the requisite showing, the trial court should consider all relevant circumstances. For example, a "pattern" of strikes against black jurors included in the particular venire might give rise to an inference of discrimination. Similarly, the prosecutor's questions and statements during *voir dire* examination and in exercising his challenges may support or refute an inference of discriminatory purpose. These examples are merely illustrative. We have confidence that trial judges, experienced in supervising *voir dire*, will be able to decide if the circumstances concerning the prosecutor's use of peremptory challenges creates a prima facie case of discrimination against black jurors.

Once the defendant makes a prima facie showing, the burden shifts to the State to come forward with a neutral explanation for challenging black jurors. Though this requirement imposes a limitation in some cases on the full peremptory character of the historic challenge, we emphasize that the prosecutor's explanation need not rise to the level justifying exercise of a challenge for cause. See *McCray* v. *Abrams*, 750 F.2d, at 1132; *Booker* v. *Jabe*, 775 F.2d 762, 773 (CA6 1985), cert. pending, No. 85–1028. But the prosecutor may not rebut the defendant's prima facie case of discrimination by stating merely that he challenged jurors of the defendant's race on the assumption—or his intuitive judgment—that they would be partial to the defendant because of their shared race. Cf. *Norris* v. *Alabama*, 294 U.S., at 598–599; see *Thompson* v. *United States*, 469 U.S. 1024, 1026 (1984) (BRENNAN, J., dissenting from denial of certiorari). Just as the Equal Protection Clause forbids the States to exclude black persons from the venire on the assumption that blacks as a group are unqualified to serve as jurors, *supra*, at 86, so it forbids the States to strike black veniremen on the assumption that they will be biased in a particular case simply because the defendant is black. The core guarantee of equal protection, ensuring citizens that their State will not discriminate on account of race, would be meaningless were we to approve the exclusion of jurors on the basis of such assumptions, which arise solely from the jurors' race. Nor may the prosecutor rebut the defendant's case merely by denying that he had a discriminatory motive or "[affirming] [his] good faith in making individual selections." *Alexander* v. *Louisiana*, 405 U.S., at 632. If these general assertions were accepted as rebutting a defendant's prima facie case, the Equal Protection Clause "would be but a vain and illusory requirement." *Norris* v. *Alabama*, *supra*, at 598. The prosecutor therefore must articulate a neutral explanation related to the particular case to be tried. n20 The trial court then will have the duty to determine if the defendant has established purposeful discrimination.

The State contends that our holding will eviscerate the fair trial values served by the peremptory challenge. Conceding that the Constitution does not guarantee a right to peremptory challenges and that *Swain* did state that their use ultimately is subject to the strictures of equal protection, the State argues that the privilege of unfettered exercise of the challenge is of vital importance to the criminal justice system.

While we recognize, of course, that the peremptory challenge occupies an important position in our trial procedures, we do not agree that our decision today will undermine the contribution the challenge generally makes to the administration of justice. The reality of practice, amply reflected in many state- and federal-court opinions, shows that the challenge may be, and unfortunately at times has been, used to discriminate against black jurors. By requiring trial courts to be sensitive to the racially discriminatory use of peremptory challenges, our decision enforces the mandate of equal protection and furthers the ends of justice. In view of the heterogeneous population of our Nation, public respect for our criminal justice system and the rule of law will be strengthened if we ensure that no citizen is disqualified from jury service because of his race.

Nor are we persuaded by the State's suggestion that our holding will create serious administrative difficulties. In those States applying a version of the evidentiary standard we recognize today, courts have not experienced serious administrative burdens, and the peremptory challenge system has survived. We decline, however, to formulate particular procedures to be followed upon a defendant's timely objection to a prosecutor's challenges.

In this case, petitioner made a timely objection to the prosecutor's removal of all black persons on the venire. Because the trial court flatly rejected the objection without requiring the prosecutor to give an explanation for his action, we remand this case for further proceedings. If the trial court decides that the facts establish, prima facie, purposeful discrimination and the prosecutor does not come forward with a neutral explanation for his action, our precedents require that petitioner's conviction be reversed. *E. g., Whitus* v. *Georgia*, 385 U.S., at 549–550; *Hernandez* v. *Texas*, 347 U.S., at 482; *Patton* v. *Mississippi*, 332 U.S., at 469. *It is so ordered.*

United States v. Dougherty
473 F.2d 1113 (D.C. Cir. 1972)(Excerpt)

OPINION BY: LEVENTHAL

Seven of the so-called "D.C. Nine" bring this joint appeal from convictions arising out of their unconsented entry into the Washington offices of the Dow Chemical Company, and their destruction of certain property therein....

Appellants urge three grounds for reversal as follows: (1) The trial judge erred in denying defendants' timely motions to dispense with counsel and represent themselves. (2) The judge erroneously refused to instruct the jury of its right to acquit appellants without regard to the law and the evidence, and refused to permit appellants to argue that issue to the jury. (3) The instructions actually given by the court coerced the jury into delivering a verdict of guilty. On the basis of defendants' first contention we reverse and remand for new trial. To provide an appropriate mandate governing the new trial, we consider the second and third contentions, and conclude that these cannot be accepted....

I. The Record in District Court

The undisputed evidence showed that on Saturday, March 22, 1969, appellants broke into the locked fourth floor Dow offices at 1030—15th Street, N.W., Washington, D.C., threw papers and documents about the office and into the street below, vandalized office furniture and equipment, and defaced the premises by spilling about a blood-like substance. The prosecution proved its case through Dow employees who testified as to the lack of permission and extent of damage, members of the news media who had been summoned to the scene by the appellants and who witnessed the destruction while recording it photographically, and police officers who arrested appellants on the scene...

On Friday, February 6, after an opening statement by Mr. Bowman, appellants O'Rourke and Malone made opening statements on their own behalf, as the other defendants had done prior to the Government's case. They directed their remarks, as had the others, to an attack on the role of Dow Chemical Company and other unspecified corporations in supporting American military efforts in the Vietnam War.... [The defense] consisted entirely of defendants' testimony.... [The trial judge] refused to instruct the jury that it could disregard the law as he gave it to them, and refused to instruct the jury that "moral compulsion" or "choice of the lesser evil" constituted a legal defense....

The Issue of Jury Nullification

Our reference to the "intensity" factor underlying the *pro se* right should not be understood as embracing the principle of "nullification" proffered by appellants. They say that the jury has a well-recognized prerogative to disregard the instructions of the court even as to matters of law, and that they accordingly have the legal right that the jury be informed of its power. We turn to this matter in order to define the nature of the new trial permitted by our mandate.

There has evolved in the Anglo-American system an undoubted jury prerogative-in-fact, derived from its power to bring in a general verdict of not guilty in a criminal case, that is not reversible by the court. The power of the courts to punish jurors for corrupt or incorrect verdicts, which persisted after the medieval system of attaint by another jury became obsolete, was repudiated in 1670 when *Bushell's* Case, 124 Eng.Rep. 1006 (C.P. 1670) discharged the jurors who had acquitted William Penn of unlawful assembly. Juries in civil cases became subject to the control of ordering a new trial; no comparable control evolved for acquittals in criminal cases.

The pages of history shine on instances of the jury's exercise of its prerogative to disregard uncontradicted evidence and instructions of the judge. Most often commended are the 18th century acquittal of Peter Zenger of seditious libel, on the plea of Andrew Hamilton, and the 19th century acquittals in prosecutions under the fugitive slave law. The values involved drop a notch when the liberty vindicated by the verdict relates to the defendant's shooting of his wife's paramour, or purchase during Prohibition of alcoholic beverages.

Even the notable Dean Pound commented in 1910 on positive aspects of "such jury lawlessness." These observations of history and philosophy are underscored and illuminated, in terms of the current place of the jury in the American system of justice, by the empirical information and critical insights and analyses blended so felicitously in H. Kalven and H. Zeisel, The American Jury.

Reflective opinions upholding the necessity for the jury as a protection against arbitrary action, such as prosecutorial abuse of power, stress fundamental features like the jury "common sense judgment" and assurance of "community participation in the determination of guilt or innocence." Human frailty being what it is, a prosecutor disposed by unworthy motives could likely establish some basis in fact for bringing charges against anyone he wants to book, but the jury system operates in fact, (see note 33) so that the jury will not convict when they empathize with the defendant, as when the offense is one they see themselves as likely to commit, or consider generally acceptable or condonable under the mores of the community.

The rulings did not run all one way, but rather precipitated "a number of classic exchanges on the freedom and obligations of the criminal jury." This was, indeed, one of the points of clash between the contending forces staking out the direction of the government of the newly established Republic, a direction resolved in political terms by reforming but sustaining the status of the courts, without radical change. As the distrust of judges appointed and removable by the king receded, there came increasing acceptance that under a republic the protection of citizens lay not in recognizing the right of each jury to make its own law, but in following democratic processes for changing the law.

The crucial legal ruling came in *United States v. Battiste*, 2 Sum. 240, 24 F. Cas. 1042 (C.C.D.Mass. 1835). Justice Story's strong opinion supported the conception that the jury's function lay in accepting the law given to it by the court and applying that law to the facts. This considered ruling of an influential jurist won increasing acceptance in the nation. The youthful passion for independence accommodated itself to the reality that the former rebels were now in control of their own destiny, that the practical needs of stability and sound growth outweighed the abstraction of centrifugal philosophy, and that the judges in the courts, were not the colonial appointees projecting royalist patronage and influence but were themselves part and parcel of the nation's intellectual mainstream, subject to the checks of the common law tradition and professional opinion, and capable, in Roscoe Pound's words, of providing "true judicial justice" standing in contrast with the colonial experience.

The tide was turned by *Battiste*, but there were cross-currents. At mid-century the country was still influenced by the precepts of Jacksonian democracy, which spurred demands for direct selection of judges by the people through elections, and distrust of the judge-made common law which enhanced the movement for codification reform. But by the end of the century, even the most prominent state landmarks had been toppled; and the Supreme Court settled the matter for the Federal courts in *Sparf v. United States,* 156 U.S. 51, 102, 15 S. Ct. 273, 39 L. Ed. 343 (1895) after exhaustive review in both majority and dissenting opinions. The jury's role was respected as significant and wholesome, but it was not to be given instructions that articulated a right to do whatever it willed. The old rule survives today only as a singular relic.

The breadth of the continuing prerogative of the jury, however, perseveres, as appears from the rulings permitting inconsistent verdicts. These reflect, in the words of Justice Holmes, an acknowledgment that "the jury has the power to bring in a verdict in the teeth of both law and facts," or as Judge Learned Hand said: "We interpret the acquittal as no more than their assumption of a power which they had no right to exercise, but to which they were disposed through lenity."

Since the jury's prerogative of lenity, again in Learned Hand's words introduces a "slack into the enforcement of law, tempering its rigor by the mollifying influence of current ethical conventions," it is only just, say appellants, that the jurors be so told. It is unjust to withhold information on the jury power of "nullification," since conscientious jurors may come, ironically, to abide by their oath as jurors to render verdicts offensive to their individual conscience, to defer to an assumption of necessity that is contrary to reality.

This so-called right of jury nullification is put forward in the name of liberty and democracy, but its explicit avowal risks the ultimate logic of anarchy. This is the concern voiced by Judge Sobeloff in *United States v. Moylan,* 417 F.2d 1002, 1009 (4th Cir. 1969), *cert. denied,* 397 U.S. 910, 90 S. Ct. 908, 25 L. Ed. 2d 91 (1970):

To encourage individuals to make their own determinations as to which laws they will obey and which they will permit themselves as a matter of conscience to disobey is to invite chaos. No legal system could long survive if it gave every individual the option of disregarding with impunity any law which by his personal standard was judged morally untenable. Toleration of such conduct would not be democratic, as appellants claim, but inevitably anarchic.

The statement that avowal of the jury's prerogative runs the risk of anarchy, represents, in all likelihood, the habit of thought of philosophy and logic, rather than the prediction of the social scientist. But if the statement contains an element of hyperbole, the existence of risk and danger, of significant magnitude, cannot be gainsaid. In contrast, the advocates of jury "nullification" apparently assume that the articulation of the jury's power will not extend its use or extent, or will not do so significantly or obnoxiously. Can this assumption fairly be made? We know that a posted limit of 60 m.p.h. produces factual speeds 10 or even 15 miles greater, with an understanding all around that some "tolerance" is acceptable to the authorities, assuming conditions warrant. But can it be supposed that the speeds would stay substantially the same if the speed limit were put: Drive as fast as you think appropriate, without the posted limit as an anchor, a point of departure?

Our jury system is a resultant of many vectors, some explicit, and some rooted in tradition, continuity and general understanding without express formulation. A constitution may be meaningful though it is unwritten, as the British have proved for 900 years.

The jury system has worked out reasonably well overall, providing "play in the joints" that imparts flexibility and avoid undue rigidity. An equilibrium has evolved—an often marvelous balance—with the jury acting as a "safety valve" for exceptional cases, without being a wildcat or runaway institution. There is reason to believe that the simultaneous achievement of modest jury equity and avoidance of intolerable caprice depends on formal instructions that do not expressly delineate a jury charter to carve out its own rules of law. We have taken due and wry note that those whose writings acclaim and invoke Roscoe Pound's 1910 recognition of the value of the jury as safety valve, omit mention of the fact that in the same article he referred to "the extreme decentralization that allows a local jury or even a local prosecutor to hold up instead of uphold the law of the state" as one of the conditions that "too often result in a legal paralysis of legal administration," that his writings of that period are expressly concerned with the evils of the "extravagant powers" of juries, and that in 1931 he joined the other distinguished members of the Wickersham Commission in this comment:

In a number of jurisdictions juries are made judges of the law in criminal cases, thus inviting them to dispense with the rules of law instead of finding the facts. The juror is made judge of the law not to ascertain what it is, but to judge of its conformity to his personal ideals and ascertain its validity on that basis.... It is significant that there is most satisfaction with criminal juries in those jurisdictions which have interfered least with the conception of a trial of the facts unburdened with further responsibility and instructed as to the law and advised as to the facts by the judge.

The way the jury operates may be radically altered if there is alteration in the way it is told to operate. The jury knows well enough that its prerogative is not limited to the choices articulated in the formal instructions of the court. The jury gets its understanding as to the arrangements in the legal system from more than one voice. There is the formal communication from the judge. There is the informal communication from the total culture—literature (novel, drama, film, and television); current comment (newspapers, magazines and television); conversation; and, of course, history and tradition. The totality of input generally convey adequately enough the idea of prerogative, of freedom in an occasional case to depart from what the judge says. Even indicators that would on their face seem too weak to notice—like the fact that the judge tells the jury it must acquit (in case of reasonable doubt) but never tells the jury in so many words that it must convict—are a meaningful part of the jury's total input. Law is a system, and it is also a language, with secondary meanings that may be unrecorded yet are part of its life.

When the legal system relegates the information of the jury's prerogative to an essentially informal input, it is not being duplicitous, chargeable with chicane and intent to deceive. The limitation to informal input is, rather a governor to avoid excess: the prerogative is reserved for the exceptional case, and the judge's instruction is retained as a generally effective constraint. We "recognize a constraint as obligatory upon us when we require not merely reason to defend our rule departures, but damn good reason." The practicalities of men, machinery and rules point up the danger of articulating discretion to depart from a rule, that the breach will be more often and casually invoked. We cannot gainsay that occasionally jurors uninstructed as to the prerogative may feel themselves compelled to the point of rigidity. The danger of the excess rigidity that may now occasionally exist is not as great as the danger of removing the boundaries of constraint provided by the announced rules.

We should also note the inter-relation of the unanimity requirement for petit juries, which was applicable to this trial, and is still the general rule though no longer constitutionally required for state courts. This is an additional reason—a material consideration, though neither a necessary nor sufficient condition—to brake the wheels of those who would tell the petit jurors they are to determine the rules of law, either directly or by telling them they are free to disregard the judge's statement of the rules. The democratic principle would not be furthered, as proponents of jury nullification claim, it would be disserved by investing in a jury that must be unanimous the function not merely of determining facts, hard enough for like-minded resolution, but of determining the rules of law.

Rules of law or justice involve choice of values and ordering of objectives for which unanimity is unlikely in any society, or group representing the society, especially a society as diverse in cultures and interests as ours. To seek unity out of diversity, under the national motto, there must be a procedure for decision by vote of a majority or prescribed plurality—in accordance with democratic philosophy. To assign the role of mini-legislature to the various petit juries, who must hang if not unanimous, exposes criminal law and administration to paralysis, and to a deadlock that betrays rather than furthers the assumptions of viable democracy.

Moreover, to compel a juror involuntarily assigned to jury duty to assume the burdens of mini-legislator or judge, as is implicit in the doctrine of nullification, is to put untoward strains on the jury system. It is one thing for a juror to know that the law condemns, but he has a factual power of lenity. To tell him expressly of a nullification prerogative, however, is to inform him, in effect, that it is he who fashions the rule that condemns. That is an overwhelming responsibility, an extreme burden for the jurors' psyche. And it is not inappropriate to add that a juror called upon for an involuntary public service is entitled to the protection, when he takes action that he knows is right, but also knows is unpopular, either in the community at large or in his own particular grouping, that he can fairly put it to friends and neighbors that he was merely following the instructions of the court.

In the last analysis, our rejection of the request for jury nullification doctrine is a recognition that there are times when logic is not the only or even best guide to sound conduct of government. For machines, one can indulge the person who likes to tinker in pursuit of fine tuning. When men and judicial machinery are involved, one must attend to the many and complex mechanisms and reasons that lead men to change their conduct—when they know they are being studied; when they are told of the consequences of their conduct; and when conduct exercised with restraint as an unwritten exception is expressly presented as a legitimate option.

What makes for health as an occasional medicine would be disastrous as a daily diet. The fact that there is widespread existence of the jury's prerogative, and approval of its existence as a "necessary counter to case-hardened judges and arbitrary prosecutors," does not establish as an imperative that the jury must be informed by the judge of that power. On the contrary, it is pragmatically useful to structure instructions in such wise that the jury must feel strongly about the values involved in the case, so strongly that it must itself identify the case as establishing a call of high conscience, and must independently initiate and undertake an act in contravention of the established instructions. This requirement of independent jury conception confines the happening of the lawless jury to the occasional instance that does not violate, and viewed as an exception may even enhance, the over-all normative effect of the rule of law. An explicit instruction to a jury conveys an implied approval that runs the risk of degrading the legal structure requisite for true freedom, for an ordered liberty that protects against anarchy as well as tyranny....

I. Horowitz, N.L. Kerr and K.E. Niedermeier (Summer 2001). Jury nullification: Legal and psychological perspectives *
Brooklyn Law Review 66: 1207 (Excerpt)

Introduction

Juries have the implicit power to acquit defendants despite evidence and judicial instructions to the contrary. The jury's right to decide a criminal case by its own merits, without fear of outside coercion and pressures, is a hallmark of Anglo-American jurisprudence. The jury's nullification power has become the subject of a resurgence of scholarly and popular interest in recent years, partly as a response to a number of high profile criminal trials. While jury nullification has more support among legal academics n1 than judges, most legal scholars strongly oppose the jury's exercise of its nullification power. The vast majority of case law also condemns nullification as lawless and arbitrary. Indeed, in a recent case, the Second Circuit emphasized that nullification is a violation of a juror's oath to apply the law as instructed by the court.[4]

While the judiciary as a general rule does not sanction the nullification power of the jury, some jurists tacitly recognize the jury's right to nullify by allowing defendants to testify about moral values and intent, but remain unwilling to directly inform jurors of their nullification powers. Indeed, Americans have historically displayed "bipolar" attitudes toward jury nullification.[6] The use of the term bipolar signifies not only that proponents and opponents

---

*   reprinted with the permission of the Brooklyn Law School's *Brooklyn Law Review*
4. *United States v. Thomas*, 116 F.3d 606, 608 (2d Cir. 1997).
6. Irwin A. Horowitz & Thomas E. Willging, Changing Views of Jury Power, *Law and Human Behavior* 15: 165 (1991).

are diametrically opposed, but also, like the affective bipolar disorder it be-speaks, the controversy is heated and emotional.[7]

The purpose of this Article is to inform this debate. This Article will begin by exploring what is meant by the term "nullification."...[T]his Article's primary tasks will be to pose a number of empirical questions relevant to the legal de-bate on nullification, to provide a selective review of the empirical research bear-ing on these questions (with an emphasis on some of our own research on this topic), and finally, to identify open empirical questions needing further research.

I. Defining jury nullification

Nullification occurs when a jury disregards or misapplies the law in reach-ing its verdict. Nullification proponents argue that the primary motive for such action should be to return an acquittal when strict interpretation of the law would result in an injustice and violate the moral conscience of the com-munity. Henceforth, this Article will use the term "conventional nullification" to refer to nullification so motivated. Such perceived injustice can arise from various concerns. One is that the defendant's behavior, while technically ille-gal, was justified to some degree. Jurors may apply a "reasonable man" stan-dard and justify a defendant's behavior, feeling that any reasonable person (in-cluding themselves, perhaps) would have acted similarly under the circumstances. Or, jurors may reason that the defendant was not a free agent but acted under compulsion or diminished capacity (e.g., Inside the Jury Room). Or, jurors may conclude that a defendant's actions were prompted by admirable motives or intentions (in some cases of euthanasia or doctor as-sisted suicide). Even if jurors do not see a defendant's behavior as justified, they could nullify because they believe that the penalty prescribed by law is disproportionate to the offense, either because the usual penalty is seen as too severe or because the defendant has "already suffered enough."

Exercise of the nullification power permits the jury to be merciful. Alan Scheflin has suggested that nullification power does not abrogate statutes or precedents (thereby creating new law), but rather it "perfects" the application of current law by adding a much needed touch of mercy. The power of juries to nullify tends to emerge as a political issue during times of national discon-tent. The nullification doctrine has struck a resonant chord in the community as evidenced by the existence of grass roots organizations whose aims are to

---

7. Id.

amend state constitutions to permit juries to be fully informed of their power to nullify.

Nullification can also be motivated by jurors' rejection of the law itself, rather than by concern for the fate of particular defendants. For example, jurors may feel that the behavior in question should not be illegal. An historic example is the unwillingness of Prohibition-era jurors to convict defendants charged with selling liquor. More contemporary examples might be cases in which the law prohibits some private sexual behavior of consenting adults or the use of certain "soft" illegal drugs. Or, jurors may have some moral objection to a law. For example, some jurors might see laws that prohibit blocking entrances to abortion clinics as countenancing legalized murder.

Critics of nullification note that jurors' motives need not be so principled; nullification may also occur because of caprice or unprincipled favoritism. An example of the latter is the apparent refusal of southern juries to convict white defendants charged with offenses against black victims despite very strong prosecution cases. Yet another dark side of nullification can be termed jury vilification. Juries may return verdicts that reflect prejudiced or bigoted community standards and convict when the evidence does not warrant a conviction. Examples of jury vilification may be found throughout American history but are most prominent in the racially charged history of the former states of the confederacy. The opponents of the nullification power have pilloried the doctrine as historically unsound, functionally unwise, and legally untenable. Gary Simson takes the position that the difference between vengeance and mercy is an unprincipled distinction and while nullification may have had some legal basis in colonial days, it is now a legal anachronism.

At times, jurors may disregard or misapply the law to meet somewhat broader goals than producing a preferred trial outcome for a particular defendant. An acquittal may be intended to voice a protest against some agency or public policy. For example, many media personalities have suggested that the verdict in the O.J. Simpson murder trial might have been, in part, an indictment of racism in the Los Angeles police department. Jurors may also nullify the law to meet very general justice goals. So, for example, some have urged juries to combat racism in the criminal justice system by acquitting minority defendants even when the necessary elements of the charge have appeared to be proven against a specific minority defendant.

There is yet another, less conventional form of nullification that this Article will consider. It occurs when jurors fail to follow some normative, legal prescription and alter their verdict because of the resultant bias. This action is called "nullification via juror bias." The prescription in question need not be a particular statute under which a defendant is charged, as the preceding, conventional views of nullification assume. Rather, any rule or instruction that proscribes jurors' selection and evaluation of information could be the locus of such nullification via juror bias. This could include rules of evidence, exclusionary instructions, or standards or burdens of proof. What is crucial in such acts of nullification is the biased use of information. Although in some contexts (such as in assigning culpability; in identifying remedies), it may be important to distinguish between willful refusals to follow the law and unintentional failures to do so, in terms of the net effect for trial outcome, it is not useful to draw such a distinction. Thus, this Article will consider juror bias arising both from unwillingness and inability to follow the law's prescriptions as types of nullification. In contrast to conventional nullification, some such instances of nullification via bias may even occur without conscious awareness.

Such juror bias may take many forms. One form is when jurors are either unwilling or unable to disregard certain information. Familiar examples would include jurors' failure to disregard evidence heard but subsequently ruled as inadmissible, or jurors' consideration of proscribed pretrial publicity. Another form occurs when jurors are unwilling or unable to limit their use of certain information. Examples would include using knowledge of a defendant's prior criminal record to infer culpability (rather than just as a source of credibility information) or taking the content of opening/closing arguments as evidence (rather than just as each side's theory of the case). Yet another form of bias consists of the inability or unwillingness to consider certain information. Examples would be a failure to consider the well-reasoned arguments of opposing jurors during deliberation or a failure to consider evidence contrary to one's initially preferred verdict.

Another broad class of juror biases arise when jurors rely upon legally-proscribed pre-existing beliefs. Racial or gender stereotypes which are treated as probative illustrate such biases. And a final type of juror bias arises from jurors' feelings about parties in the trial (e.g., defendant, victim, attorney). This Article is concerned with the impact of jurors' feelings (of sympathy or of aversion) on biasing jurors' interpretation, evaluation, and weighing of information at trial....

Empirical questions bearing on jury nullification

A. Question 1: Does conventional jury nullification occur?

As noted earlier, "conventional" nullification refers to those instances where the jury's disregard of the law is motivated by concerns with achieving a more just outcome than would occur under the strict application of the law. There is considerable non-experimental evidence that conventional nullification does achieve a more just outcome. Best known, of course, are classic case studies of historically important instances of nullification, such as the *Bushel* and *Zenger* cases. In each such case, there was unambiguous and strong evidence of the defendants' guilt under the then-current law, widespread public opposition to the defendants' conviction, and an eventual jury acquittal. Reasonable inferences of conventional nullification have also been drawn from low conviction rates for particularly unpopular statutes (e.g., violations of Prohibition, Fugitive Slave Act in the Northern states).

Other, somewhat more direct evidence comes from reports of juror behavior during trials or in post-deliberation interviews. For instance, a clear example of nullification was provided by the documentary program Inside the Jury Room, which included (with all parties' permission) a video-recording of an actual jury deliberation for an unlawful possession of a weapon case. The jurors' rationale for acquittal clearly reflected appeal to extenuating circumstances (e.g., the defendant's diminished mental capacity) unprovided for in the law.

Another line of evidence comes from geographic disparities in acquittal rates that cannot be plausibly attributed to geographic differences in applicable law or trial evidence (e.g., acquittals of black defendants in the Bronx).

There is also corroborative experimental evidence. For example, experimental jury simulation studies show that as the severity of a prescribed penalty increases (especially to extremely harsh levels), the probability of criminal conviction declines and a higher standard of proof may be applied by jurors. For instance, in a recent study Niedermeier, Horowitz, and Kerr reported an experiment in which a physician was accused of knowingly transfusing a patient with blood unscreened for the HIV virus. Although the charges, elements necessary for conviction, evidence, and prescribed standards of proof were held constant, they found that the mock jurors were less likely to judge the physician as guilty of violating the law when the penalty prescribed by law was severe (twenty-five years of imprisonment) than when it was relatively mild ($ 500 fine)....

The goal of the research summarized above was to examine, first at the individual and then at the group level, how decision makers use information when the decision criteria support results that may conflict with desires to reach outcomes that are perceived as fair, just, or equitable. To put it another way, the research was directed toward situations in which distributive justice norms were violated by the stipulated decision criteria. Previous research suggested that when people believe that their decisions may result in unfair (e.g., overly punitive) outcomes for others, these decision-makers may augment the importance of information leading to particular (i.e., fair) conclusions. In a similar vein, the group research on judgmental tasks finds that groups give disproportional attention to evidence supporting desired and commonly shared decision alternatives. Sommer, Horowitz, and Bourgeous examined the hypothesis that individuals and groups that experience conflict between legally constrained outcomes versus morally fair judgments recruit information in a manner that will enhance distributive justice outcomes....

B. Question 2: Does jury nullification via juror bias occur?

Of course, there is considerable anecdotal evidence that jurors and juries exhibit extralegal biases which functionally nullify the law. There is also a large and varied body of corroborative experimental evidence. Examples include jurors' proscribed use of prejudicial pretrial publicity and proscribed, inadmissible evidence. There is also research evidence suggesting that sometimes jurors disregard the law because they see the law (such as the laws of evidence) as unfair in the present instance. For example, Kassin and Sommers found that jurors were more likely to disregard evidence ruled as inadmissible by the judge if that inadmissibility was based on the evidence's unreliability (fair basis for exclusion) than when the inadmissibility stemmed from legal, due-process concerns (unfair basis for exclusion).

C. Question 3: What do uninstructed jurors know about their nullification powers and inclinations?

As noted above, Judge Leventhal, writing for the majority in the *Dougherty* ruling, expressed the belief that jurors knew full well—through informal channels such as the news media—that they could nullify without fear of reprisal. n134 Evidence is scant on this empirical question, but there are indications that this position is rather too sanguine. For example, one recent survey of jury-eligible adults in New York City found that no more that five percent of the population was cognizant of the jury's nullification powers.[135]

A related question is whether naive venierpersons expect to follow the law or their own personal conceptions of justice, should these prove to be in conflict. Anecdotal and survey evidence suggests that decreasing confidence in the

---

135. David C. Brody & Craig Rivera, (1997) Examining the *Dougherty* "All Knowing Assumption": Do jurors know about their nullification power? 33 *Criminal Law Bulletin* 151, 151 (1997).

legal system, a heightened distrust of lawyers, as well as an increased cynicism concerning the parties involved in civil suits, has led to concern that jurors would readily nullify in such instances. The first "Juror Outlook Survey" conducted by the National Law Journal found that three-quarters of the respondents said that they would do what they considered to be the "right thing," no matter how the judge instructed them. However, a closer look at the survey suggests that when jurors are provided with specific examples, their view is less provocative and cynical. When asked if they could be fair and impartial in a case if one of the defendants was an African-American, only 1.8% said no, and an additional 4.8% were unsure. When the hypothetical defendant was white, 1.9% were sure they could not be fair, while 5.2% were unsure. Interestingly, jurors were more likely to admit to prejudice against gays or lesbians, as well as politicians.

D. Question 4: What would the impact be of explicitly informing jurors of a power or a right to nullify?

The chaos theory advanced in *Dougherty* raises at least two related empirical questions. First, advocates and apologists for jury nullification see what this Article has called "conventional" jury nullification—avoiding unjust verdicts under the law—as a proper exercise of juridic authority. The interesting empirical question is whether explicitly informing jurors that they have the power and/or the right to nullify in this way would facilitate this "proper" form of nullification. The second question is whether such instructions might have broader, unintended effects (such as increasing juror biases, prejudice, use of stereotypes, etc.). Critics of jury nullification and adherents to the chaos theory fear that the answer to the latter question is "yes."

With respect to the first question, there is some experimental evidence that nullification instructions increase nullification verdicts in cases in which conviction or acquittal runs counter to jurors' sense of justice. Horowitz examined a number of hypothetical criminal cases, all of which had clear, strong evidence for conviction. One was a garden-variety case of murder that raised no obvious problems of injustice through the strict application of the law. The case involved the killing of a grocery store owner during a robbery, and there was ample physical and eyewitness evidence of the defendant's guilt. A second case was a (pre-Kevorkian) case of euthanasia. In it, a nurse hastened the death of a terminally ill cancer patient to relieve the patient's suffering. The facts of this case produced a highly sympathetic defendant. Here a strict application of the law (i.e., finding the nurse guilty of first-degree murder) could be expected to violate at least some jurors' sense of justice.

Jurors were given instructions by the trial judge after watching the video-tapes and before retiring to deliberate. Three sets of judicial instructions were used. One was a set of standard instructions (SI), drawn from pattern in-structions of Ohio, which made no reference to nullification. The second was drawn from pattern instructions of Maryland, one of just a few states that has any explicit provision in state law for jury nullification. These Maryland instructions (MI) indicated that the law "is not binding upon you" and "you may accept or reject it...." The third set of instructions were the most ex-pansive on jury nullification powers and were based on recommendations made by Jon Van Dyke. These "nullification" instructions (NI) admonished jurors that while they must give respectful attention to the law, they had the final authority to decide whether or not to apply the law to the acts of the de-fendant. In addition, juries were told that they were representatives of the community and they should take into account the sentiments of that com-munity as well as their conscience. Finally, the third part of these instruc-tions informed the jurors that while they must respect the law, "nothing would bar you from acquitting the defendant if you feel the law, as applied to the fact situation before you, would produce an inequitable or unjust ver-dict." Hence, these NI instructions asserted both the jury's power and the right to nullify.

Do juries who receive nullification instructions function differently than those given standard instructions? The results of this study suggest that they do. Analysis of Horowitz's mock juries' deliberations indicated that the pres-entation of radical nullification instructions engendered a different deliber-ation dynamic. Juries who received standard instruction were more focused on the evidence and the instruction while those who received strong nulli-fication instructions focused relatively more on personal experiences and in-dividual notions of justice. The latter juries also were more likely to focus on the defendant's characteristics and discuss the judge's instructions dur-ing the deliberation process. It should be noted that juries who received the Maryland instructions did not differ from those given standard instructions.

While the expansive nullification instructions appeared to have "liberated" the juries somewhat from the evidence, what effect did these instructions have on judgments of guilt?...Horowitz found that the juries given the NI instruc-tions were much more likely to be merciful in the euthanasia case. That is, in the euthanasia case, these juries were more likely to acquit in the face of the law. Also note that the type of instruction made no difference in the murder trial. This is important because it suggests that nullification instructions do not prompt a general inclination to acquit, regardless of the content of the case.

This conclusion is underscored by the results involving a third case, also examined by Horowitz. The case involved a drunk college-aged male defendant who killed one individual and severely injured another while driving under the influence of alcohol. The issue in this case was whether the defendant deliberately ignored warnings that he was not in any condition to drive. [M]ock juries given the nullification instructions were more severe in the drunk driving case, and were also more likely to convict of the most serious charge (vehicular homicide) in this case. Clearly, the effect of nullification instructions is not restricted to promoting mercy in cases where a technically-guilty defendant merits leniency. Such instructions can also prompt harshness in cases where the defendant is very unsympathetic.

In summary, an explicit nullification instruction did alter the process and the outcome of Horowitz's mock jury deliberations. When juries were instructed that they could determine both facts and law, there was a rationality to their decision making. That is, they were merciful when the community would be merciful and the law would not (the euthanasia scenario) and they were severe when the community might be expected to be severe, even when the law made a conviction on the most severe charge rather difficult.

A follow-up study was aimed at providing a demonstration as to the impact of explicit nullification information (embedded either in judicial instructions or in lawyers' arguments) on jury functioning. Lawyers are often able to insinuate nullification sentiments in arguments without an overt use of that term. Previous research has suggested that lawyers' nullification arguments can alter the jury's perception of its role. This second experiment examined the effects of what happens when a defense lawyer makes a thinly veiled nullification argument to the jury. It is quite unlikely that such a defense would go unchallenged. Previous research had indicated a tendency for unchallenged nullification arguments to exaggerate jurors' tendencies to consider non-evidentiary issues in their decision making.

In the second experiment, mock juries were again exposed to one of three trials: the drunk driving case used in the previous study, a modified version of the euthanasia case (here, with a male nurse), and a case of illegal possession of a weapon, based on a PBS documentary which demonstrated jury nullification. In addition, mock juries received standard or nullification instructions from the trial judge and they did or did not hear a plea for nullification during closing arguments by the defendant's counsel. Finally, the prosecutor did or did not challenge the defense counsel's nullification plea. The prosecutor's challenge strongly reminded the juries that they are asked to follow the law whatever their sentiments.

In trials in which the defendant was sympathetic and/or portrayed as morally upright (i.e., the euthanasia and illegal possession cases), the judge's instructions that included a nullification clause or nullification pleas from the defense counsel resulted in more merciful verdicts. But nullification information from judge or lawyer did not move the juries in the direction of mercy for the drunk driving case. This offers support for Judge Bazelon's hypothesis that a truly dangerous defendant would not go free under nullification instructions. Indeed, the data indicated that jurors had a tendency to judge the defendant in this trial more harshly than the evidence warranted, as found in the first study.

The impact of challenges to nullification arguments depressed juries' tendencies to act upon their sentiments. In the drunk driving case, juries tended to give harsher verdicts when nullification information went unchallenged. This is a curious situation: it would appear that if the defense raises the possibility of nullification when the defendant is perceived as dangerous, juries will act on that information by bringing in verdicts more severe than when not given such information. However, the prosecutor's admonitions to the jury to follow its prescribed role muted these tendencies.

These two studies suggest then that nullification instructions from the bench will alter both jury functioning and verdicts. The verdicts appear to reflect a sense of community sentiment that is willing to be merciful to morally upright individuals but is also willing to be more severe than the law in dealing with less worthy or more dangerous defendants. There seems to be a predictable calculus that juries employ when in receipt of nullification information. In addition, when reminded of their duty to adhere closely to the law as enunciated by the judge, juries tend to forgo tendencies to nullify. This explains perhaps why juries in states that have a nullification instruction (however veiled) and do remind jurors of their duty to follow the law, do not report instances of "chaos."

Implicit in the chaos theory is the fear that nullification instructions will have a much wider impact than merely promoting more merciful verdicts in a handful of exceptional cases. The fear is that such instructions create a slippery slope that will encourage jurors to ignore the law with impunity and to give full rein to their personal prejudices and biases. To examine these concerns empirically, Niedermeier, Horowitz, and Kerr conducted four additional studies. In the first three of these studies, they employed a trial that involved a morally upright defendant who was technically guilty of the charged crime.

However, the crime was committed under circumstances so extenuating that many jurors would see his behavior as justified. A doctor was charged with illegally transfusing a patient with blood unscreened for the HIV virus; this patient later died of AIDS. However, the doctor had not simply been careless, but had acted out of extreme necessity. A natural disaster, a tornado, had resulted in many injured persons. The local hospital was isolated and unable to receive emergency supplies, including blood. The patient's need for transfusion was immediate and pressing, and the only blood available to the doctor was unscreened. Therefore, there were good reasons to suspect that jurors would feel that convicting the defendant of this crime would be unjust and a violation of their sense of fairness.

As in the previous studies by Horowitz, mock jurors (or juries) received either standard instructions (SI) or expansive nullification instructions (NI)…. [M]ock jurors were more lenient (this time toward the sympathetic physician) when they received nullification instructions. But the key objective in these studies was not to show that nullification instructions could have some direct impact on verdicts, but rather to see if such instructions exacerbated the magnitude of other potential biases. Thus, in the study a number of case factors were varied which, ideally, jurors should ignore, but which research evidence suggests jurors do not completely ignore, despite the judge's instructions to the contrary or other normative pressures. Specifically, the following factors were varied: (a) the defendant's nationality (physician was born and trained in the United States versus in a foreign country), (b) the severity of the penalty prescribed for conviction ($ 500 fine versus twenty-five years of imprisonment), (c) the defendant's professional status (hospital medical director versus resident), (d) the defendant's remorse (remorse expressed versus not expressed), and (e) the defendant's gender (male versus female physician).

As much prior experimental work would suggest, the jurors' ratings of the defendant's guilt and/or verdicts were affected by several of the manipulated, extra-legal factors. Specifically, the physician/defendant was more likely to be judged guilty if (a) she was a female (rather than a male), (b) the prescribed penalty was only a $ 500 fine (rather than a twenty-five year prison sentence), (c) he was a low-status resident (rather than the hospital medical director), (d) he failed to express remorse (if a resident), and (e) he expressed remorse (if the hospital director). But more importantly, in all but one of these instances of jury bias, hearing NI instructions did not affect the magnitude of bias.

The one exception to this rule occurred for the defendant professional status factor. For jurors, the effect of status (i.e., harsher judgments for the medical resident than for the hospital medical director) was stronger if the jurors heard nullification instructions than when they had heard standard instructions. It is noteworthy that this instruction effect was not replicated among juries; that is, status did not have a stronger effect under NI than SI for mock juries, only for mock jurors.

Thus, the first three studies provided very little evidence that nullification instructions exacerbated jurors' personal biases in a case where conventional nullification might be appropriate. In the fourth study, Horowitz posed the same question for a case in which there was little conflict between jurors' sense of justice and the demands of the law. This experiment used trial materials developed for a classic study by Galen Bodenhausen. It was a garden-variety case of assault, growing out of a bar fight (girl flirts with boy in a bar; boyfriend gets angry; boy gets assaulted outside bar; boyfriend is charged; evidence against the boyfriend is circumstantial, but strong). The biasing factor examined was the defendant's ethnicity; some jurors learned that the defendant was Hispanic (his name was Carlos Ramierez), the remaining jurors were told that the defendant was Anglo (Robert Johnson). And, as in the previous studies, half of the jurors received standard instructions (SI) and the rest received nullification instructions (NI).

Overall, mock jurors were more likely to judge the Hispanic defendant as guilty than the Anglo defendant. However, this bias was not statistically stronger (or weaker) among those receiving nullification instructions than among those receiving standard instructions. Once again, there was little evidence that receipt of nullification instructions "unleashed" preexisting juror biases. This demonstration achieved more than replicating a result previously found for a nullification-relevant case to a nullification-irrelevant case. It is possible that most or even all of the biasing factors examined in the first three studies had some indirect impact on jurors' interpretation of the evidence.

For example, in Niedermeier, Horowitz, and Kerr's Experiment 2, perhaps the doctor's status affected jurors' judgment of the doctor's degree of experience, which could, in turn, have affected jurors' assessment of the reasonableness of the doctor's actions. Or, in Experiment 3, the doctor's gender might illogically have affected jurors' judgment of his/her medical competence, which again could have affected their judgment of how well justified his/her actions were. One has to strain mightily, though, to see a way that the defendant's race in the last experiment could—logically or illogically—influence jurors' interpretation of the evidence. Rather, this bias seems more readily interpreted as reflecting reliance on personal racial or ethnic stereotypes. And it is, in part, reliance on such personal, extra-legal beliefs which constitutes the "chaos" that the court predicted would follow receipt of nullification instructions. But here, there was little evidence of chaotic effects of such instructions.

Collectively, Niedermeier's studies sought to test whether explicitly informing jurors of their power to nullify invites chaos, as feared by some, or prompts jurors to rule based on their sense of fairness, as hoped for by others. Nullification instructions seemed to heighten jurors' concerns about fairness. Mock jurors reported feeling more free to avail themselves of their notions of fairness. However, except for one instance in which nullification instructions provoked individual jurors—not juries—to be more favorable to a higher status defendant, nullification instructions never interacted with any manipulation of proscribed information including defendant gender, defendant remorse, defendant nationality, extenuating circumstances, or penalty severity. It should be noted that their findings were consistent over four studies that employed a variety of participant samples (college students, jury-eligible adults, and adults drawn directly from jury rolls, both paid and unpaid), and were generally consistent (with the one exception noted above) across both individuals and groups.

Overall, the data suggests a generally prudent use of the power to nullify. When the facts of the case engaged jurors' sense of justice, there are lower conviction rates when they were in receipt of nullification instructions. This result replicates previous findings in similar research. We also found that nullification instructions, particularly when the focus was the jury, did not affect the magnitude of these biases. Juries did respond to certain biasing factors, but nullification instructions did not amplify those biases.

IV. Open empirical questions

A number of preliminary answers to key empirical questions relevant to jury nullification have been provided by the research literature reviewed above. However, for all of the empirical questions this Article posed, the empirical evidence, although largely consistent, is fragmentary and inconclusive. It is clear that more research will be required before we can confidently assert answers to these questions. Moreover, there are a number of additional nullification-relevant empirical questions for which there is practically no research available. This Article concludes by posing a few of these open questions.

A. Just how widespread is nullification in contemporary American juries?

There certainly are well-documented instances of nullification by actual and experimental juries. Thus, it is clear that nullification can and does occur.

What is not nearly so clear is just how common it is. One means of exploring this question would be through extensive post-trial interviews with jurors serving in a representative sample of jurisdictions and cases.

B. Under what conditions is nullification most likely to occur?

For example, are there certain types of cases or defenses that make nullification more or less likely? How important is the presence of a nullification advocate ("trigger") during deliberation for nullification to occur? These questions could be addressed in experimental jury simulation studies.

C. Are American jurors becoming more inclined to nullify?

For example, are the various "nonconventional" forms of nullification on the increase, such as "protest verdicts" or raciallybased nullification. If so, what are the events or sources of information that are encouraging nullification beliefs, inclinations, and behaviors? Particularly interesting in this regard is the possibility, highlighted by several prominent cases (e.g., the O. J. Simpson case; the Rodney King case), that racial factors may be playing a more important role in jury nullification.

D. What do jurors who receive standard instructions believe about their powers and rights to nullify?

Standard instructions usually instruct jurors that they must follow the law and do not mention nullification powers. Do jurors so instructed still understand the nullification powers that they possess?

E. Just what nullification instructions have what impact?

Are there instruction wordings which accurately communicate powers or rights without inviting excesses or "chaos"? Are there any kinds of bias which are exacerbated through strong nullification instructions? In this regard, there are a number of contrasting interests: (1) Conscious or intentional acquittal, motivated by goals of fairness or justice as opposed to unconscious, unintentional acquittal produced by biased evaluation of evidence or standards of proof; (2) Bias via belief (e.g., evaluation of evidence) as opposed to bias via emotion (e.g., sentiment/liking/sympathy). In this latter regard, practically all of the research showing an effect on verdicts for nullification instructions involve a sympathetic, likable defendant (e.g., the nurse charged with euthanasia in Horowitz, the doctor accused of an illegal transfusion in Niedermeier) or an unsympathetic, unlikable defendant (e.g., the drunk driver of Horowitz). Moreover, most, if not all, of the biasing factors examined to date may have had exerted their effects through the interpretation of evidence. Even the biasing effect of defendant ethnicity observed in the Niedermeier study could have been the result of such a stereotyped evidentiary inference (e.g., jurors could infer a disposition for violence from defendant ethnicity). Would the general pattern of prior studies—i.e., nullification instructions not affecting the magnitude of such biasing effects—also be replicated for biases that exert their effect through jurors' positive or negative evaluation of the defendant, or victim, such as that resulting from racial prejudice?

Conclusion

Scholarly opinions on jury nullification reveal many contradictions. Ours is a system of justice under law, not under the personal, idiosyncratic judgments of men and women. However, people recognize that there will be instances in which justice may be better served by men and women departing from the strict letter of the law. Many observers believe that instances of jury nullification are very rare and hence, not a significant issue or problem. Yet, a number of high profile cases, many touching on sensitive issues of race, have raised concerns that there might be a rather large iceberg of jury nullification beneath the surface of the relatively few, well-documented cases. Explicit instructions to jurors that they possess nullification powers (or, more controversially, nullification rights) may invite arbitrary and widespread departure from the law with profound consequences. On the other hand, it is curious to expect jurors to exert a power that they are routinely told they do not possess.

This Article has suggested that these and other aspects of the public and scholarly debate on jury nullification require answers to empirical, behavioral questions. This Article reviewed the extant empirical literature and identified a number of suggestive patterns: e.g., explicit instructions sanctioning conventional jury nullification appear to increase its incidence, such instructions do not appear to alter juror verdicts in cases where strict application of the law raises few problems of perceived injustice in jurors' minds, and such instructions do not appear to accentuate or exaggerate pre-existing juror biases. No matter where one stands on the ongoing, non-empirical disagreement about the net benefit or harm of jury nullification, obtaining clearer, more definitive answers to these and related empirical questions should do much for informing and helping to resolve such disagreements.

List of other cases and articles relevant to this topic.

Williams v. Florida, 399 U.S. 78 (1970)
Colgrove v. Battin, 413 U.S. 149 (1973)
Duncan v. Louisiana, 391 U.S. 145 (1968)
J.E.B. v. Alabama, 511 U.S. 127 (1994)
Beck v. Alabama, 447 U.S. 625 (1980)
Campbell v. Louisiana, 523 U.S. 392 (1998)
Horowitz, I., (1985). The effect of jury nullification instruction on verdicts and jury functioning in criminal trials. *Law and Human Behavior* 9(1): 25–36.
Horowitz, I., (1988). Jury nullification: The impact of judicial instruments, arguments and challenges on jury decision making. *Law and Human Behavior* 12(4): 439–453.

Discussion and Review Questions

1. There is no discussion in the United States Constitution or found in the writing of our forefathers concerning the size, composition or power of the jury to nullify. Based on your readings which issue has the most historical basis?
2. Develop a research project to answer one of the following empirical questions:
   a   Are the dynamics and deliberations of six and twelve person groups significantly different? In developing this project, it is important to define what types of "differences" are important to examine and how you would test the research question on those points.
   b   Is it important to have a racially, ethnically and gender mixed jury? In developing this project, it is important to identify how diverse and non-diverse juries may differ in terms of legitimacy as well as deliberations.
   c   Should juries be advised of their power to nullify the law? In developing this project, it is important to explore whether individuals are aware of this power as well as the ramification of this knowledge?
3. What types of cases in contemporary society do you think jurors are likely to engage in nullification? Some argue that nullification of the law based

on racial, political and moral grounds is legitimate whereas others argue that nullification is a perversion of the law. Do you think that there are any crimes that would warrant nullification by a jury? Why or why not.

References

Articles

Brody, D.C. and C. Rivera (1997). Examining the Dougherty "all knowing assumption": Do jurors know about their nullification power? *Criminal Law Bulletin* 33: 151.

Horowitz, I. (1985). The effect of jury nullification instruction on verdicts and jury functioning in criminal trials. *Law and Human Behavior* 9: 25–36.

Horowitz, I, N. L. Kerr, and K.E. Niedermeier (2001). Jury nullification: Legal and psychological perspectives. *Brooklyn Law Review* 66: 1207–1249.

Kalven, H. and Zeisel, H. (1966). *The American Jury*. NY: Little Brown Co.

Kerr, N.L., G.P. Kramer, J.S. Carroll, and J.J. Alfini (1991). On the effectiveness of voir dire in criminal cases with prejudicial pretrial publicity: An empirical study. *American University Law Review* 40, 665–701.

Melilli, K. (1996) Batson in practice: What we have learned about Batson and peremptory challenges. *Notre Dame Law Review* 71: 447–503.

Niedermeier, K.E., Horowitz, I., and N.L. Kerr (1999). Informing jurors of their nullification power: A route to a just verdict or judicial chaos? *Law and Human Behavior* 23: 313.

Pound, R. (1910). Law in books and law in action. *American Law Review* 44: 12.

Rose, M.R. (1999). The peremptory challenged accused of race or gender discrimination? Some data from one county. *Law and Human Behavior* 23: 695–702.

Saks, M.J. and M. W. Marti (1997). A meta-analysis of the effect of jury size. *Law and Human Behavior* 21: 451–467.

Case Citations

Baldwin v. New York, 399 U.S. 66 (1970)
Ballew v. Georgia, 435 U.S. 223 (1978)
Batson v. Kentucky, 476 U.S. 79 (1994)
Campbell v. Louisiana, 523 U.S. 392 (1998)
Colgrove v. Battin, 413 U.S. 149 (1973)
Duncan v. Louisiana, 391 U.S. 145 (1968)
Ex parte Milligan, 71 U.S. 2 (1886)

Georgia v. McCollum, 505 U.S. 42 (1992)

J.E.B. v. Alabama, 511 U.S. 127 (1994)

McKeiver v. Pennsylvania, 403 U.S. 528 (1971)

Peters v. Kiff, 407 U.S. 493 (1972)

Powers v. Ohio, 499 U.S. 400 (1991)

Sparf and Hansen v. United States, 156 U.S. 51 (1895)

Strauder v. West Virginia, 100 U.S. 303 (1880)

Swain v. Alabama, 380 U.S. 202 (1965)

United States v. Dougherty, 473 F. 2d 1113 (D.C. Cir. 1972)

United States v. Thomas, 116 F. 3d 606 (2d Cir. 1997)

Williams v. Florida, 399 U.S. 78 (1970)

CHAPTER 9

EYEWITNESS AND MISTAKEN IDENTIFICATIONS

"I was certain, but I was wrong."

–Jennifer Thompson (New York Times Op-Ed, June 18, 2000).

On June 18, 2000, Jennifer Thompson wrote an op-ed piece for the New York Times describing her brutal rape when she was a 22 year-old college student, how she painstakingly watched her attacker so that she could later identify him and how she found out 11 years later she was wrong. Several days after her rape, she identified a man in a photo line up and chose the same man again in a later live line-up. In the two trials (the first one was reversed by the appellate court) against Ronald Cotton, Thompson pointed him out in court as her attacker. During the second trial, a man named Bobby Poole was bragging about raping Thompson, they brought him to court and she said she had never seen him before. Cotton was convicted and sentenced to life in prison. In 1995, DNA exonerated Cotton and proved that Poole had raped Thompson.

More than 100 convicted criminals have been released due to the work of Barry Scheck and Peter Neufeld's "The Innocence Project" (http://www.innocenceproject.org/). These individuals were found innocent after years in prison based on DNA evidence. In 1996, the National Institute of Justice highlighted 26 cases (including the Cotton case) in its review of DNA exonerations. In *Actual Innocence*, a book written by Barry Scheck, Peter Neufeld, and Jim Dwyer, they found that more than 80% of the wrongful convictions involved mistaken identifications. The release of so many inmates (more than 400 nation-wide) based on exonerating DNA analysis has provoked lawyers and psychologists to begin raising questions about eyewitness identifications in general. Some courts allow expert witnesses to testify concerning the factors related to misidentifications and problematic identification procedures, however other courts continue to disallow this evidence. In 1983, the Arizona Supreme Court was the first to allow the admission of expert testimony on the problems of eyewitness identifications (Contreras 2001). A number of state courts (e.g, California and New York) have also allowed the admission of this testimony. Other courts have restricted the testimony and opted for alternative measures, discussed below, to address problems related to possible misidentifications. A few courts (e.g., the 7th Circuit Court of Appeals, the 11th Circuit Court of Appeals and the Utah Supreme Court) have disallowed this testimony completely. The courts that have rejected the introduction of this evidence do so for one of two reasons—first, they find the evidence not scientific and two, that the testimony is not necessary to educate juries because it is a matter of common-sense.

What social science may assist in the understanding of eyewitness identification?

Although the study of memory covers more than one hundred years, a great deal of research has been conducted in the last two decades. Now, psychologists understand how memory is affected by different situations (Wrightsman 2001). Memory is influenced by "reasoning processes, suggestibility and social influence, self-confidence, authoritarian submission, and conformity." (Id. at 121). Situational circumstances, e.g., the stress of an event witnessed, lighting, brevity of observation, also influence the accuracy of memory and eyewitness identification. The latest studies show that police procedures used to identify suspects may significantly influence the accuracy of identifications.

Wells (1978) categorized these two types of influencing factors as "system variables" and "estimator variables." System variables—involving police questioning, the method of identification, use of videotaping, presence of other witnesses during identifications and other procedures—involve law enforcement and are preventable (Wrightsman 2001; Wells 1993). Estimator variables—lighting, vision impairment, exposure to witness, and other factors related to the commission of the crime—do not involve law enforcement and are therefore not within the control of the criminal justice system (Wrightsman 2001; Wells 1993). General information about the factors influencing identifications is considered "social framework" evidence because it provides juries with information about "general conclusions from social science research" to assist them in making factual determinations (Monahan and Walker 1988: p. 470).

What types of "out of court" identification procedures are used by law enforcement?

There are three primary types of out-of-court identification procedures, the show-up, the line-up and the photo array. A show-up is a procedure where a single individual is presented for identification, a line-up requires several individuals for presentation for identification, and a photo array uses photographs of individuals for identification. There are a number of things that police may do to affect the accuracy of an identification using each of these procedures. In October 1999, the United States Department of Justice (1999) published a guide for law enforcement on eyewitness evidence. Janet Reno (then the Attorney General of the United States) commissioned a panel of experts to examine problems with eyewitness identification in light of the many wrongful convictions exposed by DNA testing. The group, called the Technical Working Group for Eyewitness Evidence, was comprised of 34 experts created the guide. The purpose of the guide is to ensure that law enforcement does everything possible to obtain accurate and reliable evidence from eyewitnesses.

The guide provides information concerning the initial or preliminary investigation—the initial report or first responder, the preparation of mug books, procedures for interviewing witnesses by follow-up investigators, field identification (show-ups) procedures, and procedures for eyewitness identifications (photo and live lineups). One of the primary advantages of this guide, over prior work in this area, is that it is supported by social science (p. 1). Each principle set forth in the guide is intended to reduce the chance that police actions will influence eyewitness identifications. For example, the guide recommends that compositions of line-ups be conducted so that the suspect "does not unduly standout" (1999: 29). The guide provides very specific instructions on methods to develop a "fair" line up, including but not limited to:

1. Include only one suspect in each identification procedure....
3. Consider placing suspects in different positions in each lineup, both across cases and with multiple witnesses in the same case. Position the suspect randomly unless, where local practice allows, the suspect or the suspect's attorney requests a particular position. (p. 30).

The provisions in the *Eyewitness evidence: A guide for law enforcement* are only recommendations, these procedures are not required by law, nor is it a given that experts will be permitted to testify in court concerning the fallibility of eyewitness identifications based on the influence of "system" or "estimator" factors.

Are judges willing to introduce expert witness testimony on eyewitness identifications?

Expert testimony in court on the inaccuracy of eyewitness testimony is very controversial. As noted earlier, most courts do not admit this type of "social framework" evidence at trial (Monahan and Walker (1988). Courts have generally taken one of three approaches to dealing with the admissibility of this type of expert testimony. Most courts give trial judges wide-latitude and discretion in determining whether expert testimony is admissible under current standards (discussed in chapter 2) (Dillickrath 2001). Other courts utilize a *per se* rule of exclusion concerning the introduction of the expert testimony (Dillickrath 2001). The third view from the courts is to provide a "limited admissibility" rule which restricts trial judges from excluding expert evidence when there is no other corroborating evidence to demonstrate the defendant's guilt (Dillickrath 2001).

According to a review of state and federal court decisions, Dillickrath (2001) found that the introduction of eyewitness identification expert testimony "does not enjoy a favored status in the state or federal courts" (p. 1060). Dillickrath identifies some current methods being used by the courts, far short of introducing expert testimony, "to ameliorate problems in eyewitness identifications" (p. 1061). The laundry list of alternatives include cautionary jury instructions, effective cross-examination of witnesses and argument by attorneys, and general knowledge about the flaws of identification (more or less a "this is common knowledge" approach).

Are all identifications admissible in court?

There are four methods of identification—the photographic array, the show-up, the pretrial line-up and the in-court identification. Lawyers have challenged the admissibility of each type of identification based on a variety of constitutional grounds. The Court has held that pretrial confrontations do not violate the **Fifth Amendment** provision protecting accused's from self-incrimination, however post-indictment line-ups involve a **critical stage** in the criminal court process and therefore defendants are entitled to a lawyer. *Stovall v. Denno*, 388 U.S. 293 (1967); *United States v. Wade*, 388 U.S. 218 (1967). In addition, the Court has held identifications that are "unduly and

> **Fifth Amendment:** No person... shall be compelled in any criminal case to be a witness against himself.....
>
> **Critical stage:** Critical stage in a criminal proceeding at which an accused is entitled to counsel is one in which a defendant's rights may be lost, defenses waived, privileges claimed or waived, or in which the outcome of the case is otherwise substantially affected. (Black's Law Dictionary).

unnecessarily suggestive," may violate the due process clause of the Fourteenth Amendment.

In *Stovall*, the Court found that using the show-up procedure when there was doubt as to whether the victim would recover from his wounds was not unnecessary. The standard for suggestiveness that violates due process requires that the identification at trial be preceded by an identification procedure that is "so impermissibly suggestive as to give rise to a very substantial likelihood of irreparable misidentification." *Simmons v. United States*, 390 U.S. 377 (1968). Creating situations where the identification of a suspect is virtually inevitable has been condemned by the United States Supreme Court in *Foster v. California*, 394 U.S. 440 (1969).

In subsequent cases, the court has found the suggestiveness of the pretrial identification as an issue for cross examination and reliability to be determined by jurors, not a matter of admissibility to be determined by the court. In a case involving a show-up procedure, the Court upheld the procedure but re-affirmed that a pretrial show-up or line-up must avoid a substantial likelihood of irreparable misidentification. *Neil v. Biggers*, 409 U.S. 188 (1972). In *Biggers*, the Court recognized the very real problem surrounding suggestive pre-trial show-ups that these confrontations increase the chance of a later misidentification at trial. The Court also stated that unnecessary suggestiveness alone does not require the exclusion of identification evidence. A suggestive procedure could still result in a reliable identification and therefore the identification would be admissible. To determine whether a pre-trial identification procedure meets this standard of suggestibility and unreliability, the court outlined five factors to be viewed under the "totality of the circumstances":

1. the witness's opportunity to view the criminal during the crime;
2. the witness's degree of attention;

3. the accuracy of the witness's prior description of the criminal;
4. the level of certainty demonstrated by the witness at the confrontation; and
5. the length of time between the crime and the confrontation.

(Klotter and Kanovitz 1995: 402). Interestingly, the factors set out by the United States Supreme Court in *Neil v. Biggers* and *Manson v. Braithwaite* to assess identification procedures have not been found by researhcers to be empirically reliable factors. (Wells and Seelau 1995). As one example, studies have demonstrated that "witness confidence" is not related to the accuracy of witness identifications (Penrod and Cutler 1995).

Are "in court" identifications inherently suggestive?

With this background, we turn now to a discussion of the inherent suggestibility of 'in-court' identifications. One of the primary concerns about out-of-court identifications is to assess whether the suggestibility irreparably effects later identifications. But given the dynamics of an in-court identification, there is nothing more suggestive than the defendant sitting at counsel table next to his lawyer when the prosecutor asks for a witness to identify his or her assailant. Interestingly, compared to the challenges to pre-trial "out of court" identification procedures, much less attention has been devoted to questioning the propriety of the in-court identification procedure (Mandery 1996). There has been a mix across state and federal courts on dealing with the suggestiveness of in-court identifications. Some have given in-court identification procedures no protection based on the assumption that they are not unnecessarily suggestive whereas other courts have applied the *Biggers* test and still others have ordered in-court lineups. In his review of the legal and psychological evidence, Mandery suggests that in-court identification procedures "at least be given the same protection as pre-trial identifications." (Mandery at 421).

In this chapter, *Neil v. Biggers*, 409 U.S. 188 (1972), *State v. Chapple*, 660 P. 2d 1208 (Ariz. 1983)(holding eyewitness identification testimony admissible), and *State v. Butterfield*, 27 P. 3d 1133 (Utah 2001)(holding eyewitness identification testimony inadmissible) are included.

Neil v. Biggers
409 U.S. 188 (1972)(Excerpt)

MR. JUSTICE POWELL delivered the opinion of the Court.

In 1965, after a jury trial in a Tennessee court, respondent was convicted of rape and was sentenced to 20 years' imprisonment. The State's evidence

consisted in part of testimony concerning a station-house identification of respondent by the victim. The Tennessee Supreme Court affirmed. Biggers v.
State, 219 Tenn. 553, 411 S. W. 2d 696 (1967). On certiorari, the judgment
of the Tennessee Supreme Court was affirmed by an equally divided Court.
Biggers v. Tennessee, 390 U.S. 404 (1968) (MARSHALL, J., not participating).
Respondent then brought a federal habeas corpus action raising several
claims.... We granted certiorari to decide whether...the identification procedure violated due process.... As the claim turns upon the facts, we must first
review the relevant testimony at the jury trial and at the habeas corpus hearing regarding the rape and the identification. The victim testified at trial that
on the evening of January 22, 1965, a youth with a butcher knife grabbed her
in the doorway to her kitchen:

> "A. [H]e grabbed me from behind, and grappled—twisted me on the
> floor. Threw me down on the floor.
> "Q. And there was no light in that kitchen?
> "A. Not in the kitchen.
> "Q. So you couldn't have seen him then?
> "A. Yes, I could see him, when I looked up in his face.
> "Q. In the dark?
> "A. He was right in the doorway—it was enough light from the bed-
> room shining through. Yes, I could see who he was.
> "Q. You could see? No light? And you could see him and know him
> then?
> "A. Yes."

When the victim screamed, her 12-year-old daughter came out of her bedroom and also began to scream. The assailant directed the victim to "tell her
[the daughter] to shut up, or I'll kill you both." She did so, and was then
walked at knifepoint about two blocks along a railroad track, taken into a
woods, and raped there. She testified that "the moon was shining brightly, full
moon." After the rape, the assailant ran off, and she returned home, the whole
incident having taken between 15 minutes and half an hour.

She then gave the police what the Federal District Court characterized as
"only a very general description," describing him as "being fat and flabby with
smooth skin, bushy hair and a youthful voice." Additionally, though not mentioned by the District Court, she testified at the habeas corpus hearing that
she had described her assailant as being between 16 and 18 years old and between five feet ten inches and six feet tall, as weighing between 180 and 200
pounds, and as having a dark brown complexion. This testimony was sub-

stantially corroborated by that of a police officer who was testifying from his notes.

On several occasions over the course of the next seven months, she viewed suspects in her home or at the police station, some in lineups and others in show-ups, and was shown between 30 and 40 photographs. She told the police that a man pictured in one of the photographs had features similar to those of her assailant, but identified none of the suspects. On August 17, the police called her to the station to view respondent, who was being detained on another charge. In an effort to construct a suitable lineup, the police checked the city jail and the city juvenile home. Finding no one at either place fitting respondent's unusual physical description, they conducted a show-up instead.

The show-up itself consisted of two detectives walking respondent past the victim. At the victim's request, the police directed respondent to say "shut up or I'll kill you." The testimony at trial was not altogether clear as to whether the victim first identified him and then asked that he repeat the words or made her identification after he had spoken.[4] In any event, the victim testified that she had "no doubt" about her identification. At the habeas corpus hearing, she elaborated in response to questioning.

> "A. That I have no doubt, I mean that I am sure that when I—see, when I first laid eyes on him, I knew that it was the individual, because his face—well, there was just something that I don't think I could ever forget. I believe_____
>
> "Q. You say when you first laid eyes on him, which time are you referring to?
>
> "A. When I identified him—when I seen him in the courthouse when I was took up to view the suspect."

We must decide whether, as the courts below held, this identification and the circumstances surrounding it failed to comport with due process requirements.

---

4. At trial, one of the police officers present at the identification testified explicitly that the words were spoken after the identification. The victim testified:

"Q. What physical characteristics, if any, caused you to be able to identify him?

"A. First of all,—uh—his size,—next I could remember his voice.

"Q. What about his voice? Describe his voice to the Jury.

"A. Well, he has the voice of an immature youth—I call it an immature youth. I have teen-age boys. And that was the first thing that made me think it was the boy."

The colloquy continued, with the victim describing the voice and other physical characteristics. At the habeas corpus hearing, the victim and all of the police witnesses testified that a visual identification preceded the voice identification.

We have considered on four occasions the scope of due process protection against the admission of evidence deriving from suggestive identification procedures. In *Stovall v. Denno*, 388 U.S. 293 (1967), the Court held that the defendant could claim that "the confrontation conducted...was so unnecessarily suggestive and conducive to irreparable mistaken identification that he was denied due process of law." Id., at 301–302. This, we held, must be determined "on the totality of the circumstances." We went on to find that on the facts of the case then before us, due process was not violated, emphasizing that the critical condition of the injured witness justified a show-up in her hospital room. At trial, the witness, whose view of the suspect at the time of the crime was brief, testified to the out-of-court identification, as did several police officers present in her hospital room, and also made an in-court identification.

Subsequently, in a case where the witnesses made in-court identifications arguably stemming from previous exposure to a suggestive photographic array, the Court restated the governing test:

> "[W]e hold that each case must be considered on its own facts, and that convictions based on eyewitness identification at trial following a pretrial identification by photograph will be set aside on that ground only if the photographic identification procedure was so impermissibly suggestive as to give rise to a very substantial likelihood of irreparable misidentification." *Simmons v. United States*, 390 U.S. 377, 384 (1968).

Again we found the identification procedure to be supportable, relying both on the need for prompt utilization of other investigative leads and on the likelihood that the photographic identifications were reliable, the witnesses having viewed the bank robbers for periods of up to five minutes under good lighting conditions at the time of the robbery.

The only case to date in which this Court has found identification procedures to be violative of due process is *Foster v. California*, 394 U.S. 330, 442 (1969). There, the witness failed to identify Foster the first time he confronted him, despite a suggestive lineup. The police then arranged a show-up, at which the witness could make only a tentative identification. Ultimately, at yet another confrontation, this time a lineup, the witness was able to muster a definite identification. We held all of the identifications inadmissible, observing that the identifications were "all but inevitable" under the circumstances. Id., at 443.

In the most recent case of *Coleman v. Alabama*, 399 U.S. 1 (1970), we held admissible an in-court identification by a witness who had a fleeting but "real good look" at his assailant in the headlights of a passing car. The witness testified at a pretrial suppression hearing that he identified one of the petitioners among the participants in the lineup before the police placed the participants in a formal line. MR. JUSTICE BRENNAN for four members of the Court stated that this evidence could support a finding that the in-court identification was "entirely based upon observations at the time of the assault and not at all induced by the conduct of the lineup." Id., at 5–6.

Some general guidelines emerge from these cases as to the relationship between suggestiveness and misidentification. It is, first of all, apparent that the primary evil to be avoided is "a very substantial likelihood of irreparable misidentification." Simmons v. United States, 390 U.S., at 384. While the phrase was coined as a standard for determining whether an in-court identification would be admissible in the wake of a suggestive out-of-court identification, with the deletion of "irreparable" it serves equally well as a standard for the admissibility of testimony concerning the out-of-court identification itself. It is the likelihood of misidentification which violates a defendant's right to due process, and it is this which was the basis of the exclusion of evidence in Foster. Suggestive confrontations are disapproved because they increase the likelihood of misidentification, and unnecessarily suggestive ones are condemned for the further reason that the increased chance of misidentification is gratuitous. But as Stovall makes clear, the admission of evidence of a showup without more does not violate due process.

What is less clear from our cases is whether, as intimated by the District Court, unnecessary suggestiveness alone requires the exclusion of evidence. While we are inclined to agree with the courts below that the police did not exhaust all possibilities in seeking persons physically comparable to respondent, we do not think that the evidence must therefore be excluded. The purpose of a strict rule barring evidence of unnecessarily suggestive confrontations would be to deter the police from using a less reliable procedure where a more reliable one may be available, and would not be based on the assumption that in every instance the admission of evidence of such a confrontation offends due process. Clemons v. United States, 133 U.S. App. D.C. 27, 48, 408 F.2d 1230, 1251 (1968) (Leventhal, J., concurring); cf. Gilbert v. California, 388 U.S. 263, 273 (1967); Mapp v. Ohio, 367 U.S. 643 (1961). Such a rule would have no place in the present case, since both the confrontation and the trial preceded Stovall v. Denno, supra, when we first gave notice that the suggestiveness of confrontation procedures was anything other than a matter to be argued to the jury.

We turn, then, to the central question, whether under the "totality of the circumstances" the identification was reliable even though the confrontation procedure was suggestive. As indicated by our cases, the factors to be considered in evaluating the likelihood of misidentification include the opportunity of the witness to view the criminal at the time of the crime, the witness' degree of attention, the accuracy of the witness' prior description of the criminal, the level of certainty demonstrated by the witness at the confrontation, and the length of time between the crime and the confrontation. Applying these factors, we disagree with the District Court's conclusion.

In part, as discussed above, we think the District Court focused unduly on the relative reliability of a lineup as opposed to a show-up, the issue on which expert testimony was taken at the evidentiary hearing. It must be kept in mind also that the trial was conducted before Stovall and that therefore the incentive was lacking for the parties to make a record at trial of facts corroborating or undermining the identification. The testimony was addressed to the jury, and the jury apparently found the identification reliable. Some of the State's testimony at the federal evidentiary hearing may well have been self-serving in that it too neatly fit the case law, but it surely does nothing to undermine the state record, which itself fully corroborated the identification.

We find that the District Court's conclusions on the critical facts are unsupported by the record and clearly erroneous. The victim spent a considerable period of time with her assailant, up to half an hour. She was with him under adequate artificial light in her house and under a full moon outdoors, and at least twice, once in the house and later in the woods, faced him directly and intimately. She was no casual observer, but rather the victim of one of the most personally humiliating of all crimes. Her description to the police, which included the assailant's approximate age, height, weight, complexion, skin texture, build, and voice, might not have satisfied Proust but was more than ordinarily thorough. She had "no doubt" that respondent was the person who raped her. In the nature of the crime, there are rarely witnesses to a rape other than the victim, who often has a limited opportunity of observation. The victim here, a practical nurse by profession, had an unusual opportunity to observe and identify her assailant. She testified at the habeas corpus hearing that there was something about his face "I don't think I could ever forget." App. 127.

There was, to be sure, a lapse of seven months between the rape and the confrontation. This would be a seriously negative factor in most cases. Here, however, the testimony is undisputed that the victim made no previous identification at any of the show-ups, lineups, or photographic showings. Her record for reliability was thus a good one, as she had previously resisted whatever suggestiveness inheres in a show-up. Weighing all the factors, we find no substantial likelihood of misidentification. The evidence was properly allowed to go to the jury. Affirmed in part, reversed in part, and remanded.

MR. JUSTICE MARSHALL took no part in the consideration or decision of this case.

State v. Chapple
660 P. 2d 1208 (Ariz. 1983)(Excerpt)

OPINION BY: FELDMAN

OPINION: Dolan Chapple was convicted on three counts of first degree murder, one count of unlawfully transporting marijuana and one count of conspiring to unlawfully transport marijuana. He was sentenced to a term of life imprisonment without possibility of parole for twenty-five years on each of the murder counts, to a term of imprisonment for not less than twenty-five years nor more than life on the transportation count, and to a term of imprisonment for not less than twenty-five nor more than thirty years on the conspiracy count. The sentence on each count is to run concurrently with the sentences on all other counts. The defendant appealed from this judgment and sentence....

Facts

[Essentially, defendant was implicated in a drug deal "rip off" that resulted in several homicides. Chapple was charged with the drug and homicide charges].....At his extradition hearing in Illinois, seven witnesses placed [Chapple] in Cairo, Illinois during the entire month of December 1977, three of them testifying specifically to his presence in that town on December 11, the day of the crime. The same witnesses testified for him in the trial at which he was convicted. No direct or circumstantial evidence of any kind connects defendant to the crime, other than the testimony of Malcolm Scott and Pamela Buck, neither of whom had ever met the defendant before the crime and neither of whom saw him after the crime except at the trial. Defendant was apprehended and tried only because Malcolm Scott and Pamela Buck picked his photograph out of a lineup more than one year after the date of the crime; he was convicted because they later identified both the photographs and defendant himself at trial.

The State's position was that the identification was correct, while the defendant argued at trial that the identification was erroneous for one of two reasons. The first reason advanced by defendant is that Scott and Buck were lying to save themselves by "fingering" him....These contentions were evidently rejected by the jury and are not in issue here. Defendant further argued at trial, and urges here, that even if Scott and Buck are not lying, their identification was a case of mistaken identity. The argument is that Scott and Buck picked the wrong picture out of the photographic lineup and that their subsequent photographic and in-court identifications were part of the "feedback phenomenon" and are simply continuations or repetitions of the same mistake. To support this contention of mistaken identification, defendant offered expert testimony regarding the various factors that affect the reliability of identification evidence. For the most part, that testimony was rejected by the trial court as not being within the proper sphere of expert testimony....

Expert Testimony Regarding Eyewitness Identification

On learning of Mel Coley's participation in the crime, the sheriff's office quickly procured photographs of Coley, which were shown to Scott and Buck in a photographic lineup on December 16, 1977. Both of them identified Coley, thus providing law enforcement with the first step in its efforts to apprehend Dee and Eric. The detectives then showed Scott and Buck various photographs and lineups containing pictures of known acquaintances of Mel Coley. At this same session, Scott pointed to a picture of James Logan and stated that it resembled Dee, though he could not be sure. So far as the record shows, no follow-up was made of this tentative identification. One of the photographic lineups displayed to Scott, but not to Buck, contained a picture of the defendant, Dolan Chapple, but Scott did not identify him as Dee. At a time and in a manner not disclosed by the record, both Scott and Buck made a tentative identification of a photograph of Eric. The photograph portrayed Coley's nephew, Eric Perry.

The police continued to show the witnesses photographic lineups in an attempt to obtain an identification of Dee. Police efforts were successful on January 27, 1979, when Scott was shown a nine-picture photo lineup. For the first time, this lineup included photos of both Eric Perry, who had already been tentatively identified by Scott and Buck, and of the defendant; however, James Logan's photo was not included. Upon seeing this lineup, Scott immediately recognized Eric's picture again. About ten minutes later, Scott identified defendant's picture as Dee. Scott was then shown the picture of defendant he had failed to identify at a previous session and asked to explain why he had not previously identified it. He stated that he had no recollection of having seen it before. After Scott had identified Dee and before he could talk to his sister, the police showed Buck the same lineup. Buck identified the defendant as Dee and then re-identified Eric.

Defendant argues that the jury could have found the in-court identification unreliable for a variety of reasons. The defendant argues that the identification of Dee from photographic lineups in this case was unreliable because of the time interval which passed between the occurrence of the event and the lineup and because of the anxiety and tension inherent in the situation surrounding the entire identification process. The defendant also argues that since Scott and Buck had smoked marijuana on the days of the crime, their perception would have been affected, making their identification through photographs less reliable. Further, defendant claims the January 27, 1979 identification of Dee by Scott and Buck from the photographic lineup was the product of an unconscious transfer. Defendant claims that Scott picked the picture of Dolan Chapple and identified it as Dee because he remembered that picture from the previous lineup (when he had not been able to identify defendant's picture). Defendant urges that the in-court identifications were merely reinforcements of the initial error. Defendant also argues that Eric's presence in the lineup heightened the memory transfer and increased the chance of an incorrect photographic identification. Defendant makes the further point that since the James Logan picture resembled defendant's and was not again displayed to the witnesses, the chance of misidentification was heightened. Further, defendant claims that the identification was made on the basis of subsequently acquired information which affected memory. Finally, defendant argues that the confidence and certainty which Scott and Buck displayed in making their in-court identification at trial had no relation whatsoever to the accuracy of that identification and was, instead, the product of other factors.

It is against this complicated background, with identification the one issue on which the guilt or innocence of defendant hinged, that defense counsel offered the testimony of an expert on eyewitness identification in order to rebut the testimony of Malcolm Scott and his sister, Pamela Buck. The witness called by the defense was Dr. Elizabeth Loftus, a professor of psychology at the University of Washington. Dr. Loftus specializes in an area of experimental and clinical psychology dealing with perception, memory retention and recall. Her qualifications are unquestioned, and it may fairly be said that she "wrote the book" on the subject. The trial court granted the State's motion to suppress Dr. Loftus' testimony. Acknowledging that rulings on admissibility of expert testimony are within the discretion of the trial court, defendant contends that the court erred and abused its discretion in granting the motion to suppress Dr. Loftus' testimony. The admissibility of expert testimony is governed by Rule 702, Ariz.R. of Evid. That rule states:

If scientific, technical, or other specialized knowledge will assist the trier of fact to understand the evidence or to determine a fact in issue, a witness qualified as an expert by knowledge, skill, experience, training, or education, may testify thereto in the form of an opinion or otherwise.

In what is probably the leading case on the subject, the Ninth Circuit affirmed the trial court's preclusion of expert evidence on eyewitness identification in *United States v. Amaral*, 488 F.2d 1148 (9th Cir.1973). In its analysis, however, the court set out four criteria which should be applied in order to determine the admissibility of such testimony. These are: (1) qualified expert; (2) proper subject; (3) conformity to a generally accepted explanatory theory; and (4) probative value compared to prejudicial effect. Id. at 1153. We approve this test and find that the case at bar meets these criteria. We recognize that the cases that have considered the subject have uniformly affirmed trial court rulings denying admission of this type of testimony. However, a careful reading of these cases reveals that many of them contain fact situations which fail to meet the Amaral criteria or are decided on legal principles which differ from those we follow in Arizona. For instance, in one of the cases often cited on this subject, *United States v. Watson*, 587 F.2d 365 (7th Cir.1978), the court held that the expert testimony was properly precluded by the trial court because of the lack of the witness' qualifications and the fact that identification had been "prompt and positive" so that expert testimony would be of little use. Id. at 369. Neither of those grounds is applicable to the case at bench. Similarly, in another leading case, *United States v. Brown*, 540 F.2d 1048, 1053–54 (10th Cir.1976), the court pointed out that there had been no real offer of proof and that expert evidence regarding eyewitness testimony would improperly invade the province of the jury[10] and would result in undue consumption of time. In the case presently before us, there was a detailed offer of proof, the consumption of time involved in taking the testimony of the expert witness in question was certainly not "undue" in comparison with the importance of the issue before the court, and the worry about invading the province of the jury has been solved for us by the provisions of Rule 704, Ariz.R. of Evid., which permits opinion testimony even though "it embraces an ultimate issue."

Applying the Amaral test to the case at bench, we find from the record that the State has conceded that the expert was qualified and that the question of

---

10. Several other cases hold that such testimony was properly refused on the basis that expert evidence on the reliability of eyewitness identification would invade the province of the jury. See *Caldwell v. State*, 267 Ark. 1053, 1059, 594 S.W.2d 24, 28–29 (App.1980); *People v. Johnson*, 112 Cal.Rptr. 834, 836–37, 38 Cal.App.3d 1, 6–7 (1974); *James v. State*, 232 Ga. 762, 763–64, 208 S.E.2d 850, 852–53 (1974); *Pankey v. Commonwealth*, 485 S.W.2d 513, 521–22 (Ky.App.1972).

conformity to generally accepted explanatory theory is not raised and appears not to be a question in this case. The two criteria which must therefore be considered are (1) determination of whether the probative value of the testimony outweighs its possible prejudicial effect and (2) determination of whether the testimony was a proper subject.

1. Probative Value vs. Predjudice

The State argues that there would have been little probative value to the witness' testimony and great danger of unfair prejudice. The latter problem is claimed to arise from the fact that Loftus' qualifications were so impressive that the jury might have given improper weight to her testimony. We do not believe that this raises the issue of unfair prejudice. The contention of lack of probative value is based on the premise that the offer of proof showed that the witness would testify to general factors which were applicable to this case and affect the reliability of identification, but would not express any opinion with regard to the accuracy of the specific identification made by Scott and Buck and would not express an opinion regarding the accuracy percentage of eyewitness identification in general.

We believe that the "generality" of the testimony is a factor which favors admission. Witnesses are permitted to express opinions on ultimate issues but are not required to testify to an opinion on the precise questions before the trier of fact.

> Most of the literature assumes that experts testify only in the form of opinions. The assumption is logically unfounded. [Rule 702] accordingly recognizes that an expert on the stand may give a dissertation or exposition of scientific or other principles relevant to the case, leaving the trier of fact to apply them to the facts. Since much of the criticism of expert testimony has centered upon the hypothetical question, it seems wise to recognize that opinions are not indispensable and to encourage the use of expert testimony in non-opinion form when counsel believes
> Fed.R. of Evid. 702 advisory committee note.

2. Proper Subject

The remaining criterion at issue is whether the offered evidence was a proper subject for expert testimony. Ariz.R. of Evid. 702 allows expert testi-

mony if it "will assist the trier of fact to understand the evidence or to determine a fact in issue." Put conversely, the test "is whether the subject of inquiry
is one of such common knowledge that people of ordinary education could
reach a conclusion as intelligently as the witness...." *State v. Owens*, 112 Ariz.
223, 227, 540 P.2d 695, 699 (1975). Furthermore, the test is not whether the
jury could reach some conclusion in the absence of the expert evidence, but
whether the jury is qualified without such testimony "to determine intelligently
and to the best possible degree the particular issue without enlightenment
from those having a specialized understanding of the subject...." Fed.R.Evid.
702 advisory committee note (quoting Ladd, Expert Testimony, 5 Vand.L.Rev.
414, 418 (1952)).

In excluding the evidence in the case at bench, the trial judge stated:

I don't find anything that's been presented in the extensive discussions that
I have read in your memorandum with regard to the fact that this expert is
going to testify to anything that isn't within the common experience of the
people on the jury, that couldn't really be covered in cross-examination of the
witnesses who made the identification, and probably will be excessively argued in closing arguments to the jury.

This basis for the view that eyewitness identification is not a proper subject
for expert testimony is the same as that adopted in *United States v. Amaral*,
supra, and in the great majority of cases which have routinely followed Amaral. See, e.g., *State v. Valencia*, 118 Ariz. 136, 138, 575 P.2d 335, 337 (App.1977);
People v. Guzman, 121 Cal.Rptr. 69, 71–72, 47 Cal.App.3d 380, 385–86 (1975);
Dyas v. United States, 376 A.2d 827, 831–32 (D.C.App.1977); *Nelson v. State*,
362 So.2d 1017, 1021 (Fla.App.1978); *People v. Dixon*, 87 Ill.App.3d 814, 818,
410 N.E.2d 252, 256 (1980); *State v. Porraro*, R.I., 404 A.2d 465, 471 (1979).

However, after a careful review of these cases and the record before us, we
have concluded that although the reasons cited by the trial judge would correctly permit preclusion of such testimony in the great majority of cases, it
was error to refuse the testimony in the case at bench. In reaching this conclusion, we have carefully considered the offer of proof made by the defense
in light of the basic concept of "proper subject" underlying Rule 702.

We note at the outset that the law has long recognized the inherent danger
in eyewitness testimony. See *United States v. Wade*, 388 U.S. 218, 87 S.Ct. 1926,
18 L.Ed.2d 1149 (1967). [11] Of course, it is difficult to tell whether the ordinary

---

11. "The vagaries of eye-witness identification are well known: the annals of criminal
law are rife with instances of mistaken identification.... 'What is the worth of identification
testimony even when uncontradicted? The identification of strangers is proverbially un-

juror shares the law's inherent caution of eyewitness identification. Experimental data indicates that many jurors "may reach intuitive conclusions about the reliability of [such] testimony that psychological research would show are misguided." Note, Did Your Eyes Deceive You? Expert Psychological Testimony on the Unreliability of Eyewitness Identification, 29 *Stan.L.Rev.* 969, 1017 (1977).

Even assuming that jurors of ordinary education need no expert testimony to enlighten them to the danger of eyewitness identification, the offer of proof indicated that Dr. Loftus' testimony would have informed the jury that there are many specific variables which affect the accuracy of identification and which apply to the facts of this case. For instance, while most jurors would no doubt realize that memory dims as time passes, Dr. Loftus presented data from experiments which showed that the "forgetting curve" is not uniform. Forgetting occurs very rapidly and then tends to level out; immediate identification is much more trustworthy than long-delayed identification. Thus, Scott's recognition of Logan's features as similar to those of Dee when Logan's picture was shown at the inception of the investigation is probably a more reliable identification than Scott's identification of Chapple's photograph in the photographic lineup thirteen months later. By the same token, Scott's failure to identify Chapple's photograph when it was first shown to him on March 26, 1978 (four months after the crime) and when Scott's ability to identify would have been far greater, is of key importance.

Another variable in the case is the effect of stress upon perception. Dr. Loftus indicated that research shows that most laymen believe that stressful events cause people to remember "better" so that what is seen in periods of stress is more accurately related later. However, experimental evidence indicates that stress causes inaccuracy of perception with subsequent distortion of recall.

Dr. Loftus would also have testified about the problems of "unconscious transfer," a phenomenon which occurs when the witness confuses a person seen in one situation with a person seen in a different situation. Dr. Loftus would have pointed out that a witness who takes part in a photo identification session without identifying any of the photographs and who then later sees a photograph of one of those persons may relate his or her familiarity with the picture to the crime rather than to the previous identification session.

Another variable involves assimilation of post-event information. Experimental evidence, shown by Dr. Loftus, confirms that witnesses frequently in-

---

trustworthy. The hazards of such testimony are established by a formidable number of instances in the records of English and American trials.'" Id. 388 U.S. at 228, 87 S.Ct. at 1933 (Brennan, J., quoting Frankfurter, J.).

corporate into their identifications inaccurate information gained subsequent to the event and confused with the event. An additional problem is the "feedback factor." We deal here with two witnesses who were related and who, according to Loftus' interview, engaged in discussions with each other about the identification of Dee. Dr. Loftus, who interviewed them, emphasized that their independent descriptions of Dee at times utilized identical language. Dr. Loftus would have explained that through such discussions identification witnesses can reinforce their individual identifications. Such reinforcement will often tend to heighten the certainty of identification. The same may be said of the continual sessions that each witness had with the police in poring over large groups of photographs.[13]

The last variable in this case concerns the question of confidence and its relationship to accuracy. Dr. Loftus' testimony and some experimental data indicate that there is no relationship between the confidence which a witness has in his or her identification and the actual accuracy of that identification. Again, this factor was specifically tied to the evidence in the case before us since both Scott and Buck indicated in their testimony that they were absolutely sure of their identification. Evidently their demeanor on the witness stand showed absolute confidence.

We cannot assume that the average juror would be aware of the variables concerning identification and memory about which Dr. Loftus was qualified to testify.

Depriving [the] jurors of the benefit of scientific research on eyewitness testimony force[d] them to search for the truth without full knowledge and opportunity to evaluate the strength of the evidence. In short, this deprivation prevent[ed] [the] jurors from having "the best possible degree" of "understanding the subject" toward which the law of evidence strives.

Note, supra, 29 *Stan.L.Rev.* at 1017–18. Thus, considering the standard of Rule 702, supra,—whether the expert testimony will assist the jury in determining an issue before them—and the unusual facts in this case, we believe that Dr. Loftus' offered evidence was a proper subject for expert testimony and should have been admitted.

---

13. We do not suggest that the police attempted to prejudice the identification procedure. The facts show that the police were careful to avoid the possibility of prejudice. However, as Dr. Loftus pointed out, it is not possible to discuss identification of photographs with witnesses on seven different occasions, comprising a total of over 200 pictures, without giving the witness some "feedback" with respect to what the officers anticipate or expect the witness to find.

Of course, the test is not whether we believe that under these facts the evidence was admissible, but whether the trial court abused its discretion in reaching the contrary conclusion. Our review of the record leads us to the following conclusions regarding the various factors which support admission or preclusion here. Among the factors considered are the following:

1. The facts were close and one of the key factual disputes to be resolved involved the accuracy of the eyewitness identification. The preclusion ruling undercut the entire evidentiary basis for defendant's arguments on this issue.
2. The testimony offered was carefully limited to an exposition of the factors affecting reliability, with experimental data supporting the witness' testimony and no attempt was made to have the witness render opinions on the actual credibility or accuracy of the identification witnesses. Issues of ultimate fact may be the subject of expert testimony, but witnesses are not "permitted as experts on how juries should decide cases." Ariz.R. of Evid. 704 comment.
3. On the other hand, we see no significant prejudice to the State in permitting the testimony; the problem of time is not present in this case, since time spent on the crucial issue of the case can not be considered as "undue" loss of time. No other significant factor weighing against admission of the evidence seems present.
4. No question exists with regard to three of the four criteria listed in United States v. Amaral, supra, being fulfilled by the factual situation present in this case.
5. The key issue here pertained to the fourth criterion—the question of whether Loftus' evidence was a "proper subject" for expert testimony.

As indicated above, the key to this issue is whether the testimony might assist the jury to resolve the issues raised by the facts. In making this determination, the trial court must first consider those contentions of ultimate fact raised by the party offering the evidence and supported by evidentiary facts in the record. It must then determine whether the expert testimony will assist in resolving the issues.

In our view, the record clearly shows that Dr. Loftus' testimony would have been of considerable assistance in resolving some of the factual contentions raised by the parties in this case. Examples follow:

First, the photographs in evidence show that there is a resemblance between Logan and Chapple. Scott told the police that Logan's photograph resembled

Dee. Scott then failed to identify Chapple's photograph when it was first shown to him. Considering these facts, might Scott's comments regarding the Logan photographs be considered an identification? Should it be considered more accurate than his identification of Chapple from the photographic lineup almost one year later? Loftus' testimony regarding the forgetting curve would have assisted the jury in deciding this issue.

Second, assuming the jury disregarded, as was its right, Scott's and Buck's denial of having discussed Dee's description prior to the identification of January 27, 1979, did the feedback/after-acquired information phenomena play a part in Buck's identification of defendant on the cropped-hair lineup? We cannot assume that ordinary jurors would necessarily be aware of the impact of these factors.

Third. Logan and Chapple bear some resemblance. Logan's picture had been the object of some comment between Scott and the sheriff's deputies shortly after the killing. Although he professed to have no memory of it, Scott had seen a picture of the defendant within a few months of the shooting. Was Scott's identification of defendant on the January 27, 1979 lineup therefore influenced by an unconscious transfer of memory? Since Dee evidently looked like Logan and Chapple, was this transfer phenomenon with regard to their photographs more pronounced than it was with regard to other photographs which were shown to Scott on more than one occasion?

Fourth. Since a cropped hair picture of Logan, who bore a resemblance to defendant and was tentatively identified by Scott soon after the killing, was not included in the lineup of January 1979, were Scott and Buck given a reasonable choice with respect to the photos which they examined on the occasion on which they identified Chapple?

Fifth. The opportunity for perception by the witnesses in this case was great. Most of us would assume that where the opportunity for perception has been significantly greater than the usual case, the recall of the witness and the subsequent identification must be correspondingly more accurate than in most cases. The expert testimony may well have led to the opposite conclusion, though Dr. Loftus admitted that none of her experiments had been based upon situations where the opportunity for perception had been similar to that of the case at bench. Nevertheless, it is implicit in Loftus' testimony that even in cases such as this, the other factors described by her can have a significant impact on the accuracy of later identification.

Sixth, did the witnesses' absolute confidence in the identification bear any relationship to the accuracy of that identification? Again, contrary to Dr. Loftus' opinion, most people might assume that it would.

Each of the factual issues described above is raised by evidentiary facts in the record or reasonable inferences from those facts. In effect, the trial judge ruled that all of the information necessary to resolve the conflicting factual contentions on these issues was within the common experience of the jurors and could be covered in cross-examination of the identification witnesses and argued to the jury.

It is difficult to support this conclusion. For instance, while jurors are aware that lapse of time may make identification less reliable, they are almost certainly unaware of the forgetting curve phenomenon and the resultant inference that a prompt tentative identification may be much more accurate than later positive identification. Similarly, cross-examination is unlikely to establish any evidentiary support for argument that eyewitnesses who have given similar nonfactual descriptions of the criminal may have been affected by the feedback phenomenon. Again, experimental data provides evidentiary support to arguments which might otherwise be unpersuasive because they seem contrary to common "wisdom."

The phrase "within the discretion of the trial court" is often used but the reason for that phrase being applied to certain issues is seldom examined. One of the primary reasons an issue is considered discretionary is that its resolution is based on factors which vary from case to case and which involve the balance of conflicting facts and equitable considerations. *Walsh v. Centeio*, 692 F.2d 1239, 1242 (9th Cir.1982). Thus, the phrase "within the discretion of the trial court" does not mean that the court is free to reach any conclusion it wishes. It does mean that where there are opposing equitable or factual considerations, we will not substitute our judgment for that of the trial court. Thus, while we have no problem with the usual discretionary ruling that the trier of facts needs no assistance from expert testimony on the question of reliability of identification, the unusual facts of this case compel the contrary conclusion. The preclusion ruling here was based upon a determination that the jury would not be assisted by expert testimony because the subjects embraced by that testimony could be elicited on cross-examination and argued without the evidentiary foundation. Preclusion here was not predicated upon a balancing of conflicting factual contentions or equitable considerations;[17] it was based upon the court's own conclusion that scientific theory regarding the working of human memory could be developed on cross-examination and effectively argued without evidentiary foundation. The examples listed above

---

17. E.g.: consumption of time, delay in trial or undue prejudice to the State.

demonstrate that under the facts here this conclusion was incorrect; there were a number of substantive issues of ultimate fact on which the expert's testimony would have been of significant assistance. Accordingly, we hold that the order precluding the testimony was legally incorrect and was unsupported by the record. It was, therefore, an abuse of discretion. *Grant v. Public Service Company*, 133 Ariz. 434, 652 P.2d 507 (1982).

In reaching this conclusion, we do not intend to "open the gates" to a flood of expert evidence on the subject. We reach the conclusion that Dr. Loftus should have been permitted to testify on the peculiar facts of this case and have no quarrel with the result reached in the vast majority of cases which we have cited above. The rule in Arizona will continue to be that in the usual case we will support the trial court's discretionary ruling on admissibility of expert testimony on eyewitness identification. Nor do we invite opinion testimony in even the most extraordinary case on the likelihood that a particular witness is correct or mistaken in identification or that eyewitness identification in general has a certain percentage of accuracy or inaccuracy.....

State v. Butterfield
27 P. 3d 1133 (Utah 2001)(Excerpt)

OPINION: RUSSON, Associate Chief Justice:

Defendant Raymond Butterfield ("Butterfield") appeals from convictions of aggravated burglary, rape of a child, sodomy on a child, and three counts of aggravated sexual abuse of a child, all first degree felonies. See Utah Code Ann. §§ 76–6–203 & 76–5–402.1, –403.1, –404.1 (1999). Butterfield contends that his convictions should be reversed because the trial court...(2) abused its discretion in excluding Butterfield's proposed expert testimony on the inherent deficiencies of eyewitness identification....We affirm.

BACKGROUND

I. Facts

On May 17, 1998, two sisters, V.R. and M.R., and their friend B.M.—all under the age of fourteen—decided to sleep outside in a tent in V.R. and M.R.'s backyard. Sometime between 8:00 and 9:00 p.m., the three girls took some blankets, CDs, and a board game into the tent. A short time later, M.R. left the tent and went inside the house to sleep on the couch. After M.R. left the tent, V.R. and B.M. turned off a light that hung inside the tent and went to sleep.

Later that night, V.R. awoke to the barking of her neighbor's dogs. Almost immediately thereafter, a man ripped a hole in the side of the tent. V.R. and B.M. screamed and hid under the blankets. The man then entered the tent and jumped on top of V.R. stating, "Shut up or I'll slice your throat." The man then proceeded to remove V.R.'s clothes and, while doing so, demanded that B.M. remove her clothes as well. When the man had removed V.R.'s sweat pants and underwear, he forced "his finger inside of [her] vagina," "licked" her chest, kissed her "on the mouth," and forced his "tongue into [her] mouth." The man also forced his penis inside V.R.'s "mouth" and "vagina." During the assault, B.M.—lying only inches from V.R.—could hear V.R. pleading and crying, "Please don't, please don't."

After raping and sexually assaulting V.R., the man then proceeded to sexually assault B.M., forcing his finger into her vagina, fondling her chest, and ordering her to take his penis and "move it up and down." The attacker then proceeded to move from one girl to the next with his groping and molestation. Throughout the assault, the man repeatedly ordered the girls to keep quiet or he would "slice [their] throats."

At some point in the ordeal, which lasted nearly an hour and a half, the girls' attacker turned on the light that hung inside the tent and rummaged through the girls' belongings. The light was on for nearly ten minutes. Although the attacker demanded that the girls close their eyes, V.R. peeked from the blankets and could see different portions of the man's face. As he searched through the girls' belongings, the man commented on their CDs, talked to B.M., and remarked how "cute" her braids were.

Thereafter, the man asked V.R. and B.M. to tell him who was inside the house, threatening that if they did not tell him he would "slit [their] throats." Both V.R. and B.M. responded that they "didn't know." The attacker then stated, "I'm going inside right now, and if I catch you guys out of the tent or if somebody is out here with you, I'll kill you and then I'll kill whoever is with you."

After leaving the tent, the attacker broke into the house and proceeded to sexually assault and molest M.R., who was sleeping on a couch in the living room. When M.R. yelled for her father, the man told her that he would "stab [her]" if she was not quiet. The man then lifted her shirt and bra and "licked [her] chest." After warning her not to peek, he lowered her shorts and underwear and forced his "finger in[to her vagina]." The man then threw a pillow over M.R.'s face and left through the back door. M.R. estimated that the sexual assault lasted for nearly ten minutes.

After the attacker left the house, M.R. went downstairs and told her parents what had happened. M.R.'s parents immediately called the police. When the police arrived, they found B.M. screaming and M.R. in shock. B.M. told the police that the attacker was a man who lived in an apartment down the street from V.R. and M.R.'s house, and who had spoken with the girls earlier in the day while they were riding their bikes around their neighborhood. The three girls were then transported to the South Salt Lake Police Department where V.R. and M.R.were interviewed by Detective William Hogan. Consistent with B.M.'s statements at the house, V.R. told Detective Hogan that the attacker was a man who lived near her neighborhood, and who had spoken with the girls earlier in the day. Specifically, V.R. explained that prior to the attack, a man on a bike approached the girls, stated that he was a "cop," and then rode to an apartment down the street from V.R. and M.R.'s house. A short while later, the man returned, again asserting that he was a policeman and that, therefore, they could not call the police on him. V.R. thought this behavior "weird." V.R. told Detective Hogan that the next time she saw the man was in her tent that night. From their various conversations, and after further investigation, Detective Hogan identified the attacker as defendant Raymond Butterfield.... The day after the incident, Detective Hogan, accompanied by another police officer, went to Butterfield's apartment. Butterfield answered the door wearing a white undershirt and blue jeans. After identifying himself as a policeman, Detective Hogan asked Butterfield if he would come to the South Salt Lake Police Department for questioning regarding the sexual assault of V.R., M.R., and B.M. Butterfield agreed. Upon their arrival at the police station, Butterfield waived his Miranda rights, and therefore Detective Hogan conducted a formal interview. Butterfield was then transported to the Salt Lake County Jail where his clothes were retained after a policeman noticed blood on his undershirt.

After interviewing Butterfield, Detective Hogan assembled a six-photo array, including a photograph of Butterfield that he obtained from the Salt Lake County Jail. All the photographs were black and white and depicted similarly looking individuals. Detective Hogan then separately presented V.R., M.R., and B.M. with the photo array. V.R. and M.R. each identified Butterfield as the attacker, although B.M. did not....

Based upon the eyewitness identifications and the DNA evidence, Butterfield was charged with aggravated burglary, rape of a child, sodomy on a child, and three counts of aggravated sexual abuse of a child, all first degree felonies. After a jury trial, Butterfield was convicted on all counts and sentenced to statutory five-to-life terms for aggravated burglary and aggravated sexual abuse of a child, and fifteen-to-life terms for rape of a child and sodomy on a child—all terms to run consecutively and with a recommendation that no parole be granted....

B. Butterfield's Eyewitness Identification Expert

Pursuant to section 77–17–13 of the Utah Code, Butterfield gave notice that he intended to call an expert witness at trial to testify concerning memory and various factors that can affect the accuracy of eyewitness identification. In response, the State moved to preclude the proposed expert testimony. The State argued that Butterfield's proffered expert testimony on eyewitness identification should not be allowed because it did not concern the specific facts of the case; because expert testimony regarding the reliability of eyewitness identification would infringe on the jury's responsibility to weigh the credibility of the witnesses; and because the jurors would be presented with an instruction that would adequately and thoroughly explain how to evaluate eyewitness identification presented at trial. The trial court granted the State's motion, excluding the proposed expert testimony....

ANALYSIS....

II. Expert Eyewitness Identification Testimony

Butterfield's second argument on appeal is that the trial court erred in excluding his proposed expert testimony on the inherent deficiencies of eyewitness identification. Specifically, Butterfield argues that the cautionary jury instruction given by the trial court in this case, listing criteria for the jury to consider in evaluating the eyewitness identification testimony presented, was insufficient because of the limitations inherent in eyewitness identification.

As Butterfield correctly notes, this court has previously recognized the vagaries of eyewitness identification. Indeed, in *State v. Long*, this court stated:

Research has convincingly demonstrated the weaknesses inherent in eyewitness identification[; however,] jurors are, for the most part, unaware of these problems. People simply do not accurately understand the deleterious effects that certain variables can have on the accuracy of the memory processes of an honest eyewitness. Moreover, the common knowledge that people do possess often runs contrary to documented research findings. 721 P.2d 483, 490 (Utah 1986) (citations omitted). Because of the inherent deficiencies in eyewitness identification recognized in Long, trial courts are required to give a cautionary jury instruction when eyewitness identification "is a central issue in a case and such an instruction is requested by the defense." Id. at 492. However, as the Utah Court of Appeals correctly noted in *State v. Kinsey*, this court "has not extended the cautionary instruction requirement tos include additional expert testimony concerning eyewitness identification." 797 P.2d 424, 427 (Utah Ct. App.), cert. denied, 800 P.2d 1105 (Utah 1990).

Whether expert testimony on the inherent deficiencies of eyewitness identification should be allowed is within the sound discretion of the trial court. *State v. Malmrose*, 649 P.2d 56, 61 (Utah 1982); 31A Am. Jur. 2d Expert and Opinion Evidence § 370 (1989) ("Expert testimony concerning the reliability of eyewitness identification is not automatic but conditional."). Although a defendant has the right to have witnesses, including experts, testify on his or her behalf, the calling of expert witnesses to testify as to matters which would apply to any crime or any trial does not in the true sense offer testimony of a witness who has knowledge of the facts of the case. Rather, it would be in the nature of a lecture to the jury as to how they should judge the evidence. *State v. Griffin*, 626 P.2d 478, 481 (Utah 1981). Accordingly, a trial court's determination that expert testimony would amount to a lecture to the jury as to how they should judge the evidence, and its subsequent refusal to admit such testimony into evidence "is not an abuse of discretion, particularly where there has been no showing that the excluded evidence would probably have had a substantial influence in bringing about a different verdict." *Malmrose*, 649 P.2d at 61; accord *United States v. Brown*, 540 F.2d 1048, 1054 (10th Cir. 1976) (affirming trial court's exclusion of expert testimony regarding inherent deficiencies of eyewitness identification); *State v. Reed*, 226 Kan. 519, 601 P.2d 1125, 1128 (Kan. 1979) (same); *State v. Helterbridle*, 301 N.W.2d 545, 547 (Minn. 1980) (same); *State v. Porraro*, 121 R.I. 882, 404 A.2d 465, 471 (R.I. 1979) (same).

In this case, the trial court found that the proposed testimony of Butterfield's expert witness, Dr. David Dodd, "did not deal with the specific facts from this case but rather would constitute a lecture to the jury about how it should judge the evidence." Moreover, the trial court concluded that "such evidence could cause confusion of the issues and could cause undue delay or waste of time during the trial." The trial court's finding is supported by ample evidence. Indeed, it is undisputed that Dr. Dodd was not familiar with Butterfield, the victims, or the facts of this case. As Butterfield himself stated, Dr. Dodd "would not have offered an opinion concerning whether any witness' identification was accurate. Instead, he would outline for the jury the general principles of psychological knowledge which illuminate the problems of eyewitness performance." (Emphasis added.) Moreover, Butterfield has made no showing that the proffered testimony would have had a substantial influence in bringing about a different verdict, especially considering the fact that the jurors in this case were presented with a cautionary instruction that met the requirements of Long, adequately and thoroughly explaining how to evaluate eyewitness identifications presented at trial. Therefore, we conclude that the trial court did not abuse its discretion in excluding Butterfield's proposed expert testimony regarding eyewitness identification....

Accordingly, we affirm the jury's verdict and the trial court's subsequent sentence.

List of other cases and articles relevant to this topic.

United States v. Wade, 388 U.S. 218 (1967)
Simmons v. United States, 390 U.S. 377 (1968)
Manson v. Brathwaite, 432 U.S. 98 (1977)
Gilbert v. California, 388 U.S. 263 (1967)
Watkins v. Sowders, 449 U.S. 341 (1981)

Discussion and Review Questions

1. Which court decision—*Chapple* or *Butterfield*—is more persuasive, and why?
2. What types of precautions could trial judges implement to ensure the reliability and fairness of in-court identifications?
3. What precautions should police officers take to ensure a fair identification procedure?

References

Articles

Contreras, R. (2001). More Courts Allow Witnesses Debunk Eyewitness Accounts. Wall Street Journal, Friday, August 10, 2001.

Dillickrath, T. (2001). Evidence of innocence offered by the criminal defendant, not so fast: Expert testimony on eyewitness identification: Admissibility and alternatives. *University of Miami Law Review* 55: 1059–1150.

Klotter, J.C. and J.R. Kanovitz (1995). *Constitutional Law, Seventh Edition.* Cincinnati, OH: Anderson Publishing.

Mandery, E. (1996). Legal development: Due process considerations of in-court identifications. *Albany Law Review* 60: 389–424.

Monahan, J. and L. Walker (1988). Social science research in law: A new paradigm. *American Psychologist* 43: 465.

Penrod, S. and B. Cutler (1995). Witness confidence and witness accuracy: Assessing the Forensic Relationship" *Psychology, Public Policy and Law* 1: 817.

Scheck, B., P. Neufeld, and J. Dwyer (2000). *Actual innocence: Five days to execution, and other dispatches from the wrongly convicted*. NY: Doubleday.

United States Department of Justice (1999). *Eyewitness Evidence: A Guide for Law Enforcement*. Washington DC: NIJ.

Wells, G.L. (1978). Applied eyewitness testimony research: System variables and estimator variables. *Journal of Personality and Social Psychology* 36: 1546–1557.

Wells, G. L. (1993). What do we know about eyewitness identification? *American Psychologist* 48: 553–571.

Wells, G.L. and E.P. Seelau (1995). Eyewitness Identification: Psychological Research and Legal Policy on Lineups. *Psychology, Public Policy and Law* 1: 765.

Wrightsman, L.S. (2001). *Forensic psychology*. Belmont, CA: Wadsworth Publishing.

Case Citations

Foster v. California, 394 U.S. 440 (1969)

Manson v. Braithwaite, 432 U.S. 98 (1977).

Neil v. Biggers, 409 U.S. 188 (1972)

Simmons v. United States, 390 U.S. 377 (1968)

State v. Butterfield, 27 P. 3d 1133 (Utah 2001)

State v. Chapple, 660 P. 2d 1208 (Ariz. 1983)

Stovall v. Denno, 388 U.S. 293 (1967)

United States v. Wade, 388 U.S. 218 (1967)

CHAPTER 10

MIRANDA AND FALSE CONFESSIONS

You have the right to remain silent, anything you say can and will be used against you in a court of law. You have the right to an attorney. If you cannot afford an attorney, one will be appointed for you.

–*Miranda v. Arizona*, 384 U.S. 436 (1966).

These, as most people know, are the *Miranda* warnings. These warning made famous by television police shows were developed by the Court in *Miranda v. Arizona*. In this 1966 case, the United States Supreme Court held that to ensure an individual's **Fifth Amendment** right against self-incrimination an accused who is "**in custody**" and subjected to police "**interrogation**" must be advised of his rights. The court reasoned that an atmosphere dominated by law enforcement—like a police station—unduly pressures suspects. Thus, *Miranda* warnings are intended to even the playing field. The right to remain silent may be knowingly, voluntarily and intelligently waived as long as the individual is advised that he has the right not to speak to the police or to have a lawyer present during the discussion.

When does law enforcement have to read individuals the Miranda warnings?

The *Miranda* decision was very controversial. Prior to *Miranda*, the Court had excluded confessions that were procured by physical coercion because these tactics resulted in involuntary statements. (See *Brown v. Mississippi*, 297 U.S. 278 (1936); *Chambers v. Florida*, 309 U.S. 277 (1940); and *Spano v. New York*, 360 U.S. 315 (1959). The *Miranda* decision was intended by the Court to diminish the impact of psychological coercion to induce involuntary confessions. "*Miranda* marked the end of *third degree* interrogations and the es-

> **Fifth Amendment:** No person shall…be compelled in any criminal case to be a witness against himself.…
>
> **Custodial interrogation:**…means questioning initiated by law enforcement officers after person has been taken into custody or otherwise deprived of his freedom in any significant way; custody can occur without formality of arrest and in areas other than in police station. (Black's Law Dictionary).

tablishment of a new era of psychological interrogation techniques and strategies.…Recognizing that psychological interrogation methods can produce both involuntary and unreliable confessions, the Court created a bright-line rule to more clearly and more effectively regulate the admissibility of psychologically-induced confession statements." (Leo and Ofshe 1998: 434 fn10).

In *Miranda*, the court significantly changed the everyday practices of law enforcement. There was an almost immediate outcry from law enforcement that the *Miranda* decision would be a significant impediment to the solving of crimes. "Legislators and 'law and order' proponents condemned the Court for 'strait-jacketing' the police and 'coddling' criminals with the *Miranda* requirements." (Barker and Barker 1990). Later decisions extended the application of *Miranda* to non-police station interrogations (*Orozco v. Texas*, 394 U.S. 324 (1967) and routine questioning, while in custody, for another charge (*United States v. Mathis*, 391 U.S. 1 (1968).

In the 1970s and 1980s there was a slight retreat on the wide application of *Miranda*. First, the United States Supreme Court held that statements made in violation of the *Miranda* decision may be used to **impeach** a defendant who takes the stand in his own defense. *Harris v. New York*, 401 U.S. 222 (1971). The Court also re-defined the term "custodial" to exclude discussions with suspects in their home (*Beckwith v. United States*, 425 U.S. 319 (1976), when a suspect voluntarily appears at a police station to talk to the police (*Oregon v. Mathiason*, 435 U.S. 492 (1977) and during normal traffic encounters (*Pennsylvania v. Bruder*, 488 U.S. 9 (1988). The Court has also not applied *Miranda* to discussions with probation officers (*Minnesota v. Murphy*, 104 S. Ct. 1136 (1984) and held that it is not a violation of *Miranda* to fail to tell a suspect that an attorney was attempting to contact him prior to his police inter-

> **Impeachment:** To call in question the veracity of a witness, by means of evidence adduced for such purpose, or the adducing of proof that a witness is unworthy of belief. (Black's Law Dictionary).

view (*Moran v. Burbine*, 106 S. Ct. 1135 (1986). In 1984, the Court also developed a "public safety" exception to *Miranda*. When there is an immediate issue concerning public safety, law enforcement will not be held to the rigors of *Miranda*. *New York v. Quarles*, 467 U.S. 649 (1984). In *Quarles*, the police were chasing a suspect believed to have raped a woman at gunpoint. They followed him into a grocery store, stopped him and conducted a frisk. They found an empty shoulder holster and asked him (without *Miranda* warnings) where the gun was. The suspect indicated where the gun was located and it was retrieved. Under these circumstances, the Court found that the exigency of the circumstances justified the limited questioning to locate an abandoned firearm without satisfying the *Miranda* requirement. The statement and gun were admissible as evidence against Quarles.

In *Illinois v. Perkins*, 496 U.S. 292 (1990), the Court upheld the introduction of a confession to an under-cover police officer posing as an inmate. The Court reasoned that *Miranda* warnings were not necessary when a suspect is unaware that she is voluntarily confessing to a law enforcement officer. The interests protected by the *Miranda* decision—custodial interrogation in a police dominated atmosphere—were not implicated by this confession. The suspect had no reason to feel that the undercover agent held any legal authority over the inmate, whatsoever.

In addition to the prophylactic protections of *Miranda*, the Court has held that the right to counsel, when requested, is inviolate. Police must end the questioning of a suspect when a request for counsel is made. Police officers may not reinitiate a custodial interrogation without counsel present after an accused has requested counsel. *Minnick v. Mississippi*, 498 U.S. 146 (1990). Confessions obtained after a request for counsel and after or before consultation with a lawyer are inadmissible. *Minnick v. Mississippi*, 498 U.S. 146 (1990); *Michigan v. Jackson*, 475 U.S. 625 (1986). It is not necessary, however, that a suspect be aware of all possible subjects of questioning to assess the validity of a waiver of the right against self-incrimination and counsel. *Colorado v. Spring*, 479 U.S. 564 (1987).

The request for counsel or to terminate an interrogation and request for counsel, however, must be unequivocal. In *Davis*, the Court held that Naval Investigative Service agents were not required, with respect to the *Miranda* right to counsel, to stop questioning of a Navy member after he made the ambiguous remark, "Maybe I should talk to a lawyer." (*Davis v. United States*, 512 U.S. 452 (1994). Moreover, requests for probation officers are not the same as requests for counsel and do not require police to cease an interrogation. *Fare v. Michael C.*, 482 U.S. 707 (1979). The Court has also held that the Fifth Amendment does not require the suppression of an oral confession where, after *Miranda* warnings, a suspect agreed to speak, but would not make a written statement without an attorney. *Connecticut v. Barrett*, 479 U.S. 523 (1987).

After more than thirty years of litigation, the United States Supreme Court was confronted by a challenge to the validity of the *Miranda* decision in *United States v. Dickerson*, 530 U.S. 428 (2000). Congress, in 1968, passed a statute (18 USCS 3501) intended to overrule the *Miranda* decision in federal criminal prosecutions by asserting that the admissibility of statements turned on whether it was voluntarily made under the totality of the circumstances. The law also omitted any requirement of warnings to suspects. This law was not enforced, that is until the late 1990s when the prosecutors in the *Dickerson* case attempted to use it to prevent the suppression of a confession obtained by the Federal Bureau of Investigation without *Miranda* warnings. The United States Supreme Court got the case and rejected the statute by holding that Congress over-stepped its authority in attempting to overrule a constitutional decision of the Court.

What, if any, affect did the Miranda decision have on obtaining confessions?

Despite the outcry from members of the law enforcement community, there is no empirical evidence that demonstrates that the police have been "straightjacketed" in terms of not solving crimes by eliciting confessions from suspects. In fact, there is some evidence that suggests that *Miranda* has fallen far short of its goal to reduce the number of unreliable confessions extracted by law enforcement because "false confessions" even after the requirements of *Miranda* remain a problem (Leo and Ofshe 1998). The extent of the number of false confessions is hotly debated (Leo and Ofshe 1998; Cassell 1998). Leo and Ofshe argue that "[d]espite additional safeguards, police continue to elicit false confessions in the post-*Miranda* era, and juries continue to convict false confessors at an alarmingly high rate." (Leo and Ofshe 1998: 481). In a review of 60 cases where individuals falsely confessed to crimes, Leo and Oshe identify the common denominators that make false confessions more likely and suggest policy changes in the methods of police interrogation and the admissibility of these confessions in court to reduce the numbers and effect of false confessors. In his rejoinder, Paul Cassell (1998) argues that Leo and Oshe (1998) fail to consider how important the tool of interrogation is to solving crime and their suggestion to regulate interrogation further would harm "another category of innocents: victims of crime." (p. 499). By blocking truthful confessions, Cassell argues guilty criminals will be released to further victimize. In his essay, Cassell attempts to empirically analyze the "risk to the innocent from false confessions, lost confessions, and lost convictions." (p. 501). Cassell concludes that the risk from false confessions is less frequent when compared to causes (e.g., eyewitness identification) that lead to false convictions. Cassell argues that regulations precluding the use of false evidence of guilt and restrictions on interviewing vulnerable suspects (e.g., mentally handicapped individuals) would disproportionately disadvantage the prosecution of guilty offenders. In addition, Cassell is very critical of the *Miranda* decision. He asserts that this decision does nothing to avoid the problem of false confessions and simultaneously reduces the number of truthful confessions. The first step necessary in protecting the innocent and prosecuting the guilty, he suggests, is to repeal the *Miranda* decision.

What does social science say about law enforcement techniques and false confessions?

Some courts have become more willing to introduce expert testimony concerning false confessions,[1] while others have not.[2] In *Crane v. Kentucky*, 476 U.S. 683 (1986), the United States Supreme Court held that the Confrontation Clause of the Sixth Amendment and the Due Process Clause entitled a defendant to "a meaningful opportunity to present a complete defense," and this is "entirely independent" from the voluntariness of the confession. Prohibiting a jury from hearing evidence about the circumstances surrounding a

---

1. *U.S. v. Hall (Hall I)*, 93 F. 3d 1337, 1344–45 (7th Cir. 1996) *on remand*, 974 F. Supp 1198 (1997) and appeal *(Hall II)* 165 F. 3d 1095 (1999); *United States v. Shay*, 57 F. 3d 126, 130–134 (1st Cir. 1995); *Carter v. State*, 697 So. 2d 529 (Fla. App. 1997); *Callis*, 684 NE 2d 233 (Ind 1997); *Bixler v. State*, 568 N.W. 2d 880 (Minn. App. 1997); *State v. Koskela*, 536 N.W. 2d 625 (Minn. 1995); *State v. Buechler*, 572 NW 2d 65 (Neb 1998); *State v. Baldwin*, 482 SE 2d 1 (NC 1997); *State v. Aldridge*, 697 N.E.2d 228 (Ohio App. 1997); *State v. Caulley*, LEXIS (Ohio App. 2002); *State v. Miller*, 1997 Wash. App. LEXIS 960 (Wash. App. 1997) see also *Cassell*, 1998: p. 526 fn. 144. See also *United States v. Hall (Hall II)*, 165 F. 3d 1095 (7th Cir. 1999)(allowing the prosecution to rebut the admission of false confession testimony with damaging evidence that the characteristics that create the likelihood of falsely confessing are also consistent with the characteristics of a sex offender).

2. *U.S. Mazzeo*, LEXIS (2d Cir. 2000); *Beltran v. Florida*, 700 So. 2d 132 (Fla. 1997); *People v. Gilliam*, 670 N.E. 2d 606, 619 (Il. 1996); *People v. Slago*, 374 N.E. 2d 1270 (Il. 1978); *MacDonald* 718 A. 2d 195 (Maine 1998); *State v. Green* 250 AD 2d 143 (NY 1998)(apply *Frye* test); *Green v. State*, 55 S.W.3d 633 (Tex. App. 2001); *Ruckman v. State*, LEXIS (Tex. App. 2000); *Madrid* 910 P. 2d 1340 (Wyo 1996).

confession essentially disables a defendant "from answering the one question every rational juror needs answered: If the defendant is innocent, why did he previously admit his guilt?" 476 U.S. at 689–90. Several states have admitted expert testimony on this question when the courts have held that their testimony was necessary to educate jurors about information beyond the ken of their knowledge. For example, in *State v. Buechler*, 253 Neb. 727, 739, 572 N. W. 2d 65, (1998), the Supreme Court of Nebraska held that it was an abuse of discretion for the trial court to exclude the testimony of a psychologist concerning the effect of drug withdrawal combined with several other psychological disorders on his suggestibility to confess, to process information, and to reach faulty conclusions. This rationale has guided the several other courts that have concluded that expert testimony is admissible, for example see *U.S. v. Shay*, 57 F. 3d 126 (1st Cir. 1995)(holding it was error to exclude expert testimony on Maunchausen's Disease, a mental disorder characterized by extreme pathological lying because a jury is unqualified, without assistance, to determine whether the defendant falsely confessed due to his mental disorder).

Some states permit the introduction of the general testimony concerning the phenomena of false confessions and the circumstances that influence the coercion necessary to falsely confess, however they disallow direct testimony concerning the particular interrogation and confession. *Callis v. State*, 684 N.E. 2d 233 (Ct. Apps. Ind. 1997) *See also Miller v. State*, 770 N.E. 2d 763 (Ind. 2002). In other words, in these decisions courts have permitted experts to testify about the correlation between false confessions and the various factors associated with the inducement of false confessions. Under these circumstances, experts have been allowed to testify that false confessions exist, that they are associated with the use of certain police interrogation techniques, and that those techniques were used in the particular instance during interrogation. These court have disallowed testify about matters of causation, i.e., whether the interrogation methods used in the particular case caused a false confession. The reason for this limitation concerns the lack of "experimental verification" to determine whether a particular defendant falsely confessed.

In one case, where the appeals court held expert testimony inadmissible, the pivotal issue concerned the lack of a claim of "false confession" by the defendant. *Beltran v. State*, 700 So. 2d 132 (Fla. 4th DCA 1997). Moreover, the *Beltran* court was critical of the particular expert's opinion and testimony being proffered. The expert failed to provide appropriate methodology and factors for the trial court to make its determination of admissibility. In another case, the Maine Supreme Court was critical of the expert as well as the lack of scientific support for and the questionable value of "false confession" expert testimony. *State v. MacDonald*, 718 A. 2d 195 (Maine 1998). In this particular case, the expert witness acknowledged that there were few published studies by mental health professionals concerning false confession hypothesis and he had not conducted any studies on the subject. Several courts, similar to *MacDonald*, have been reluctant to introduce evidence of this kind when an expert is not qualified to render an opinion about false confessions. *See also Beltran v. State*, 700 So. 2d 132 (Fla. 1997); *Green v. State*, 55 S.W. 3d 633 (Tex. App. 2001).

What interrogation techniques have been found to increase the risk of a false confession?

Several techniques used regularly by law enforcement and promoted in the text "Criminal Interrogation and Confession, Fourth Edition" have been found to increase the risk of obtaining a false confession. (Kassin 2002). This text, cited the United State Supreme Court in *Miranda*, instructs interrogators to "isolate suspects, confront them with their guilt with dogged persistence, present evidence (such as faked hair, blood or fingerprint specimens, phony witnesses or supposedly failed lie detector tests), put the suspect in a state of helplessness where his denials do not achieve escape for him, and present a palatable alternative that minimizes the crime and makes it seem in the suspect's best interest to make a confession." (Kassin 2002). Using an "accident" scenario, offering an excuse to the suspect, communicating leniency if the suspect confesses, and suggestions of impairment of the suspect that prevents them from remembering that they committed the crime (e.g., alcohol or drug consumption) are suggested examples of methods to elicit a confession. The key to false confessions, according to Kassin, is the police presumption of suspect guilt. He argues that when interrogators believe a suspect is guilty, they use techniques to get a confession, ignore evidence or statements that contradict guilt and stop investigating any other leads.

Kassin identifies three types of false confessions—voluntary, coerced-compliant and coerced internalized (Kassin 2002). "In voluntary confessions there is no external pressure and they occur typically in high profile cases.... In coerced-compliant confessions, the confessor knows he is innocent but confesses to get out of the interrogation situation, to get a promised reward or to avoid a threat. Usually they will immediately recant the confession. In coerced-internalized confession innocent suspects come to believe they actually committed the crime and that they have repressed all memory of the act." (Kassin 2002)[3]

In this chapter excerpts from *Miranda v. Arizona*, 384 U.S. 436 (1966), *U.S. v. Hall*, 974 F. Supp. 1198 (Cent. Dist. Ill. 1997) and Leo and Ofshe's (1998) *The consequences of false confessions: Deprivations of liberty and miscarriages of justice in the age of psychological interrogation* are included.

Miranda v. Arizona
384 U.S. 436 (1966)(Excerpt)

MR. CHIEF JUSTICE WARREN delivered the opinion of the Court.

The cases before us raise questions which go to the roots of our concepts of American criminal jurisprudence: the restraints society must observe consistent with the Federal Constitution in prosecuting individuals for crime. More specifically, we deal with the admissibility of statements obtained from an individual who is subjected to custodial police interrogation and the necessity for procedures which assure that the individual is accorded his privilege under the Fifth Amendment to the Constitution not to be compelled to incriminate himself.

We dealt with certain phases of this problem recently in *Escobedo v. Illinois*, 378 U.S. 478 (1964). There, as in the four cases before us, law enforcement officials took the defendant into custody and interrogated him in a police station for the purpose of obtaining a confession. The police did not effectively advise him of his right to remain silent or of his right to consult with his attorney. Rather, they confronted him with an alleged accomplice who accused him of having perpetrated a murder. When the defendant denied the accusation and said "I didn't shoot Manuel, you did it," they handcuffed him and took him to an interrogation room. There, while handcuffed and standing, he was questioned for four hours until he confessed. During this interrogation, the police denied his request to speak to his attorney, and they prevented his retained attorney, who had come to the police station, from consulting with him. At his trial, the State, over his objection, introduced the confession against him. We held that the statements thus made were constitutionally inadmissible.

---

3. The lecture by Kassin is discussed at the University of Virginia Law School web site: *http://www.law.virginia.edu/home2002/html/news2002_fall/falseconfession.htm*. At this site are more examples of the techniques and findings from his experimental research.

This case has been the subject of judicial interpretation and spirited legal debate since it was decided two years ago. Both state and federal courts, in assessing its implications, have arrived at varying conclusions. A wealth of scholarly material has been written tracing its ramifications and underpinnings. Police and prosecutor have speculated on its range and desirability. We granted certiorari in these cases...in order further to explore some facets of the problems, thus exposed, of applying the privilege against self-incrimination to in-custody interrogation, and to give concrete constitutional guidelines for law enforcement agencies and courts to follow.

We start here, as we did in *Escobedo*, with the premise that our holding is not an innovation in our jurisprudence, but is an application of principles long recognized and applied in other settings. We have undertaken a thorough re-examination of the *Escobedo* decision and the principles it announced, and we reaffirm it. That case was but an explication of basic rights that are enshrined in our Constitution—that "No person...shall be compelled in any criminal case to be a witness against himself," and that "the accused shall... have the Assistance of Counsel"—rights which were put in jeopardy in that case through official overbearing. These precious rights were fixed in our Constitution only after centuries of persecution and struggle. And in the words of Chief Justice Marshall, they were secured "for ages to come, and...designed to approach immortality as nearly as human institutions can approach it," *Cohens v. Virginia*, 6 Wheat. 264, 387 (1821)....

This was the spirit in which we delineated, in meaningful language, the manner in which the constitutional rights of the individual could be enforced against overzealous police practices. It was necessary in *Escobedo*, as here, to insure that what was proclaimed in the Constitution had not become but a "form of words," *Silverthorne Lumber Co. v. United States*, (1920), in the hands of government officials. And it is in this spirit, consistent with our role as judges, that we adhere to the principles of *Escobedo* today.

Our holding will be spelled out with some specificity in the pages which follow but briefly stated it is this: the prosecution may not use statements, whether exculpatory or inculpatory, stemming from custodial interrogation of the defendant unless it demonstrates the use of procedural safeguards effective to secure the privilege against self-incrimination. By custodial interrogation, we mean questioning initiated by law enforcement officers after a person has been taken into custody or otherwise deprived of his freedom of action in any significant way. As for the procedural safeguards to be employed, unless other fully effective means are devised to inform accused persons of their right of silence and to assure a continuous opportunity to exercise it, the following measures are required. Prior to any questioning, the person must be warned that he has a right to remain silent, that any statement he does make may be used as evidence against him, and that he has a right to the presence of an attorney, either retained or appointed. The defendant may waive effectuation of these rights, provided the waiver is made voluntarily, knowingly and intelligently. If, however, he indicates in any manner and at any stage of the process that he wishes to consult with an attorney before speaking there can be no questioning. Likewise, if the individual is alone and indicates in any manner that he does not wish to be interrogated, the police may not question him. The mere fact that he may have answered some questions or volunteered some statements on his own does not deprive him of the right to refrain from answering any further inquiries until he has consulted with an attorney and thereafter consents to be questioned.

The constitutional issue we decide in each of these cases is the admissibility of statements obtained from a defendant questioned while in custody or otherwise deprived of his freedom of action in any significant way. In each, the defendant was questioned by police officers, detectives, or a prosecuting attorney in a room in which he was cut off from the outside world. In none of these cases was the defendant given a full and effective warning of his rights at the outset of the interrogation process. In all the cases, the questioning elicited oral admissions, and in three of them, signed statements as well which were admitted at their trials. They all thus share salient features—incommunicado interrogation of individuals in a police-dominated atmosphere, resulting in self-incriminating statements without full warnings of constitutional rights....

As we have stated before, "Since *Chambers v. Florida*, this Court has recognized that coercion can be mental as well as physical, and that the blood of the accused is not the only hallmark of an unconstitutional inquisition." *Blackburn v. Alabama*, (1960). Interrogation still takes place in privacy. Privacy results in secrecy and this in turn results in a gap in our knowledge as to what in fact goes on in the interrogation rooms. A valuable source of information about present police practices, however, may be found in various police manuals and texts which document procedures employed with success in the past, and which recommend various other effective tactics. These texts are used by law enforcement agencies themselves as guides. It should be noted that these texts professedly present the most enlightened and effective means presently used to obtain statements through custodial interrogation. By considering these texts and other data, it is possible to describe procedures observed and noted around the country.

The officers are told by the manuals that the "principal psychological factor contributing to a successful interrogation is privacy—being alone with the person under interrogation." The efficacy of this tactic has been explained as follows:

> "If at all practicable, the interrogation should take place in the investigator's office or at least in a room of his own choice. The subject should be deprived of every psychological advantage. In his own home he may be confident, indignant, or recalcitrant. He is more keenly aware of his rights and more reluctant to tell of his indiscretions or criminal behavior within the walls of his home. Moreover his family and other friends are nearby, their presence lending moral support. In his own office, the investigator possesses all the advantages. The atmosphere suggests the invincibility of the forces of the law."

To highlight the isolation and unfamiliar surroundings, the manuals instruct the police to display an air of confidence in the suspect's guilt and from outward appearance to maintain only an interest in confirming certain details. The guilt of the subject is to be posited as a fact. The interrogator should direct his comments toward the reasons why the subject committed the act, rather than court failure by asking the subject whether he did it. Like other men, perhaps the subject has had a bad family life, had an unhappy childhood, had too much to drink, had an unrequited desire for women. The officers are instructed to minimize the moral seriousness of the offense, to cast blame on the victim or on society. These tactics are designed to put the subject in a psychological state where his story is but an elaboration of what the police purport to know already—that he is guilty. Explanations to the contrary are dismissed and discouraged.

The texts thus stress that the major qualities an interrogator should possess are patience and perseverance. One writer describes the efficacy of these characteristics in this manner:

"In the preceding paragraphs emphasis has been placed on kindness and stratagems. The investigator will, however, encounter many situations where the sheer weight of his personality will be the deciding factor. Where emotional appeals and tricks are employed to no avail, he must rely on an oppressive atmosphere of dogged persistence. He must interrogate steadily and without relent, leaving the subject no prospect of surcease. He must dominate his subject and overwhelm him with his inexorable will to obtain the truth. He should interrogate for a spell of several hours pausing only for the subject's necessities in acknowledgment of the need to avoid a charge of duress that can be technically substantiated. In a serious case, the interrogation may continue for days, with the required intervals for food and sleep, but with no respite from the atmosphere of domination. It is possible in this way to induce the subject to talk without resorting to duress or coercion. The method should be used only when the guilt of the subject appears highly probable."

The manuals suggest that the suspect be offered legal excuses for his actions in order to obtain an initial admission of guilt. Where there is a suspected revenge-killing,

> "Joe, you probably didn't go out looking for this fellow with the purpose of shooting him. My guess is, however, that you expected something from him and that's why you carried a gun—for your own protection. You knew him for what he was, no good. Then when you met him he probably started using foul, abusive language and he gave some indication that he was about to pull a gun on you, and that's when you had to act to save your own life. That's about it, isn't it, Joe?"

Having then obtained the admission of shooting, the interrogator is advised to refer to circumstantial evidence which negates the self-defense explanation. This should enable him to secure the entire story. One text notes that "Even if he fails to do so, the inconsistency between the subject's original denial of the shooting and his present admission of at least doing the shooting will serve to deprive him of a self-defense 'out' at the time of trial."

When the techniques described above prove unavailing, the texts recommend they be alternated with a show of some hostility. One ploy often used has been termed the "friendly-unfriendly" or the "Mutt and Jeff" act:

> "...In this technique, two agents are employed. Mutt, the relentless investigator, who knows the subject is guilty and is not going to waste any time. He's sent a dozen men away for this crime and he's going to send the subject away for the full term. Jeff, on the other hand, is obviously a kindhearted man. He has a family himself. He has a brother who was involved in a little scrape like this. He disapproves of Mutt and his tactics and will arrange to get him off the case if the subject will cooperate. He can't hold Mutt off for very long. The subject would be wise to make a quick decision. The technique is applied by having both investigators present while Mutt acts out his role. Jeff may stand by quietly and demur at some of Mutt's tactics. When Jeff makes his plea for cooperation, Mutt is not present in the room."

The interrogators sometimes are instructed to induce a confession out of trickery. The technique here is quite effective in crimes which require identification or which run in series. In the identification situation, the interrogator may take a break in his questioning to place the subject among a group of men in a line-up. "The witness or complainant (previously coached, if necessary) studies the line-up and confidently points out the subject as the guilty party." Then the questioning resumes "as though there were now no doubt about the guilt of the subject." A variation on this technique is called the "reverse line-up":

"The accused is placed in a line-up, but this time he is identified by several fictitious witnesses or victims who associated him with different offenses. It is expected that the subject will become desperate and confess to the offense under investigation in order to escape from the false accusations."

The manuals also contain instructions for police on how to handle the individual who refuses to discuss the matter entirely, or who asks for an attorney or relatives. The examiner is to concede him the right to remain silent. "This usually has a very undermining effect. First of all, he is disappointed in his expectation of an unfavorable reaction on the part of the interrogator. Secondly, a concession of this right to remain silent impresses the subject with the apparent fairness of his interrogator." After this psychological conditioning, however, the officer is told to point out the incriminating significance of the suspect's refusal to talk:

"Joe, you have a right to remain silent. That's your privilege and I'm the last person in the world who'll try to take it away from you. If that's the way you want to leave this, O. K. But let me ask you this. Suppose you were in my shoes and I were in yours and you called me in to ask me about this and I told you, 'I don't want to answer any of your questions.' You'd think I had something to hide, and you'd probably be right in thinking that. That's exactly what I'll have to think about you, and so will everybody else. So let's sit here and talk this whole thing over."

Few will persist in their initial refusal to talk, it is said, if this monologue is employed correctly.

In the event that the subject wishes to speak to a relative or an attorney, the following advice is tendered:

"[T]he interrogator should respond by suggesting that the subject first tell the truth to the interrogator himself rather than get anyone else involved in the matter. If the request is for an attorney, the interrogator may suggest that the subject save himself or his family the expense of any such professional service, particularly if he is innocent of the offense under investigation. The interrogator may also add, 'Joe, I'm only looking for the truth, and if you're telling the truth, that's it. You can handle this by yourself.'"

From these representative samples of interrogation techniques, the setting prescribed by the manuals and observed in practice becomes clear. In essence, it is this: To be alone with the subject is essential to prevent distraction and to deprive him of any outside support. The aura of confidence in his guilt undermines his will to resist. He merely confirms the preconceived story the police seek to have him describe. Patience and persistence, at times relentless questioning, are employed. To obtain a confession, the interrogator must "patiently maneuver himself or his quarry into a position from which the desired objective may be attained." When normal procedures fail to produce the needed result, the police may resort to deceptive stratagems such as giving false legal advice. It is important to keep the subject off balance, for example, by trading on his insecurity about himself or his surroundings. The police then persuade, trick, or cajole him out of exercising his constitutional rights....

In the cases before us today, given this background, we concern ourselves primarily with this interrogation atmosphere and the evils it can bring. In No. 759, *Miranda v. Arizona*, the police arrested the defendant and took him to a special interrogation room where they secured a confession. In No. 760, *Vignera v. New York*, the defendant made oral admissions to the police after interrogation in the afternoon, and then signed an inculpatory statement upon being questioned by an assistant district attorney later the same evening. In No. 761, *Westover v. United States*, the defendant was handed over to the Federal Bureau of Investigation by local authorities after they had detained and interrogated him for a lengthy period, both at night and the following morning. After some two hours of questioning, the federal officers had obtained signed statements from the defendant. Lastly, in No. 584, *California v. Stewart*, the local police held the defendant five days in the station and interrogated him on nine separate occasions before they secured his inculpatory statement.

In these cases, we might not find the defendants' statements to have been involuntary in traditional terms. Our concern for adequate safeguards to protect precious Fifth Amendment rights is, of course, not lessened in the slightest. In each of the cases, the defendant was thrust into an unfamiliar atmosphere and run through menacing police interrogation procedures. The potentiality for compulsion is forcefully apparent, for example, in Miranda, where the indigent Mexican defendant was a seriously disturbed individual with pronounced sexual fantasies, and in Stewart, in which the defendant was an indigent Los Angeles Negro who had dropped out of school in the sixth grade. To be sure, the records do not evince overt physical coercion or patent psychological ploys. The fact remains that in none of these cases did the officers undertake to afford appropriate safeguards at the outset of the interrogation to insure that the statements were truly the product of free choice.

It is obvious that such an interrogation environment is created for no purpose other than to subjugate the individual to the will of his examiner. This atmosphere carries its own badge of intimidation. To be sure, this is not physical intimidation, but it is equally destructive of human dignity. The current practice of incommunicado interrogation is at odds with one of our Nation's most cherished principles—that the individual may not be compelled to incriminate himself. Unless adequate protective devices are employed to dispel the compulsion inherent in custodial surroundings, no statement obtained from the defendant can truly be the product of his free choice....

At the outset, if a person in custody is to be subjected to interrogation, he must first be informed in clear and unequivocal terms that he has the right to remain silent. For those unaware of the privilege, the warning is needed simply to make them aware of it—the threshold requirement for an intelligent decision as to its exercise. More important, such a warning is an absolute prerequisite in overcoming the inherent pressures of the interrogation atmosphere. It is not just the subnormal or woefully ignorant who succumb to an interrogator's imprecations, whether implied or expressly stated, that the interrogation will continue until a confession is obtained or that silence in the face of accusation is itself damning and will bode ill when presented to a jury. Further, the warning will show the individual that his interrogators are prepared to recognize his privilege should he choose to exercise it....

The warning of the right to remain silent must be accompanied by the explanation that anything said can and will be used against the individual in court. This warning is needed in order to make him aware not only of the privilege, but also of the consequences of forgoing it. It is only through an awareness of these consequences that there can be any assurance of real understanding and intelligent exercise of the privilege. Moreover, this warning may serve to make the individual more acutely aware that he is faced with a phase of the adversary system—that he is not in the presence of persons acting solely in his interest.

The circumstances surrounding in-custody interrogation can operate very quickly to overbear the will of one merely made aware of his privilege by his interrogators. Therefore, the right to have counsel present at the interrogation is indispensable to the protection of the Fifth Amendment privilege under the system we delineate today. Our aim is to assure that the individual's right to choose between silence and speech remains unfettered throughout the interrogation process. A once-stated warning, delivered by those who will conduct the interrogation, cannot itself suffice to that end among those who most require knowledge of their rights. A mere warning given by the interrogators is not alone sufficient to accomplish that end. Prosecutors themselves claim that the admonishment of the right to remain silent without more "will benefit only the recidivist and the professional." Brief for the National District Attorneys Association as amicus curiae, p. 14. Even preliminary advice given to the accused by his own attorney can be swiftly overcome by the secret interrogation process. Cf. *Escobedo v. Illinois.* Thus, the need for counsel to protect the Fifth Amendment privilege comprehends not merely a right to consult with counsel prior to questioning, but also to have counsel present during any questioning if the defendant so desires....

Accordingly we hold that an individual held for interrogation must be clearly informed that he has the right to consult with a lawyer and to have the lawyer with him during interrogation under the system for protecting the privilege we delineate today. As with the warnings of the right to remain silent and that anything stated can be used in evidence against him, this warning is an absolute prerequisite to interrogation. No amount of circumstantial evidence that the person may have been aware of this right will suffice to stand in its stead: Only through such a warning is there ascertainable assurance that the accused was aware of this right.

If an individual indicates that he wishes the assistance of counsel before any interrogation occurs, the authorities cannot rationally ignore or deny his request on the basis that the individual does not have or cannot afford a retained attorney. The financial ability of the individual has no relationship to the scope of the rights involved here. The privilege against self-incrimination secured by the Constitution applies to all individuals. The need for counsel in order to protect the privilege exists for the indigent as well as the affluent....In order fully to apprise a person interrogated of the extent of his rights under this system then, it is necessary to warn him not only that he has the right to consult with an attorney, but also that if he is indigent a lawyer will be appointed to represent him. Once warnings have been given, the subsequent procedure is clear. If the individual indicates in any manner, at any time prior to or during questioning, that he wishes to remain silent, the interrogation must cease....If the individual states that he wants an attorney, the interrogation must cease until an attorney is present. At that time, the individual must have an opportunity to confer with the attorney and to have him present during any subsequent questioning. If the individual cannot obtain an attorney and he indicates that he wants one before speaking to police, they must respect his decision to remain silent....

United States v. Hall
974 F. Supp. 1198 (Cent. D. Ill 1997)(Excerpt)

OPINION BY: JOE BILLY McDADE

Before the Court is the Government's Motion to Preclude Dr. Ofshe's Testimony at Trial. Dr. Richard Ofshe is a social psychologist operating in the field of coercive police interrogation techniques and the phenomenon of false or coerced confessions. He is prepared to testify that experts in his field agree that false confessions exist, that individuals can be coerced into giving false confessions, and that there exist identifiable coercive police interrogation techniques which are likely to produce false confessions....

Admissibility of False Confession Expert Testimony

Dr. Ofshe has been proffered by Defendant as an expert on false confessions and the factors which allow them to occur. He has a doctoral degree in social psychological from Stanford University and has taught psychological research methods at the University of California at Berkeley. He has received a number of prestigious honors in his field. He also serves on the editorial boards of numerous publications dealing with sociology and social psychology and has engaged in peer reviews of such articles. In addition, he has served as a consultant on the issue of influence in interrogations for federal and state law enforcement agencies across the country.

Throughout his 35-year academic career, Dr. Ofshe has researched the subject of influence and decision-making. For the past 25 years, he has focused on extreme forms of influence, such as coercion, and for the past 10 years, he has dealt specifically with the use of coercion in police interrogations. He has also written numerous articles on these topics and presented papers at the meetings of various scientific associations. He has personally evaluated at least 126 separate interrogations and has testified about the subject of influence in interrogation at least 68 times in state and federal courts throughout the country.

At the Rule 104(a) hearing, Dr. Ofshe testified at length about the development of the study of false confessions within the field of social psychology. He testified that social psychology is a hybrid between sociology and psychology, with some influence drawn from modern economic theory. The use of coercive techniques in interrogation is an established topic within the field of social psychology and draws on principles of rational decision making, perception and interpersonal influence. As an example of how vast the studies of this particular topic have been, Dr. Ofshe cited to Professor Gisli H. Gudjonsson's textbook entitled, "The Psychology of Interrogations, Confessions and Testimony" (Def. Ex. # 7) which references between 900 and 1,000 separate articles on the subject. Defendant also introduced into evidence over thirty separate articles and formal presentations about false confessions.

According to Dr. Ofshe, the study of false confessions generally involves the systematic observation of real-world interrogations. This is a method generally accepted as reliable by the community of social psychologists in this field. The researcher initially obtains documented cases in which an innocent person has confessed to the crime. For instance, the researcher may look at cases in which another person subsequently confesses and is convicted of the crime or in which it is revealed, through DNA evidence or otherwise, that the defendant could not have committed the crime. Dr. Ofshe hypothesizes, and his peers appear to agree, that the major analytical method for determining the existence of a false confession is the post-admission narrative statement. In this technique, the confessor is asked about the details of the crime about which he has just confessed. If he relates facts that only the murderer would know, he must be guilty. If he relates facts inconsistent with the evidence at the crime scene, he is probably confessing falsely.

Once it is established through a post-admission narrative statement that a false confession has occurred, the researcher then analyzes the interrogation process, either by reviewing it on audio or videotape or by having the parties recall the details of the interrogation. Documented factors are systematically analyzed to see whether they correlate with the existence of a false confession. Dr. Ofshe testified that no one factor or combination of factors could guarantee a false confession but that some factors might heighten the likelihood of one. While a number of factors were present in both true and false confession cases, a major distinguishing factor for false confessions is the interrogator's continued use of coercion either through false accusations or false promises of leniency. The idea is that a guilty person will more likely "crack" under the pressure or make a rational decision to choose the more lenient option sooner than an innocent person would.

In analyzing this type of data, some researchers have utilized statistical correlational techniques whereby they divide individuals by their personality traits or by their intelligence and then demonstrate the probability of those subjects complying with the interrogator. This is not an experimental method because the researcher does not manipulate the variables. Rather, it involves the use of observation and systematic analysis of persons with different traits.

Dr. Ofshe also testified that low-level laboratory experimentation has been conducted in this field. However, he admits that these experiments alone are not sufficiently reliable to support his findings. Even Professor Saul M. Kassin, who conducted many of these experiments, points out that various factors may have skewed the results, such as the use of college students as subjects (Govt. Ex. # 2, at 249–50) and the nature of the acts involved (Def. Ex. # 19, at 127). Professor Kassin even goes so far as to admit that "the current empirical foundation may be too meager to support recommendations for reform or qualify as a subject of 'scientific knowledge' according to the criteria recently articulated by the U.S. Supreme Court" in *Daubert*. (Govt. Ex. # 1, at 231).

Dr. Ofshe explained that the reason no laboratory studies could be conducted in real life situations is that it would be unethical. He stated that "people think of experiments as the be all and end all of science...That is simply not the case. And the entire social science enterprise is based on the use of a variety of different methods, that's so fundamental, and...I'm simply saying that...given the problems that arise in doing particularly social science research, we cannot do the things to people that we can even do to animals." He concluded that "observation in the organization of reliable, of regular phenomenon...is fundamental to the whole social science enterprise."

Dr. Ofshe testified that the studies based upon observational data are subjected to a process of peer review within the social psychologist community. Authors generally respond to the criticisms of their peers before actually publishing the paper. He further testified that there is no dispute in the scientific community that false confessions do exist and that studying things such as coercion and the post-admission narrative statement is the proper method of analyzing whether and why they occur.

The Government's witness, Dr. Frank Horvath, who has a doctoral degree in criminal justice and criminology, claims that there is no scientific basis for the use of the post-admission narrative statement as a method by which to determine the falsity of a confession. However, it is only common sense that a person who does not give accurate information about the crime may in fact not be guilty of that crime. While such a person may simply be withholding evidence or purposely giving false details, this risk does not destroy the validity of the original hypothesis that more likely than not, the person is innocent. The Court does not require a separate scientific basis for the use of post-admission narrative statements, which is only a technique by which social psychologists in this field gather their data.

Dr. Ofshe discussed his reluctance to state an ultimate opinion in the courtroom as to whether a false confession has actually occurred in any particular case. He would rather indicate to the jury the possibility of such a confession given the factors which have been systematically correlated to the existence of a false confession. Such restraint in the area of causation increases the reliability of Dr. Ofshe's testimony.

In light of this testimony, the Court finds that Dr. Ofshe is qualified as an expert in the field of coercive police interrogation techniques which may lead to false confessions. The Court further finds that the science of social psychology, and specifically the field involving the use of coercion in interrogations, is sufficiently developed in its methods to constitute a reliable body of specialized knowledge under Rule 702. While Dr. Ofshe and his peers utilize observational, as opposed to experimental, techniques, this is wholly acceptable in the established field of social psychology.

The Court cautions Defendant, however, that it will hold Dr. Ofshe to his word that he will only testify to the correlation between false confessions and the various factors espoused by him. Thus, he can testify that false confessions do exist, that they are associated with the use of certain police interrogation techniques, and that certain of those techniques were used in Hall's interrogation in this case. Dr. Ofshe cannot explicitly testify about matters of causation, specifically, whether the interrogation methods used in this case caused Hall to falsely confess. Without experimental verification, such testimony would be speculative and prejudicial. Dr. Ofshe will simply provide the framework which the jury can use to arrive at its own conclusions.

Just as important, Dr. Ofshe cannot testify about the specifics of the post-admission narrative statement in this case. Such an endeavor would require Dr. Ofshe to assess the inconsistencies between Hall's statements to the police and the evidence presented at trial. Dr. Ofshe has no more expertise to perform this task than any juror. It is beyond Dr. Ofshe's knowledge as a social psychologist to assess the weight of the evidence and the credibility of witnesses. Of course, Dr. Ofshe can speak of the post-admission narrative statement as a technique by which social psychologists screen out true from false confessions in order to form systematic observations about them. He may even hypothesize to the jury that the post-admission narrative statement is a valid method by which to test the truth or falsity of a confession. However, he cannot go so far as to analyze Hall's post-admission narrative statement in this manner. That task is for the jury alone.

One final limitation, and one which the Court does not believe is in dispute, is that Dr. Ofshe cannot testify to Hall's psychological or psychiatric impairments or the effect of these impairments upon his likelihood of confessing falsely. Dr. Ofshe is not a clinical psychologist nor a psychiatrist and has no expertise in this area.

Helpful to the Trier of Fact

In addition to requiring that the proposed expert be knowledgeable about the particular matter at issue and that his methods be reliable, Rule 702 also requires that his testimony "will assist the trier of fact to understand the evidence or to determine a fact in issue." Fed. R. Evid. 702. The Seventh Circuit has indicated that social scientists in particular may be able to show that commonly accepted explanations for behavior are, when studied more closely, inaccurate. *Tyus*, 102 F.3d at 263; Hall, 93 F.3d at 1345.

Dr. Ofshe testified that a common misperception among the public is that once a person confesses to his guilt, he must be guilty. Dr. Ofshe's expert testimony challenges this perception based on systematic observation of data to which the jury is not privy. If Defendant presents admissible testimony to show that the police used coercive interrogation techniques in his case, this would make Dr. Ofshe's expert testimony helpful to the trier of fact.

The problem is that Hall's account of the interrogation was given to his lawyer without having him swear under oath to the truth of that testimony. Moreover, Hall's testimony was not subject to cross-examination by the Government. Thus, the interview is not presently admissible. Unless Defendant can introduce some admissible testimony regarding the manner in which the interrogation occurred, such as testifying on the stand, the jury will not hear any evidence of coercive interrogation techniques and Dr. Ofshe's testimony would be rendered irrelevant.

Even if admissible evidence of coercive interrogation techniques are introduced, the Court reminds Defendant that Dr. Ofshe cannot testify about the significance of the post-admission narrative statement in Hall's case. Far from assisting the jury, such testimony would unduly usurp the jury's role as the trier of fact and cloak his factual determinations in the guise of expert testimony. Such testimony would simply be too prejudicial under Fed. R. Evid. 403 and will not be allowed.

Conclusion

IT IS THEREFORE ORDERED that the Government's Motion to Preclude Dr. Ofshe'sTestimony at Trial is DENIED except to the extent discussed in this Order.

ENTERED this 13th day of August 1997.

JOE BILLY McDADE, United States District Judge

R.A. Leo and R.J. Ofshe.
The Consequences of false confessions: Deprivations of liberty and miscarriages of justice in the age of psychological interrogation. *

The Journal of Criminal Law and Criminology 88: 429–496 (1998)

I. Introduction

A. Defining the problem

Because a confession is universally treated as damning and compelling evidence of guilt, it is likely to dominate all other case evidence and lead a trier of fact to convict the defendant. A false confession is therefore an exceptionally dangerous piece of evidence to put before anyone adjudicating a case. In a criminal justice system whose formal rules are designed to minimize the frequency of unwarranted arrest, unjustified prosecution, and wrongful conviction, police-induced false confessions rank amongst the most fateful of all official errors.

As many investigators have recognized, the problems caused by police-induced false confessions are significant, recurrent, and deeply troubling. Police elicit false confessions so frequently that social science researchers, legal scholars, and journalists have discovered and documented numerous case examples in this decade alone. Yet no one knows precisely how often false confessions occur in the United States, how frequently false confessions lead to wrongful convictions, or how much personal and social harm false confessions cause. This is because: (1) no organization collects statistics on the annual number of interrogations and confessions or evaluates the reliability of confession statements; (2) most interrogations leading to disputed confessions are not recorded; and (3) the ground truth (what really happened) may remain in genuine dispute even after a defendant has pled guilty or been convicted. These problems prevent researchers from defining a universe of confession cases, sampling a subset, and confidently determining the truth or falsity of each underlying confession.

Until these methodological obstacles are overcome, no one can authoritatively estimate the rate of police-induced false confessions or the annual number of wrongful convictions caused by false confessions. The lack of such information also prevents researchers from estimating the full magnitude of

---

* reprinted with permission of R.A. Leo, author.

personal and social harm that police-induced false confessions cause: the days and months innocent persons spend in pre-trial incarceration; the resources, time, and dollars wasted prosecuting and defending them; the months and years defendants languish in prison after wrongful conviction; and the additional crimes carried out by the true perpetrators.

Although it is presently not possible to estimate the magnitude of harm caused by false confessions, this article sheds light on another dark corner of the problem by addressing the following questions: What is the impact of demonstrably unreliable confession evidence on criminal justice officials? What are the consequences of false confessions on defendants as they move through the criminal justice system? And how much influence does a false confession alone exert on the decision-making of jurors?

B. False confessions and the administration of justice

...This article explores whether contemporary American psychological interrogation practices continue to induce false confessions like the third degree methods that preceded them. This article also analyzes how likely police-induced false confessions are to lead to the wrongful arrest, prosecution, conviction, and incarceration of the innocent. And this article examines with field data n13 whether confession evidence substantially biases a trier of fact even when the defendant's statement was elicited by coercive methods. We explore this issue with cases in which the defendant's statement has not only been coerced but is also demonstrably unreliable, and in which other evidence proves or strongly supports the defendant's innocence.... [T]he findings of our research [and]...the deprivations of liberty and miscarriages of justice associated with the sixty cases described in this article [as well as]....the import of this research [with] some concluding remarks [are discussed]....

C. Police-induced false confession

Police-induced false confessions arise when a suspect's resistance to confession is broken down as a result of poor police practice, overzealousness, criminal misconduct and/or misdirected training. Interrogators sometimes become so committed to closing a case that they improperly use psychological interrogation techniques to coerce or persuade a suspect into giving a statement that allows the interrogator to make an arrest. Sometimes police become so certain of the suspect's guilt that they refuse to even-handedly evaluate new evidence or to consider the possibility that a suspect may be innocent, even when all the case evidence has been gathered and overwhelmingly demonstrates that the confession is false. Once a confession is obtained, investigation often ceases, and convicting the defendant becomes the only goal of both investigators and prosecutors. As the investigative process progresses, some interrogators, who overstepped procedural boundaries to obtain a false confession, engage in criminal conduct to cover up their procedural violations (e.g., coerce false witness statements, suborn perjured testimony from snitches, or perjure themselves at suppression hearings or at trial). Furthermore, some prosecutors who are determined to convict obstruct justice by withholding exculpatory evidence from the defense.

American police are poorly trained about the dangers of interrogation and false confession. Rarely are police officers instructed in how to avoid eliciting confessions, how to understand what causes false confessions, or how to recognize the forms false confessions take or their distinguishing characteristics. Instead, some interrogation manual writers and trainers persist in the unfounded belief that contemporary psychological methods will not cause the innocent to confess—a fiction so thoroughly contradicted by all of the research on police interrogation that it can be labeled a potentially deadly myth. This fiction perpetuates the commonly held belief that only torture can cause an innocent suspect to confess, and it allows some police to rationalize accepting coerced and demonstrably unreliable confession statements as

III. Findings

A. Proven false confessions

There are four sub-types of proven false confessions: the suspect confessed to a crime that did not happen; the evidence objectively demonstrates that the defendant could not possibly have committed the crime; the true perpetrator was identified and his guilt established; or the defendant was exonerated by scientific evidence....

IV. False confessions and case outcomes

A. Deprivations of liberty and miscarraiges of justice

Cases involving suspected or established false confessions typically result in some deprivation of the false confessor's liberty. The amount of deprivation may vary from a brief wrongful arrest and detention to lifelong incarceration or execution. The harms of false confessions can be measured by the amount of liberty deprived in each case.... Each case outcome is classified into one of four categories (wrongful arrest/detention, wrongful prosecution, wrongful incarceration and wrongful execution) corresponding to the amount of harm done.

B. Classifying case outcomes

In general, false confession cases can be usefully divided into two categories: those that result in pre-trial deprivations of liberty (Type I cases); and those that result in miscarriages of justice and wrongful deprivation of many years of liberty and/or of life (Type II cases). Type I cases occur when police, prosecutors, trial judges or juries correct the initial error of relying on a questionable confession. There are multiple points in the trial process at which the criminal justice system has the potential to be self-correcting. Indeed, the rules of American criminal procedure are structured to allocate the risk of error so as to minimize the possibility of convicting the innocent.

1. *Type I cases: False confessions that do not lead to conviction (52%)*

a. *General*

Sometimes police extract a confession from an innocent suspect that they initially believe to be true, but either they or the prosecutors realize is false before the filing of charges. In other instances, police and prosecutors realize that an innocent suspect has confessed because it is physically impossible for the suspect to have committed the crime. Sometimes officials do not come to the realization that the confession is false until after another suspect has confessed to the crime. And sometimes police and prosecutors never come to this realization even though the confession is demonstrably not true (i.e., contradicts the known facts of the crime)....

b. *Confessions from the true perpetrator*

Often police or prosecutors only discover and acknowledge their error in eliciting a false confession or charging an innocent defendant prior to conviction because they have accidentally or unintentionally obtained a reliable confession from the true perpetrator(s) of the crime....

c. *Prosecutorial intervention*

Though it appears to happen relatively infrequently, prosecutors sometimes drop charges against a defendant who has confessed because the confession does not match the facts of the crime and the prosecutor thus recognizes that it is of no evidentiary value....

d. Judicial suppression

Sometimes prosecutors are forced to drop charges after a judge suppresses a confession because there is no physical or even uncompromised testimonial evidence to implicate the defendant....

e. Jury acquittals

If police fail to detect that a confession is unreliable, prosecutors fail to dismiss charges and the judge fails to suppress the confession, the defendant may still be able to persuade a jury of his innocence. Though juries tend to regard confessions as the most probative and damning evidence of guilt possible, they sometimes acquit defendants who have confessed falsely....

2. Type II cases: False confessions that lead to wrongful conviction and imprisonment (48%)

a. General

Type II cases are those in which miscarriages have occurred and the justice system has clearly failed: not only have innocent individuals been made to confess to crimes they did not commit, but they have also been wrongly prosecuted, convicted, and imprisoned. False confessions may lead to wrongful conviction either when a suspect pleads guilty to avoid an anticipated harsher punishment or when a judge or jury convicts at trial....Following Type II errors, some suspects are eventually released and exonerated; some are released after serving a prison term but are never exonerated; and some false confessors are sentenced to life terms and remain incarcerated to this day. Several false confessors in this study were sentenced to death, and in one case the defendant was executed.

Confession evidence is sufficient to produce wrongful arrests, convictions and incarceration. In practice, criminal justice officials and lay jurors often treat confession evidence as dispositive, so much so that they often allow it to outweigh even strong evidence of a suspect's factual innocence. All of the police-induced false confessions documented here resulted in some deprivation of liberty. Fifty-two percent of the false confessors' wrongful deprivation of liberty ended before conviction, while 48% of the defendants suffered miscarriages of justice.

b. Plea bargains

If it seems counter-intuitive that an innocent person would confess falsely, the specter of an innocent false confessor pleading guilty seems fantastic. Yet this is not uncommon. n412 As Table B2 indicates, in 12% (7) of the cases reported here, the false confessor chose to plead guilty to avoid an anticipated harsher punishment—typically the death penalty....

c. Jury convictions

i. General

The history of criminal justice in America prior to the Miranda decision is replete with instances of juries convicting innocent defendants who were linked to the crime only by a false confession. Despite additional safeguards, police continue to elicit false confessions in the post-Miranda era, and juries continue to convict false confessors at an alarmingly high rate....Even an unsupported and disconfirmed confession is often sufficient to lead a trier of fact to judge the defendant guilty beyond a reasonable doubt. [T]he thirty false confessors whose cases proceeded to trial had a 73% chance of being convicted. Despite the absence of any physical or other significant credible evidence corroborating a confession, a false confessor was approximately three times more likely to be found guilty at trial than to be acquitted (73% vs. 27%). These data demonstrate that a false confession is an exceptionally dangerous piece of evidence to put before a jury even when the other case evidence weighs heavily in favor of the defendant's innocence....

Not surprisingly, the false confessors who are ever going to be proven innocent are likely to have this proof come to light shortly after their confession. Slightly over half (53%) of the proven false confessors have charges dismissed prior to trial, while 47% of proven false confessors must make a decision about pleading to an offer of lesser punishment or undergoing trial. The high percentage of pre-trial dismissals is likely due to proof of a confessor's innocence coming to light early in the pre-trial discovery process (e.g., when scientific test results become available) or when the defense establishes the defendant's alibi (e.g., the alibi the police ignored when the defendant offered it during interrogation) or for other strong reasons (e.g., the victim turns up alive).

Absent the discovery of evidence dispositively proving the defendant's innocence, only 19% of defendants classified as highly probable or probable false confessors are spared having to choose to undergo trial or to plead guilty. The vast majority (81%) of these false confessors find themselves having to choose either to plead guilty to a crime they did not commit or go to trial and risk the harshest possible punishment.

[T]here is a strong likelihood that a miscarriage of justice will occur if a false confessor undergoes a trial. It is alarming that about three-quarters (73%) of all false confessors who went to trial were convicted. Table 4 reports that when proven and classified confession cases (i.e., highly probable + probable) are separated there is a 27% higher level of risk of conviction at trial for those whose innocence will be proven much later. Further, while 63% of the classified false confessors are convicted at their trials, 90% of the defendants who would someday be proven innocent are convicted when their false confessions are brought into court.

If tried, 37% of those classified as false confessors are acquitted, while only 10% of those belatedly proven innocent are acquitted. It appears that at the time of trial the exculpatory evidence favoring those who were destined to someday be proven innocent was weaker than the exculpatory evidence supporting those who even today can only be classified as false confessors. Some of those who were later proven to be false confessors were only saved from their sentences of execution or life imprisonment by new scientific developments such as DNA analysis or a true perpetrator's long-delayed decision to confess.

V. Conclusion

This article has documented that American police continue to elicit false confessions even though the era of third degree interrogation has passed. This study has also demonstrated with field data what Kassin and Wrightsman have established in the laboratory: that confession evidence substantially biases the trier of fact's evaluation of the case in favor of prosecution and conviction, even when the defendant's uncorroborated confession was elicited by coercive methods and the other case evidence strongly supports his innocence. With near certainty, false confessions lead to unjust deprivations of liberty. Often they also result in wrongful conviction and incarceration, sometimes even execution.

For those concerned with the proper administration of justice, the important issue is no longer whether contemporary interrogation methods cause innocent suspects to confess. Nor is it to speculate about the rate of police-induced false confession or the annual number of wrongful convictions they cause. Rather, the important question is: How can such errors be prevented? If police and prosecutors wish to prevent wrongful deprivations of liberty and miscarriages of justice, they must acknowledge the reality of false confessions, seek to understand their causes and consequences, and work to implement policies that will both reduce the likelihood of eliciting false confessions and increase the likelihood of detecting them.

The sixty false confessions described in this article dispel the myth promoted by interrogation manual authors and police trainers that the psychological interrogation methods they advocate do not cause suspects to confess to crimes they did not commit. In fact, the opposite is true. Our analysis almost always reveals evidence of shoddy police practice and/or police criminality. Shoddy police practice derives in large part from poor interrogation training. Influential manuals such as Criminal Interrogation and Confessions n534 and Practical Aspects of Interview and Interrogation teach police to use tactics that have been shown to be coercive and to produce false confessions. Such texts also mislead interrogators into believing that a suspect's guilt can be inferred on the basis of pseudoscientific claims about the meaning of demeanor and behavior analysis, and they fail to educate police about the social psychology, variety and distinguishing characteristics of interrogation-induced false confessions.

Police criminality (e.g., coercing false witness statements, suborning perjured testimony from snitches, perjury at suppression hearings or at trial and/or obstruction of justice by withholding exculpatory evidence) often stems from ill-conceived efforts to save prosecutions that never should have commenced. The blood sport attitude that often develops in high profile criminal prosecutions — "get the guilty party no matter what" — sometimes causes significant harm to innocent individuals who police and prosecutors have identified as guilty solely because they were coerced or persuaded to make a false confession. During the investigation and prosecution of every wrongful conviction documented in this article, police and prosecutors should have realized that the confession was almost certainly, if not demonstrably, false.

The American criminal justice system has not yet developed adequate safeguards to prevent police-induced false confessions from leading to the wrongful deprivation of liberty and conviction of the innocent. False confessions threaten the quality of criminal justice in America by inflicting significant and unnecessary harms on the innocent. In 52% of the cases reported here, the false confessor suffered, at a minimum, unjust and needless pre-trial deprivations of liberty. For these defendants, the safeguards built into the criminal justice system limited the false confessor's harms to pre-trial incarceration, the cost of defending their innocence, and the damage to their careers and reputations. Forty-eight percent of the false confession cases studied resulted in a miscarriage of justice. In these prosecutions, the safeguards built into the criminal justice system failed to prevent lengthy incarceration, years of imprisonment on death row and in one case a wrongful execution.

False confessions are likely to lead to unjust deprivations of liberty and miscarriages of justice because criminal justice officials and lay jurors treat confession evidence with such deference that it outweighs strong evidence of a defendant's innocence. It bears emphasizing that in none of the disputed confessions documented in this article was there any reliable evidence corroborating the defendant's confession, and in most of these cases there was compelling, if not overwhelming, evidence establishing his innocence. Nevertheless, criminal justice officials treated these confession statements as the most probative evidence of the defendant's guilt and permitted the "I did it" statement to override evidence of his innocence. Absent the uncorroborated and unreliable statement, none of these individuals would likely have been arrested, charged, convicted, incarcerated, or executed.

The risk of harm caused by false confessions could be greatly reduced if police were required to video- or audio-record the entirety of their interrogations. Presently, only Alaska and Minnesota require recording custodial interrogations.The practice of recording creates an objective and exact record of the interrogation process that all parties—police, prosecutors, defense attorneys, judges, juries—can review at any time. The existence of an exact record of the interrogation is crucial for determining the voluntariness and reliability of any confession statement, especially if the confession is internally inconsistent, is contradicted by some of the case facts, or was elicited by coercive methods or from highly suggestible individuals.

Taping also allows third parties to resolve the courtroom "swearing contests" that arise when the suspect and the police offer conflicting testimony about what occurred during interrogation. In disputed confession cases the discrepancies between police officers' and defendants' accounts clearly indicate that one of the parties is either lying or mistaken. Of course, interrogators are sometimes falsely accused of deviant conduct. In the usual case, however, the police officer's testimony is treated as far more credible than the citizen's, whose reputability is compromised by his status as a criminal defendant. In many of the cases documented in this article, however, the interrogator claimed that the confessor supplied information that only the perpetrator could have known—only to have the suspect subsequently proven innocent and his ignorance of the crime facts revealed. To more accurately resolve whether the interrogator used coercion, whether the suspect knew the facts of the crime, and/or whether he was made to confess falsely, one conclusion is inescapable: interrogations must be recorded in their entirety.

The cases discussed above also illustrate the compelling need for police, prosecutors, judges and juries to carefully scrutinize and evaluate a suspect's post admission narrative against the known facts of the crime. Confessions should be evaluated on the basis of the quality of the post-admission narratives they produce, and police should be trained to recognize that it is this information—not the words "I did it"—that discriminates between the innocent and the guilty. In investigations in which hard evidence linking a person to a crime is missing, only the analysis of the suspect's post-admission narrative provides a basis for objectively assessing his personal knowledge of a crime (assuming contamination is eliminated). In each of the recorded false confessions studied here, the account the suspect offered after saying the words "I did it" was significantly at odds with the crime facts and indicated that the suspect was ignorant of information the true perpetrator would have known.

When police are trained to seek both independent evidence of a suspect's guilt and internal corroboration for every confession before making an arrest; when state's attorneys demand that "I did it" statements be corroborated by the details of a suspect's post-admission narrative before undertaking a prosecution; when courts insist on a minimal indicia of reliability before admitting confession statements into evidence; and when legislators mandate the recording of interrogations in their entirety, the damage wrought and the lives ruined by the misuse of psychological interrogation methods will be significantly reduced. The sixty cases discussed in this article illustrate that when there is no independent evidence against a defendant and only a factually inaccurate confession, the risk of justice miscarrying is so great that the case should never be allowed to proceed to trial.

List of other cases and articles relevant to this topic

P. Cassell (1998) Protecting the innocent from false confessions and lost confessions—and from Miranda. *Journal of Criminal Law and Criminology* 88: 429–496.

R.A. Leo and R. Ofshe (1998). Using the innocent to scapegoat Miranda: Another reply to Paul Cassell. *Journal of Criminal Law and Criminology* 88: 429–496.

Beltran v. Florida, 700 So. 2d 132 (Fla. 1997)

Bixler v. State, 568 N.W. 2d 880 (Minn. App. 1997)

Callis, 684 NE 2d 233 (Ind 1997)

Carter v. State, 697 So. 2d 529 (Fla. App. 1997)

Green v. State, 55 S.W.3d 633 (Tex. App. 2001)

MacDonald 718 A. 2d 195 (Maine 1998)

Madrid 910 P. 2d 1340 (Wyo 1996).

People v. Gilliam, 670 N.E. 2d 606, 619 (Il. 1996)

People v. Slago, 374 N.E. 2d 1270 (Il. 1978)
Ruckman v. State, LEXIS (Tex. App. 2000)
State v. Aldridge, 697 N.E.2d 228 (Ohio App. 1997)
State v. Baldwin, 482 SE 2d 1 (NC 1997)
State v. Buechler, 572 NW 2d 65 (Neb 1998)
State v. Caulley, LEXIS (Ohio App. 2002)
State v. Green 250 AD 2d 143 (NY 1998)(apply *Frye* test)
State v. Koskela, 536 N.W. 2d 625 (Minn. 1995)
State v. Miller, 1997 Wash. App. LEXIS 960 (Wash. App. 1997)
U.S. Mazzeo, LEXIS (2d Cir. 2000)
United States v. Shay, 57 F. 3d 126, 130–134 (1st Cir. 1995)

Discussion and Review Questions

1. Applying *Daubert* et al., do you think the Court should allow the introduction of expert testimony on false confession hypothesis?
2. What policy measures do you think that police departments could take to reduce the incidence of false confessions?
3. Should the police be permitted to use trickery to get suspects to confess? A Missouri case, pending before the United States Supreme Court, raises an interesting question about a particular type of trickery to get a confession. In this case, a police officer admitted that he violates Miranda (i.e., intentionally interrogates suspects without reading them their warnings) in the hope of obtaining a confession. The officer then uses the admissions in a second interview that is tape-recorded and Miranda warnings are provided. The question before the Court is whether this technique violates the Fifth Amendment? How do you think the Court will rule? Do you think this technique is psychologically coercive?

References

Articles

Barker, Lucius and Twiley W. Barker (1990). *Civil liberties and the constitution: Cases and commentaries.* Englewood Cliffs, NJ: Prentice Hall.
Cassell, Paul G. (1998). Protecting the innocent from false confessions and lost confessions—and from *Miranda. The Journal of Criminal Law and Criminology* 88: 497–556.
Kassin, Saul (November 12, 2002). Police presumption of guilt: Key in false confessions—Lecture at University of Virginia Law School. Discussion at:

http://www.law.virginia.edu/home2002/html/news/2002_fall/falseconfession.htm

Leo, Richard A. and Richard J. Ofshe (1998). The consequences of false confessions: Deprivations of liberty and miscarriages of justice in the age of psychological interrogation. *The Journal of Criminal Law and Criminology* 88: 429–496.

Leo, Richard A. and Richard J. Ofshe (1998). Using the innocent to scapegoat Miranda: Another reply to Paul Cassell. *The Journal of Criminal Law and Criminology* 88(2): 429–496.

Case Citations

Beckwith v. United States, 425 U.S. 319 (1976).

Beltran v. Florida, 700 So. 2d 132 (Fla. 4th DCA 1997).

Brown v. Mississippi, 297 U.S. 278 (1936).

Callis v. State, 684 N.E. 2d 233 (Ct. App. Ind. 1997).

Chambers v. Florida, 309 U.S. 277 (1940).

Colorado v. Spring, 479 U.S. 564 (1987).

Connecticut v. Barrett, 479 U.S. 523 (1987).

Crane v. Kentucky, 476 U.S. 683 (1986).

Davis v. United States, 512 U.S. 452 (1994).

Fare v. Michael C., 482 U.S. 707 (1979).

Green v. State, 55 S.W.3d 633 (Tex. App. 2001).

Harris v. New York, 401 U.S. 222 (1971).

Illinois v. Perkins, 496 U.S. 292 (1990).

Michigan v. Jackson, 475 U.S. 625 (1986).

Miller v. State, 770 N.E. 2d 763 (Ind. 2002).

Minnesota v. Murphy, 105 S.Ct. 1136 (1984).

Minnick v. Mississippi, 498 U.S. 146 (1990).

Miranda v. Arizona, 384 U.S. 436 (1966).

Moran v. Burbine, 106 S. Ct. 1135 (1986).

New York v. Quarles, 467 U.S. 649 (1984).

Oregon v. Mathiason, 435 U.S. 492 (1977).

Orozco v. Texas, 394 U.S. 324 (1967).

Pennsylvania v. Bruder, 488 U.S. 9 (1988).

Spano v. New York, 360 U.S. 315 (1959).

State v. Buechler, 253 Neb. 727, 572 N.W.2d 65 (1998).

State v. MacDonald, 718 A.2d 195 (Maine 1998).

United States v. Dickerson, 530 U.S. 428 (2000).
United States v. Hall, 974 F. Supp. 1198 (Cent. Dist. Ill. 1997).
United States v. Mathis, 391 U.S. 1 (1968).
United States v. Shay, 57 F. 3d 126 (1st Cir. 1995).

CHAPTER 11

FUTURE DANGEROUSNESS AND THE OFFENDER

On September 29, 1994, [Jesse Timmendequas] lured his seven-year old neighbor, Megan Kanka, into his house, ostensibly to play with his puppy. [Timmendequas] drew her into his bedroom where he attempted to sexually assault her. Megan screamed and tried to escape but [Timmendequas], fearing detection, would not let her leave. [He] strangled Megan with a belt and, during the struggle, hit her face on a dresser and her head on the floor, causing bleeding. To avoid stains on the carpet, Timmendequas placed a plastic bag over Megan's head. [Timmendequas] then sexually assaulted her. Believing Megan to be dead, [Timmendequas] placed her body in a toy box and carried it downstairs. When he put the box in his truck, he thought he heard Megan cough. [Timmendequas] drove to Mercer County Park, took Megan's body out of the box, and placed her in tall weeds. Before he left, he sexually assaulted her again.

–State of New Jersey v. Timmendequas, 773 A. 2d 18 (NJ 2001).

Timmendequas had two prior convictions—a 1980 conviction for attempted aggravated sexual contact and a 1982 conviction for sexual assault and aggravated assault. *Id.* at 32. In response to this horrifying and nationally publicized child abduction, rape and homicide by a twice-convicted felon, every state has passed sexual offender notification laws (commonly known as Megan's Law). The underlying assumption of sexual offender notification laws, as well as civil commitment laws and the use of a defendants' predilection to offending in the sentencing phase of capital cases is that the future dangerousness of these offenders can be presumed or predicted. These laws were intended to achieve the laudable goal of protecting society. The legal parameters of these laws, the ability of social scientists to predict future dangerousness of offenders and the societal benefits from these laws will be discussed.

What are sexual offender notification laws?

In general, these laws require the registration of sexual offenders with their local police, and to varying degrees, the notification of communities that a convicted sexual offender intends to live in their neighborhood (Kabat 1998). The initial attempts by the states to introduce registration and notification laws resulted in vast variations in the laws across the United States involving the duration of the notification and registration, the ability to petition for termination of the registration and notification requirements, the ability of an offender to review his record for accuracy, variations in the definition of "public records" effecting what information is available to the public, the method of notification, who is notified, whether notification is discretionary or mandatory, and the specific information released to the public (Kabat 1998: 340–347).

In 1996, Congress passed the federal "Megan's Law" and broadened the scope of information provided to the public (Kabat 1998; see also H.R. 2137). This law provides that information may be disclosed for any purpose permitted under state law and law enforcement agencies shall release relevant information necessary to protect the public (Kabat 1998). This latter provision superseded those states with "discretionary" notification provisions (Kabat 1998).

Also in 1996, Congress enacted the "Pam Lyncher Act" providing for an FBI database for all individuals convicted of sexual offenses against children. This law requires community notification by state and federal authorities and allows for a nationwide database to monitor sex offenders throughout the country (Kabat 1998). States must be in compliance with the federal statutory scheme for registration and notification. This means that registration and notification laws have retroactive application, i.e., sexual offenders who were released prior to the adoption of Megan's Law are still subject to registration and notification. There is a minimum, but not maximum time frame for registration and notification, the minimum number of years is ten. Sex offenders are not permitted to petition for termination of registration or notification within the ten year period and there is no provision allowing for offenders to review their records for accuracy. Database information on sexual offenders is public not private, and if permitted by state statute, information may be disclosed upon request. Community notification as necessary to protect the public is required and this notification is mandatory, not discretionary. However, states may establish a tier system of notification. The tier system is based on the risk assessed to the particular offender and thus, the type of notification given to the public may vary based on this assessment. The information

> **Ex Post Facto Law:** A law passed after the occurrence of a fact or commission of an act, which retrospectively changes the legal consequences or relations of such fact or deed. By article 1, section 10 of the U.S. Const., the states are forbidden to pass "any ex post facto law."...An "ex post facto law" is defined as a law which provides for the infliction of punishment upon a person for an act done which, when it was committed, was innocent.... (Black's Law Dictionary)
>
> **Procedural Due Process:** Those safeguards to one's liberty and property mandated by the 14th Amendment...Central meaning of procedural due process is that parties whose rights are to be affected are entitled to be heard and, in order that they may enjoy that right they must be notified.... (Black's Law Dictionary)

released to the public is the name of the offender, the offender's address, a description of the offender, and a photograph of the offender (Kabat 1998).

There remains debate about the efficacy of "Megan's law." Some argue that these laws cannot be reconciled with rights of privacy and that the law fails to protect victims (Kabat 1998). Others argue the laws do not promote rehabilitation and encourage vigilantism (Kabat 1998). The counter-arguments suggest that registration and notification laws are not a form of punishment and are necessary to enhance community safety. (Feldman 1997). Moreover, Feldman (1997) argues that community notification laws simply make "public" otherwise "public" information. The law saves citizens the "trouble of attending trials, spending hundreds of hours searching through court records to compile lists of offenders, or paying the Department of Motor Vehicles and the Office of Court Administration for requested information." (Feldman 1997: p. 1112). Vigilantism is not, according to Feldman, a legitimate basis to disallow the notification laws. Most laws impose penalties for the misuse of the information and of course crimes against sexual offenders are violations of the criminal law.

Are sexual offender notification laws legal?

Yes. In two decisions rendered on March 5, 2003, the United States Supreme Court approved sexual notification laws. In *Smith v. Doe*, 123 S. Ct. 1140 (2003), the Court held that retroactive application of an Alaskan notification law did not violate the **ex post facto** prohibition. In *Connecticut v. Smith*, 123 S. Ct. 1160 (2003), the Court held that Connecticut's law did not violate **procedural due process** by not allowing convicted sex offenders a hearing on current dangerousness prior to the disclosure of information to the public.

In the two cases that have reached the Court, the Court has approved statutory schemes allowing the registration of offenders and the notification of the public about these offenders. In essence, the Court upheld the Alaska statute against an ex post facto argument because it found sexual notification laws are not punishment, thus the prohibition against retroactive punishments, i.e., punishing someone for past wrongs is not applicable. The Court determined that these laws were a regulatory scheme "civil" in nature and not intended to punish convicted criminals.

The Connecticut statute was upheld because the Court found that "future dangerousness" was not a material component of the sexual offender notification law. In essence, the State of Connecticut posted information about convicted sex offenders on its web site to make the sexual offender registry widely available to the public. It was not an assessment of future risk of the offenders, those on the registry were listed simply by virtue of their status as a convicted sex offender.[1]

In addition, a number of Circuit Courts of Appeal have also upheld challenges to the constitutionality of Megan's Laws. The Third Circuit Court for example has held, in a series of decisions, that sexual notification laws do not violate offenders' rights of privacy, due process and do not constitute cruel and unusual punishment. *Artway v. Attorney General*, 81 F. 3d 1235 (3d Cir. 1996); *E.B. v. Verniero*, 119 F. 3d 1077 (3d Cir. 1997), *Paul P. v. Verniero*, 170 F. 3d 396 (3d Cir. 1999); and *Paul P. v. Farmer*, 227 F. 3d 98 (3d Cir. 2000).

Another measure to protect society against sexual predators or is it—civil commitment laws?

Sexual offender notification laws have been passed in all 50 states. The swiftness of the passage of these laws speaks to the interest society has in protecting children from dangerous sex offenders. In addition to the sexual offender registration and notification laws, several states have enacted laws that make notification seem like a much less punitive alternative for sex offenders. At least thirteen states (Florida, Iowa, Missouri, South Carolina, Arizona, Cal-

---

1. In this decision, the Court does not examine whether the Connecticut statute violates principles of substantive due process because that issue was not raised by the respondent.

> **Double jeopardy**: Commonlaw and constitutional (Fifth Amendment) prohibition against a second prosecution after a first trial for the same offense.... (Black's Law Dictionary)

ifornia, Illinois, Kansas, Minnesota, North Dakota, New Jersey, Washington and Wisconsin) have enacted sexual offender civil commitment laws.

These laws allow for the involuntary confinement of individuals determined to be a danger to the public because they are sexual predators likely to re-offend if not detained. *Kansas v. Hendricks*, 521 U.S. 346, 357 (1997). As an example of the effect of these laws, an offender preparing for release from prison after serving his sentence of 10 years for a sexual offense may be involuntarily confined by civil commitment in a psychiatric hospital indefinitely if a court finds that he suffers from a "mental abnormality or personality disorder which makes the person likely to engage in the predatory acts of sexual violence" and their is a "likelihood of such conduct in the future if the person is not incapacitated".

In *Kansas v. Hendricks*, the United States Supreme Court upheld the constitutionality of these laws and rejected Hendricks' claims that the law violated the Constitution's **double jeopardy** prohibition (i.e., the prohibition of being tried twice for the same crime) and the ban on ex post facto lawmaking (i.e., prohibiting the application of punishments for past crimes, i.e., retroactive punishments). Similar to the Court's decision in *Smith v. Doe* on sexual offender notification laws, the Court found that involuntary confinement was not criminal in nature because the confinement was not based on two primary objectives of criminal punishment: retribution or deterrence. The Court reasoned that involuntary commitment is not based on a criminal conviction (conviction is not necessary) nor is the commitment intended to punish the sexual predator for past behavior but to prevent future dangerousness. Second, the Court found that the sexual predators are unable to be deterred by the threat of confinement and the purpose of the confinement is not punishment but to hold the person until he recovers and is no longer a threat to others. Since the confinement is not criminal in nature, the statute in *Hendricks* does not violate the double jeopardy or ex post facto clauses.

The concept of future dangerousness and the death penalty.

The Court utilizes the concept of "future dangerousness" in the context of death penalty cases as well. In *Jurek v. Texas*, 428 U.S. 262 (1976), the Court held that the likelihood of a defendant's committing a future crime was an acceptable criterion for imposing the death penalty and that it was appropriate to utilize expert witnesses to assist in making this assessment. In *Jurek*, a majority of the Court rejected the notion that it was impossible to predict "future dangerousness" to invalidate this criterion in death penalty cases. This position was re-affirmed in *Estelle v. Barefoot*, 463 U.S. 880 (1983).

Justice Blackmun in a dissenting opinion was very critical of this finding. Justice Blackmun stated: "The Court holds that psychiatric testimony about a defendant's future dangerousness is admissible, despite the fact that such testimony is wrong two times out of three." *Id.* at 916. Based on the lack of reliability of the testimony, Justice Blackmun would hold that greater reliability should prevail, particularly in capital cases. *Id.* A limitation on the introduction of this evidence was found in *Powell v. Texas*, 492 U.S. 680 (1989). The Court held the taking of evidence on the accused's future dangerousness during pretrial psychiatric examinations without notifying defendant's counsel and without advising the defendant of his *Miranda* rights violate the Sixth Amendment right to assistance of counsel in death penalty cases.

In another case, the United States Supreme Court has held that a defendant, in a death penalty case during the sentencing phase of the trial, was entitled to a jury instruction that he was not eligible for parole (if sentenced to life in prison) when the prosecutor argues to the jury, in favor of the death penalty, the future dangerousness of the defendant. *Simmons v. South Carolina*, 512 U.S. 154 (1994). This decision was re-affirmed in two later cases – *Shafer v. South Carolina*, 532 U.S. 36 (2001) and *Kelly v. South Carolina*, 534 U.S. 246 (2002)(holding that arguments by the prosecutor were sufficient to raise the issue of future danger for the jury). In *Simmons v. South Carolina*, the Court reasoned that it was a violation of due process under the Fourteenth Amendment to refuse to allow the capital sentencing jury to be informed that the defendant was ineligible for parole under state law. This information would allow jurors to make better-informed decisions about the appropriate sentence because jurors would understand that they would not necessarily be releasing a dangerous criminal into society by voting against the death penalty.

Do sexual offender notification and civil commitment laws protect the public?

The study of "future dangerousness" is relatively new. No studies were cited by the United States Supreme Court in its decisions in *Kansas v. Hendricks* (civil commitment case) or in *Jurek v. Texas* and *Estelle v. Barefoot* (future dangerousness cases). However, Justice Blackmun noted in *Jurek* that studies indicated measures of future dangerousness were wrong two out of three times.

Recent studies have begun to examine the impact of Megan's Law, indefinite civil commitment and the potential of future dangerousness in death penalty cases. Some have explored whether these measures – community notification and civil confinement – prevent future crime (Menzies, Webster, McMain et al. 1994; Cunningham and Reidy 1999; Petrosino and Petrosino 1999). A recent study by the National Institute of Justice (2000) studied the sex offender community notification law in Wisconsin and found mixed results. (Zevitz and Farkas 2000). In part, the study found that there remained some misconceptions by the public on the purpose of the notification laws. Equal numbers of citizens felt more concerned and less concerned about the offender after notification. In addition, they found that although law enforcement had few problems with implementing the law, the law increased the workload of probation and parole officers, housing resources for released offenders were scarce and more research was necessary to assess its impact on recidivism.

Although psychiatrists are instrumental in assessing sexual predators for indefinite and involuntary commitment, the American Psychiatric Association opposes the development and implementation of civil commitment laws. (Fitch and Ortega 2000; Post 1999). One disagreement among psychiatric and psychology professionals is the ability to predict future dangerousness. Some argue that risk assessments of future dangerousness are inaccurate, whereas others make the case that prediction is not "impossible or unethical" (Post 1999: 235–236). In Preventative victimization: Assessing future dangerousness in sexual predators for purposes of indeterminate civil commitment (1999), Dawn Post argues that some risk assessment instruments are accurate in predicting violent behavior and that recidivism rates are particularly high among sexual offenders.

In this article, excerpted in your text, she reviews the studies and tools available to assist in assessing the future dangerousness of individuals. The list of factors, identified by John Monahan (1995), necessary for an assessment are: precipitating events, context of events at time of violence, demographic characteristics, history of violence, base rate of violence among individual's with similar backgrounds, sources of environmental stress confronted by person, comparisons of current and past violent behavior, predisposition to cope with stress, availability of victims, means to commit violence in the future (Post 1999).

When is future dangerousness in death penalty cases an issue?

According to the United States Supreme Court in *Simmons v. South Carolina*, 512 U.S. 154 (1994), a defendant is only entitled to a jury instruction informing them that if the defendant is not sentenced to death, he will spend the rest of his life in prison when the prosecution makes an argument about the defendant's future dangerousness. In other words, if the prosecutor does not argue that a defendant should be put to death because he remains a threat, the jury is not instructed about the meaning of life imprisonment versus death. The reason for the Court's decision rests on the presumption that jurors do not "worry about the defendant's future dangerousness, and about what a sentence of life imprisonment really means [unless] the state injects the issue of future dangerous into the proceedings." (Blume et al. 2001: 398). Thus a remedial instruction is not necessary. John Blume, Stephen Garvey and Sheri Johnson disagree with the Court's assumption in their article *Future Dangerousness in Capital Cases: Always at Issue.*

In a study of over 100 jurors who served on capital cases in South Carolina (as part of the Capital Jury Project),[2] Blume et al. (2001: 398–9) found "that future dangerousness is on the minds of most capital jurors, and is thus "at issue" in virtually all capital trials, no matter what the prosecution says or does not say." After interviewing 187 jurors, the researchers identified 53 that indicated that prosecutors did not emphasize defendant's danger to the public in its evidence or argument to the jury. The focus of their research was on these 53 jurors and they found that a high percentage of these jurors had discussed future dangerousness during deliberations on the penalty phase and that they were concerned about the defendant reintegrating into society to kill again. In essence, even in the absence of evidence or prosecutorial argument, jurors remain concerned about defendants' future dangerousness.

Blume et al. raised these concerns with the United States Supreme Court by way of an amicus brief in *Shafer v. South Carolina*, 532 U.S. 36 (2001).[3] But the Court avoided answering the question whether a 'no parole eligibility' instruction when the prosecution does not argue the future dangerousness of the defendant is necessary because this issue was not directly raised on appeal. In other words, this remains an open question.

In this chapter excerpts from *Smith v. Doe*, 123 S. Ct. 1140 (2003), *Simmons v. South Carolina*, 512 U.S. 154 (1994), Post's (1999) *Preventative vic-*

---

2. To find out more about the capital jury project go to: http://www.lawschool.cornell.edu/lawlibrary/death/cjp.htm

3. No amicus brief was found using Lexis-Nexis in the *Kelly* case from the Capital Jury Project.

timization: Assessing future dangerousness in sexual predators for purposes of in-determinate civil commitment and Blume et al.'s *Future dangerousness in capi-tal cases: Always at issue* are included.

Smith v. Doe
123 S. Ct. 1140 (2003)(Excerpt)

OPINION: JUSTICE KENNEDY delivered the opinion of the Court.

The Alaska Sex Offender Registration Act requires convicted sex offenders to register with law enforcement authorities, and much of the information is made public. We must decide whether the registration requirement is a retroactive punishment prohibited by the Ex Post Facto Clause.

The State of Alaska enacted the Alaska Sex Offender Registration Act (Act) on May 12, 1994.... The Alaska law...contains two components: a registra-tion requirement and a notification system. Both are retroactive. 1994 Alaska Sess. Laws ch. 41, § 12(a). The Act requires any "sex offender or child kid-napper who is physically present in the state" to register, either with the De-partment of Corrections (if the individual is incarcerated) or with the local law enforcement authorities (if the individual is at liberty). Alaska Stat. §§ 12.63.010(a), (b) (2000). Prompt registration is mandated. If still in prison, a covered sex offender must register within 30 days before release; otherwise he must do so within a working day of his conviction or of entering the State. § 12.63.010(a). The sex offender must provide his name, aliases, identifying features, address, place of employment, date of birth, conviction information, driver's license number, information about vehicles to which he has access, and postconviction treatment history. § 12.63.010(b)(1). He must permit the authorities to photograph and fingerprint him. § 12.63.010(b)(2).

If the offender was convicted of a single, nonaggravated sex crime, he must provide annual verification of the submitted information for 15 years. §§ 12.63.010(d)(1), 12.63.020(a)(2). If he was convicted of an aggravated sex offense or of two or more sex offenses, he must register for life and verify the information quarterly. §§ 12.63.010(d)(2), 12.63.020(a)(1). The offender must notify his local police department if he moves. § 12.63.010(c). A sex offender who knowingly fails to comply with the Act is subject to criminal prosecution. §§ 11.56.835, 11.56.840.

The information is forwarded to the Alaska Department of Public Safety, which maintains a central registry of sex offenders. § 18.65.087(a). Some of the data, such as fingerprints, driver's license number, anticipated change of address, and whether the offender has had medical treatment afterwards, is kept confidential. §§ 12.63.010(b), 18.65.087(b). The following information is made available to the public: "the sex offender's or child kidnapper's name, aliases, address, photograph, physical description, description[,] license [and] identification numbers of motor vehicles, place of employment, date of birth, crime for which convicted, date of conviction, place and court of conviction, length and conditions of sentence, and a statement as to whether the offender or kidnapper is in compliance with [the update] requirements... or cannot be located." § 18.65.087(b). The Act does not specify the means by which the registry information must be made public. Alaska has chosen to make most of the nonconfidential information available on the Internet.

Respondents John Doe I and John Doe II were convicted of sexual abuse of a minor, an aggravated sex offense. John Doe I pleaded nolo contendere after a court determination that he had sexually abused his daughter for two years, when she was between the ages of 9 and 11; John Doe II entered a nolo contendere plea to sexual abuse of a 14-year-old child. Both were released from prison in 1990 and completed rehabilitative programs for sex offenders. Although convicted before the passage of the Act, respondents are covered by it. After the initial registration, they are required to submit quarterly verifications and notify the authorities of any changes. Both respondents, along with respondent Jane Doe, wife of John Doe I, brought an action under Rev. Stat. § 1979, 42 U.S.C. § 1983, seeking to declare the Act void as to them under the Ex Post Facto Clause of Article I, § 10, cl. 1, of the Constitution and the Due Process Clause of § 1 of the Fourteenth Amendment. The United States District Court for the District of Alaska granted summary judgment for petitioners. In agreement with the District Court, the Court of Appeals for the Ninth Circuit determined the state legislature had intended the Act to be a nonpunitive, civil regulatory scheme; but, in disagreement with the District Court, it held the effects of the Act were punitive despite the legislature's intent. In consequence, it held the Act violates the Ex Post Facto Clause. *Doe v. Otte*, 259 F.3d 979 (2001). We granted certiorari. 534 U.S. 1126 (2002).

This is the first time we have considered a claim that a sex offender registration and notification law constitutes retroactive punishment forbidden by the Ex Post Facto Clause. The framework for our inquiry, however, is well established. We must "ascertain whether the legislature meant the statute to establish 'civil' proceedings." *Kansas v. Hendricks*, 521 U.S. 346, 361 (1997). If the intention of the legislature was to impose punishment, that ends the inquiry. If, however, the intention was to enact a regulatory scheme that is civil and nonpunitive, we must further examine whether the statutory scheme is "'so punitive either in purpose or effect as to negate [the State's] intention' to deem it 'civil.'" Ibid. (quoting *United States v. Ward*, 448 U.S. 242, 248–249, 65 L. Ed. 2d 742, 100 S. Ct. 2636 (1980)). Because we "ordinarily defer to the legislature's stated intent," *Hendricks*, supra, at 361, "'only the clearest proof' will suffice to override legislative intent and transform what has been denominated a civil remedy into a criminal penalty," *Hudson v. United States*, 522 U.S. 93, 100 (1997) (quoting Ward, supra, at 249); see also *Hendricks*, supra, at 361; *United States v. Ursery*, 518 U.S. 267, 290 (1996); *United States v. One Assortment of 89 Firearms*, 465 U.S. 354, 365 (1984).

Whether a statutory scheme is civil or criminal "is first of all a question of statutory construction." *Hendricks*, supra, at 361 (internal quotation marks omitted); see also *Hudson*, supra, at 99. We consider the statute's text and its structure to determine the legislative objective. *Flemming v. Nestor*, 363 U.S. 603, 617 (1960). A conclusion that the legislature intended to punish would satisfy an ex post facto challenge without further inquiry into its effects, so considerable deference must be accorded to the intent as the legislature has stated it.

The courts "must first ask whether the legislature, in establishing the penalizing mechanism, indicated either expressly or impliedly a preference for one label or the other." *Hudson*, supra, at 99 (internal quotation marks omitted). Here, the Alaska Legislature expressed the objective of the law in the statutory text itself. The legislature found that "sex offenders pose a high risk of reoffending," and identified "protecting the public from sex offenders" as the "primary governmental interest" of the law. 1994 Alaska Sess. Laws ch. 41, § 1. The legislature further determined that "release of certain information about sex offenders to public agencies and the general public will assist in protecting the public safety." *Ibid.* As we observed in *Hendricks*, where we examined an ex post facto challenge to a post-incarceration confinement of sex offenders, an imposition of restrictive measures on sex offenders adjudged to be dangerous is "a legitimate nonpunitive governmental objective and has been historically so regarded." 521 U.S., at 363. In this case, as in *Hendricks*, "nothing on the face of the statute suggests that the legislature sought to create anything other than a civil...scheme designed to protect the public from harm." Id., at 361.

Respondents seek to cast doubt upon the nonpunitive nature of the law's declared objective by pointing out that the Alaska Constitution lists the need for protecting the public as one of the purposes of criminal administration. Brief for Respondents 23 (citing Alaska Const., Art. I, § 12). As the Court stated in *Flemming v. Nestor*, rejecting an ex post facto challenge to a law terminating benefits to deported aliens, where a legislative restriction "is an incident of the State's power to protect the health and safety of its citizens," it will be considered "as evidencing an intent to exercise that regulatory power, and not a purpose to add to the punishment." 363 U.S., at 616 (citing *Hawker v. New York*, 170 U.S. 189 (1898))....

Other formal attributes of a legislative enactment, such as the manner of its codification or the enforcement procedures it establishes, are probative of the legislature's intent. See *Hendricks*, supra, at 361; *Hudson*, supra, at 103; 89 Firearms, supra, at 363. In this case these factors are open to debate. The notification provisions of the Act are codified in the State's "Health, Safety, and Housing Code," § 18, confirming our conclusion that the statute was intended as a nonpunitive regulatory measure. Cf. *Hendricks*, supra, at 361 (the State's "objective to create a civil proceeding is evidenced by its placement of the Act within the [State's] probate code, instead of the criminal code" (citations omitted)). The Act's registration provisions, however, are codified in the State's criminal procedure code, and so might seem to point in the opposite direction. These factors, though, are not dispositive. The location and labels of a statutory provision do not by themselves transform a civil remedy into a criminal one....

Title 12 of Alaska's Code of Criminal Procedure (where the Act's registration provisions are located) contains many provisions that do not involve criminal punishment, such as civil procedures for disposing of recovered and seized property, Alaska Stat. § 12.36.010 et seq. (2000); laws protecting the confidentiality of victims and witnesses, § 12.61.010 et seq.; laws governing the security and accuracy of criminal justice information, § 12.62.110 et seq.; laws governing civil postconviction actions, § 12.72.010 et seq.; and laws governing actions for writs of habeas corpus, § 12.75.010 et seq., which under Alaska law are "independent civil proceedings," *State v. Hannagan*, 559 P.2d 1059, 1063 (Alaska 1977). Although some of these provisions relate to criminal administration, they are not in themselves punitive. The partial codification of the Act in the State's criminal procedure code is not sufficient to support a conclusion that the legislative intent was punitive....

The policy to alert convicted offenders to the civil consequences of their criminal conduct does not render the consequences themselves punitive. When a State sets up a regulatory scheme, it is logical to provide those persons subject to it with clear and unambiguous notice of the requirements and the penalties for noncompliance. The Act requires registration either before the offender's release from confinement or within a day of his conviction (if the offender is not imprisoned). Timely and adequate notice serves to apprise individuals of their responsibilities and to ensure compliance with the regulatory scheme. Notice is important, for the scheme is enforced by criminal penalties. See §§ 11.56.835, 11.56.840. Although other methods of notification may be available, it is effective to make it part of the plea colloquy or the judgment of conviction. Invoking the criminal process in aid of a statutory regime does not render the statutory scheme itself punitive.

Our conclusion is strengthened by the fact that, aside from the duty to register, the statute itself mandates no procedures. Instead, it vests the authority to promulgate implementing regulations with the Alaska Department of Public Safety, §§ 12.63.020(b), 18.65.087(d)—an agency charged with enforcement of both criminal and civil regulatory laws.... We conclude, as did the District Court and the Court of Appeals, that the intent of the Alaska Legislature was to create a civil, nonpunitive regime.

In analyzing the effects of the Act we refer to the seven factors noted in *Kennedy v. Mendoza-Martinez*, 372 U.S. 144, 168–169 (1963), as a useful framework.... The factors most relevant to our analysis are whether, in its necessary operation, the regulatory scheme: has been regarded in our history and traditions as a punishment; imposes an affirmative disability or restraint; promotes the traditional aims of punishment; has a rational connection to a nonpunitive purpose; or is excessive with respect to this purpose.

A historical survey can be useful because a State that decides to punish an individual is likely to select a means deemed punitive in our tradition, so that the public will recognize it as such. The Court of Appeals observed that the sex offender registration and notification statutes "are of fairly recent origin," 259 F.3d at 989, which suggests that the statute was not meant as a punitive measure, or, at least, that it did not involve a traditional means of punishing. Respondents argue, however, that the Act—and, in particular, its notification provisions—resemble shaming punishments of the colonial period. Brief for Respondents 33–34 (citing A. Earle, Curious Punishments of Bygone Days 1–2 (1896)).

Some colonial punishments indeed were meant to inflict public disgrace. Humiliated offenders were required "to stand in public with signs cataloguing their offenses."...At times the labeling would be permanent: A murderer might be branded with an "M," and a thief with a "T."...The aim was to make these offenders suffer "permanent stigmas, which in effect cast the person out of the community."...The most serious offenders were banished, after which they could neither return to their original community nor, reputation tarnished, be admitted easily into a new one. T. Blomberg & K. Lucken, American Penology: A History of Control 30–31 (2000). Respondents contend that Alaska's compulsory registration and notification resemble these historical punishments, for they publicize the crime, associate it with his name, and, with the most serious offenders, do so for life.

Any initial resemblance to early punishments is, however, misleading. Punishments such as whipping, pillory, and branding inflicted physical pain and staged a direct confrontation between the offender and the public. Even punishments that lacked the corporal component, such as public shaming, humiliation, and banishment, involved more than the dissemination of information. They either held the person up before his fellow citizens for face-to-face shaming or expelled him from the community....By contrast, the stigma of Alaska's Megan's Law results not from public display for ridicule and shaming but from the dissemination of accurate information about a criminal record, most of which is already public. Our system does not treat dissemination of truthful information in furtherance of a legitimate governmental objective as punishment. On the contrary, our criminal law tradition insists on public indictment, public trial, and public imposition of sentence. Transparency is essential to maintaining public respect for the criminal justice system, ensuring its integrity, and protecting the rights of the accused. The publicity may cause adverse consequences for the convicted defendant, running from mild personal embarrassment to social ostracism. In contrast to the colonial shaming punishments, however, the State does not make the publicity and the resulting stigma an integral part of the objective of the regulatory scheme.

The fact that Alaska posts the information on the Internet does not alter our conclusion. It must be acknowledged that notice of a criminal conviction subjects the offender to public shame, the humiliation increasing in proportion to the extent of the publicity. And the geographic reach of the Internet is greater than anything which could have been designed in colonial times. These facts do not render Internet notification punitive. The purpose and the principal effect of notification are to inform the public for its own safety, not to humiliate the offender. Widespread public access is necessary for the efficacy of the scheme, and the attendant humiliation is but a collateral consequence of a valid regulation.

The State's Web site does not provide the public with means to shame the offender by, say, posting comments underneath his record. An individual seeking the information must take the initial step of going to the Department of Public Safety's Web site, proceed to the sex offender registry, and then look up the desired information. The process is more analogous to a visit to an official archive of criminal records than it is to a scheme forcing an offender to appear in public with some visible badge of past criminality. The Internet makes the document search more efficient, cost effective, and convenient for Alaska's citizenry.

We next consider whether the Act subjects respondents to an "affirmative disability or restraint." *Mendoza-Martinez*, 372 U.S., at 168. Here, we inquire how the effects of the Act are felt by those subject to it. If the disability or restraint is minor and indirect, its effects are unlikely to be punitive.

The Act imposes no physical restraint, and so does not resemble the punishment of imprisonment, which is the paradigmatic affirmative disability or restraint. *Hudson*, 522 U.S., at 104. The Act's obligations are less harsh than the sanctions of occupational debarment, which we have held to be nonpunitive. See ibid. (forbidding further participation in the banking industry); *De Veau v. Braisted*, 363 U.S. 144, 4 L. Ed. 2d 1109, 80 S. Ct. 1146 (1960) (forbidding work as a union official), *Hawker v. New York*, 170 U.S. 189 (1898) (revocation of a medical license). The Act does not restrain activities sex offenders may pursue but leaves them free to change jobs or residences....Although the public availability of the information may have a lasting and painful impact on the convicted sex offender, these consequences flow not from the Act's registration and dissemination provisions, but from the fact of conviction, already a matter of public record. The State makes the facts underlying the offenses and the resulting convictions accessible so members of the public can take the precautions they deem necessary before dealing with the registrant....It suffices to say the registration requirements make a valid regulatory program effective and do not impose punitive restraints in violation of the Ex Post Facto Clause.

The State concedes that the statute might deter future crimes. Respondents seize on this proposition to argue that the law is punitive, because deterrence is one purpose of punishment. Brief for Respondents 37. This proves too much. Any number of governmental programs might deter crime without imposing punishment. "To hold that the mere presence of a deterrent purpose renders such sanctions 'criminal'...would severely undermine the Government's ability to engage in effective regulation.."..

The Court of Appeals was incorrect to conclude that the Act's registration obligations were retributive because "the length of the reporting requirement appears to be measured by the extent of the wrongdoing, not by the extent of the risk posed." 259 F.3d at 990. The Act, it is true, differentiates between individuals convicted of aggravated or multiple offenses and those convicted of a single nonaggravated offense. Alaska Stat. § 12.63.020(a)(1) (2000). The broad categories, however, and the corresponding length of the reporting requirement, are reasonably related to the danger of recidivism, and this is consistent with the regulatory objective.

The Act's rational connection to a nonpunitive purpose is a "most significant" factor in our determination that the statute's effects are not punitive. *Ursery, supra*, at 290. As the Court of Appeals acknowledged, the Act has a legitimate nonpunitive purpose of "public safety, which is advanced by alerting the public to the risk of sex offenders in their community." 259 F.3d at 991. Respondents concede, in turn, that "this alternative purpose is valid, and rational." Brief for Respondents 38. They contend, however, that the Act lacks the necessary regulatory connection because it is not "narrowly drawn to accomplish the stated purpose." Ibid. A statute is not deemed punitive simply because it lacks a close or perfect fit with the nonpunitive aims it seeks to advance. The imprecision respondents rely upon does not suggest that the Act's nonpunitive purpose is a "sham or mere pretext."...

Alaska could conclude that a conviction for a sex offense provides evidence of substantial risk of recidivism. The legislature's findings are consistent with grave concerns over the high rate of recidivism among convicted sex offenders and their dangerousness as a class. The risk of recidivism posed by sex offenders is "frightening and high." *McKune v. Lile*, 536 U.S. 24, 34, 153 L. Ed. 2d 47, 122 S. Ct. 2017 (2002); see also id., at 33 ("When convicted sex offenders reenter society, they are much more likely than any other type of offender to be rearrested for a new rape or sexual assault") (citing U.S. Dept. of Justice, Bureau of Justice Statistics, *Sex Offenses and Offenders* 27 (1997); U.S. Dept. of Justice, Bureau of Justice Statistics, *Recidivism of Prisoners Released in 1983*, p. 6 (1997)).

The Ex Post Facto Clause does not preclude a State from making reasonable categorical judgments that conviction of specified crimes should entail particular regulatory consequences. We have upheld against ex post facto challenges laws imposing regulatory burdens on individuals convicted of crimes without any corresponding risk assessment. See *De Veau*, 363 U.S. at 160; *Hawker*, 170 U.S., at 197. As stated in *Hawker*: "Doubtless, one who has violated the criminal law may thereafter reform and become in fact possessed of a good moral character. But the legislature has power in cases of this kind to make a rule of universal application...." Ibid. The State's determination to legislate with respect to convicted sex offenders as a class, rather than require individual determination of their dangerousness, does not make the statute a punishment under the Ex Post Facto Clause.

Our decision in *Hendricks*, on which respondents rely, Brief for Respondents 39, is not to the contrary. The State's objective in *Hendricks* was involuntary (and potentially indefinite) confinement of "particularly dangerous individuals." 521 U.S., at 357–358, 364. The magnitude of the restraint made individual assessment appropriate. The Act, by contrast, imposes the more minor condition of registration. In the context of the regulatory scheme the State can dispense with individual predictions of future dangerousness and allow the public to assess the risk on the basis of accurate, nonprivate information about the registrants' convictions without violating the prohibitions of the Ex Post Facto Clause.

The duration of the reporting requirements is not excessive. Empirical research on child molesters, for instance, has shown that, "contrary to conventional wisdom, most reoffenses do not occur within the first several years after release," but may occur "as late as 20 years following release." R. Prentky, R. Knight, and A. Lee, U.S. Dept. of Justice, National Institute of Justice, *Child Sexual Molestation: Research Issues* 14 (1997).

The Court of Appeals' reliance on the wide dissemination of the information is also unavailing. The Ninth Circuit highlighted that the information was available "world-wide" and "broadcas[t]" in an indiscriminate manner. 259 F.3d at 992. As we have explained, however, the notification system is a passive one: An individual must seek access to the information. The Web site warns that the use of displayed information "to commit a criminal act against another person is subject to criminal prosecution." http://www.dps. state.ak.us/nSorcr/asp/ (as visited Jan. 17, 2003) (available in the Clerk of Court's case file). Given the general mobility of our population, for Alaska to make its registry system available and easily accessible throughout the State was not so excessive a regulatory requirement as to become a punishment. See D. Schram & C. Milloy, Community Notification: A Study of Offender Characteristics and Recidivism 13 (1995) (38% of recidivist sex offenses in the State of Washington took place in jurisdictions other than where the previous offense was committed).

The excessiveness inquiry of our ex post facto jurisprudence is not an exercise in determining whether the legislature has made the best choice possible to address the problem it seeks to remedy. The question is whether the regulatory means chosen are reasonable in light of the nonpunitive objective. The Act meets this standard.

The two remaining *Mendoza-Martinez* factors—whether the regulation comes into play only on a finding of scienter and whether the behavior to which it applies is already a crime—are of little weight in this case. The regulatory scheme applies only to past conduct, which was, and is, a crime. This is a necessary beginning point, for recidivism is the statutory concern. The obligations the statute imposes are the responsibility of registration, a duty not predicated upon some present or repeated violation.

Our examination of the Act's effects leads to the determination that respondents cannot show, much less by the clearest proof, that the effects of the law negate Alaska's intention to establish a civil regulatory scheme. The Act is nonpunitive, and its retroactive application does not violate the Ex Post Facto Clause. The judgment of the Court of Appeals for the Ninth Circuit is reversed, and the case is remanded for further proceedings consistent with this opinion.

It is so ordered.

D. Post. Preventive victimization: Assessing future dangerousness in sexual predators for purposes of indeterminate civil commitment. *

Hamline Journal of Public Law and Policy volume 21, page 177 (Excerpt)(Fall 1999).

I. Introduction.

...There are two types of "law." There is the type we are most familiar with, namely "black letter law," the "law on the books." This is the law that legislators enact, the law that was set down by the Founding Fathers in the Constitution, the law that evolves through common law cases and appeals decisions. It is the law that law school students study, judges interpret, and jurisprudens' analyze. But there is another law—although "law" may be too lofty or lowly a term to describe it: I call it commonsense justice, and it reflects what ordinary people think is just and fair. It is embedded in the intuitive notions jurors bring with them to the jury box when judging both a defendant and the law. It is what ordinary people think the law ought to be....

What we need to see—if we are to understand violence and to prevent it— is that human agency or action is not only individual; it is also, unavoidably, familial, societal, and institutional. Each of us is inextricably bound to others— in relationship. All human action (even the act of a single individual) is relational.

Such a conflict is particularly apparent with respect to the civil commitment of sexual predators. Over one hundred fifty articles have been published opposing the development and application of sexual predator legislation. This

---

* reprinted with permission of Hamline University School of Law & Hamline Journal of Public Law and Policy

article takes the minority position, and presents arguments in support of the development and application of laws providing for the civil commitment of sexual predators...

II. Sexual predators in general

Sexual predators are sexually violent offenders who are perceived to be a readily identifiable class of offenders, more likely to re-offend than others. Sexual predator laws center around the perceived threat these offenders present to the community at large based on their criminal history, present behavior, and future dangerousness. These laws originated with several highly publicized cases which led to greater public sensitivity, general interest, and more visible expressions of community outrage at crimes in general, and, in particular, violent sex crimes. For lawmakers focusing on recidivism and future dangerousness, polls indicated that the public wanted harsher, stiffer, and deadlier penalties. The health care industry identified violence as a prominent contributor to mortality and morbidity. The public envisioned widening and worsening of crimes by repeat offenders....

With fear of crime at all-time high levels, legislators and the judiciary responded to public concern by being hard on sex offenders to protect the safety of the public. Dramatic solutions to the crime epidemic included focus on capital punishment, "three strikes and you're out" incarceration policies, construction of more prisons, tighter gun control, and increasing the number of police on the streets. Legislative effort also focused on controlling sexual violence, including longer sentencing, registration and notification, and civil commitment of sexual predators in treatment centers after they have served their criminal sentence. Society had finally reached a point where it feared crime more than the state and favored individual safety over the liberty of the individual: "Today, law-abiding Americans are likely to fear crime more, and so they find it increasingly difficult to accept a constitution written by men who feared the state."...

Some scholars suggest that public opinion and relatively high press coverage may have influence, not only over our legislatures, but even over our highest court. The question remains, then, should courts ignore community values and expectations? Arguably, the Supreme Court, and judges in general, follow public opinion in order to maintain popular support and "create an image of legitimacy." Undeniably "judges read newspapers, watch television, and engage in social interaction." Chief Justice William Rehnquist explained the influence of public opinion in this way:

Judges, so long as they are relatively normal human beings, can no more escape being influenced by public opinion in the long run than can people working at other jobs. In addition, if a judge on coming to the bench were to decide to seal himself off hermetically from all manifestations of public opinion, he would accomplish very little; he would not be influenced by the state of public opinion at the time he came to the bench.

Logically, one cannot expect judges to ignore the risk that if sexual predators are released new victims will pay the price....

V. The law's emphasis on future dangerousness and the use of experts

A. The expert

The use of forensic psychologists in the courtroom is controversial. In part, because:

through both their report and testimony, the expert is usually the only individual asked to provide his or her opinion as to the degree to which a respondent satisfies the statutory criteria for commitment, based on record review, direct assessment of the respondent, knowledge and previous experience, and/or the testimony of other witnesses.

In fact, some authors have gone so far as to refer to forensic psychologists as "whores" of the court. Others view the profession as a self-serving institution designed to "...extend its influence, expand its markets and increase its overall profits" leaving in its wake "damaged people, divided families, distorted justice, destroyed companies, and a weakened nation". Opponents of forensic psychology also feel that, "behind the benevolent facade is a voracious self-serving industry that proffers facts which are often unfounded, provides "therapy' which can be damaging to its recipients, and exerts influence which is having devastating effects on the social fabric."

However, the real focus should be "...not whether as experts forensic psychologists can make better decisions than judges; their critical role regards whether a court can do a better job with their input rather than without it". Thus, the following is absolutely essential to maintain the legitimacy and integrity of the civil commitment process. They "...should adhere to, and be held to, a higher level of accountability, both in their collection of data and in their interpretation and explanation of data and opinion in court." In addition, "both those in favor and those opposed to these statutes must carefully and thoughtfully scrutinize their belief systems and their ability to conduct a neutral evaluation and render an impartial opinion." Perhaps most important, forensic psychologists "have an obligation to maintain current knowledge of scientific, professional and legal developments within their area of claimed competence. They are obligated also to use that knowledge, consistent with accepted clinical and scientific standards, in selecting data collection methods and procedures for evaluation, treatment, consultation or scholarly/empirical investigation." Lastly, assessors should adhere to a "forensic ethic."

Forensic Psychologists remain dispassionate as to the legal issues they examine; they are skeptical rather than accepting of the information presented to them; they work to avoid forming a therapeutic alliance with the people they examine; and the people examined by forensic psychologists bear the burden of convincing the psychologist of the accuracy and the merit of what they say [they]...are wary of the vested interests of the parties they examine and of the lawyers who represent those parties; maintain a belief system that encompasses fairness, impartiality, and objectivity toward each of the participants in the legal dispute; are expected to tell others, in a very public forum, about what they have learned form those parties they have examined; and have the responsibility to respect the rights of all parties to a dispute.

B. The importance of prediction

Consider a community that is governed by a set of just laws. These laws ensure that a just distribution of burdens, benefits, and opportunities is maintained, provided each person complies with the laws. Let us also suppose that, in this community each person always does comply with the law, and that this state of affairs has obtained for a long period of time. In a just community, we are all entitled to this state of affairs. If anyone changes this situation for the worse, he has wrongfully harmed us.

In order to civilly commit a sex offender, the state must show that the likelihood of the harmful sexual conduct reoccurring must be great enough so that the state's interest in civil commitment is legitimate and compelling, and outweighs the Respondent's liberty interest. As the gravity of the anticipated harm increases, the required likelihood decreases. For example, if there is a 75-percent chance that a person will sexually touch several children and cause years of emotional pain and confusion, the state believes that civil commitment would be justified. In such a case, society's interest in acting would be sufficiently compelling to justify the limitation of the committed person's liberty. However, if there were only a 51-percent chance that such conduct would occur, the need for civil commitment would be more questionable. Thus, whether the likelihood of future harm is sufficient to justify civil commitment depends not only on how likely the harm is to occur, but also the seriousness of the anticipated harm. Prediction regarding future dangerousness is not solely confined to sex offenders.

As in disease, in violence a victim may lose liberty, and possibly life. If nothing else a victim may be imprisoned by the fear of violence. In such a situation, "suppose that someone has smallpox, and that the chance of being contagious at all is 50 percent and that the chance of dying for contagion is 50 percent. Under these conditions we would, I think, unhesitantly insist on the enforced isolation of the carrier, until such time as he no longer posed a threat to others." While, the most obvious type of harm is felt by victims and their families "violence is increasingly taking its toll in terms of fear and frustration for many communities", creating secondary harm.

Those who commit crimes also inflict a loss on members of their community, regardless of whether these community members have experienced any primary harm as a result of a crime. Those who commit a particular type of criminal violation provide grounds for the members of the community to infer that they may become the victims of this type of violation in the future and that they therefore should take steps to protect themselves. As more and more crimes are committed, the members of the community suffer a substantial loss in this respect.

Simply, prediction and law "ensures that each person has the opportunity to live his own life to the fullest extent possible."

C. Arguments against prediction

Arguably, "there are four statistical outcomes that can occur when one is faced with making a prediction of future dangerousness."

Monahan describes the issue in the following way:

If one predicts that violence will occur and later finds that, indeed, it has occurred, the prediction is called a True Positive. One has made a positive prediction, and it turned out to be correct or true. Likewise, if one predicts that violence will not occur and it in fact does not, the prediction is called a True Negative, since one has made a negative prediction of violence and it turned out to be true. These, of course, are the two outcomes one wishes to maximize in making predictions. There are also two kinds of mistakes that can be made. If one predicts that violence will occur and it does not, the outcome is called a False Positive. One made a positive prediction of violence, and it turned out to be incorrect or false. In practice, this kind of mistake usually means that a person has been unnecessarily detained to prevent an act of violence that would not have occurred in any event. If one predicts that violence will not occur, and it does occur, the outcome is called a False Negative. In practice, this kind of mistake often means that someone who is not detained, or who is released from detention, commits an act of violence in the community. These two outcomes, obviously, are what predictors of violence try to minimize.

According to critics, risk assessment cannot be accurate. They argue it is inherently difficult to establish risk of harm presented by a certain individual and "illegal or unethical to use group data to make statements about individuals." Generally, graphs or studies cannot address a political question how costs are perceived, either by society, the victim, or the sex offender. However, the following studies illustrate the need and the legitimacy of prediction using proven scientific method.

D. Studies addressing rates of re-offending and predictive factors

Prediction of future dangerousness by sex offenders has become a highly specialized area with specific ethical standards. Experts in this field have their own process of evaluation, areas of evaluation, and specific instruments designed to facilitate evaluation. A determination of future dangerousness is critical in sexual predator cases. Indeed, it could be said that it is the primary focus.

In broad terms, risk management consists of treatment, the application of some intervention designed to reduce a person's risk of violent re offending, and supervision, anything that reduces the person's opportunity to re offend. To the extent that treatment reduces a person's risk, less supervision is necessary. The key to determining the extent to which an offender requires treatment or supervision is an accurate appraisal of his dangerousness.

Contrary to the critic's arguments, it is not impossible or unethical to make predictions:

In our opinion it is moral, indeed desirable, for authorities to use information on those individuals who have already done harm to prevent further harm. The prevention of future victimization is, in our view, a moral good, and it is appropriate and desirable that science be used to aid in this enterprise.

A variety of studies have provided researchers with tools to assist in prenticing future dangerousness in sexual predators. One checklist that is frequently is the Hare Revised Psychopathy Checklist. In reference to the issue of violent recidivism, research has utilized the Hare score alone and in combination with other variables to examine the relationship to recidivism. The mean Hare score for any prisoner in a state correctional facility has been found to be 22. Using the Hare with a sample of both rapists and child molesters, one study found a mean score for this group to be 29 (with a standard of 6.5). Using a cutoff score of 32, they also reported that 45% of the incarcerated rapists and 31% of the incarcerated child molesters were classified as psychopaths.

A number of years ago, in a classic monograph, Monahan listed a number of factors for the clinical assessment for the purpose of predicting violent behavior. These factors included the precipitating events and context of such events at the time of the index violent event, demographic characteristics, the person's history of violent behavior, the base rate of violent behavior among individual's of this particular person's background, the sources of stress in the environment the person might be released into, the similarity of the current context to past context in which violent behavior has been manifested, cognitive and affective factors which characterize an individual's predisposition to cope with stress, the likely victims or victim pool and their availability, and the means available to the individuals under consideration to commit violence. Similar criteria for assessing the risk of future dangerousness have been adopted by Minnesota courts. More recent studies have applied similar factors upholding the validity of their use.

For example, recidivism of prisoners in 1983 studies by Beck and Shipley was as follows:

- 63% re-arrested for a felony or serious misdemeanor within three years
- 46% re-convicted
- 41% returned to prison or jail

The study identified the following variables as increasing the risk of future criminal behavior: the number of previous arrest, prior escape or revocation, most serious offense, prior incarceration, younger age at first arrest, prior violent arrest, and prior drug arrest. While researchers found that the amount of time incarcerated was not systematically related to likelihood of re-arrest, they also found that released prisoners were often re-arrested for the same type of crime which they had served time in prison: "The relative likelihood of re-arrest for a similar crime was highest among prisoners for rape [and] sexual assault." In addition, rapists were found to be 10.5 times more likely than non-rapists, and other sexual offenders 7.5 times more likely, to be re-arrested for similar crimes.

In recent years an actuarial instrument (Violence Risk Appraisal Guide (VRAG)) has been developed, significantly predicting violent behavior in groups of mentally disordered offenders. Using a sample of formerly incarcerated individuals, researchers found that the base rate of severe violent recidivism for a ten year follow up was 29% for the total sample and 57% for the subsequent sample of sex offenders.

In a subsequent study that attempted to cross-validate the VRAG, researchers examined child molesters and rapists over a period averaging 10 years. The base rate for overall sexual recidivism was 35%. The VRAG was again successful at identifying those at greatest risk of violent recidivism; however, the prediction of specifically sexual recidivism was poorer than that of more general violent recidivism. This discrepancy can be explained by the fact that, for a variety of reasons, many offenses that appear to be non-sexual actually have a sexual component or motivation.

All in all, quite a few psychological studies have found recidivism in follow-up studies to be high. One found that over a nearly 5 year period, 38% of sex offenders were convicted of a new sex offense and 40% were arrested, convicted or returned to the psychiatric facility for a new violent (including sexual) offense. In addition, rapists were more likely to recidivate in the study compared to child molesters, despite a shorter follow-up period. However, existing data reveal increasing recidivism over an extended follow-up period; for untreated child molesters, rates of re-offending had risen substantially after four year periods. In a study of recidivism of child molesters released from prison, researchers found that 42% of their sample was re-convicted for sexual crimes, violent crimes or both. Similarly, another study found that in only a 6 year follow-up period, 31% of the subjects who were child molesters were convicted of a new sex offense, 43% committed a violent or sexual offense, and 58% were arrested for some offense or returned to an institution. In a study over a 25 year period, the cumulative recidivism of child molesters followed who committed another sexual offense was 52%.

In general, it has been found that subjects convicted of a new sexual offense had previously committed more sex offenses, had been admitted to correctional institutions more frequently, were more likely to have been diagnosed as personality disordered, and had shown more inappropriate sexual preferences. In addition, sexual recidivists had more serious sexual offense histories, higher psychopathy scores, and more phallometrically measured sexual interest in non-consensual violence against women.

Using largely the same sample followed for a longer period of time, another researcher found that sexual recidivists were significantly differentiated by their previous record of sexual offenses, previous general criminal history, non-married status, Hare score, and phallometric deviance index. Rice and Harris showed that sexual recidivism rates for sex offenders were substantially higher among identified psychopaths; the combination of deviant sexual arousal and psychopathy produced the most pronounced rates for sexual recidivism.

VI. Community safety and preventive victimization

First, under a system of just law each individual is guaranteed certain fundamental interests—bodily integrity security, control over his property etc. These are benefits to which a person is entitled in a just distribution of burdens and benefits. Under a system of just law, each individual is also obligated to respect the rights of others. That is, a person is obligated to refrain from depriving others of the benefits to which they are entitled.

Therefore, even though to live one's life free of physical restraint by the state is a fundamental right, individual liberty rights are not absolute. The "liberty of the individual" may be outweighed by the "demands of an organized society."…

True rates of sexual recidivism are estimated to be very high. However, determining the true rate of actual offenses committed by sexual offenders is problematic. To be forthright and honest about the actual number of such offenses places the offender at risk of more extensive incarceration and other negative consequences. A unique study which addresses this issue was conducted in 1990. Sexual offenders voluntarily sought assessment for their paraphilia's, and their anonymity was guarded by a Federal Certificate of Confidentiality. The study concluded that in the criminal justice system, offenders report only 5% of the sex crimes they admit to within the mental health system. In addition, this study found that the great majority of sex offenders had multiple paraphilias and were involved in substantial criminal behavior. Another study notes that relying on the self report of sex offenders regarding prior offenses is unwise because such reports are so unreliable. The authors found that even official police records of charges indicate a rate of reoffending 42% less than that obtained via unofficial records (i.e. reports to child protection or the police). Similarly, merely reviewing parole records produced a 33% increase in estimates of the number of serious crimes committed by sex offenders. Further, it has been reported that in a controlled study, 62% of paraphilics confronted with their physiologic measurements admitted to paraphilia diagnoses that they had previously denied or not revealed. The following statistics are also very informative:

1. It is possible that an untreated juvenile sex offender can be expected to commit an average of 380 sexual crimes in his lifetime.
2. The mean number of victims of adult homosexual pedophiles is 150.

3. Overall, the chance of getting caught for child molestation is only approximently 3%.

We must ask, who must society sacrifice so that the sexually dangerous persons can be controlled through the criminal system? How many victims must there be? To suggest that society's interest in protecting its members is vindicated by waiting for such dangerous persons to reoffend, and then dealing with them through the criminal justice system is hideous and absurd. Simply, many "people are victims of violence purely by accident, or because of circumstances which they did not cause, could not have foreseen or prevented, and cannot by any reasonable criterion be held responsible for."

The fact that members of the community have to make substantial sacrifices to defend themselves against crime after these violations occur is clearly the fault of the persons who have committed them. We make these sacrifices to protect ourselves against crime because, on the basis of what has happened in the past, we believe we need to do so. In the end, "those who are guilty of criminal violations create this need, and they are responsible for the fact that we have to cope with it, at least insofar as they have violated just laws."

Simmons v. South Carolina
512 U.S. 154 (1994)(Excerpt).

OPINION: JUSTICE BLACKMUN.

This case presents the question whether the Due Process Clause of the Fourteenth Amendment was violated by the refusal of a state trial court to instruct the jury in the penalty phase of a capital trial that under state law the defendant was ineligible for parole. We hold that where the defendant's future dangerousness is at issue, and state law prohibits the defendant's release on parole, due process requires that the sentencing jury be informed that the defendant is parole ineligible.

In July 1990, petitioner beat to death an elderly woman, Josie Lamb, in her home in Columbia, South Carolina. The week before petitioner's capital murder trial was scheduled to begin, he pleaded guilty to first-degree burglary and two counts of criminal sexual conduct in connection with two prior assaults on elderly women. Petitioner's guilty pleas resulted in convictions for violent offenses, and those convictions rendered petitioner ineligible for parole if convicted of any subsequent violent-crime offense. S. C. Code Ann. §24–21–640 (Supp. 1993).

Prior to jury selection, the prosecution advised the trial judge that the State "obviously [was] going to ask you to exclude any mention of parole throughout this trial." App. 2. Over defense counsel's objection, the trial court granted the prosecution's motion for an order barring the defense from asking any question during voir dire regarding parole. Under the court's order, defense counsel was forbidden even to mention the subject of parole, and expressly was prohibited from questioning prospective jurors as to whether they understood the meaning of a "life" sentence under South Carolina law. After a 3-day trial, petitioner was convicted of the murder of Ms. Lamb....

In its closing argument the prosecution argued that petitioner's future dangerousness was a factor for the jury to consider when fixing the appropriate punishment. The question for the jury, said the prosecution, was "what to do with [petitioner] now that he is in our midst." 496 U.S. at 110. The prosecution further urged that a verdict for death would be "a response of society to someone who is a threat. Your verdict will be an act of self-defense." Ibid....

Concerned that the jury might not understand that "life imprisonment" did not carry with it the possibility of parole in petitioner's case, defense counsel asked the trial judge to clarify this point by defining the term "life imprisonment" for the jury in accordance with S. C. Code Ann. §24–21–640 (Supp. 1993)....

Petitioner then offered into evidence, without objection, the results of a statewide public-opinion survey conducted by the University of South Carolina's Institute for Public Affairs. The survey had been conducted a few days before petitioner's trial, and showed that only 7.1 percent of all jury-eligible adults who were questioned firmly believed that an inmate sentenced to life imprisonment in South Carolina actually would be required to spend the rest of his life in prison. See App. 152–154. Almost half of those surveyed believed that a convicted murderer might be paroled within 20 years; nearly three-quarters thought that release certainly would occur in less than 30 years. Ibid. More than 75 percent of those surveyed indicated that if they were called upon to make a capital sentencing decision as jurors, the amount of time the convicted murderer actually would have to spend in prison would be an "extremely important" or a "very important" factor in choosing between life and death. Id., at 155.

Petitioner argued that, in view of the public's apparent misunderstanding about the meaning of "life imprisonment" in South Carolina, there was a reasonable likelihood that the jurors would vote for death simply because they believed, mistakenly, that petitioner eventually would be released on parole.

The prosecution opposed the proposed instruction, urging the court "not to allow...any argument by state or defense about parole and not charge the jury on anything concerning parole." Id., at 37. Citing the South Carolina

Supreme Court's opinion in *State v. Torrence*, 305 S.C. 45, 406 S.E.2d 315 S.E.2d 315 (1991), the trial court refused petitioner's requested instruction.... The trial judge also refused to give this instruction, but indicated that he might give a similar instruction if the jury inquired about parole eligibility.

After deliberating on petitioner's sentence for 90 minutes, the jury sent a note to the judge asking a single question: "Does the imposition of a life sentence carry with it the possibility of parole?" *Id.*, at 145. Over petitioner's objection, the trial judge gave the following instruction:

"You are instructed not to consider parole or parole eligibility in reaching your verdict. Do not consider parole or parole eligibility. That is not a proper issue for your consideration. The terms life imprisonment and death sentence are to be understood in their plan [sic] and ordinary meaning." Id., at 146.

Twenty-five minutes after receiving this response from the court, the jury returned to the courtroom with a sentence of death.

On appeal to the South Carolina Supreme Court, petitioner argued that the trial judge's refusal to provide the jury accurate information regarding his parole ineligibility violated the Eighth Amendment and the Due Process Clause of the Fourteenth Amendment. The South Carolina Supreme Court declined to reach the merits of petitioner's challenges. With one justice dissenting, it concluded that, regardless of whether a trial court's refusal to inform a sentencing jury about a defendant's parole ineligibility might be error under some circumstances, the instruction given to petitioner's jury "satisfied in substance [petitioner's] request for a charge on parole ineligibility," and thus there was no reason to consider whether denial of such an instruction would be constitutional error in this case. 310 S. C. 439, 444, 427 S.E.2d 175, 179 (1993). We granted certiorari, 510 U.S. 811 (1993).

The Due Process Clause does not allow the execution of a person "on the basis of information which he had no opportunity to deny or explain." *Gardner v. Florida*, 430 U.S. 349, 362, 51 L. Ed. 2d 393, 97 S. Ct. 1197 (1977). In this case, the jury reasonably may have believed that petitioner could be released on parole if he were not executed. To the extent this misunderstanding pervaded the jury's deliberations, it had the effect of creating a false choice between sentencing petitioner to death and sentencing him to a limited period of incarceration. This grievous misperception was encouraged by the trial court's refusal to provide the jury with accurate information regarding petitioner's parole ineligibility, and by the State's repeated suggestion that petitioner would pose a future danger to society if he were not executed. Three times petitioner asked to inform the jury that in fact he was ineligible for parole under state law; three times his request was denied. The State thus succeeded in securing a death sentence on the ground, at least in part, of petitioner's future dangerousness, while at the same time concealing from the sentencing jury the true meaning of its noncapital sentencing alternative, namely, that life imprisonment meant life without parole. We think it is clear that the State denied petitioner due process.

A

This Court has approved the jury's consideration of future dangerousness during the penalty phase of a capital trial, recognizing that a defendant's future dangerousness bears on all sentencing determinations made in our criminal justice system. See *Jurek v. Texas*, 428 U.S. 262, 275, 49 L. Ed. 2d 929, 96 S. Ct. 2950 (1976) (joint opinion of Stewart, Powell, and STEVENS, JJ.) (noting that "any sentencing authority must predict a convicted person's probable future conduct when it engages in the process of determining what punishment to impose"); *California v. Ramos*, 463 U.S. 992, 1003, n. 17, 77 L. Ed. 2d 1171, 103 S. Ct. 3446 (1983) (explaining that it is proper for a sentencing jury in a capital case to consider "the defendant's potential for reform and whether his probable future behavior counsels against the desirability of his release into society").

Although South Carolina statutes do not mandate consideration of the defendant's future dangerousness in capital sentencing, the State's evidence in aggravation is not limited to evidence relating to statutory aggravating circumstances.... Thus, prosecutors in South Carolina, like those in other States that impose the death penalty, frequently emphasize a defendant's future dangerousness in their evidence and argument at the sentencing phase; they urge the jury to sentence the defendant to death so that he will not be a danger to the public if released from prison. Eisenberg & Wells, Deadly Confusion: Juror Instructions in Capital Cases, 79 *Cornell L. Rev.* 1, 4 (1993)....

B

.... [P]etitioner was prevented from rebutting information that the sentencing authority considered, and upon which it may have relied, in imposing the sentence of death. The State raised the specter of petitioner's future dangerousness generally, but then thwarted all efforts by petitioner to demonstrate that, contrary to the prosecutor's intimations, he never would be released on parole and thus, in his view, would not pose a future danger to society. The logic and effectiveness of petitioner's argument naturally depended on the fact that he was legally ineligible for parole and thus would remain in prison if afforded a life sentence. Petitioner's efforts to focus the jury's attention on the question whether, in prison, he would be a future danger were futile, as he repeatedly was denied any opportunity to inform the jury that he never would be released on parole. The jury was left to speculate about petitioner's parole eligibility when evaluating petitioner's future dangerousness, and was denied a straight answer about petitioner's parole eligibility even when it was requested....

III

There remains to be considered whether the South Carolina Supreme Court was correct in concluding that the trial court "satisfied in substance [petitioner's] request for a charge on parole ineligibility," 310 S. C. at 444, 427 S.E.2d at 179, when it responded to the jury's query by stating that life imprisonment was to be understood in its "plain and ordinary meaning," ibid. In the court's view, petitioner basically received the parole-ineligibility instruction he requested. We disagree.

It can hardly be questioned that most juries lack accurate information about the precise meaning of "life imprisonment" as defined by the States. For much of our country's history, parole was a mainstay of state and federal sentencing regimes, and every term (whether a term of life or a term of years) in practice was understood to be shorter than the stated term. See generally Lowenthal, Mandatory Sentencing Laws: Undermining the Effectiveness of Determinate Sentencing Reform, 81 *Calif. L. Rev.* 61 (1993) (describing the development of mandatory sentencing laws). Increasingly, legislatures have enacted mandatory sentencing laws with severe penalty provisions, yet the precise contours of these penal laws vary from State to State. See Cheatwood, The Life-Without-Parole Sanction: Its Current Status and a Research Agenda, 34 *Crime & Delinq.* 43, 45, 48 (1988). Justice Chandler of the South Carolina Supreme Court observed that it is impossible to ignore "the reality, known to the 'reasonable juror,' that, historically, life-term defendants have been eligible for parole." *State v. Smith,* 298 S.C. 482, 489–490, 381 S.E.2d 724, 728 (1989) (opinion concurring and dissenting), cert. denied, 494 U.S. 1060 (1990).[9]

---

9. Public opinion and juror surveys support the commonsense understanding that there is a reasonable likelihood of juror confusion about the meaning of the term "life imprisonment." See Paduano & Smith, Deadly Errors: Juror Misperceptions Concerning Parole in the Imposition of the Death Penalty, 18 *Colum. Human Rights L. Rev.* 211, 222–225 (1987); Note, The Meaning of "Life" for Virginia Jurors and Its Effect on Reliability in Capital Sentencing, 75 *Va. L. Rev.* 1605, 1624 (1989); Eisenberg & Wells, Deadly Confusion: Juror Instructions in Capital Cases, 79 *Cornell L. Rev.* 1 (1993); Bowers, Capital Punishment and Contemporary Values: People's Misgivings and the Court's Misperceptions, 27 *Law & Society* 157, 169–170 (1993).

An instruction directing juries that life imprisonment should be understood in its "plain and ordinary" meaning does nothing to dispel the misunderstanding reasonable jurors may have about the way in which any particular State defines "life imprisonment."…

….Because petitioner's future dangerousness was at issue, he was entitled to inform the jury of his parole ineligibility. An instruction directing the jury not to consider the defendant's likely conduct in prison would not have satisfied due process in *Skipper v. South Carolina*, 476 U.S. 1, 90 L. Ed. 2d 1, 106 S. Ct. 1669 (1986), and, for the same reasons, the instruction issued by the trial court in this case does not satisfy due process.

IV

The State may not create a false dilemma by advancing generalized arguments regarding the defendant's future dangerousness while, at the same time, preventing the jury from learning that the defendant never will be released on parole. The judgment of the South Carolina Supreme Court accordingly is reversed, and the case is remanded for further proceedings. It is so ordered.

Blume, Garvey and Johnson (January 2001). Future dangerousness in capital cases: Always "at issue". *Cornell Law Review* volume 86, page 397 (Excerpt).

The empirical results we describe below…were presented to the United States Supreme Court in a brief amicus curiae submitted by the Cornell Death Penalty Project in support of the petitioner in *Shafer v. South Carolina*. See Brief Amicus Curiae of the Cornell Death Penalty Project in Support of Petitioner, *Shafer v. South Carolina*, No. 00–5250 (U.S. filed Nov. 13, 2000).

J.H. Blume, S.P. Garvey, and S.L. Johnson (Jan. 2001). Future dangerousness in capital cases: Always at issue. *
Cornell Law Review Volume 86 page 397 (excerpt)

Introduction

Capital jurors face a hard choice. They must impose a sentence of death, or a sentence of life imprisonment. One or the other. But for many jurors the choice is even harder.

---

* reprinted with the permission of the Cornell Law Review.

The problem is this: Even where the alternative to death is life imprison-ment, and where life imprisonment means life imprisonment without any possibility of parole, jurors may nonetheless believe that the defendant, if not sentenced to death, will one day find his way to freedom. In the minds of these jurors, the choice is really between death and something less than life impris-onment, and this imagined but false choice will prompt them to cast their vote for death. Forced to choose, jurors would prefer to see the defendant executed rather than run the risk that he will someday be released.

In *Simmons v. South Carolina*, the Supreme Court tried to craft a solution to this problem. A plurality of the Simmons Court held that when state law authorizes the jury to impose a life sentence without the possibility of parole, due process entitles a capital defendant to inform the jury about his parole in-eligibility. But Simmons came with a catch: A capital defendant was entitled to this remedy only if the state placed his future dangerousness "at issue." Oth-erwise, the jury was to be left to its own devices, forced to rely on its own un derstanding, however far off the mark, of what life imprisonment really meant.

But why the "at issue" requirement? The most likely explanation is ulti-mately empirical. On this account, the rule in Simmons is designed to obvi-ate juror misapprehension about parole ineligibility and thereby promote re-liability in capital sentencing. The "at issue" requirement, in turn, reflects the empirical assumption that capital jurors worry about the defendant's future dangerousness, and thus about what a sentence of life imprisonment really means, only if the state injects the issue of future dangerous into the pro-ceedings. If not, jurors will think little, if at all, about future dangerousness, and no remedial instruction is needed.

We disagree. Based on the results of interviews with over a hundred jurors who served on capital cases in South Carolina, all conducted in connection with the nationwide Capital Jury Project (CJP), we argue that the "at issue" requirement is misguided because the empirical assumption on which it rests is false: We find that future dangerousness is on the minds of most capital ju-rors, and is thus "at issue" in virtually all capital trials, no matter what the prosecution says or does not say....

....Based on data collected from CJP interviews with jurors who sat on over one hundred capital cases tried in South Carolina, we argue that Simmons' second condition—that the prosecution by word or deed place the defendant's future dangerousness "at issue"—should be eliminated. We make this sug-gestion not because we believe the "at issue" requirement is unimportant, but rather because we find that future dangerousness is "at issue" in virtually all capital cases, even when the prosecution says or does nothing to put it there. A case-by-case resolution of the "at issue" requirement is therefore a waste of judicial time and energy, not to mention the unfairness it produces when jurors, uninformed about a defendant's ineligibility for parole because the prosecutor chose to remain silent, vote for death out of fear that the defendant will otherwise someday be released.

The Capital Jury Project

The Capital Jury Project is a National Science Foundation-funded, multistate research effort designed to better understand the dynamics of juror decision making in capital cases. Toward that end, the CJP began in 1990 to interview in a number of different states jurors who had actually served on capital cases. Analyses of the data collected during the interviews began appearing in 1993.

Prior to the work of the CJP, our understanding of juror decision making in capital cases—and in particular of the sentencing phase of the trial—was based primarily on mock jury studies, and on inferences drawn from the conduct of individual cases. Each of these methodologies, though valuable, has limitations. Mock studies are open to a variety of criticisms, not the least of which is that the experience of mock jurors is substantially removed from that of actual jurors, perhaps especially so in capital cases. Likewise, inferences based on an individual case or series of cases may not lend themselves to generalization; worse, they may reflect little more than the preconceptions of the person drawing them....

The results we present below are based on the CJP's efforts in South Carolina. The data from South Carolina are the most extensive of all the states included in the CJP, encompassing interviews with 187 jurors in 53 cases tried in South Carolina between 1988 and 1997. Of the 187 jurors interviewed thus far, 100 sat on one of 28 cases that resulted in a death sentence, and 87 sat on one of 25 cases that resulted in a sentence of life imprisonment.

Always "At Issue"

Our focus here is limited to the *Simmons* "at issue" requirement. But in order to set the context, we begin with a brief review of existing CJP findings that highlight the important role future dangerousness plays in capital sentencing. We then present the results of the simple analysis that lead us to urge the Court to abandon the "at issue" requirement.

A. Future Dangerousness

The results that have so far emerged from the research efforts of the CJP support the following three propositions related to the role of future dangerousness in capital sentencing:

First, "jurors grossly underestimate how long capital murderers not sentenced to death usually stay in prison." In South Carolina, for example, the median juror estimate of years usually served by capital murderers not sentenced to death was only seventeen years. Based on these results, the typical South Carolina juror, told only that the alternative to a death sentence was a sentence of "life imprisonment," would have thought that nineteen-year-old Wesley Shafer would be released at the still-threatening age of thirty-six. Less than one percent would have thought he would never be released.

Second, future dangerousness plays a highly prominent role in the jury's discussions during the penalty phase. One of the earliest CJP studies, which relied on South Carolina data, found that topics related to the defendant's dangerousness should he ever return to society (including the possibility and timing of such a return) are second only to the crime itself in the attention they receive during the jury's penalty phase deliberations. Future dangerousness overshadows evidence presented in mitigation (such as the defendant's intelligence, remorse, alcoholism, mental illness), as well as any concern about the defendant's dangerousness in prison.

Third, these misconceptions about parole eligibility have predictable and deadly consequences. The shorter the period of time a juror thinks the defendant will be imprisoned, the more likely he or she is to vote for death on the final ballot. Moreover, aggregate data from all eleven states of the CJP show that even in cases in which the prosecution's evidence and argument at the penalty phase did "not at all" emphasize the defendant's future dangerousness, jurors who believed the defendant would be released in under twenty years if not sentenced to death were still more likely to cast their final vote for death than were jurors who thought the alternative to death was twenty years or more.

We believe these findings provide strong support for a rule broader than Simmons. Those findings suggest that a capital defendant should have a right to tell the jury how long he will remain in prison if not sentenced to death, even if the term of his imprisonment under state law is less than death, and even if the prosecution does nothing to place his future dangerousness "at issue." In other words, we believe these findings cast serious doubt on both of the requirements set forth in Simmons.

For now, however, we concentrate on the second requirement: Does it makes sense, in light of how capital jurors decide capital cases, to require the right Simmons recognizes—the right of a capital defendant to honestly tell the jury that, if its members do not sentence him to death, he will in accordance with state law never be released from prison—to turn on the prosecution's decision to put future dangerousness "at issue?"

B. Testing the Empirical Assumption Behind the "At Issue" Requirement

The "at issue" requirement, as we construe it here, is based on the Court's empirical assumption that jurors only worry about future dangerousness if and when the prosecution broaches the subject. However, we would have assumed just the opposite: that capital jurors worry about future dangerousness no matter what the prosecution says. Here we put these competing assumptions to two empirical tests.

First, if the Court's assumption is correct, then we would expect the jury's discussions during the penalty phase to reflect worries about future dangerousness only when the prosecution makes a point of it; in contrast, if our assumption is correct, then we would expect the jury's discussions to reflect worries about future dangerousness even when the prosecution says nothing about it at all. Second, if the Court's assumption is correct, we would expect jurors to say that future dangerousness influenced their sentencing decisions only when the prosecution raised questions about it; in contrast, if our assumption is correct, then we would expect jurors to say that future dangerousness was a significant factor in their sentencing decisions regardless of the prosecution's focus.

One question the CJP asked jurors was the following: "How much did the prosecutor's evidence and arguments at the punishment stage of the trial emphasize the danger to the public if the defendant ever escaped or was released from prison?" The possible responses were: a "great deal," a "fair amount," "not much," and "not at all." Of the 187 South Carolina jurors we interviewed, fifty-three said that the prosecutor's evidence and argument at the penalty phase emphasized the defendant's danger to the public if he was ever released or escaped from prison "not at all." It is on this group of fifty-three that we focus the remainder of our analysis. If future dangerousness matters to this group, then it matters even when the prosecution has not placed the defendant's dangerousness "at issue."

We next look at the responses this group of jurors gave when asked a series of questions about the topics the jury discussed during the course of its penalty phase deliberations. We focus in particular on how much the jury discussed various topics related to the defendant's future dangerousness....

Even among jurors who said the prosecution made no effort whatsoever to emphasize the defendant's future dangerousness, anywhere between twenty-one and thirty-two percent reported that the jury's discussions during the penalty phase focused "a great deal" on a variety of topics related to worries about the defendant's future dangerousness. Moreover, anywhere between fifty-three and sixty-six percent of these same jurors reported that the jury's discussions focused at least a "fair amount" on topics related to the defendant's future dangerousness.

....Concentrating once again on those jurors who said the prosecutor emphasized "not at all" the defendant's danger to the public if he was ever released or escaped from prison, we asked how important it was to them in deciding the defendant's punishment to "keep[ ] the defendant from ever killing again." Forty-three percent said it was "very" important; twenty-six percent said it was "fairly" important. In other words, nearly seventy percent of the jurors who served on cases in which the prosecution did not put the defendant's future dangerousness "at issue" nonetheless reported that keeping the defendant from ever killing again was at least fairly important to them in deciding how to vote.

Of course, the jury's concern about "keeping the defendant from ever killing again" might include concerns about keeping him from killing again in prison, as well as outside of it. Accordingly, we also analyzed responses to a narrower question: How concerned was the juror that the defendant might get back into society if not given the death penalty. Thirty-one percent said they were "greatly concerned," and another twenty-nine percent said they were "somewhat concerned." That makes a total of sixty percent. Put differently, on an average jury in which the prosecutor emphasized the defendant's future dangerousness "not at all," seven members would be at least somewhat concerned that, unless sentenced to death, the defendant might get back into society....

Conclusion

Under existing doctrine, due process entitles a capital defendant to inform the jurors who will decide his fate that, if not sentenced to death, he will never be eligible for parole—but only if his future dangerousness is "at issue." Yet the fact of the matter is that future dangerousness is on the minds of most capital jurors and thus "at issue" in virtually all capital trials, even if the prosecution says nothing about it. Ironically, a capital defendant is therefore better off, all else being equal, if the prosecutor argues that he will pose a danger to society—in which case the defendant would be entitled to a Simmonsinstruction—than if the prosecutor remains silent. Indeed, the prosecutor in Shafer was well aware of this irony; otherwise, he would not have gone to such lengths to avoid a Simmons instruction. The better approach—one not only more closely attuned to the empirical realities of capital sentencing but also more in keeping with the spirit of *Simmons* itself—would be to eliminate the "at issue" requirement altogether.

List of other cases and articles relevant to this topic.

Kansas v. Crane, 534 U.S. 407 (2002)
Selig v. Young, 531 U.S. 250 (2001)
Powell v. Texas, 492 U.S. 680 (1989)

Information about Megan's Law can be found on the KlaasKids foundation website at www.klaaskids.org. In addition, more information about the "scarlet letter laws" as referred to by some scholars can be found by reading the following articles:

Feldman, D. (1997). "The scarlet letter laws of the 1990s: A response to critics" at *Albany Law Review* 60: 1081

Kabat, A.R., (1998). Scarlet letter sex offender databases and community notification: Sacrificing personal privacy for a symbol's sake. *American Criminal Law Review* 35: 333

Pallone, N.J., J.J. Hennessy, and G.T. Voelbel (1998). Identifying pedophiles "eligible" for community notification under Megan's Law: A multivariate model for actuarially anchored decisions. *Journal of Offender Rehabilitation* 28: 41–60.

Discussion and Review Questions

1. Find the statutes for three states (other than Wisconsin) with a sexual offender community notification requirement. Compare those statutes with the Wisconsin statute examined by the National Institute of Justice. What are the similarities an differences in the laws and do you think that the differences, if any, would have an impact on the studies findings if a study similar to the Wisconsin study was conducted in those three states.

2. Outline the arguments for and against the civil commitment of sexual predators. Choose a partner and debate the issue.

3. On June 21, 2003, the Associated Press reported that a sexual offender released from civil commitment when a psychiatrist testified in court that he was no longer a threat was arrested for sexual battery when DNA from semen matched his DNA profile in the national database of convicted felons. This sexual offender's case had previously gone to the United States Supreme Court in *Kansas v. Crane*—a decision upholding the constitutionality of civil commitment laws. What problems might this incident provoke for the criminal justice system, the psychiatric community and society?

4. In death penalty cases, should experts be permitted to testify or is future dangerousness a concept within the common understanding of jurors?

References

Blume, J.H., S.P. Garvey and S.L. Johnson (2001). Future dangerousness in capital cases: Always at issue. *Cornell Law Review* 86: 397.

Cunningham, M.D. and T.J. Reidy (1999). Don't confuse me with the facts: Common errors in violence and risk assessment in capital sentencing. *Criminal Justice and Behavior* 26: 20–43.

Feldman, D.L. (1997). The scarlet letter laws of the 1990s: A response to critics. *Albany Law Review* 60: 1081–1125.

Fitch, L.W. and R.J. Ortega (2000). Law and the Confinement of psychopaths. *Behavioral Sciences and the Law* 18: 663–678.

Kabat, A.R. (1998). Scarlet letter sex offender databases and community notification: Sacrificing personal privacy for a symbol's sake. *American Criminal Law Review* 35: 333–368.

Menzies, R., C. Webster, S. McMain et al. (1994). The dimensions of dangerousness revisited: Assessing forensic predictions about violence. *Law and Human Behavior* 18(1): 1–28.

Monahan, J., (1995). The Clinical Prediction of Violent Behavior.

Petrosino, A.J., and C. Petrosino (1999). The public safety potential of Megan's Law in Massachusetts: An assessment from a sample of criminal sexual psychopaths. *Crime and Deliquency* 45: 140–158

Post, D.J., (1999) Assessing future dangerousness in sexual predators for purposes of indeterminate civil commitment. *Hamline Journal of Public Law and Policy* 21: 177.

Zevitz, R.G., and M.A. Farkas (2000). *Sex offender community notification: Assessing the impact in Wisconsin.* Washtington DC: National Institute of Justice.

Case Citaions

Artway v. Attorney General, 81 F. 3d 1235 (3d Cir. 1996).
Connecticut v. Smith, 123 S. Ct. 1160 (2003).
E.B. v. Verniero, 119 F. 3d 1077 (3d Cir. 1997).
Estelle v. Barefoot, 463 U.S. 880 (1983).
Jurek v. Texas, 428 U.S. 262 (1976).
Kansas v. Hendricks, 521 U.S. 346 (1997).
Kelly v. South Carolina, 534 U.S. 246 (2002).
Paul P. v. Farmer, 227 F. 3d 98 (3d Cir. 2000).
Powell v. Texas, 492 U.S. 680 (1989).
Shafer v. South Carolina, 532 U.S. 36 (2001).
Simmons v. South Carolina, 512 U.S. 154 (1994).
Smith v. Doe, 123 S. Ct. 1140 (2003).
State of New Jersey v. Timmendequas, 773 A. 2d 18 (NJ 2001).

CHAPTER 12

THE DEATH PENALTY

In 82 percent of the studies, race of victim was found to influence the likelihood of being charged with a capital murder or receiving the death penalty, i.e., those who murdered whites were found to be more likely to be sentenced to death than those who murdered blacks.... The evidence for the influence of the race of the defendant on death penalty outcomes was equivocal. Although more than half of the studies found that race of defendant influenced the likelihood of being charged with a capital crime or receiving the death penalty, the relationship between race of defendant and outcome varied across studies.

–U.S. General Accounting Office, 1990

Prior to 1986, the United States Supreme Court avoided rendering any decisions that directly confronted the question of race and the death penalty. The Court's capital punishment decisions before 1968 primarily concerned questions about the method of executions, not the imposition of the sanction (Bohm 1999). In 1972, however, the Court held capital punishment statutes in Georgia and Texas were unconstitutional because jurors were permitted to engage in unfettered, arbitrary and capricious decisions about the imposition of the sentence of death or life (*Furman v. Georgia*, 408 U.S. 238 (1972). The *Furman* case invalidated the death penalty statutes in 38 states, and many believed the death penalty was a "dead" issue. However, death penalty proponents quickly went to work revising death penalty statutes.

In 1976, the Court was confronted with issues about the constitutionality of the revised statutes in several cases. In *Woodson v. North Carolina* 428 U.S. 280 (1976) and *Roberts v. Louisiana*, 428 U.S. 325 (1976), the Court struck down statutes that provided for mandatory sentences of death for certain capital crimes, and in *Gregg v. Georgia*, 428 U.S. 153 (1976), *Jurek v. Texas*, 428 U.S. 262 (1976), and *Proffitt v. Florida*, 428 U.S. 242 (1976) the Court ap-

> **Eighth Amendment:** Excessive bail shall not be required, nor excessive fines imposed, nor cruel and unusual punishments inflicted.

proved capital punishment statutes that provided guidelines for jurors to render decisions on death versus life in the sentencing phase.

During this same time, the Court decided several cases (including *Furman v. Georgia*) where the issue of racial discrimination in capital cases was raised. However, the Court avoided this issue by deciding cases on other grounds (See for example: *Coker v. Georgia*, 433 U.S. 584 (1977); *Maxwell v. Bishop*, 398 U.S. 262 (1970) and *Furman v. Georgia*, 408 U.S. 238 (1972). It was not until *McCleskey v. Kemp*, 481 U.S. 279 (1987) that the Court directly confronted the "race" question. The issue in *McCleskey* was "whether a complex statistical study [the Baldus' study] that indicates a risk that racial considerations enter into capital sentencing determinations proves that petitioner McCleskey's capital sentence is unconstitutional under the **Eighth** or Fourteenth Amendment."

In assessing the Baldus[1] statistical study, the Court distinguished several cases that relied on statistics to establish racial discrimination. In those cases, the court accepted the same statistical methods employed by Baldus to demonstrate that systemic racial discrimination existed in the selection of jurors and in employment cases. In *McCleskey*, the Court imposed a much higher burden of showing racial discrimination in capital case sentencing decisions, a standard that made it seem virtually impossible to attain using statistical methods. The Court found that to establish a constitutional violation, McCleskey had to demonstrate "purposeful racial discrimination" in the particular case under review. The Court opinion "suggests that since 'statistics at most may show only a likelihood that a particular factor entered into some decision,' statistical proof can never provide a sufficient base for inferring a constitutional risk of excessiveness [under the Eighth Amendment] in an individual case." (Baldus et al. 1998). The Court also rejected the statistical proof to establish an Equal Protection challenge as follows:

> McCleskey's statistical proffer must be viewed in the context of his challenge. McCleskey challenges decisions at the heart of the State's criminal justice system. 'One of society's most basic tasks is that of

---

1. Baldus, David C., Charles Pulaski, and George Woodworth (1983). Comparative Review of Death Sentences: An Empirical Study of the Georgia Experience. *Journal of Criminal Law and Criminology* 74: 661–753.

protecting the lives of its citizens and one of the most basic ways in which it achieves the task is through criminal laws against murder.' Implementation of these laws necessarily requires discretionary judgments. Because discretion is essential to the criminal justice process, we would demand exceptionally clear proof before we would infer that the discretion has been abused. The unique nature of the decisions at issue in this case also counsels against adopting such an inference from the disparities indicated by the Baldus study. Accordingly, we hold that the Baldus study is clearly insufficient to support an inference that any of the decision makers in McCleskey's case acted with discriminatory purpose. *McCleskey*, 481 U.S. at 281–282.

As Baldus et al. (1998) later stated the Court, unlike the trial court, did not discount the statistical proofs on their merit. The Court discounted statistical evidence as a whole in proving purposeful discrimination. To achieve these proofs, a defendant is required to show a "smoking gun," e.g., by a showing that a prosecutor or juror made racist remarks that impacted the outcome of the death determination.

Is race still an issue?

Although it appears that the *McCleskey* decision foreclosed the federal courts as a venue for challenging capital punishment based on racial discrimination, there remain several avenues for future challenges. Challenging prosecutors' decisions on seeking the death penalty, pursuing attacks on the death penalty in state courts or attempting to legislate change may be viable. (Baldus et al. 1998; Sorenson and Wallace 1999).

Sorenson and Wallace (1999) examined prosecutorial discretion in seeking the death penalty and found that racial disparities existed in a mid-west county on determinations of who is subject to the sanction of death. In fact, they found that the probability that a prosecutor seeks a sentence of death is 2½ times greater when a black defendant kills a white victim. Sorenson and Wallace argue that this type of challenge to capital punishment is allowable under the *McCleskey* ruling. This is a challenge to the decisions made by a single actor—a prosecutor—during the death penalty process as opposed to a challenge based on the findings from a multitude of prosecutors and jurors.

In 1990, the General Accounting Office (GAO) published its findings from a review of the available studies assessing the affect of race on death penalty decision-making. The GAO found "a pattern of evidence indicating racial disparities in the charging, sentencing, and imposition of the death penalty." Baldus and his colleagues found the odds of receiving a death sentence in Philadelphia are almost four times higher when the defendant is black. (Baldus et al. 1998). In 2000 and 2001, the United States Department of Justice issued a report on the federal death penalty finding that there was no evidence of bias against racial and ethnic minorities in the federal courts. However this same report also instituted procedures for the continued collection of data on race and the death penalty. It also developed protocols for the selection of death cases to maintain public confidence in the fairness of the death penalty process.

The findings from these studies along with recent revelations of the many innocent persons on death row (see Chapters 9 and 10) have been presented to state courts, state legislatures and Congress in an attempt to pass a moratorium on capital punishment. Only one state, —the State of Kentucky— has passed the "Racial Justice Act." This law allows defendants to use the statistical evidence of racial discrimination rejected in *McCleskey* to demonstrate that race contributed to the decision to seek the death penalty by prosecutors. If race is found to have contributed to the decision, the use of the death penalty is prohibited. Several states have considered a moratorium on executions to allow for more study of the implementation of the death penalty (Hansen 2000). The Governor of Illinois in January of 2000 declared a moratorium in his state. In announcing this decision, Governor Ryan stated:

> I now favor a moratorium, because I have grave concerns about our state's shameful record of convicting innocent people and putting them on death row, And, I believe, many Illinois residents now feel that same deep reservation. I cannot support a system, which, in its administration, has proven to be so fraught with error and has come so close to the ultimate nightmare, the state's taking of innocent life. Thirteen people have been found to have been wrongfully convicted.

There are several other state and nationwide movements calling for a moratorium in light of the social science findings about the influence of race and the numbers of wrongful convictions.

After McCleskey, is social science still relevant in death cases?

There are numerous intersections between law and social science relating to the death penalty. Numerous studies and cases have discussed the deterrent effect of the sentence of death (*Gregg v. Georgia*, 428 U.S. 153 (1976), the cost of execution versus life in prison, the impact and the causes of miscarriages of justice, i.e., when innocent defendants are placed on death row or to death (Radelet and Bedau 1992; Sorenson, Wrinkle, Brewer, and Marquart 1999; Harmon 2001; Poveda 2001). Each of these issues involves social science. Social science evidence has also been instrumental in individual cases where "adjudicative facts" are necessary for judges and jurors to make determinations of fact. For example, chapter 11 provided information about the use of social science, i.e., psychiatric and psychological testimony in capital cases concerning the future dangerousness of defendants to assist jurors in rendering decisions between life and death. Psychologists are also instrumental in assisting the courts in assessing the mental competence of defendants, to assist in the selection of juries as consultants, and in testifying about the mitigating circumstances surrounding the life events of the defendant in an effort to persuade the jury to render a decision of life versus death. (Wrightsman 2001). In 2002, the United States Supreme Court held that the Sixth Amendment right to a jury trial required that a jury and not a judge make findings on the aggravating circumstances to justify the imposition of a death sentence. *Ring v. Arizona*, 122 S.Ct. 2428 (2002). In doing so, the Court may have increased the role that social science experts play in participating in the sentencing hearings in capital cases. Experts may play a larger role by assisting the juries in death cases to make informed decisions about the appropriateness of death or life in individual cases.

One justification for the continued acceptance of capital punishment by our courts is that there is public support for this penalty. Social science has been influential in assessing public support for the death penalty. The Gallup poll and others continuously assess Americans views on their support for capital punishment. In a survey of 1,012 adults, the Gallup poll reported in May 2002 that 72% of those surveyed were in favor of the death penalty for a person convicted of murder, 25% were against and 3% did not respond to the question. Social science researchers, however, have found that public opinion varies based on the amount of information given during the survey. The more information about the crime, the defendant, the victim and the circumstances provided to respondents reduces the support for capital punishment in those cases. (Wright, Bohm and Jamieson 1995). Some demographic characteristics also influence support and non-support for the death penalty (Krzycki 2000). Gender (Whitehead and Blankenship 2000) as well as political affiliation, race, wealth and religion (Krzycki 2000) have been found to be factors in discerning whether individuals support or oppose the death penalty.

In this chapter, excerpts from *McCleskey v. Kemp* and Baldus et al. (1998) *Racial discrimination and the death penalty in the post-Furman era: An empirical and legal overview* are included.

McCleskey v. Kemp
481 U.S. 279 (1987)

JUSTICE POWELL delivered the opinion of the Court.

This case presents the question whether a complex statistical study that indicates a risk that racial considerations enter into capital sentencing determinations proves that petitioner McCleskey's capital sentence is unconstitutional under the Eighth or Fourteenth Amendment.

McCleskey, a black man, was convicted of two counts of armed robbery and one count of murder in the Superior Court of Fulton County, Georgia, on October 12, 1978. McCleskey's convictions arose out of the robbery of a furniture store and the killing of a white police officer during the course of the robbery....At the penalty hearing, the jury heard arguments as to the appropriate sentence....The jury in this case found two aggravating circumstances to exist beyond a reasonable doubt: the murder was committed during the course of an armed robbery; and the murder was committed upon a peace officer engaged in the performance of his duties, 17–10–30(b)(8). In making its decision whether to impose the death sentence, the jury considered the mitigating and aggravating circumstances of McCleskey's conduct. McCleskey offered no mitigating evidence. The jury recommended that he be sentenced to death on the murder charge and to consecutive life sentences on the armed robbery charges. The court followed the jury's recommendation and sentenced McCleskey to death....

McCleskey...filed a petition for a writ of habeas corpus in the Federal District Court for the Northern District of Georgia. His petition raised 18 claims, one of which was that the Georgia capital sentencing process is administered in a racially discriminatory manner in violation of the Eighth and Fourteenth Amendments to the United States Constitution. In support of his claim, McCleskey proffered a statistical study performed by Professors David C. Baldus, Charles Pulaski, and George Woodworth (the Baldus study) that purports to show a disparity in the imposition of the death sentence in Georgia based on the race of the murder victim and, to a lesser extent, the race of the defendant. The Baldus study is actually two sophisticated statistical studies that examine over 2,000 murder cases that occurred in Georgia during the

1970's. The raw numbers collected by Professor Baldus indicate that defendants charged with killing white persons received the death penalty in 11% of the cases, but defendants charged with killing blacks received the death penalty in only 1% of the cases. The raw numbers also indicate a reverse racial disparity according to the race of the defendant: 4% of the black defendants received the death penalty, as opposed to 7% of the white defendants.

Baldus also divided the cases according to the combination of the race of the defendant and the race of the victim. He found that the death penalty was assessed in 22% of the cases involving black defendants and white victims; 8% of the cases involving white defendants and white victims; 1% of the cases involving black defendants and black victims; and 3% of the cases involving white defendants and black victims. Similarly, Baldus found that prosecutors sought the death penalty in 70% of the cases involving black defendants and white victims; 32% of the cases involving white defendants and white victims; 15% of the cases involving black defendants and black victims; and 19% of the cases involving white defendants and black victims.

Baldus subjected his data to an extensive analysis, taking account of 230 variables that could have explained the disparities on nonracial grounds. One of his models concludes that, even after taking account of 39 nonracial variables, defendants charged with killing white victims were 4.3 times as likely to receive a death sentence as defendants charged with killing blacks. According to this model, black defendants were 1.1 times as likely to receive a death sentence as other defendants. Thus, the Baldus study indicates that black defendants, such as McCleskey, who kill white victims have the greatest likelihood of receiving the death penalty.

The District Court held an extensive evidentiary hearing on McCleskey's petition. Although it believed that McCleskey's Eighth Amendment claim was foreclosed by the Fifth Circuit's decision in *Spinkellink v. Wainwright*, it nevertheless considered the Baldus study with care. It concluded that McCleskey's "statistics do not demonstrate a prima facie case in support of the contention that the death penalty was imposed upon him because of his race, because of the race of the victim, or because of any Eighth Amendment concern." *McCleskey v. Zant*, 580 F. Supp. 338, 379 (ND Ga. 1984). As to McCleskey's Fourteenth Amendment claim, the court found that the methodology of the Baldus study was flawed in several respects. Because of these defects, the court held that the Baldus study "fail[ed] to contribute anything of value" to McCleskey's claim. Id., at 372 (emphasis omitted). Accordingly, the court denied the petition insofar as it was based upon the Baldus study.

The Court of Appeals for the Eleventh Circuit, sitting en banc, carefully reviewed the District Court's decision on McCleskey's claim. 753 F.2d 877 (1985). It assumed the validity of the study itself and addressed the merits of McCleskey's Eighth and Fourteenth Amendment claims. That is, the court assumed that the study "showed that systematic and substantial disparities existed in the penalties imposed upon homicide defendants in Georgia based on race of the homicide victim, that the disparities existed at a less substantial rate in death sentencing based on race of defendants, and that the factors of race of the victim and defendant were at work in Fulton County." Id., at 895. Even assuming the study's validity, the Court of Appeals found the statistics "insufficient to demonstrate discriminatory intent or unconstitutional discrimination in the Fourteenth Amendment context, [and] insufficient to show irrationality, arbitrariness and capriciousness under any kind of Eighth Amendment analysis." Id., at 891. The court noted:

> "The very exercise of discretion means that persons exercising discretion may reach different results from exact duplicates. Assuming each result is within the range of discretion, all are correct in the eyes of the law. It would not make sense for the system to require the exercise of discretion in order to be facially constitutional, and at the same time hold a system unconstitutional in application where that discretion achieved different results for what appear to be exact duplicates, absent the state showing the reasons for the difference....
> "The Baldus approach...would take the cases with different results on what are contended to be duplicate facts, where the differences could not be otherwise explained, and conclude that the different result was based on race alone....This approach ignores the realities.... There are, in fact, no exact duplicates in capital crimes and capital defendants. The type of research submitted here tends to show which of the directed factors were effective, but is of restricted use in showing what undirected factors control the exercise of constitutionally required discretion." Id., at 898–899.

The court concluded:

> "Viewed broadly, it would seem that the statistical evidence presented here, assuming its validity, confirms rather than condemns the system....The marginal disparity based on the race of the victim tends to support the state's contention that the system is working far differently from the one which *Furman* [*v. Georgia*, (1972)] condemned.

In pre-Furman days, there was no rhyme or reason as to who got the death penalty and who did not. But now, in the vast majority of cases, the reasons for a difference are well documented. That they are not so clear in a small percentage of the cases is no reason to declare the entire system unconstitutional." Id., at 899.

The Court of Appeals affirmed the denial by the District Court of McCleskey's petition for a writ of habeas corpus insofar as the petition was based upon the Baldus study, with three judges dissenting as to McCleskey's claims based on the Baldus study. We granted certiorari, (1986), and now affirm.

McCleskey's first claim is that the Georgia capital punishment statute violates the Equal Protection Clause of the Fourteenth Amendment. He argues that race has infected the administration of Georgia's statute in two ways: persons who murder whites are more likely to be sentenced to death than persons who murder blacks, and black murderers are more likely to be sentenced to death than white murderers. As a black defendant who killed a white victim, McCleskey claims that the Baldus study demonstrates that he was discriminated against because of his race and because of the race of his victim. In its broadest form, McCleskey's claim of discrimination extends to every actor in the Georgia capital sentencing process, from the prosecutor who sought the death penalty and the jury that imposed the sentence, to the State itself that enacted the capital punishment statute and allows it to remain in effect despite its allegedly discriminatory application. We agree with the Court of Appeals, and every other court that has considered such a challenge, that this claim must fail.

Our analysis begins with the basic principle that a defendant who alleges an equal protection violation has the burden of proving "the existence of purposeful discrimination." *Whitus v. Georgia*, (1967). A corollary to this principle is that a criminal defendant must prove that the purposeful discrimination "had a discriminatory effect" on him. *Wayte v. United States*, (1985). Thus, to prevail under the Equal Protection Clause, McCleskey must prove that the decision makers in his case acted with discriminatory purpose. He offers no evidence specific to his own case that would support an inference that racial considerations played a part in his sentence. Instead, he relies solely on the Baldus study. McCleskey argues that the Baldus study compels an inference that his sentence rests on purposeful discrimination. McCleskey's claim that these statistics are sufficient proof of discrimination, without regard to the facts of a particular case, would extend to all capital cases in Georgia, at least where the victim was white and the defendant is black.

The Court has accepted statistics as proof of intent to discriminate in certain limited contexts. First, this Court has accepted statistical disparities as proof of an equal protection violation in the selection of the jury venire in a particular district. Although statistical proof normally must present a "stark" pattern to be accepted as the sole proof of discriminatory intent under the Constitution, *Arlington Heights v. Metropolitan Housing Dev. Corp.*, (1977), "[b]ecause of the nature of the jury-selection task,...we have permitted a finding of constitutional violation even when the statistical pattern does not approach [such] extremes." Id., at 266, n. 13. Second, this Court has accepted statistics in the form of multiple-regression analysis to prove statutory violations under Title VII of the Civil Rights Act of 1964. *Bazemore v. Friday*, (1986) (opinion of BRENNAN, J., concurring in part).

But the nature of the capital sentencing decision, and the relationship of the statistics to that decision, are fundamentally different from the corresponding elements in the venire-selection or Title VII cases. Most importantly, each particular decision to impose the death penalty is made by a petit jury selected from a properly constituted venire. Each jury is unique in its composition, and the Constitution requires that its decision rest on consideration of innumerable factors that vary according to the characteristics of the individual defendant and the facts of the particular capital offense. See *Hitchcock v. Dugger*, post, at 398–399; *Lockett v. Ohio*, (1978) (plurality opinion of Burger, C.J.). Thus, the application of an inference drawn from the general statistics to a specific decision in a trial and sentencing simply is not comparable to the application of an inference drawn from general statistics to a specific venire-selection or Title VII case. In those cases, the statistics relate to fewer entitics, and fewer variables are relevant to the challenged decisions.

Another important difference between the cases in which we have accepted statistics as proof of discriminatory intent and this case is that, in the venire-selection and Title VII contexts, the decision maker has an opportunity to explain the statistical disparity. See *Whitus v. Georgia*; *Texas Dept. of Community Affairs v. Burdine*, (1981); *McDonnell Douglas Corp. v. Green*, (1973). Here, the State has no practical opportunity to rebut the Baldus study. "[C]ontrolling considerations of...public policy," *McDonald v. Pless*, (1915), dictate that jurors "cannot be called...to testify to the motives and influences that led to their verdict." *Chicago, B. & Q. R. Co. v. Babcock*, (1907). Similarly, the policy considerations behind a prosecutor's traditionally "wide discretion" suggest the impropriety of our requiring prosecutors to defend their decisions to seek death penalties, "often years after they were made."...Moreover, absent far stronger proof, it is unnecessary to seek such a rebuttal, because a legitimate and unchallenged explanation for the decision is apparent from the record: McCleskey committed an act for which the United States Constitution and Georgia laws permit imposition of the death penalty.

Finally, McCleskey's statistical proffer must be viewed in the context of his challenge. McCleskey challenges decisions at the heart of the State's criminal justice system. "[O]ne of society's most basic tasks is that of protecting the lives of its citizens and one of the most basic ways in which it achieves the task is through criminal laws against murder." *Gregg v. Georgia*, (1976) (WHITE, J., concurring). Implementation of these laws necessarily requires discretionary judgments. Because discretion is essential to the criminal justice process, we would demand exceptionally clear proof before we would infer that the discretion has been abused. The unique nature of the decisions at issue in this case also counsels against adopting such an inference from the disparities indicated by the Baldus study. Accordingly, we hold that the Baldus study is clearly insufficient to support an inference that any of the decision makers in McCleskey's case acted with discriminatory purpose.

McCleskey also suggests that the Baldus study proves that the State as a whole has acted with a discriminatory purpose. He appears to argue that the State has violated the Equal Protection Clause by adopting the capital punishment statute and allowing it to remain in force despite its allegedly discriminatory application. But "'[d]iscriminatory purpose'...implies more than intent as volition or intent as awareness of consequences. It implies that the decision maker, in this case a state legislature, selected or reaffirmed a particular course of action at least in part 'because of,' not merely 'in spite of,' its adverse effects upon an identifiable group."...For this claim to prevail, McCleskey would have to prove that the Georgia Legislature enacted or maintained the death penalty statute because of an anticipated racially discriminatory effect. In Gregg v. Georgia, supra, this Court found that the Georgia capital sentencing system could operate in a fair and neutral manner. There was no evidence then, and there is none now, that the Georgia Legislature enacted the capital punishment statute to further a racially discriminatory purpose.

Nor has McCleskey demonstrated that the legislature maintains the capital punishment statute because of the racially disproportionate impact suggested by the Baldus study. As legislatures necessarily have wide discretion in the choice of criminal laws and penalties, and as there were legitimate reasons for the Georgia Legislature to adopt and maintain capital punishment, see *Gregg v. Georgia*, supra, at 183–187 (joint opinion of Stewart, POWELL, and STEVENS, JJ.), we will not infer a discriminatory purpose on the part of the State of Georgia. Accordingly, we reject McCleskey's equal protection claims.

McCleskey also argues that the Baldus study demonstrates that the Georgia capital sentencing system violates the Eighth Amendment.... Two principal decisions guide our resolution of McCleskey's Eighth Amendment claim. In *Furman v. Georgia*, (1972), the Court concluded that the death penalty was so irrationally imposed that any particular death sentence could be presumed excessive. Under the statutes at issue in Furman, there was no basis for determining in any particular case whether the penalty was proportionate to the crime: "[T]he death penalty [was] exacted with great infrequency even for the most atrocious crimes and...there [was] no meaningful basis for distinguishing the few cases in which it [was] imposed from the many cases in which it [was] not." Id., at 313 (WHITE, J., concurring).

In *Gregg*, the Court specifically addressed the question left open in Furman—whether the punishment of death for murder is "under all circumstances, 'cruel and unusual' in violation of the Eighth and Fourteenth Amendments of the Constitution." We noted that the imposition of the death penalty for the crime of murder "has a long history of acceptance both in the United States and in England." Id., at 176 (joint opinion of Stewart, POWELL, and STEVENS, JJ.). "The most marked indication of society's endorsement of the death penalty for murder [was] the legislative response to Furman." Id., at 179. During the 4-year period between Furman and Gregg, at least 35 States had reenacted the death penalty, and Congress had authorized the penalty for aircraft piracy. The "actions of juries" were "fully compatible with the legislative judgments." Id., at 182. We noted that any punishment might be unconstitutionally severe if inflicted without penological justification, but concluded:

> "Considerations of federalism, as well as respect for the ability of a legislature to evaluate, in terms of its particular State, the moral consensus concerning the death penalty and its social utility as a sanction, require us to conclude, in the absence of more convincing evidence, that the infliction of death as a punishment for murder is not without justification and thus is not unconstitutionally severe." Id., at 186–187.

The second question before the Court in *Gregg* was the constitutionality of the particular procedures embodied in the Georgia capital punishment statute. We explained the fundamental principle of *Furman*, that "where discretion is afforded a sentencing body on a matter so grave as the determination of whether a human life should be taken or spared, that discretion must be suitably directed and limited so as to minimize the risk of wholly arbitrary and capricious action.". Numerous features of the then new Georgia statute met the concerns articulated in *Furman*.... Thus, "while some jury discretion still exists, 'the discretion to be exercised is controlled by clear and objective standards so as to produce non-discriminatory application.'...

Finally, where the objective indicia of community values have demonstrated a consensus that the death penalty is disproportionate as applied to a certain class of cases, we have established substantive limitations on its application. In *Coker v. Georgia*, (1977), the Court held that a State may not constitutionally sentence an individual to death for the rape of an adult woman. In *Enmund v. Florida*, (1982), the Court prohibited imposition of the death penalty on a defendant convicted of felony murder absent a showing that the defendant possessed a sufficiently culpable mental state. Most recently, in *Ford v. Wainwright*, (1986), we prohibited execution of prisoners who are insane.

In sum, our decisions since *Furman* have identified a constitutionally permissible range of discretion in imposing the death penalty. First, there is a required threshold below which the death penalty cannot be imposed. In this context, the State must establish rational criteria that narrow the decision-maker's judgment as to whether the circumstances of a particular defendant's case meet the threshold. Moreover, a societal consensus that the death penalty is disproportionate to a particular offense prevents a State from imposing the death penalty for that offense. Second, States cannot limit the sentencer's consideration of any relevant circumstance that could cause it to decline to impose the penalty. In this respect, the State cannot channel the sentencer's discretion, but must allow it to consider any relevant information offered by the defendant.

In light of our precedents under the Eighth Amendment, McCleskey cannot argue successfully that his sentence is "disproportionate to the crime in the traditional sense." See *Pulley v. Harris*, (1984). He does not deny that he committed a murder in the course of a planned robbery, a crime for which this Court has determined that the death penalty constitutionally may be imposed. *Gregg v. Georgia*. His disproportionality claim "is of a different sort." *Pulley v. Harris*, supra, at 43. McCleskey argues that the sentences in his case is disproportionate to the sentences in other murder cases.

On the one hand, he cannot base a constitutional claim on an argument that his case differs from other cases in which defendants did receive the death penalty. On automatic appeal, the Georgia Supreme Court found that McCleskey's death sentence was not disproportionate to other death sentences imposed in the State. *McCleskey v. State*, 245 Ga. 108, 263 S. E. 2d 146 (1980).

The court supported this conclusion with an appendix containing citations to 13 cases involving generally similar murders. See Ga. Code Ann. 17–10–35(e) (1982). Moreover, where the statutory procedures adequately channel the sentencer's discretion, such proportionality review is not constitutionally required. *Pulley v. Harris*, supra, at 50–51.

On the other hand, absent a showing that the Georgia capital punishment system operates in an arbitrary and capricious manner, McCleskey cannot prove a constitutional violation by demonstrating that other defendants who may be similarly situated did not receive the death penalty. In *Gregg*, the Court confronted the argument that "the opportunities for discretionary action that are inherent in the processing of any murder case under Georgia law,", specifically the opportunities for discretionary leniency, rendered the capital sentences imposed arbitrary and capricious. We rejected this contention:

> "The existence of these discretionary stages is not determinative of the issues before us. At each of these stages an actor in the criminal justice system makes a decision which may remove a defendant from consideration as a candidate for the death penalty. Furman, in contrast, dealt with the decision to impose the death sentence on a specific individual who had been convicted of a capital offense. Nothing in any of our cases suggests that the decision to afford an individual defendant mercy violates the Constitution. Furman held only that, in order to minimize the risk that the death penalty would be imposed on a capriciously selected group of offenders, the decision to impose it had to be guided by standards so that the sentencing authority would focus on the particularized circumstances of the crime and the defendant." Ibid.

Because McCleskey's sentence was imposed under Georgia sentencing procedures that focus discretion "on the particularized nature of the crime and the particularized characteristics of the individual defendant," id., at 206, we lawfully may presume that McCleskey's death sentence was not "wantonly and freakishly" imposed, id., at 207, and thus that the sentence is not disproportionate within any recognized meaning under the Eighth Amendment.

Although our decision in *Gregg* as to the facial validity of the Georgia capital punishment statute appears to foreclose McCleskey's disproportionality argument, he further contends that the Georgia capital punishment system is arbitrary and capricious in application, and therefore his sentence is excessive, because racial considerations may influence capital sentencing decisions in Georgia. We now address this claim.

To evaluate McCleskey's challenge, we must examine exactly what the Baldus study may show. Even Professor Baldus does not contend that his statistics prove that race enters into any capital sentencing decisions or that race was a factor in McCleskey's particular case. Statistics at most may show only a likelihood that a particular factor entered into some decisions. There is, of course, some risk of racial prejudice influencing a jury's decision in a criminal case. There are similar risks that other kinds of prejudice will influence other criminal trials. See infra, at 315–318. The question "is at what point that risk becomes constitutionally unacceptable," *Turner v. Murray*, (1986). McCleskey asks us to accept the likelihood allegedly shown by the Baldus study as the constitutional measure of an unacceptable risk of racial prejudice influencing capital sentencing decisions. This we decline to do.

Because of the risk that the factor of race may enter the criminal justice process, we have engaged in "unceasing efforts" to eradicate racial prejudice from our criminal justice system. *Batson v. Kentucky* (1986). Our efforts have been guided by our recognition that "the inestimable privilege of trial by jury...is a vital principle, underlying the whole administration of criminal justice,"...Thus, it is the jury that is a criminal defendant's fundamental "protection of life and liberty against race or color prejudice." *Strauder v. West Virginia*, (1880). Specifically, a capital sentencing jury representative of a criminal defendant's community assures a "'diffused impartiality,'" *Taylor v. Louisiana*, (1975) (quoting *Thiel v. Southern Pacific Co.*, (1946) (Frankfurter, J., dissenting)), in the jury's task of "express[ing] the conscience of the community on the ultimate question of life or death," *Witherspoon v. Illinois*, (1968).

Individual jurors bring to their deliberations "qualities of human nature and varieties of human experience, the range of which is unknown and perhaps unknowable." *Peters v. Kiff*, (1972) (opinion of MARSHALL, J.). The capital sentencing decision requires the individual jurors to focus their collective judgment on the unique characteristics of a particular criminal defendant. It is not surprising that such collective judgments often are difficult to explain. But the inherent lack of predictability of jury decisions does not justify their condemnation. On the contrary, it is the jury's function to make the difficult and uniquely human judgments that defy codification and that "buil[d] discretion, equity, and flexibility into a legal system." H. Kalven & H. Zeisel, *The American Jury* 498 (1966).

McCleskey's argument that the Constitution condemns the discretion allowed decision makers in the Georgia capital sentencing system is antithetical to the fundamental role of discretion in our criminal justice system. Discretion in the criminal justice system offers substantial benefits to the criminal defendant. Not only can a jury decline to impose the death sentence, it can decline to convict or choose to convict of a lesser offense. Whereas decisions against a defendant's interest may be reversed by the trial judge or on appeal, these discretionary exercises of leniency are final and unreviewable. Similarly, the capacity of prosecutorial discretion to provide individualized justice is "firmly entrenched in American law." 2 W. LaFave & J. Israel, Criminal Procedure 13.2(a), p. 160 (1984). As we have noted, a prosecutor can decline to charge, offer a plea bargain, or decline to seek a death sentence in any particular case. See n. 28, supra. Of course, "the power to be lenient [also] is the power to discriminate," K. Davis, Discretionary Justice 170 (1973), but a capital punishment system that did not allow for discretionary acts of leniency "would be totally alien to our notions of criminal justice." *Gregg v. Georgia*.

At most, the Baldus study indicates a discrepancy that appears to correlate with race. Apparent disparities in sentencing are an inevitable part of our criminal justice system. The discrepancy indicated by the Baldus study is "a far cry from the major systemic defects identified in Furman," *Pulley v. Harris*, As this Court has recognized, any mode for determining guilt or punishment "has its weaknesses and the potential for misuse."…Specifically, "there can be 'no perfect procedure for deciding in which cases governmental authority should be used to impose death.'"…Despite these imperfections, our consistent rule has been that constitutional guarantees are met when "the mode [for determining guilt or punishment] itself has been surrounded with safeguards to make it as fair as possible." *Singer v. United States*, supra, at 35. Where the discretion that is fundamental to our criminal process is involved, we decline to assume that what is unexplained is invidious. In light of the safeguards designed to minimize racial bias in the process, the fundamental value of jury trial in our criminal justice system, and the benefits that discretion provides to criminal defendants, we hold that the Baldus study does not demonstrate a constitutionally significant risk of racial bias affecting the Georgia capital sentencing process.

Two additional concerns inform our decision in this case. First, McCleskey's claim, taken to its logical conclusion, throws into serious question the principles that underlie our entire criminal justice system. The Eighth Amendment is not limited in application to capital punishment, but applies to all penalties....Thus, if we accepted McCleskey's claim that racial bias has impermissibly tainted the capital sentencing decision, we could soon be faced with similar claims as to other types of penalty. Moreover, the claim that his sentence rests on the irrelevant factor of race easily could be extended to apply to claims based on unexplained discrepancies that correlate to membership in other minority groups, and even to gender. Similarly, since McCleskey's claim relates to the race of his victim, other claims could apply with equally logical force to statistical disparities that correlate with the race or sex of other actors in the criminal justice system, such as defense attorneys or judges. Also, there is no logical reason that such a claim need be limited to racial or sexual bias. If arbitrary and capricious punishment is the touchstone under the Eighth Amendment, such a claim could—at least in theory—be based upon any arbitrary variable, such as the defendant's facial characteristics, or the physical attractiveness of the defendant or the victim, that some statistical study indicates may be influential in jury decision making. As these examples illustrate, there is no limiting principle to the type of challenge brought by McCleskey. The Constitution does not require that a State eliminate any demonstrable disparity that correlates with a potentially irrelevant factor in order to operate a criminal justice system that includes capital punishment. As we have stated specifically in the context of capital punishment, the Constitution does not "plac[e] totally unrealistic conditions on its use." *Gregg v. Georgia.*

Second, McCleskey's arguments are best presented to the legislative bodies. It is not the responsibility—or indeed even the right—of this Court to determine the appropriate punishment for particular crimes. It is the legislatures, the elected representatives of the people, that are "constituted to respond to the will and consequently the moral values of the people." *Furman v. Georgia,* (Burger, C.J., dissenting). Legislatures also are better qualified to weigh and "evaluate the results of statistical studies in terms of their own local conditions and with a flexibility of approach that is not available to the courts," *Gregg v. Georgia,* supra, at 186. Capital punishment is now the law in more than two-thirds of our States. It is the ultimate duty of courts to determine on a case-by-case basis whether these laws are applied consistently with the Constitution. Despite McCleskey's wide-ranging arguments that basically challenge the validity of capital punishment in our multiracial society, the only question before us is whether in his case, see supra, at 283–285, the law of Georgia was properly applied. We agree with the District Court and the Court of Appeals for the Eleventh Circuit that this was carefully and correctly done in this case. Accordingly, we affirm the judgment of the Court of Appeals for the Eleventh Circuit. It is so ordered.

D.C. Baldus, G. Woodworth, D. Zuckerman, N. Weiner and B. Broffitt
Racial discrimination and the death penalty in the post-Furman era: An empirical and legal overview, with recent findings from Philadelphia. *
Cornell Law Review volume 83, page 1638. (1998)

Introduction

Racial discrimination and the death penalty has been a matter of scholarly interest since the 1930s. The nation's legal system has been aware of the issue since the civil rights movement of the 1960s. Every court that has addressed the issue has condemned the idea of race influencing the administration of the death penalty. The courts agree that this practice has no place in a society dedicated to the rule of law. Nevertheless, in this century, no American court has upheld a legal claim alleging racial discrimination in the use of the death penalty. Only one American legislative body has adopted a law that would give murder defendants the right to advance claims of racial discrimination in the same manner available to racial minorities in the employment, housing, and public accommodations contexts.

This Article focuses on the following four issues related to racial discrimination in the use of the death penalty in post-*Furman* America: (1) the link between discretion and discrimination; (2) ethical, moral, and legal concerns associated with racial discrimination in the administration of the death penalty; (3) evidence of this discrimination with special reference to recent empirical findings from Philadelphia, Pennsylvania; and (4) judicial and legislative responses to claims of racial discrimination.

I. Discretion and discrimination

The potential influence of race in the administration of the death penalty takes root in the broad exercise of discretion that state laws grant prosecutors and juries. State laws give prosecutors and juries the power to treat similarly situated "death-eligible" defendants differently because of either their race or the race of the victim in the case.

---

* reprinted with permission of the Cornell Law Review.

The law gives prosecutors complete discretion either to seek a death sentence in death-eligible cases or to waive the death penalty—unilaterally or by way of a negotiated plea bargain. For cases that advance to a penalty trial, the typical jury exercises virtually complete discretion on the life or death decision once it finds a statutory aggravating circumstance present in the case. In addition, the governor or board of pardons and parole generally has complete discretion to commute a death sentence to either life without possibility of parole or a term of years....

Most striking about the exercise of both prosecutorial and jury discretion in this process is that the decisions to seek and impose death sentences are essentially unreviewable with respect to the issue of discrimination. In the absence of an admission by the prosecutor or individual jurors that race was a factor in their decision (which is virtually unheard of), discriminatory behavior by either of these actors is essentially outside the scope of review in the numerous appeals that generally follow the imposition of a death sentence....

B. Ethical, Moral, and Legal Concerns Implicated by Racial Discrimination in the Administration of the Death Penalty

1. Ethical and moral concerns

The issue of racial discrimination in the administration of the death penalty is not whether juries sentenced factually innocent defendants to death because of their race. To be sure, there is evidence that many of these miscarriages of justice both before and after *Furman* were racially motivated. For example, in the famous recent case *McMillian v. State*, Walter McMillian, an African American, was framed and sentenced to death in Alabama for the murder of a white woman based on false testimony generated by law enforcement officials.

It is clear that both McMillian's race, his history of dating a white woman, and his victim's race made him an easier target. Nevertheless, the best research suggests that both white and black defendants who are factually innocent of any crime are at equal risk of being falsely convicted and sentenced to death.

In contrast to the factual-innocence issue, the principal concern about racial discrimination in the administration of the death penalty relates to the unequal treatment of similarly situated defendants who are in fact guilty of capital murder. The core ethical concern is fairness—treating like cases alike —especially when the consequences of the decision are so severe. Governments, in particular, have a profound duty to treat all defendants with equal care and concern and without regard to factors that have no bearing on their criminal culpability. Given the legacy of slavery and race discrimination in our history, this concern has special force with respect to discrimination based on the defendant's race, a factor over which he has no control. However, when a defendant alleges discrimination based on the victim's race, the claim's moral appeal may weaken with a simple reminder that the defendant, not society, selected the victim.

Concerns about racial discrimination may also resonate at the group level. Claims of race-of-victim discrimination (for example, that nonblack-victim cases are treated more punitively than black-victim cases) raise an ethical concern that the state's failure to allocate resources equally in the prosecution of both black and nonblack cases denies the black community equitable access to any possible benefits the death penalty may provide. Even if it were clear that America's death-sentencing system treated black and nonblack defendants fairly and consistently, concerns remain about the substantial overrepresentation of blacks on death row in America. While blacks make up only thirteen percent of the nation's civilian population, blacks make up forty-one percent of the nation's death row population. Many consider it insensitive and unseemly, if not immoral, for a country with our historical record on slavery and racial discrimination to persist in using a punishment that whites almost exclusively administer and control, that serves no demonstrated penological function, and has a profound adverse impact—physically, psychologically, and symbolically—on its black citizens.

For others, ethical concerns about race discrimination relate strictly to the extent to which the death-sentencing system treats equally culpable defendants differently because of either their race or the race of the victim. Moreover, for some people within this group, the level of ethical and moral concern depends on the extent to which the cause of the unequal treatment is the product of conscious racial animus, the influence of stereotypical or non-conscious perceptions of the comparative dangerousness of black and nonblack defendants, or the influence of community perceptions of the heinousness of crimes that happen to be correlated with the racial aspects of the cases.

Proponents of the death penalty respond to these concerns with several ethical arguments. Principally, they argue that society's interest in retribution, justice, and concern for the victims of crime and their families trump equal treatment concerns. They further argue that racial discrimination in no way diminishes either the culpability of the defendants who are sentenced to death or society's justification for executing them.

Proponents of the death penalty offer two additional arguments, which proceed from quite different premises. First, they assert that concerns about racial discrimination are misplaced because no convincing evidence suggests that race is an influence in the system. Second, they argue that racial discrimination is inevitable and endemic in all of our social institutions (the death penalty being no exception), and the law can do nothing about it, short of abolishing the death penalty, which in their view, cannot be morally justified on this ground. Advocates of this second argument believe that the costs of eliminating the death penalty clearly outweigh any harms caused by racial discrimination. This belief no doubt explains why most citizens who support the death penalty in opinion polls would maintain that support even if they believed that the system were racially discriminatory.

2. Legal concerns

At a strictly doctrinal level, the law is less conflicted than ethical and moral opinion on the question. First, the Supreme Court has repeatedly stated that the Fourteenth Amendment forbids "purposeful" discrimination by all public officials, which includes prosecutorial and jury decisions to seek and impose death sentences. This position rests on the proposition that the Fourteenth Amendment prohibits consideration of race as a basis for official decisions unless the consideration can be justified by a compelling state interest. (One could never establish a compelling state interest to justify race discrimination in the death-sentencing context.)

The Court has explicitly ruled that this standard applies to purposeful race-of-defendant and race-of-victim discrimination. Thus, even though defendants claiming race-of-victim discrimination may not be able to show a nexus between their race and the adverse decision in their particular case, they may raise the issue because they are entitled to decisions that are not influenced by any person's race, including the victim's.

Legal consensus also exists that decisions to either seek or impose the death penalty that are consciously motivated by racial animus qualify as purposeful discrimination under the Fourteenth Amendment. At issue, however, is whether decisions that treat black defendants more punitively than similarly situated nonblack defendants constitute purposeful discrimination under the Fourteenth Amendment when stereotypical ideas about black defendants and white victims drive those decisions. A similar issue arises when the decisions of prosecutors or juries to seek or to impose the death penalty represent a response to the community's demand for more punitive action in cases involving, for example, black defendants and white victims.

The Supreme Court has also implied that purposeful racial discrimination violates the Eighth Amendment's "cruel and unusual punishments" provision. Indeed, the Court has held that even a demonstrated "risk" that racial considerations may have influenced a death-sentencing decision suffices as a basis for judicial relief. The theory underlying this rule is that a decision either to seek or impose a death sentence that bears a substantial risk of being influenced by the race of the defendant or victim is arbitrary within the meaning of the Eighth Amendment because it is not based on the criminal culpability of the defendant (the only constitutionally permissible basis for a sentence of death).

II Post-*Furman* evidence of arbitrariness and discrimination

A. Issues of proof and interpretation

It is useful to draw a threshold distinction between claims of purposeful "systemic" racial discrimination and claims of purposeful discrimination in individual cases. A claim of systemic discrimination alleges that race is a factor in prosecutorial decisions to seek or jury decisions to impose the death sentence. Normally, one proves systemic discrimination with statistical evidence demonstrating that, on average, the system treats black defendants or defendants with nonblack victims more punitively than similarly situated nonblack defendants or defendants with black victims. This proof is circumstantial, and its inferential power depends on (1) the magnitude of the disparities in the treatment of the different, racially defined groups of cases and (2) the plausibility that the differences in treatment are not the product of either chance or different case characteristics within the two racial groups that could reasonably explain the disparities on legitimate grounds.

One proves discrimination in an individual case by establishing that the race of the defendant or victim was a "motivating factor," a "substantial or significant factor," or a "but-for factor" in the claimant's case. This proof may be accomplished by presenting (1) "direct," smoking-gun evidence (for example, an admission or racial slur by a prosecutor or juror) or (2) a combination of both quantitative and qualitative evidence. Proof of discrimination in individual cases finds its best illustration in class-wide employment discrimination cases alleging claims of race or gender discrimination in either hiring or promotion. Proof in these cases typically commences with a statistical demonstration of systemic discrimination among a large group of cases (including the cases of the plaintiffs in the particular lawsuit). The evidence of systemic discrimination supports an inference of purposeful discrimination in the case of each minority or woman who experienced adverse effects from a decision of the defendant in hiring or promotion. At this point, Title VII, a federal law that prohibits racial and gender discrimination in employment, shifts the focus to the individual claimants and places on the defendant-employer the burden of establishing that neither race nor gender was a factor in each adversely affected case. This final inquiry, therefore, focuses on the legitimate facts of the individual case that are offered to rebut the inference of discrimination. In other words, it asks whether these facts plausibly explain the adverse decision in the plaintiff's case. For example, if a rejected minority-group member demonstrated very weak qualifications for the job, the "rival" nondiscriminatory hypothesis would likely appear quite plausible, and a court would deny relief. On the other hand, if the minority group member demonstrated qualifications exceeding those of most of the whites hired, the rival nondiscriminatory hypothesis would appear implausible, and a court probably would grant relief.

When considering claims of systemic purposeful discrimination in the application of the death penalty, one must distinguish between evidence of "gross unadjusted" racial disparities and "adjusted" racial disparities. Adjusted disparities account for the presence of aggravating and mitigating factors that clearly influence the decisions of prosecutors and juries. Adjusted disparities permit one to compare the treatment of offenders who share similar levels of aggravation and mitigation, which, when considered together, determine a defendant's criminal culpability and blameworthiness. The failure of a statistical analysis to use adjusted disparities introduces a significant risk of erroneous inferences about the influence of race in the system....

Unadjusted gross racial disparities in death sentence rates are a highly suspect basis for inferring racial discrimination in the treatment of similarly situated defendants, especially when one bases the disparities on the entire nation. For example, some occasionally offer evidence that blacks constitute thirteen percent of the national population, but forty-one percent of the nationwide death row population, to prove systemic race-of-defendant discrimination. However, this unadjusted disparity is highly misleading because it fails to control for the disproportionately high percentage of blacks (about fifty-five percent) among citizens arrested for homicide nationally. As a result, the comparison fails to control for the differential rates at which black and nonblack citizens commit death-eligible homicides.

Apologists for the current system make a similarly misleading argument when they assert that the system discriminates nationally against nonblack defendants because blacks constitute fifty-five percent of homicide arrestees but only forty-one percent of the death-row population. This argument fails to compare the treatment of similarly situated black and white defendants in death-eligible cases. (In most death sentencing states, only about ten to fifteen percent of defendants arrested for homicide have committed death-eligible crimes.) Moreover, the comparison fails to control for the widely different levels of criminal culpability among death-eligible defendants. Finally, the argument fails to account for race-of-victim discrimination. Race-of-victim discrimination also reduces the overall rate of death sentencing for black defendants because they commit the vast majority of black-victim murders. Only by comparing the differential treatment of black and nonblack defendants whose victims are of the same race, can one accurately test for race-of-defendant discrimination in the system.

Thus, unadjusted disparities are suggestive at best, and one should use them with caution. Also, experience indicates that when one adjusts the disparities in death-sentencing rates for legitimate case characteristics, the unadjusted disparities often, but not always, decline. The most reliable evidence of discrimination, therefore, consists of racial disparities that are adjusted to reflect the different levels of culpability of the cases in the different racial groups. But, here one must beware of the "average overall culpability" fallacy, which can be illustrated with two examples.

First, assume the evidence reveals that the death-sentencing rate is higher for black defendants than for nonblack defendants. However, some allege that one can refute the suggested inference of discrimination with evidence that, overall, the black-defendant cases are more aggravated than the nonblack-defendant cases. This difference in average culpability for the two groups allegedly explains the unadjusted racial disparity in death-sentencing rates. Second, assume there is evidence that the death-sentencing rate is greater in nonblack-victim cases than in black-victim cases. However, evidence shows that the nonblack-victim cases are more aggravated than the black-victim cases, which allegedly explains the unadjusted race-of-victim disparity.

Both of these arguments are flawed because no necessary correlation exists between the average culpability level for the different racial groups of cases and the extent to which similarly situated defendants in the different racial groups are treated similarly or differently. For example, the average culpability level of the black- and nonblack-victim cases may be quite different, but that disparity sheds no light on the question of whether the system treats similarly or differently black- and nonblack-victim cases with the same level of culpability. Nor does evidence that black-defendant cases are on average more aggravated than nonblack-defendant cases tell us anything about the extent to which the system treats similarly or differently subgroups of black and nonblack defendants with, for example, high or low levels of culpability.

Evidence from Georgia clearly revealed that white-victim cases were, on average, more aggravated than black-victim cases. Nevertheless, when comparing similarly culpable cases, the defendants in white-victim cases were more likely to receive a death sentence than the defendants in black-victim cases. The strongest race-of-victim effects were observed among the cases with average levels of defendant culpability.

Good practice suggests, therefore, that the results of statistically controlled studies which estimate racial disparities among cases with similar levels of criminal culpability are the most reliable. Unfortunately, well-controlled studies are expensive and time consuming. As a result, researchers have conducted relatively few. It is necessary, therefore, in speculating about the American system as a whole, to consider all of the available evidence, including unadjusted disparities and anecdotal testimony provided by the principal participants in the process—defense lawyers, prosecutors, and judges. However, the small number of systematic studies of any kind encourages skepticism about sweeping claims concerning the level of racial discrimination, especially in jurisdictions in which no one has conducted systematic studies.

B. An overview of the post-*Furman* data

The best overview of the post-*Furman* evidence about race discrimination and the death penalty appeared in 1990. The General Accounting Office ("GAO"), at the request of the United States Senate, published the results of a systematic review of the empirical studies conducted by a variety of investigators in the 1970s and 1980s. The GAO initially considered conducting one or more empirical studies itself, but finally opted for "an evaluative synthesis," which consisted of a review and critique of existing research. Toward that end, the agency evaluated twenty-eight empirical studies. It sought, in its review, to assess the extent to which the existing literature supported claims of (1) race-of-defendant discrimination and (2) race-of-victim discrimination. On the issue of race-of-victim discrimination, the agency reported that:

In 82 percent of the studies, race of victim was found to influence the likelihood of being charged with capital murder or receiving the death penalty, i.e., those who murdered whites were found to be more likely to be sentenced to death than those who murdered blacks. This finding was remarkably consistent across data sets, states, data collection methods, and analytic techniques. The finding held for high, medium, and low quality studies.

The race of victim influence was found at all stages of the criminal justice system process, although there were variations among studies as to whether there was a race of victim influence at specific stages. The evidence for the race of victim influence was stronger for the earlier stages of the judicial process (e.g., prosecutorial decision to charge defendant with a capital offense, decision to proceed to trial rather than plea bargain) than in later stages. This was because the earlier stages were comprised of larger samples allowing for more rigorous analyses. However, decisions made at every stage of the process necessarily affect an individual's likelihood of being sentenced to death.

The largest of the studies the GAO reviewed was based on a stratified sample of 1066 cases drawn from a universe of 2484 cases processed in the Georgia charging and sentencing system in the period 1973–80 ("the Baldus study"). These results, which were the basis of the petitioner's claim of racial discrimination in *McCleskey v. Kemp*, indicated that, after controlling for the presence or absence of hundreds of legitimate case characteristics, defendants with white victims faced, on average, odds of receiving a death sentence that were 4.3 times higher than the odds of similarly situated defendants whose victims were black. This study also demonstrated that in Fulton County, where the jury sentenced McCleskey to death, significant race-of-victim disparities existed.

On the issue of race-of-defendant discrimination, the GAO study concluded:

The evidence for the influence of the race of defendant on death penalty outcomes was equivocal. Although more than half of the studies found that race of defendant influenced the likelihood of being charged with a capital crime or receiving the death penalty, the relationship between race of defendant and outcome varied across studies. For example, sometimes the race of defendant interacted with another factor. In one study researchers found that in rural areas black defendants were more likely to receive death sentences, and in urban areas white defendants were more likely to receive death sentences. In a few studies, analyses revealed that the black defendant/white victim combination was the most likely to receive the death penalty. However, the extent to which the finding was influenced by race of victim rather than race of defendant was unclear.

C. Geographic scope of the post-*Furman* race disparities

To document the geographic scope of race disparities in the American death-sentencing system, we examined, on a state-by-state basis, both (1) the literature published prior to the GAO report and (2) the evidence since the GAO report. This survey, the results of which we present in Appendix B, reveals that relevant data are not available on charging and sentencing practices for all death-sentencing states. Nevertheless, for 78% (29/37) of the nation's death-sentencing states in which a death sentence has been imposed (no sentences have been imposed in New Hampshire), we located some relevant data for at least one period of time since 1973. In 90% (26/29) of these states, we observed some evidence of race-of-victim disparities and in 55% (16/29) of the states, we observed some evidence of race-of-defendant disparities (although not all of the disparities were in the normally observed direction).

As the GAO survey points out, considerable differences exist in the extent to which empirical studies of racial discrimination control for legitimate case characteristics. Because reasonably well-controlled empirical studies are expensive and quite complex, such studies have been conducted in only nine states (California, Colorado, Georgia, Kentucky, Mississippi, New Jersey, North Carolina, Pennsylvania, and South Carolina).

Additionally, for each of these states, data are available from less-well-controlled studies. In six states (Colorado, North Carolina, New Jersey, Kentucky, Pennsylvania, and South Carolina), the racial disparities were stronger in the well-controlled studies than in the less-well-controlled studies. In three states (California, Georgia, and Mississippi), the race effects were weaker in the well-controlled studies than in the less-well-controlled studies, but remained statistically significant. These results indicate that, while well-controlled studies are a more reliable basis for measuring race effects in a given jurisdiction, the results from less-well-controlled studies also can be relevant and instructive....

3. Theoretical explanations for race and SES disparities
in philadelphia and elsewhere

The statistical analyses in the preceding section [the discussion of the Philadephia analysis is omitted from this excerpt] offer some insight into the most likely explanations for the racial and SES disparities that the Philadelphia data document. However, a considerable body of psychological, sociological, and political science literature, the reported experience of legal practitioners, newspaper reports, and common experiences suggest other possible explanations. In this section, we consider these theories and evaluate their applicability in post-*Furman* Philadelphia.

a. Overt, conscious racial discrimination

One theory, particularly prominent in the pre-*Furman* South, is that the observed racial disparities were likely the product of overt racial animus—

hostility toward black defendants. This animus appeared most fervently if the victim was a "more worthy" white. During the post-Furman period, the level of overt racial animus appears to have declined throughout the nation, including Philadelphia. Although one cannot completely discount the possibility of overt conscious discrimination in Philadelphia, the mechanisms producing race effects there and elsewhere in the country appear to be more complex.

b. Community outrage

Conventional wisdom holds that community outrage is the most important determinant of race disparities among similarly situated cases. Community outrage pressures prosecutors, judges, and juries to avenge highly visible murders. One often correlates high visibility with racial composition of both the defendant and victim of the cases. White-victim cases, especially if they are interracial cases, continue to attract the most media coverage. This attention in turn influences prosecutors to allocate their scarce resources to those cases, especially if reelection or a run for higher political office is probable. Additionally, when the victim is white, some prosecutors are more solicitous of a request by the victim's family to seek a death sentence. Moreover, prosecutors consult the families of black victims less often, and when they do, the families generally are less likely to seek a death sentence.

While the outrage theory may be salient in suburbs and rural communities, both of which tend to have relatively small black populations, particularly in the South, it appears to have little applicability in Philadelphia. Surely, the Philadelphia District Attorney supports and aggressively pursues the death penalty, in part with an eye to its political implications in a community with a very high homicide rate. However, no evidence suggests that this support for the death penalty produces the racial disparities documented in the Philadelphia research.

In Philadelphia, seventy-eight percent of the capital defendants and sixty-seven percent of the victims are black. Very few of the Philadelphia victims were high-status whites murdered by black defendants. The only cases that appear to produce an uncompromising, prosecutorial hard line are those involving police victims. Indeed, in virtually all other case categories, the Commonwealth is willing to negotiate a guilty plea in exchange for a penalty of life without possibility of parole. Finally, there is little to support the idea that Philadelphia prosecutors are more deferential to the wishes of family members concerning whether the death sentence should be sought in nonblack-victim cases.

c. The perceived unimportance of Black-on-Black murder cases

The prevailing view in many communities, particularly in the South and large cities, is that black-on-black homicides do not warrant the resources required for capital trials, and therefore, plea bargains with relatively light sentences are appropriate. These perceptions may result in perfunctory investigations by law enforcement officials in black-victim cases, which in turn may lead some prosecutors to believe that the prospects of obtaining a death sentence are too low to justify the cost. In addition, some prosecutors may believe that the black community will provide a low level of cooperation in the investigation of these cases, significantly reducing the chance of obtaining a capital murder conviction at trial. This belief may encourage the acceptance of a plea to a lesser offense. Furthermore, the black community's perception that defendants in black-on-black cases probably will receive light sentences and return to the streets in a relatively short period of time may inhibit witnesses from coming forward with incriminating evidence against the defendants.

None of this analysis appears applicable to Philadelphia. The District Attorney's office generally supports the death penalty across the board even though sixty-seven percent of the murder victims and seventy-eight percent of the defendants are black.

d. The predominance of White control of the criminal justice system

In many places in the United States, prosecutors, judges, and penalty-trial jurors are predominantly white even though the defendants whose cases they hear are not. The conventional wisdom is that white jurors are less likely to sympathize with black defendants or to identify with black victims. Convincing evidence also suggests that many participants in the system, both black and nonblack, consider young black males more deserving of severe punishment because they are violence prone, morally inferior, and a threat to the community. The danger for black defendants in the system is particularly acute when the attorneys who represent them entertain racial stereotypes that diminish the quality and vigor of their representation.

The risk of both race-of-defendant and race-of-victim discrimination is also enhanced when the jury selection processes result in the serious underrepresentation of blacks on criminal trial juries. This underrepresentation is a widespread problem. First, blacks are often underrepresented on both the voter and automobile registration lists from which most jury venires are drawn. Second, low-income citizens are less likely to appear for jury service, and courts are more likely to excuse them for hardship. Third, and most important, prosecutors have the wide-ranging discretion to strike prospective jurors through the exercise of "peremptory" challenges. The result is that many black defendants receive sentences from juries with only a few or no blacks. This problem is particularly acute when the attorneys assigned to represent indigent defendants are inexperienced or indifferent, making it easier for prosecutors to strike blacks because their strikes are not effectively challenged. We are currently investigating the levels of African American representation on the Philadelphia juries referred to in this Article.

Finally, explicit prosecutorial references to the jury of the race of the defendant or the victim (e.g., " 'Can you imagine her state of mind...staring into the muzzle of a gun held by this black man?' ") as well as racial slurs and other appeals to racial prejudice, such as the use of animal metaphors in describing the defendant (e.g., "this animal" who "shouldn't be out of his cell unless he has a leash on him") exacerbate the risk of racial discrimination. Slurs of this type have come from prosecutors, judges, and defense counsel.

E. The magnitude and practical consequences of post-*Furman* race disparities

A question of obvious importance concerns the "practical" consequences and the "impact" of the disparities researchers have documented in Philadelphia and elsewhere. In this section, we consider several ways of assessing these consequences.

1. The impact of racial disparities on death-sentencing "odds" and "probabilities"

One approach is to focus on the impact of the disparities on the odds that the average member of the disadvantaged group will receive a death sentence (e.g., one can compare the odds of a death sentence for black defendants to the odds faced by similarly situated nonblack defendants)....

2. Excess death sentence rates and death sentences

But, what are the practical consequences of these disparities in death-sentencing rates? On this issue, it is useful to focus first on the extent to which the death-sentencing rate for the disadvantaged group exceeds what one would expect in an evenhanded system....

3. Impact on the community and death row population

Some observers have noted that the principal beneficiaries of race-of-victim discrimination are black defendants because the vast majority of death-eligible cases involving black victims also involve black defendants. Thus, if on average, the system treats black-victim cases less punitively than nonblack-victim cases, black defendants will be sentenced to death at a lower rate than would be the case in a system that sentenced all cases at the white-victim rate. However, if a system sentenced all cases at the black-victim rate, there would be no increase in the number of black defendants sentenced to death, but there would be a decline in the number of nonblack defendants sentenced to death. Nevertheless, it is clear that if an evenhanded policy were applied to the black- and nonblack-victim cases (at the current rate for either black- or nonblack-victim cases), the proportion of black defendants on death row would increase.

In places that currently treat black defendants more punitively, like Philadelphia, an evenhanded system would reduce the number of black defendants sentenced to death. Moreover, an evenhanded system that applied the current death-sentencing rate for either black or nonblack defendants would reduce the proportion of black defendants on death row....

IV. Judicial and legislative responses to claims of racial discrimination

A. The United States Supreme Court

The Supreme Court did not directly address a constitutional claim that states administer the death penalty in a racially discriminatory pattern until *McCleskey v. Kemp*....The Supreme Court....declared that, because the Baldus study did not establish with "exceptionally clear proof...that any of the decision makers in McCleskey's case acted with discriminatory purpose," McCleskey failed to establish an equal protection violation....*McCleskey* has drawn considerable criticism. Numerous commentators have expressed serious concern about the Court's placement of an implicit imprimatur on racial discrimination in such an important area of the criminal law. Particularly offensive to blacks is the perception, based upon *McCleskey*, that the Constitution authorizes prosecutors and jurors to provide minority communities with less protection than it provides white communities. In spite of these criticisms, however, *McCleskey* is still the law.

B. Congressional reform efforts

Although *McCleskey* has, for the time being, largely closed down federal-court discussion of race in capital cases, it did not block further congressional consideration of the issue. Indeed, Justice Powell's opinion in *McCleskey* suggested that one should present claims of discrimination for corrective action to legislatures.

In *McCleskey's* wake, congressional concerns stimulated a formal assessment of the scope of the problem in American capital-charging and sentencing systems. This assessment produced the previously mentioned GAO report, which clearly suggested that a problem existed, especially with respect to race-of-victim discrimination. Continuing congressional concerns led to a series of efforts to bypass *McCleskey* by relying on the legislative power the Enabling Clause of the Fourteenth Amendment grants Congress. The two resulting proposals were known as the Racial Justice Act and the Fairness in Death Sentencing Act. Neither addressed the specific situation in Georgia or in any other state. Nor did they specifically seek to impose structural remedies on the states that would limit the exercise of both prosecutorial and jury discretion to the most highly aggravated cases in which no race effect was apparent, which Justices Blackmun and Stevens suggested in *McCleskey*. Instead, Congress designed the measures to give offenders the right to challenge their individual death sentences as racially motivated, just as individuals who can claim discrimination under federal employment and housing laws.

Under the two proposals, a black defendant or a defendant whose victim was white could establish a prima facie case by showing a racially discriminatory pattern of death sentencing, presumably after adjustment for the leading aggravating circumstances. The State could rebut this showing by demonstrating, by a preponderance of the evidence, that identifiable and pertinent nonracial factors persuasively explain the observable racial disparities comprising the pattern. Absent such a rebuttal by the State, defendants would be entitled to relief from their death sentences if their cases fell within a category of cases in which a racial disparity existed to their disadvantage.

The U.S. House of Representatives adopted the second proposal, the Fairness in Death Sentencing Act, in 1990 and again with only slight modification, in 1994. In each instance, however, the Senate rejected it in a House-Senate Conference Committee. On both occasions, the measure attracted strong opposition from state Attorneys General and from prosecutors in death-penalty states. They argued, on the one hand, that racial discrimination did not exist and therefore the act was unnecessary, and, on the other hand, that the provision would necessarily result in either the use of quotas or the de facto abolition of capital punishment in America. They premised the latter argument on claims that racial discrimination in the use of the death penalty was inevitable and impossible to prevent, detect, or remedy. Thus, we would be left with the choice between quotas or abolition. Although we consider those arguments spurious red herrings, they had considerable force with legislators, who feared that their constituents might perceive a vote in support of the Act as an action that could lessen the viability of the death penalty in their states.

C. State court claims

Although *McCleskey* does not bind state supreme courts and they are free to entertain claims of racial discrimination under their state constitutions, the idea is distinctly unappealing to nearly all such courts. The reasons are quite clear. Most important among these reasons is the power of the death penalty as a symbol in contemporary American life, especially in the South.

Indeed, many judges are reluctant to vacate death sentences even on "technical" legal grounds when the Constitution clearly calls for such action. Elected judges are familiar with the unpleasant fate of some of their colleagues whom the public perceived to be resistant or unsympathetic to the death penalty. The idea of upsetting even a single death penalty on racial grounds, particularly in the South, would carry unacceptable risks for most judges.

It is no surprise, therefore, that the two state supreme courts (Connecticut, New Jersey) and the one state legislature (New York) that thus far have expressed a possible interest in the issue are located in northeastern jurisdictions with strong traditions of concern about racial discrimination. Moreover, the members of the only supreme court actually to have heard a race claim (New Jersey) enjoy the protection of life tenure until retirement at age seventy. In the first New Jersey case, *State v. Marshall*, the court rejected the *McCleskey* approach and ruled that, under the equal protection clause of the New Jersey constitution, claims of both race-of-victim and race-of-defendant discrimination are cognizable. It also recognized the standing of a white defendant to present "a structural challenge to the constitutional fairness" of New Jersey's death-sentencing system as the state's prosecutors and juries actually apply it.

The operative test asks whether the race of either the victim or the defendant "played a significant part in capital-sentencing decisions" in New Jersey. The Marshall case focused on the constitutional legitimacy of the system as a whole, rather than on the risk that race might adversely have influenced the decision of either the prosecutor or the jury in an individual case.

The New Jersey court barely developed potential remedies in the Marshall opinion because the court did not find evidence of unconstitutional discrimination. The court did state, however, that if it found discrimination to exist, it would "seek corrective measures" whose impact the court could observe through judicial oversight. The most likely possibilities would be the following: (1) a limitation on the class of death-eligible cases or (2) the promulgation of more objective and detailed standards to guide the exercise of prosecutorial discretion. The court further stated that if the corrective measures failed to correct the discrimination, it "could not…tolerate" such a system and would presumably declare it unconstitutional. However, in spite of the New Jersey court's willingness to consider race claims, it has rejected all of the claims it has heard thus far.

Conclusion

The century's history of race discrimination and the death penalty has been a tale of both denial and avoidance by both state and federal courts, by Congress, and by state legislatures. As a result, the civil-rights movement, which hardly has touched the American criminal justice system in general, almost has completely by-passed the core discretionary decisions of the American capital-sentencing system. Given the importance of the death penalty as a symbol in American life and the perceived political risk to public officials who appear unsympathetic to the use of the death penalty, this record comes as no great surprise. Nevertheless, for a nation with a historical commitment to equal justice under the law, the story is a disappointment. In particular, the empirical findings from Philadelphia and New Jersey reported in this Article, indicate that the problem of arbitrariness and discrimination in the administration of the death penalty is a matter of continuing concern and is not confined to southern jurisdictions. We also believe that the record of the last twenty-five years demonstrates that the issue of racial discrimination in the use of death penalty is as susceptible to identification, to adjudication, and to correction as are practices of discrimination in other areas of American life that the civil rights movements and the law have addressed for more than 30 years.

List of other cases and articles relevant to this topic.

Gregg v. Georgia, 428 U.S. 153 (1976)

Stanford v. Kentucky, 109 S. Ct. 2969 (1989)

Tison v. Arizona (1987)

Finkel, N.J., and K.B. Duff (1991). Felony-murder and community sentiment: Testing the Supreme Court's assertion. Law and Human Behavior 15(4): 405–429;

Howells, G., K. Flanagan and V. Hagan (1999). Does viewing a televised execution affect attitudes toward capital punishment? Criminal Justice and Behavior 22: 131–144;

Sorenson, J.R., and D.H. Wallace (1999). Prosecutorial discretion in seeking death: An analysis of racial disparity in the pretrial stage of case processing in a midwestern county. Justice Quarterly 16: 559–578;

Wright, H., R. Bohm, and K. Jamieson (1995). A comparison of uninformed and informed death penalty opinions: A replication and expansion. American Journal of Criminal Justice 20: 57–87.

Discussion and Review Questions

1. After reading the Court decision in McCleskey, and the more recent discussion of the topic in "Racial discrimination and the death penalty in the post-Furman era: An empirical and legal overview, with recent findings from Philadephia", do you think the Court might reconsider its decision in McCleskey or would be willing to consider another race-based challenge, e.g., statistics demonstrating that a single prosecutor has engaged in racial discrimination? Why or why not?

2. Review several opinion polls, available through the internet, that have examined public support for the death penalty. What do you think explains variations in support and opposition for capital punishment?

3. Race discrimination is an important and divisive issue in our society. Is there any way to guarantee a completely just and fair criminal justice system? Why or why not?

References

Articles

Baldus, D.C., C. Pulaski, and G. Woodworth (1983). Comparative review of death sentences: An empirical study of the Georgia experience. Journal of Criminal Law and Criminology 74: 661–753.

Baldus, D.C., G. Woodworth, D. Zuckerman, N. Weiner and B. Broffitt. (1998) Racial Discrimination and the Death Penalty in the Post-Furman Era: An Empirical and Legal Overview, with Recent Findings from Philadelphia. *Cornell Law Review* 83: 1638–1769.

Bohm , R.M. (1999). *Deathquest: An introduction to the theory and practice of capital punishment in the United States.* Cincinnati, OH: Anderson Publishing.

Hansen, M. (2000). More for moratorium. American Bar Association Journal 86: 92–94.

Harmon, T.R. (2001). Predictors of miscarriages of justice in capital cases. *Justice Quarterly* 18: 949–968.

Krzycki, L. (2000). A case study of the death penalty in Tennessee: History, attitudes, and mechanisms for critical interpretation. *Social Pathology* 6: 284–301.

Poveda, T. (2001). Estimating wrongful convictions. *Justice Quarterly* 18: 689–708.

Radelet, M.L., H.A. Bedau, and C.E. Putnam (1992). *In Spite of Innocence: The ordeal of 400 americans wrongly convicted of crimes punishable by death.* Boston, MA: Northeastern Univ. Press.

Sorenson, J. and D. Wallace (1999). Prosecutorial discretion in seeking death: An analysis of racial disparity in the pretrial stage of case processing in a midwestern county. *Justice Quarterly* 16: 559–578.

Sorenson, J., R. Wrinkle, V. Brewer, and J. Marquart (1999). Capital punishment and deterrence: Examining the effect of executions on murder in Texas. *Crime and Delinquency* 45: 481–493.

United States Department of Justice (2000). *The federal death penalty system: A statistical survey.* Washington DC: Department of Justice.

United States Department of Justice (2001). *The federal death penalty system: Supplementary data, analysis and revised protocols for capital case review.* Washington DC: Dept of Justice.

United States General Accounting Office (1990). *Death penalty sentencing: Research indicates pattern of racial disparities.* Washington DC.

Whitehead, J.T. and M.B. Blankenship (2000). The gender gap in capital punishment attitudes: An analysis of support and opposition. *American Journal of Criminal Justice* 25: 1–13.

Wright, H., R. Bohm and K. Jamieson (1995). A comparison of uninformed and informed death penalty opinions: A replication and expansion. *American Journal of Criminal Justice* 20 57–87.

Wrightsman, L.S. (2001). *Forensic Psychology.* Belmont, CA: Wadsworth Publishing.

Case Citations

Coker v. Georgia, 433 U.S. 584 (1977)
Furman v. Georgia, 408 U.S. 238 (1972)
Gregg v. Georgia, 428 U.S. 153 (1976)
Jurek v. Texas, 428 U.S. 262 (1976)
Maxwell v. Bishop, 398 U.S. 262 (1970)
McCleskey v. Kemp, 481 U.S. 279 (1987)
Proffitt v. Florida, 428 U.S. 242 (1976)
Ring v. Arizona, 122 S. Ct. 2428 (2002)
Roberts v. Louisiana, 428 U.S. 325 (1976)
Woodson v. North Carolina, 428 U.S. 280 (1976)

Index